GREGARIOUS SAINTS

GREGARIOUS SAINTS

SELF AND COMMUNITY IN
AMERICAN ABOLITIONISM, 1830–1870

LAWRENCE J. FRIEDMAN
Bowling Green State University

CAMBRIDGE UNIVERSITY PRESS

Cambridge
London   New York   New Rochelle
Melbourne   Sydney

Published by the Press Syndicate of the University of Cambridge
The Pitt Building, Trumpington Street, Cambridge CB2 1RP
32 East 57th Street, New York, NY 10022, USA
296 Beaconsfield Parade, Middle Park, Melbourne 3206, Australia

First published 1982

Printed in the United States of America

Library of Congress Cataloging in Publication Data
Friedman, Lawrence Jacob, 1940 –
Gregarious saints, self and community in
American abolitionism, 1830–1870

Bibliography: p.

Includes index.

1. Abolitionists – United States.
2. Slavery – United States – Anti-slavery
movements.   I. Title.
E449.F86   326'.0973   81–15454
ISBN 0 521 24429 3 hard cover   AACR2
ISBN 0 521 27015 4 paperback

To Walling Mariea and
Karl Menninger

But if the world separate itself from us, it leads us to find a world in ourselves and in each other . . .

Charles Follen, 1835

Reproached as infidels by a pro-slavery Church, we have found by experience that those who devote themselves to the cause of humanity "walk with God," and in the fellowship of his saints.

Oliver Johnson, 1863

One of the greatest trials in the pathway of reformers is the necessity of estranging so many who would otherwise be friends, or else of being untrue to our convictions of duty.

Lydia Maria Child, 1868

CONTENTS

PREFACE

When I began general research on the antebellum abolitionists early in 1972, few of my colleagues were encouraging. The last thing that Clio required, most of them insisted, was another wide-ranging study of abolitionists. After all, modern biographies of major figures in the movement had been written and impressive studies of abolitionist thought had been completed, while the politics of antislavery had been thoroughly covered. Indeed, the major details in the crusade against slavery were said to be known. Moreover, because scholars of the 1960s had repudiated the harsh, unsympathetic characterizations with which earlier generations of historians had portrayed the abolitionists, interpretive revision no longer seemed to be necessary.

Despite these warnings, I found, exciting and important monographs on abolitionism continued to be published throughout the 1970s. Fourteen highly innovative essays in Lewis Perry's and Michael Fellman's 1979 anthology *Antislavery Reconsidered: New Perspectives on the Abolitionists* culminated a most productive decade. During these years Perry and David Davis uncovered important dimensions of abolitionist thought, Ronald Walters demonstrated close affinity between abolitionists and Protestant benevolent reform culture, Blanche Hersh and Ellen DuBois "legitimized" systematic study of female abolitionists, James Stewart and Richard Sewell made important discoveries regarding abolitionist political strategies, Alan Kraut conducted the first truly sophisticated analysis of Liberty party voters at the local level, Peter Walker demonstrated the insights that can accrue from sensitive analysis of abolitionist autobiographies, and James McPherson published a pioneering work on the children and grandchildren of antebellum generations. These and other studies were successful because they deployed new methodologies, explored new topics, or asked new questions. To be sure, for every truly innovative study of the 1970s, many more, dull and plodding, laid out the old quotations and events roughly as they had been set down by prior generations of historians, but such contrasts were hardly unique to abolitionist studies.

If this volume helps, in some small way, to extend the innovative spirit of abolitionist studies of the 1970s into the 1980s, it is largely a result of the company that I was able to keep. The antebellum "friends of freedom" thrived on intellectual and social association, and so have their historians. In my years in academia, I had never before experienced such friendly, open, and exciting exchanges of ideas and historical documents. It was enormously stimulating. Consequently, I must note my deep gratitude to abolitionist historians Robert Abzug, Merton Dillon, David French, Larry Gara, Louis Gerteis, Lawrence Goodheart, James Horton, Reinhard Johnson, Alan Kraut, Robert McGlone, James McPherson, Jane and William Pease, Lewis Perry, Richard Sewell, Ronald Walters, and especially Bertram Wyatt-Brown. Without Bert's remarkable understanding of the subtleties of the abolitionist experience and his eagerness to share his insights, *Gregarious Saints* would have been a very different book.

I do not mean to slight the assistance of a number of scholars who are not antislavery specialists. Edmund Danziger, Joseph and Lani Gerson, Kenneth Kiple, Elizabeth Kryder, David Roller, Don Rowney, Arthur Shaffer, Eliane and Sheldon Silverman, Bernard Sternsher, and Stephen Whitfield regularly urged me to extend the scope of my observations – to relate my abolitionist research to broader issues in American history. Ronald Takaki was particularly helpful here, as he has been on two previous occasions.

I also owe a large debt to certain scholars and clinicians for any psychological insights that might inform these pages. G. J. Barker-Benfield, Lawrence Friedman, M.D., Richard King, Donald Meyer, Charles Strozier, and Jane Van Buren made me aware of a considerable body of relevant psychological literature and provided judicious criticisms. Walling Mariea taught me how to read, think, and feel about psychological issues in ways that I had never imagined were possible. Although Walling had not read a page of this manuscript before it was accepted for publication, her remarkable intellectual and personal qualities had a decided impact upon the entire volume.

Librarians and archivists were, of course, indispensable throughout a decade of antislavery research. John Dann of the Clements Library regularly uncovered useful documents and offered cogent suggestions during my many visits to his fine facility. Robert Sparks of the Massachusetts Historical Society was also very helpful. Along with the fine staff of the Boston Public Library manuscript division, he made my research trips to the Boston – Cambridge area fruitful and enjoyable. I must also thank the Bowling Green State University Interlibrary Loan Department, and particularly Kausalya Padmarajan, for substantial assistance.

The outstanding efforts of others at Bowling Green State University must be acknowledged. Ronald Etzel of the Research Services Office encouraged me to look into a year-long National Endowment for the

Humanities research fellowship and a supplementary grant from the American Council of Learned Societies. He helped me with the appropriate applications, and we were both exceedingly pleased when they were accepted. Judith Gilbert, Phyllis Wulff, and especially Connie Montgomery of the history department at Bowling Green were indispensable in typing, retyping, and duplicating the chapters of this manuscript over many years. A climate conducive to serious scholarly endeavor was also promoted by the Faculty Research Committee and by Michael Ferrari and Gary Hess, two outstanding university administrators.

Gerard McCauley was responsible for the placement of this manuscript, while Steve Fraser, Elizabeth Welch, Frank Smith, Rhona Johnson, and Steven Tenney of Cambridge University Press must be thanked for skillfully seeing it through production.

I must conclude by once again acknowledging work by my wife, Sharon Friedman, who criticized chapter after chapter and draft after draft of this manuscript as she had done on two previous occasions. Her judgment on scholarship (and so much else) remains quite remarkable. This time I must also thank my thirteen-year-old daughter, Beth, for persistently and cogently arguing that an abolitionist could not be both gregarious and saintlike.

Bowling Green, Ohio   Lawrence J. Friedman
June 1981

INTRODUCTION

In large measure scholars' definitions of an abolitionist determine the nature of their data and the scope of their interpretations. Historians have usually operated under one of two alternative conceptions. Betty Fladeland most clearly enunciated the broader – that it is best "to define an abolitionist in terms of his goal: the ending of slavery, no matter what method he advocated."[1] Some scholars, such as Dwight Dumond and Richard Sewell, have substantially concurred. Reformers were abolitionists whether they sought gradual and indirect or immediate and direct overthrow of the "peculiar institution." A second and narrower view, advanced by David Davis, James McPherson, and Aileen Kraditor, among others, distinguishes between antislavery and immediatist abolition. "Antislavery" stands for the hope that slavery might ultimately disappear as a result of various developments and tactics, but immediatist "abolition" is a more precise term: An abolitionist had a compelling desire for immediate, complete, uncompensated emancipation and was at least moderately committed to civil equality for free Negroes.

Interestingly, the antebellum advocates of immediate emancipation and civil equality thought of themselves as antislavery people and usually called their organizations antislavery societies. Nevertheless, I shall hold to the narrower definition. Indeed, I shall try to demonstrate that immediatist abolitionists showed a decidedly different cast of mind and personality from that of antislavery gradualists. Immediatists refused to temporize with evil. They craved a sense of inner grace and moral sincerity by conquering temptations toward selfish and calculating expediency. They sensed that by plying slow, calculating gradualist measures, such as African colonization and nonextensionism, in the hope of ending slavery eventually, one compromised with sin.

This book is restricted by more than the narrower definition of "abolitionist." It focuses entirely upon the first generation of immediatist abolitionists – those who took up the cause during the 1830s. The reasons for this limitation are three. First, it permits me to consider the substantial span of time that was necessary for broad, gradual changes in abolitionist attitudes, tactics, and social behavior to appear. Measure-

1

ment of fundamental change over time becomes considerably more problematic when one considers those who joined the crusade later. Second, those who embraced immediatism during the 1830s – when abolitionists faced mob attacks and other forms of fierce hostility – shared personality characteristics and values that often differed in important respects from those who took up the cause when it became safer and less reproachable to do so. Third, whereas it is easy to differentiate immediatist abolitionists from other types of antislavery advocates in the 1830s, the task becomes more difficult for recruits of the 1840s and 1850s. By then there were many cooperative efforts between certain immediatists, on the one hand, and Conscience Whigs, Free Soilers, Independent Democrats, and Republicans, on the other hand. Consequently, it is often difficult to determine whether or not a new antislavery recruit was an immediatist abolitionist.

The matter of race also required me to limit the scope of this study. Although I sometimes discuss black abolitionists, my focus is on whites. As Benjamin Quarles has demonstrated, black reformers represented abolitionism's different drummers. Unlike their white counterparts, they were sometimes ex-slaves, they often experienced poverty firsthand, and they were rarely able to escape racial discrimination. To be sure, many black abolitionists did cooperate with whites in antislavery societies. But they were usually far more attentive to the concrete everyday economic and social struggles of black Northerners generally. Consequently, in addition to their participation in white-dominated antislavery ventures, most black abolitionists felt compelled to devote considerable time to the Negro convention movement and to diverse other black initiated responses to the specific problems of the Northern Negro. Differences between black and white abolitionists in backgrounds and activities illuminate differences in memories, ideas, and strategies.

Not only is my study generally restricted to first-generation white immediatist abolitionists, but it focuses rather heavily upon internal dimensions of their crusade against slavery – private social and emotional relationships between them. Although I do not discount the importance of formal and sustained expressions of abolitionist thought such as William Goodell's *The Democracy of Christianity*, I do not explore such documents as comprehensively as I might have. Nor have I offered intensive analysis of abolitionist responses to major public issues of the day such as the Compromise of 1850. Two considerations compelled me to make these trade-offs. First, a number of historians have already published outstanding studies of formal abolitionist thought and responses to leading public questions. Second, although the preponderance of the abolitionists' private writing on antislavery (and even much of their public writing) concerned their everyday personal social and emotional relationships with each other, historians have often been reluctant to take this sort of evidence seriously; some scholars have dismissed it as insignificant gossip. Yet the abolitionists regarded their daily interactions as vitally important and considered their writings about personal relationships as crucial documents in the crusade against slavery. We are on potentially hazardous ground when we make little of the everyday feelings of our historical characters or of most of the evidence that they have left behind.

A final limitation of this book must be noted. It attempts neither to support the favorable historical assessment of antebellum abolitionists that emerged since the early 1960s nor to refurbish the more hostile pre-1960s historiographical tradition. Rather, I argue that the two are not mutually exclusive. As many historians of the 1930s, 1940s, and 1950s maintained, antebellum abolitionists tended to be impatient moralists who were not amenable to compromise. And as historians since have insisted, abolitionists tended to be psychologically stable, tactically shrewd, and quite cordial. They combined these diverse qualities, and individuals showed considerable variation in the mix.

This brings us to the central theme of *Gregarious Saints* – the blend of conviviality and austere piety at the roots of immediatist social psychology. In an interpretive tradition highlighted by Gilbert Barnes, Timothy Smith, and Bertram Wyatt-Brown, I place immediatism within the early nineteenth-century American evangelical missionary crusade to propagate Gospel truths and supplant heathenism throughout the globe. I go on, however, to characterize the immediatist missionary perspective as a merger of gregarious social aspirations and intense desires to improve the level of one's personal devotion. On the one hand, immediatists pursued what they perceived to be a time-worn tradition of Christian fellowship. On the other hand, they embraced a Wesleyan outlook on New Testament holiness; they strove for the impeccable moral fabric of saints. Like missionaries who championed temperance, Sabbath observance, Bible and tract distribution, and conversion of "savage" societies, immediatists constantly sought rapport with those whom they sought to proselytize; they embraced fellow immediatist abolitionists, more moderate antislavery Northerners, and even a few Southerners. Indeed, they persistently tried to forge personal bonds with the socially respectable, churchgoing, evangelically disposed middle-class elements everywhere as they attempted to win these elements over to immediatist abolitionism through missionary appeals. But if immediatists, like other evangelical missionaries, were usually socially outgoing reformers, they also shared with other missionaries the hope of personally pressing on toward sanctification, toward full obedience to the divine command. Although they were sure that man suffered from a depraved will and a disinclination to obey God, immediatists felt compelled to struggle against their own depravity and to follow God through their "natural ability" to discern and obey moral law. More generally, they wanted desperately to see themselves as a duplication of God's elect even as they defied the notion of election through their confidence in a salvageable human fate. If their lives became exemplary, there was greater cause to believe that God had chosen them as his special agents to uplift the nation morally – that this was their principal calling. Surely, God would not want his most faithful missionary agents to be tainted by the sins of certain associates. So whereas devout immediatists could hope that their "sincere and hearty" fellow reformers would "labor *with us* in our efforts to civilize and Christianize," they had to break their connection with those evangelicals who persisted in unholy cooperation with slaveholders or with other sinners. After all, it was hazardous for pious immediatists "to meet & mingle with them [tainted evangelical reformers] in all the most sacred acts of worship, as though they were Saints of the most High."[2]

This proclivity of first-generation immediatists, to move toward the devout and to draw away from sinners, helps us to judge the extent of their influence. Before the 1970s, historians most concerned with the abolitionist role in the coming of the Civil War generally assumed that their impact had been substantial – that they did much to mobilize the North against the Southern "slavocracy." On the other hand, scholars most interested in abolitionism as a chapter in the failure of an American radical tradition necessarily concluded that their influence had been considerably less substantial. In the course of the 1970s, however, most students of abolitionism appeared reticent to make any general assertions. The few who did seemed to be moving toward an abolitionist push–Southern shove interpretation that George Fort Milton, Henry Simms, and a few other scholars had vaguely suggested during the 1930s and early 1940s. Abolitionists, according to this view, were a numerically small and underfunded minority that failed to convert the North to immediatism. Many influential proslavery Southerners erroneously assumed that the abolitionists had captured Northern public opinions, however, and the belief moved them toward an aggressive sectional defense of the "peculiar institution" against Yankee interference. As proslavery Southerners lashed out at the "abolitionized" North, their attacks and demands produced strong anti-Southern, antislavery feelings among Northerners generally. Although abolitionists gratuitously claimed credit for the transformation of Northern attitudes, the Southern shove (not the prior abolitionist push) represented the principal force promoting the heated sectional conflict that led to war.

This study supports the push–shove interpretation not only because it is compatible with the most serious recent investigations of the rise of sectionalism and the secessionist impulse in the slave states that have come from scholars as diverse as Steven Channing, Michael Johnson, William Barney, David Potter, and John McCardell. Such a view also accords with the fact that many immediatists curtailed their work among the less devout when they feared that they were compromising their personal piety. While this conduct on the part of immediatists might have fostered apprehensions among Southerners who were able to view abolitionist outcries only from a distance, it was not likely fully to mobilize many Northerners against slavery. Indeed, even in an area like New York City, where immediatists were successful during the 1830s at gathering signatures on antislavery petitions, they did not persuade a substantial portion of the signers to endorse their middle-class evangelical values or to rally consistently behind their other anti-slavery activities. Finally, confirmation for the push–shove notion awaits the reader in many private letters and diary notations of immediatists themselves. While boasting publicly of mobilizing the North against the South and slavery, privately they often fretted over declining revenues, thinning membership ranks, and drastically curtailed lists of abolitionist publications. A few even acknowledged confidentially that Southerners had exaggerated the impact of abolitionists within the North.

In sum, immediatist abolitionists must be studied neither as figures of influence nor as radicals who failed. They were evangelical missionaries who contributed quite inadvertently and secondarily to sectional tensions and the Civil War. For the most part, they were not radicals but representatives of the broad Northern middle-class benevolent reform community, subscribers to the pervasive values of market capitalism and Christian self-help. It is certainly noteworthy that members of their highly diverse local constituencies sometimes did not share their class allegiance or all of their ideological proclivities, and much will be gained if historians explore those disparities more thoroughly. But the most revealing aspects of the immediatist experience concern the ways in which they reflected the values of the Northern middle class generally and the evangelical missionary community in particular, as well as the factors that caused them to depart in important respects from those whom they most closely resembled. Within the broad theme of gregarious sainthood, my book centers on these topics.

Chapter 1 concerns the missionary origins of immediatist abolitionism during the late 1820s and early 1830s. The evangelical missionary impulse was rooted in a complex nationwide (but preponderantly Northern middle-class) reform movement that emerged in the aftermath of the War of 1812. Early immediatism represented at once an abstract affirmation of the broad redemptive goals of this benevolent movement and a reaction to certain of its less than pious actions. More specifically, immediatism stood for a retreat of certain exceedingly devout missionaries from the apparent compromises and sins as well as the power-broker machinations of the American Colonization Society – the organization within the larger benevolent movement that sought to remedy the slavery controversy. Because the Colonization Society was thought to have serious moral deficiencies, the benevolent movement was seen to be tainted. Yet different abolitionists withdrew in different degrees and for different reasons. Consequently, the immediatist crusade was neither united nor monolithic in its early years. Indeed, factionalism reflecting a variety of attitudes and social needs existed at the outset.

Chapters 2 through 4 elaborate on diversity among early immediatists as well as on their common disposition to draw away from the larger benevolent reform community. I consider these traits in the context of the personal sanctuaries, or clusters, that immediatists forged as they launched their mission for the slaves independent of the Colonization Society and the larger benevolent reform movement. The terms "sanctuaries" and "clusters" refer to the small, highly personalized, almost familial, if relatively powerless, groups in which immediatists tended to seek refuge. Garrison's friend Charles Follen called each of these groups "a world in ourselves and in each other." There were many dozens of them, and I examine three of the most important – the Boston Clique loyal to Garrison, Lewis Tappan's informal New York City-Oberlin circle of evangelical churchgoing intimates, and a small group from upstate New York that gathered about Gerrit Smith and became deeply involved in the Liberty party. I have sought in my analysis to provide a more precise understanding than that suggested by the standard labels of "Garrisonian," "Tappanite," and "political abolitionist" usually invoked to distinguish types of abolitionists. Members of the three clusters were leaders in the sense that they often directed or advised the more occasional and part-time participants in the immediatist crusade. But they were also followers in that they tended to defer to Garrison, Tappan, or Smith. Those in the Boston Clique shared Unitarian–Quaker religious proclivities, while the Tappan and Smith clusters had broad Presbyterian–Congregationalist loyalties. The thoughts and actions of the members of these clusters provide basic information for the entire book, and Baptist and Methodist abolitionists are less central to the study. Nonetheless, the goals and the style of personal relationships within the three clusters differed significantly and plainly indicate the enormous variety that existed among first-generation immediatists.

To the themes of convivial piety, relative powerlessness, diversity, and sanctuary, Chapters 5 through 7 add the dimension of transformation. Three types of change are explored as they impinged on the everyday lives of immediatist abolitionists, particularly on those from our three sanctuaries. Chapter 5 considers changes over time in the nature of gender relationships among abolitionists, while Chapter 6 addresses shifting relationships between white and black abolitionists. The seventh chapter explores the increasing willingness of immediatists to justify force and violence. In each of these specific areas, immediatists may be seen to draw sometimes nearer to and at other times further from various dominant northern middle-class ideas, values, and social associations. As they shifted back and forth, their personal sanctuaries lost considerable emotional attraction and gradually eroded.

Chapter 8 extends the measurement of movements by first-generation immediatists toward and away from other middle-class Northerners, comparing the immediatists to radical Republicans – those Northerners with whom they felt perhaps the strongest missionary kinship during the late 1850s and early 1860s. Specifically, the radical Republicans serve to sharpen my analysis by throwing into greater relief the unique qualities of immediatists. Chapter 8 focuses on personal and ideological contacts and communications between immediatists and radicals in the 1850s. Although they shared a number of common social characteristics and views about antislavery, different temperaments and concepts of slavery and freedom often made cooperative efforts difficult. Consequently, an immediatist such as Elizur Wright, Jr., was never able to gain acceptance in a radical intimacy group such as the Bird Club. And although there were important exceptions, first-generation immediatist influence generally did not expand to the point where it significantly influenced even the radical wing of the Republican party. Despite sundry transformations and the slow disintegration of their personal sanctuaries, even those immediatists who came to support the Republican party were usually distinguishable from most radicals.

The ninth and final chapter in this book deals with first-generation immediatists during the 1860s. It focuses on the intramural controversy that transpired from the issuance of the Emancipation Proclamation in January 1863 until spring 1870. The controversy concerned the appropriate moment to proclaim success and dissolve antislavery societies. The deeper issue at stake was whether, with slavery legally abolished, there was cause to modify drastically, if not abandon, the broad patterns of abolitionist existence that involved gregarious sainthood, the sanctuary of various declining intimacy circles, and the results of various transformations. When members of the American Anti-Slavery Society adjourned their annual business meeting *sine die* in April 1870, they had essentially decided to dissolve those patterns. To be sure, some first-generation immediatists who attended that meeting continued to participate modestly in the American Missionary Association and in other freedmen's aid organizations. But they did not feel that they were going back on their 1870 decision.

Part I

Origins

CHAPTER 1

YOUNG MISSIONARIES: VARIETIES OF EARLY IMMEDIATISM

The two decades that followed the War of 1812 constituted a great age for Protestant missionary activity in the new nation. Like their progenitors in England, American missionary societies before that time had operated on very small budgets. They had employed few agents, and these agents rarely went beyond their own immediate localities. Organized entirely on a state and local basis, missionary work before 1815 had amounted to little more than individual preaching and itinerancy, much as it had throughout the colonial period. After America's second war with England, however, Protestant reformers organized church-wide societies that drew funds from members in all regions of the country. More money permitted larger staffs at more missionary stations. An improved transportation network, cheap mails, and the revolution in printing technology facilitated communication between these stations and regular exchanges of missionary brethren. These developments also promoted interdenominational benevolent societies with substantial treasuries, numerous workers, and extensive operations.[1]

The new interdenominational missionary societies had an even greater impact upon Northern culture than the church-based missionary agencies. They spread evangelical Protestant values far and wide among the Northern middle classes and, to a lesser degree, among the poor. Consider, for example, the impact they had upon a number of Northern businessmen who worked irregular hours, consumed enormous quantities of alcohol, tyrannized over their wives and children, seldom voted, and rarely attended church. After the evangelical missionaries, their interdenominational societies, and their church agencies had reached these businessmen, some started to attend church twice a week, while several businessmen contributed generously to benevolent reform causes. More generally, a surprising number of Northern businessmen worked regular hours for the first time. They required their employees to do so as well, drank only water, treated their families with gentleness and affection, and sometimes even campaigned for the Whig party.[2]

In large measure, the interdenominational benevolent societies were effective because they cooperated closely, especially in New York, Philadelphia, and Boston, where many of their activities centered. They often shared financial assets. Meetings frequently occurred in the same city at the same time. The composition of boards of directors at the national as well as the local level frequently overlapped. And it was not infrequent for missionaries to labor for several of the societies in the course of their careers – often at the same time.[3]

While formally interdenominational, these new missionary societies had specific church ties that were complex and varied. "Particular" Baptists, Methodists, and Episcopalians tended to contribute to their own sectarian societies. Consequently, the more Arminian "General" Baptists, joined by Presbyterians and Congregationalists, became the principal financial contributors. Presbyterians dominated the executive boards of two of the most powerful of these societies – the American Bible Society and the American Sunday School Union – but tried earnestly to include Methodists, Baptists, Congregationalists, Dutch Reformed, Episcopalians, and a few stray Moravians and Quakers in important governing roles. Two other extremely influential societies – the American Board of Commissioners for Foreign Missions and the American Education Society – were dominated by Congregationalists and made few efforts to draw in others. In contrast, the American Bible Society attracted prosperous missionary reformers from many diverse denominations into positions of leadership. It was the only unequivocally interdenominational if also the most class-based national benevolent society. From the standpoint of religious composition, then, most of the professedly interdenominational benevolent societies were simply somewhat less sectarian than the overtly sectarian societies. Hence, generalizations applicable to the interdenominational societies are usually equally applicable to those which were explicitly sectarian. It was the professedly interdenominational societies, frequently joined by diverse sectarian societies, that made up the benevolent society movement.[4]

What sparked the many missionaries who labored within the diverse benevolent societies, interdenominational and sectarian, in the aftermath of the War of 1812? In recent years scholars have appraised these missionaries along broadly similar lines. Attentive to the strange symbols of the Book of Revelation, they set out to universalize personal and often recently acquired values of piety, temperance, prudence, order, and stability – to wage war on sin wherever it appeared and in all of its manifestations. Often only marginally middle-class, they sometimes struggled tenaciously for the Lord because they were apprehensive; if they relaxed their activities, they could conceivably fall back into the slothful, immoral lower-class life from which they had risen. By converting sinners, these missionaries therefore proved to themselves that they were part of the genteel evangelical middle class. Perhaps more fundamentally, benevolent society missionaries sought out the sort of morally accountable freedom that was implicit in Finneyite notions of self-ability and immediate transcendence of all barriers between man and God. By warring against such evils as intemperance, theater attendance, indolence, and lust – all of which detracted from diligent labor and regular church attendance – missionaries could move their society and themselves toward a millennial Christian freedom. If a more closely controlled and economically efficient Northern middle-class labor force often sprang from evangelical missionary ventures on behalf of the benevolent societies, that result derived from a Finneyite perfectionist religious orientation intent on freeing the human soul to obey God.[5]

In essence, then, missionaries hoped that they might one day become saints as they labored together within the benevolent societies and at the affiliated way stations of those societies in the "heathen" world. The collective nature of such missionary endeavors cannot be overemphasized. Even in isolated locations in the American West, T. Scott Miyakawa reminds us, missionaries felt compelled to come together in what were essentially voluntary associations. To gain much-needed social camaraderie and strength in climates where sin was rampant and evangelical churches were few, missionaries who sought to be saintlike felt compelled to associate.[6] The coming together of the faithful also represented a means through which God's missionaries hoped to cleanse themselves from the "contaminations" of the sinners with whom they struggled. Memoirs honoring early nineteenth-century missionary agents regularly allude to the invaluable purifying benefits of social association for the Lord's vulnerable workers. In a general sense, then, the missionary imaged himself as convivial yet devout; he was an agent of the Lord who craved contacts with his brethren.[7]

Samuel Bacon, first missionary to the Liberian outpost of the American Colonization Society (A.C.S.), and Jehudi Ashmun, a subsequent missionary, certainly carried this self-image. Like Bacon, Ashmun moved about from one benevolent undertaking to another, finding greater meaning in missionary outposts with evangelical brethren than in marriage and family. Bacon ultimately decided to conduct a final pilgrimage. He drew inspiration and support from those Colonization Society associates who had tried to help him deal with his alcoholism and his fits of depression; then he went to his post in Monrovia to "uplift Africa's heathen" and to die. Ashmun wrote a memorial volume on Bacon and emulated Bacon's association with missionary comrades. Then he decided to die Bacon's death. Aware that his lungs were weak, Ashmun departed to his Liberian missionary outpost, where he quickly fell victim to consumption, assured of immortality in a benevolent cause.[8]

If Bacon and Ashmun had understood the complexities of the organization for whose mission they had given their lives, they would have been distressed. To be sure, the American Colonization Society was organized in 1816 with the benevolent goal of securing the gradual and voluntary emancipation of America's black bondsmen and sending them to Africa, where they would morally uplift that "heathen" continent. Missionaries in most of the other benevolent societies readily supported the A.C.S. for offering the proper way to atone for America's historic sins against both Africans and Afro-Americans. Those in the powerful American Bible Society, American Tract Society, and American Home Missionary Society were particularly supportive. Yet the A.C.S. was different from the other benevolent societies; it had a considerably more diverse supportive base. Certainly it followed the pattern of several of the other missionary societies with large treasuries and sizable influence in drawing considerable Congregational, Presbyterian, and Methodist financial backing. By the 1826–27 fiscal year, upper- and middle-class evangelical champions of moral reform within these three denominations had made the A.C.S. the benevolent society with the seventh highest income in the country. But the A.C.S. also attracted considerable support from Old School Federalists such as Noah Webster, who felt that colonization could defuse the potentially explosive slavery issue by making emancipationists of the Southern planter class. Webster, and others like him, assumed that planters would free their slaves and thus abort the slavery controversy, once systematic African deportation had eliminated the risk of a "troublesome" free Negro population. In addition to evangelicals and more Calvinistic Old School Federalists, the A.C.S. was supported by several Southern slaveholders. Because colonization promised to eliminate the free Negro population that gave their bondsmen hopes for emancipation, these slaveholders believed that A.C.S. efforts would shore up the "peculiar institution." Still others, North and South, supported the A.C.S. simply because they did not want Negros around, whether free or slaves. Finally, certain ambitious cultural and political leaders backed the society because of its large and diverse following; they hoped advocacy might garner support from whites of diverse ideologies. Thus, the A.C.S. was a complex multi-interest organization whose supporters perceived slavery in widely diverse ways. Only one of several constituencies in the society consisted of evangelical missionaries. But because early A.C.S. officers, organizational postures, and publications emphasized Christian evangelism and missionary endeavor, it was easy for young reformers such as Samuel Bacon and Jehudi Ashmun to assume that the A.C.S. was just like any other benevolent society that they supported. Their understanding was of short duration.[9]

To comprehend the initial manifestations of immediatist abolitionism in the early 1830s, we must keep in mind that those who turned to this cause were not simply young evangelical missionaries who commenced reform careers working within the benevolent empire of sectarian and interdenominational benevolent societies. Like Bacon and Ashmun, they found the cause of emancipation and African uplift particularly appealing and had devoted a considerable portion of their missionary activity to the Colonization Society. Young reformers and immediatists-to-be such as Elizabeth Chandler, Amos Phelps, Simeon Jocelyn, and Joshua Leavitt had labored vigorously as fund raisers for this "cause of humanity and justice." Gerrit Smith and Lewis and Arthur Tappan had ranked among the society's chief donors, and James Birney had been its major agent in the Southwest. Samuel J. May had organized an A.C.S. auxiliary in Windham County, Connecticut. Even Theodore Weld and William Lloyd Garrison had been supporters.[10]

Thus, young immediatists-to-be differed from most of their missionary colleagues in the sense of having devoted at least an important part of their early reform careers to uplifting blacks in America and Africa through Colonization Society ventures. In time they discovered that this very organization was perhaps the most deceptive of all benevolent societies. Although it professed to eliminate slavery and to Christianize Africa, they learned that it was partially bankrolled by slaveholders and other "sinners." Their shock was understandably intense, and their reaction was strong. In large measure, the cry for immediatism was their reaction to this deep and profound sense of betrayal.

The late 1820s and the early 1830s were the years when these young missionaries first became suspicious of A.C.S. intentions. Garrison offers a case in point. In September 1829 Benjamin Lundy offered him the co-editorship of his antislavery newspaper, the *Genius of Universal Emancipation*. Garrison gladly accepted. Whereas the older reformer was no opponent of the A.C.S. colony in Liberia, he favored Western hemisphere repatriation projects as a less costly and more practical way to eliminate American slavery. But when coeditor Garrison learned, through his research on repatriation and his conversations with blacks, that slaveholders supported the A.C.S. and that the whole organization was morally tainted, personal outrage caused him to question the propriety of all colonization projects. Only complete, total, and immediate emancipation could satisfy the imperatives of Christian behavior; thus Garrison refused to allow his name to be associated with Lundy's procolonization editorials. The older reformer understood the young missionary's moral indignation and offered a solution: "Well, thee may put thy initials to thy articles and I will put my initial to mine, and each will bear his own burden." This only temporarily satisfied Garrison. As the months passed he sensed, increasingly, that colonization was sin – even the well-intended variety that Lundy espoused – and that he had to break from even as mildly tainted a missionary publication as the *Genius of Universal Emancipation* if he was to be a true advocate of divinity. Consequently, young Garrison left Lundy's offices and established his own antislavery newspaper in Boston, where he could fully articulate the sins of colonization in general and of the "deceptive" Colonization Society in particular. Not long after Garrison departed for Boston, Theodore Weld, the Tappans,

Samuel J. May, Elizur Wright, Jr., Beriah Green, and many other young missionary reformers made similar discoveries about the sins of the A.C.S. Shocked, enraged, and with a sense that they had been led down the devil's path, they left colonization and championed the only "undefiled" path to emancipation – immediate abolition.[11]

II

Pious young evangelical missionaries active in the benevolent society movement, interested in the plight of blacks, and at least mildly supportive of the A.C.S. were the sort that embraced immediatism. Yet this characterization of the first immediatist abolitionists is altogether too imprecise. Most young missionaries active in the other benevolent societies regarded the A.C.S. as the agency that should uplift blacks and retained this view even as Garrison, the Tappans, and others denounced the sins of the Colonization Society. Nor did the immediatist exposé deter most A.C.S. agents in the field. Indeed, only a small minority of young missionaries turned against the Colonization Society and went on to help launch the crusade for immediate abolition. If the Colonization Society permitted expediency and sin by embracing slaveholders and self-seeking politicians, why did so few of the young benevolent society missionaries feel compelled to preserve the virtue of their calling by repudiating the A.C.S. and embracing immediatism?

Scholars have rarely confronted this question and for understandable reasons. It essentially asks why people reaching adulthood under similar conditions and expectations went different ways. One can describe the phenomenon, yet any explanation is exceedingly difficult. Sarah Tappan, for example, reared six sons quite similarly and in almost identical social circumstances. But historians have not been able to explain the different paths that they took. We do not know why two (Lewis and Arthur) repudiated colonization and became abolitionists, why three participated in other missionary causes but stayed clear of immediatism, or why the sixth son spent his life in steady drinking. Similarly, given that Gerrit Smith and his brother were both attracted to benevolent society causes, why did one shrug off the A.C.S. and become a slaveholder while the other supported the A.C.S. and then moved on to immediatism? By the same token, as Theodore Weld concentrated his missionary efforts on abolitionism, why was his brother Lewis more attracted to education of the deaf?[12]

Although we may never be able to fathom the reasons for such differences among siblings, there are a number of more general ways in which immediatists of the early 1830s can be distinguished from other young evangelical missionaries who never felt compelled to leave the Colonization Society. First, perhaps owing to their intense interest in the supposed improvement of Negroes in America and Africa, those missionaries who became immediatists had considerably more contact with the free blacks about them than did those who concentrated in causes like tract distribution and temperance. Usually free blacks informed young immediatists-to-be, as they informed other missionaries in the Colonization Society who sought out candidates for Liberian deportation, that they did not regard Africa as their homeland and wanted to remain in America. Some free blacks also warned that Liberia was the scene of intemperance, price extortion, and other questionable moral practices. Missionaries who remained supportive of the A.C.S. tended to assume that the free blacks were ignorant and hence wrong about Liberia; they contemplated strategies to convince these blacks that their race would benefit by African repatriation. But those colonizationists who became immediatists considered the protestations of free blacks much more seriously. They empathized with the Negro's desire to remain in America, and they investigated the charges that sinful activities were carried on in Liberia. Whereas young colonizationists such as M. L. Fullerton and David I. Burr, who remained devoted to the A.C.S., regarded the Negro as a heathen to be uplifted no matter what the Negro said, those such as Lewis Tappan and William Lloyd Garrison who became immediatists clearly considered blacks to have sensibilities and feelings akin to their own. For abolitionists-to-be, the distance between missionary and heathen was much less pronounced.[13]

Empathy and partial identity of feelings and emotions with the Negro was hazardous in an early nineteenth-century North where racial segregation, job discrimination, and black disfranchisement were becoming increasingly prevalent. Racial empathy was even hazardous within the missionary community of the benevolent societies. The Colonization Society's assumption that the presumed heathen should dwell in their own territory was much more consistent with missionary premises. According to these premises, converted savages frequently had the potential to revert to barbarism; hence Christian purity was most safely preserved if they remained in their own lands. When early immediatists opposed African deportations and found moral rectitude in the Negro's claim that America was his homeland, they were therefore taking issue not only with white Northern society in general but with the empire of benevolent reform organizations that they so deeply prized.

There was a second general distinction between the nonimmediatist missionary like Henry Lyman, who was determined to stand his ground for Christ against "a tribe of cannibals" in far-off Sumatra, and an emerging immediatist, like Amos Phelps, who fretted over Cherokee removal, Jacksonian "tyranny," and "Fanny Wrightism" as well as the "peculiar institution." The emerging immediatist was more political. Rather than approach the heathen in some distant rain forest, as Lyman had, the young missionary-turned-immediatist followed Phelps's example and struggled to convert fellow reformers in his own country against slavery and other domestic ills. Indeed, by charging that instant uncompensated emancipation without repatriation was guaranteed by the semireligious ideals of the Declaration of Independence, he was introducing an issue into national political debate that also had basic repercussions for Americans who were not missionaries. There was, then, a more down-to-earth, close-to-home quality that distinguished those missionaries who were moving toward immediatism from their colleagues. They were more political in that they seemed to care about the sins of people and institutions within their own country.[14]

In some measure, the political orientation of early immediatists was either kindled or intensified by the experiences that many of them had had during the late 1820s with the General Union for Promoting the Observance of the Christian Sabbath. This interdenominational benevolent society set out to ban mail delivery on Sundays so that postal workers could observe the Sabbath. As Sabbatarianism failed and the Sabbath Union collapsed, participants such as the Tappans, Garrison, Theodore Weld, Joshua Leavitt, and William Jay saw the emerging Jacksonian party system of secret bribes, coarse self-congratulation, and the evasion of fundamental moral problems as the enemy. The major parties had not simply failed to take a firm stand on the Sabbath. They were thought to be subversive of Christian statesmanship and the moral ideals of the Declaration of Independence. Not only did the Sabbatarian experience make these immediatists-to-be feel that the dominant parties were the great institutional evils of the time; it deeply inculcated in them self-perceptions of being despised participants in an unpopular cause. Just as the Sabbatarian caused ebbed, many of the young missionaries who had battled against the dominant political parties in the Sabbath Union began to leave the Colonization Society and to launch attacks against that organization. Thus, Sabbatarianism represented a prelude to immediate abolitionism. It helped to politicize certain young reformers in the sense that it made them active if unpopular antagonists of the nation's dominant political parties. They persisted in this role as they turned against the powerful and respected Colonization Society – the organ for racial reform that drew support from many politicians of the dominant parties.[15]

Early immediatists can also be distinguished from most other young evangelical missionaries in terms of their careers. More than other missionaries active in the benevolent society movement, they tended to be ministers or candidates for the ministry. It is crucial to note that most of them were experiencing at least some disillusionment with the ministerial calling at the time that they embraced immediatism, and one can understand why. By the 1820s the minister had ceased to be the most learned and respected individual in the community – the moral leader he once had been. Immediatists-to-be perceived this only after they had committed themselves to ministerial careers. They watched established gentlemen of the cloth seek out the higher salary and the approval of equally acquisitive laymen, and they sensed that there must be a higher calling for those truly intent on serving God. Consequently, Elizur Wright, Jr., resisted strong parental pressures and decided not to complete his ministerial training. Stephen S. Foster dropped out of Union Theological Seminary. Charles T. Torrey finished his study for the Congregationalist ministry beset with doubts about the vocation he was about to enter. Amos Phelps assumed pastoral duties but found them exceedingly monotonous and sometimes inconsequential. So did Simeon S. Jocelyn, Orange Scott, Joshua Leavitt, Samuel J. May, La Roy Sunderland, and others. The traditional work of the church had to be combined with or replaced by some higher calling; otherwise they feared that they would imbibe the hypocrisy and errors of their ecclesiastical brethren. God's faithful risked moral taint. Because immediatist abolitionism appeared to be morally impeccable – because the cause was mocked by compromising politicians and self-serving colonizationists – it represented the sort of higher calling that missionaries of the cloth required. As historian Donald Scott has thoroughly demonstrated, immediatism rekindled the missionary's early but flagging moral commitment to the Gospel ministry. It reawakened the sense of a sacred moral vocation that had come upon hard times since the young reformer had initially chosen to pursue the ministry. Whether he combined his pastoral duties with his new immediatist career or left the ministry entirely, the young missionary sensed that abolitionism afforded a second chance at a calling that involved more than remote or feigned service to God.[16]

What, then, are we to conclude about the difference between the few missionaries who embraced immediatism in the early 1830s and the many who did not? Robert Berkhofer has perceptively noted that evangelical missionaries at large had an important social and cultural impact during the early nineteenth century because they held the basic values of the society that surrounded them. They formed a subculture only because they emphasized theology and morals more than others. They adhered more vigorously, for example, to the professed sexual code and were more concerned with the moral taboos of drink, obscenity, and blasphemy. They differed with their neighbors only in the intensity of their moral concerns.[17] If evangelical missionaries represented a subculture based on moral intensity, those missionaries who turned to immediatism constituted a subculture within a subculture. Whereas most missionaries in the Colonization Society, for example, made little of claims by free Negroes that they wanted to remain in America and that life in the Liberian colony was morally reprehensible, those who became immediatists found these charges disturbing. Investigation of moral conditions in Liberia was required. Even if conditions there were salubrious, early immediatists found the reluctance of blacks to be colonized a much more serious moral problem than their missionary colleagues did. Similarly, whereas most young missionaries were relatively apolitical – more concerned with Bible truths in the Sandwich Islands than in congressional refusal to ban Sunday mail delivery in America – those who became immediatists were deeply concerned with the immorality of the politicians and parties who ran the country. This sense of outrage at political immorality was intensified by their Sabbath Union experiences and the knowledge that expedient office seekers and slaveholders supported the Colonization Society. Finally, much more than most other missionaries, early immediatists were deeply disturbed by the self-seeking ways and ebbing moral leadership of the ministry. They were upset that their village parishes could no longer content them; they required a more rigorously pietistic vocation.

Thus, early immediatists seem to have been most fundamentally distinguishable from other young missionaries by the intensity of their moral commitments. A nonimmediatist such as Henry Lyman was able to envision his life's work accomplished reading Scripture to the children of Sumatra's cannibals, while Jehudi Ashmun died content with the realization that he had arrived at an A.C.S. missionary station in Liberia. In contrast, the moral goals of Amos Phelps, Lewis Tappan, and others who turned to immediatism seemed insatiable. Almost any taint of moral vacillation anywhere – whether in Liberia, in the A.C.S. national office, or in the halls of Congress – had to be confronted and reversed. Early in the 1830s, for example, young Garrison begged an influential missionary in the benevolent empire to join his immediatist crusade against the sins of slavery. The man courteously replied that he had so many irons in the fire of missionary reform that he could not think of putting in another. "Then you had better let all the others go, and attend to this one," Garrison sharply retorted.[18]

Much more than their fellow missionaries, early immediatists were thus involved in a social and emotional process under which personal piety required expression through concrete moral activism. Moral activism, in turn, brought them to new and different moral problems that required solutions. Like Lyman and Ashmun, most missionaries who eschewed immediatism seemed to be able to concentrate upon a limited number of problems; they were therefore able to envisage the completion of their pursuits. But immediatists found themselves within a type of emotional spiral that increased in intensity and never ended as long as there were any disturbing immoralities to eliminate.

Once immediatists decided to engage the Colonization Society in moral debate, they then had to decide how far their criticisms were to go. Did personal piety require them to renounce the A.C.S. leadership, to seek to destroy the whole organization, or to repudiate the entire benevolent society movement? How far did God's most devout have to disengage themselves from their missionary colleagues? Answers to these questions did not turn young skeptics of A.C.S. benevolence into immediatists; their search for a morally rigorous antislavery alternative to the A.C.S. had done that. Rather, the answers to these questions helped to give precise doctrinal shape to their immediatism and to determine the specific reform associates each immediatist could embrace without fear of moral taint.

This, in turn, suggests that though early immediatists constituted the most intense moral expression of a larger evangelical missionary subculture, there were significant differences among them from the start. These differences were detectable within their earliest criticisms of the A.C.S. and the larger benevolent society movement. Moreover, when these differences combined with other variables in the course of the 1830s, serious factional squabbles among abolitionists became quite visible. We therefore turn to early immediatist commentary on the Colonization Society not so much to learn how immediatists differed from other missionaries as to make important distinctions among participants in this subculture within a subculture as it began to form.

III

According to traditional historical accounts, young Garrison commenced the immediatist assault on the A.C.S. through his 1832 essay, *Thoughts on African Colonization*. Within nine months of publication, 2,750 copies of that pamphlet were sold – it was a great success by contemporary standards. Young reformers who had been supportive of the Colonization Society read it, also turned against the colonization cause, and endorsed Garrison's immediatist alternative. In very short order, then, the crusade for immediatist abolition had been launched. Immediatists began to define their new crusade against slavery through a vigorous and relatively uniform array of charges against the Colonization Society.[19]

There is some truth to this standard account of the early immediatist critique. In a certain sense, the arguments advanced by young missionaries-turned-immediatists were broadly similar. They almost always cited Garrison's *Thoughts* approvingly despite the pamphlet's harsh and condemnatory tone. As well, most of these young reformers apologized for having been duped into supporting the A.C.S.; they had mistakenly believed that it was an evangelical agency for antislavery missionary uplift. They all noted the impracticality and illogic of African colonization. Repatriation of large numbers of Negroes was economically unfeasible, and it was ludicrous to assume that poor uneducated blacks could Christianize Africa. In addition, nearly all early immediatists questioned the benevolence of a society that sought to repatriate a black population that wanted to remain in America. In essence, colonizationists were refusing to recognize the Negro's desires and thus his humanity. With a great deal of fervor, young missionaries-turned-immediatist also noted that colonizationists had given up on the egalitarian pledge of the Declaration of Independence and were willing to tolerate the perpetual degradation of all blacks who resided in America. Clearly, the A.C.S. fortified anti-Negro practices in the land. Finally, and most forcefully, all early 1830s immediatists charged that the Colonization Society had to be repudiated because it had failed to condemn openly the grossest immorality in universal history – chattel bondage. Thus Southern planters were able to continue to own slaves with "slumbering consciences" and little guilt.[20]

This general chain of arguments can be found within almost every critical immediatist discussion of the A.C.S. during the early 1830s. The arguments constituted objections to colonization that all young missionaries-turned-immediatists felt comfortable enunciating under almost any circumstance. They generally conveyed what early immediatism stood for: opposition to the A.C.S. and to its Liberian colonization ventures, recognition of the humanity and the desires of Afro-Americans, dedication to the proposition that degraded blacks should be uplifted, and unambiguous denunciation of the "peculiar institution." At this early stage of its existence, immediatist abolitionism seemed to stand for a set of priorities that were largely antithetical to the priorities of the Colonization Society. At a deeper level, however, this impression of early immediatist unity and similarity quickly breaks down. First, we shall find that the standard arguments were actually used in distinct ways and with varied emphases. Second, it becomes clear that various immediatists made major and unique additions. These differences in emphasis and in substantive argument itself demonstrate that immediatists stood apart in important essentials at the commencement of their crusade to build a moral antislavery alternative to the Colonization Society. There was a broad spectrum of attitudes.

At one end of the spectrum during the early 1830s were youthful New Englander missionary reformers such as Garrison, Samuel J. May, George Benson, Lydia Maria Child, Samuel Sewall, Ellis Gray Loring, Henry and Maria Weston Chapman, Arnold Buffum, Oliver Johnson, Nathaniel Peabody Rogers, and Henry Clarke Wright. They tended to be religious liberals and mainly Unitarian friends of William Ellery Channing; this affiliation differentiated them from most other evangelical missionaries in the benevolent movement. To be sure, Garrison had been a Baptist before he sloughed off denominationalism entirely. But even in his churchgoing years, he never joined the Baptist Church of Christ. More significant than their formal denominational ties, these people tended to embrace Antinomian religious styles; they were suspicious of accepted dogma, bored by religious ritual, and sometimes even intolerant of the compromises inherent in the Christian fellowship of the benevolent societies. Consequently, their involvement in the benevolent empire had always been limited. With the exception of

Wright, who had been an agent of the Home Missionary Society and the American Sunday School Union, a delegate to Massachusetts Temperance Society conventions, and a participant in the New York anniversary meetings of national Bible, Tract, and Peace societies, none of these reformers had been deeply involved in the broad benevolent society movement. Occasional and often highly qualified support for the American Peace Society, for the Colonization Society, and for various temperance societies generally constituted the extent of their activity. Benson and May, for example, helped form the Windham County auxiliary of the American Peace Society and participated modestly in the county A.C.S. auxiliary, while May also joined the American Total Abstinence Society. Garrison was never a direct participant in any benevolent society. As a young Newburyport editor, he voiced mild approval of the aims of Bible, home mission, and Sunday school societies. Then, in 1829, he delivered an antislavery speech at an A.C.S. rally in Boston's Park Street Church. The next year he considered buying the *American Spectator and Washington City Chronicle*, organ of the colonizationist African Education Society, and he vainly sought out the secretary of the Board of Commissioners for Foreign Missions to help him found an antislavery newspaper. But this was the extent of his contact with the benevolent empire. From time to time, all of these young New England missionary reformers actually seemed to view the old and defunct Federalist party more than benevolent societies as the appropriate agency to remove national sin and malaise.[21]

Owing in some measure to their Antinomian proclivities, then, these young New England reformers had only very modest connections with the benevolent society movement that deferred to the A.C.S. on matters of racial policy. The limited nature of their ties with this movement is crucial to an understanding of their initial critique of the Colonization Society. They were able to offer a more mutinous and drastic commentary on the A.C.S. and its benevolent movement affiliates than most other early immediatists because they did not feel closely tied to those bodies; they had not promoted the "evil" organizations that they now attacked. Because they sensed that they had little stake in the success of the benevolent societies, and owing to their strong Antinomian proclivities, these young immediatists preferred destruction of the A.C.S. and its supporting missionary organizational structure to reform.

Whereas most other early immediatists were intent on pulling away from colonization and charting an abolitionist alternative during the early 1830s, these New Englanders focused on the A.C.S. They often expressed their concerns in Garrison's *Liberator*. In the course of 1831, its first year of publication, the *Liberator* allocated ten times more space to anticolonizationist diatribes than to justifications for immediate emancipation. By 1834 and 1835 most immediatists felt that the A.C.S. was falling apart. Still, at least 20 percent of the space in the *Liberator* accommodated exposés of colonization and attacks on the A.C.S.[22] Indeed, whenever and wherever these young missionaries wrote during the early 1830s, their focus was heavily, if not exclusively, on the Colonization Society.

Their attacks were bold, loud, and polemical. By quoting the personal opinions of specific A.C.S. leaders out of context, the New Englanders made prominent colonizationists seem to be excessively racist and hypocritical. Personal opinions of well-known colonizationists were treated as official declarations of A.C.S. policy. Editorial views expressed in the *African Repository,* a major procolonization publication, were treated as if they had issued from the A.C.S. executive board. Over and over, without specific supporting documentation and in the name of "open, free & fearless exposition of its policy & effects," the Colonization Society was accused of falsehood and deception. The society was "the most specious and wicked disguise ever assumed by Satan to dupe the benevolent." It wore different masks before different audiences: It was a missionary society before the pious, a commercial venture in Africa before the merchants, a crusade in "progressive emancipation" before proponents of gradual abolition, and a mode of preserving slavery and its profits before the Southern planter class. Ralph Randolph Gurley, a prominent national organizer of the A.C.S., was singled out as particularly hypocritical: "He ranges from topic to topic along his crooked ecliptic – from New Orleans on the south to – the old town hall in Concord on the north – shifting his disk, like the changing moon." Finally, the insincerity of colonizationists was underscored through a parody on their logic. They proposed, said the mocking critics, to uplift Africa by sending depraved Afro-Americans armed with liquor, guns, and lies to redeem the so-called dark continent.[23]

One is struck, then, by the rather heavy-handed propaganda techniques that these young New England missionaries deployed against the A.C.S. Because they themselves had been captivated by Colonization Society appeals only a few years, months, or even weeks earlier, they seemed to need to lash out at the agency that had misled them; the denunciations smacked vaguely of a purification rite. The first necessity was for the young immediatist to demonstrate that he was no longer deceived, and therefore no longer morally "tainted," through a vigorous attack upon the A.C.S.; later he could corroborate his changes. The level of moral intensity that distinguished immediatists from other young missionary reformers was clearly evident.

As Garrison, May, Benson, Rogers, and the other New England rebels launched the most extreme form of all early immediatist attacks on the Colonization Society, they came to feel that the cost of moving toward sainthood was increased social isolation. They were separating themselves from their countrymen. Moreover, although they had never been exceedingly active in the benevolent empire, they had nonetheless cultivated a number of warm friendships among missionary colleagues who continued to participate in several of the benevolent societies. These friendships were put under enormous strain, if they were not in fact undermined, when the young insurgents characterized all participants in the benevolent movement as tainted and sinful. "The whole nation is against me," Garrison proclaimed as he gained notoriety as an anti-colonizationist. "The friendship of good men is to be turned into enmity, and their support into opposition." Samuel J. May noted that he and his friends who had joined Garrison in his rabid denunciations of the A.C.S. and its allies had all been denounced as infidels and characterized as enemies of their country. Amasa Walker compared the A.C.S. with the New England Anti-Slavery Society, which he, Garrison, May, and the others had helped to organize: "The former is supported by a formidable array of great names, of judges, governors, and members of Congress, and of course flourishes in wealth under the smiles of public opinion. The latter has nothing to support it, but truth and justice." Apprehensive that she and her New England colleagues were venturing too far from the established missionary community, Lydia Child publicly insisted that they were at least friendly to "peace societies." There were at least some moral reformers within the tainted benevolent empire whom they could continue to befriend. Although they had to redeem their piety, it continued to be possible to embrace at least a few of the missionaries with whom they had formerly associated.[24]

In some measure, Garrison, May, Child, Johnson, Rogers, and the other insurgents were pained by the moral deceptions of the A.C.S. because they themselves had not entirely broken from all of the missionary premises inherent in colonization. Since 1816 when the Colonization Society was founded, its spokesmen had proclaimed that American blacks sent to Africa would act as Christian missionaries and would help uproot heathenism. The New Englanders acknowledged that they had continued to be impressed with this benevolent missionary goal; above all, it partially atoned for the horrid slave trade in which Africa's sons had been removed from their native soil. Still, they noted, the A.C.S. was only hypocritically committed; it said nothing about the material and moral poverty of Afro-Americans, their lack of religious education, and their hesitancy to migrate to Africa. Hence, despite its solid missionary professions, and despite the fact that it was supported by national, state, and local missionary societies, the A.C.S. was not really committed to the spread of Christianity. Rather, the fact that the Colonization Society commanded widespread national support despite false pretenses proved that it was destroying the nation's claim to genuine missionary zeal. Through this assertion, the young New England abolitionists were clearly moving beyond the standard early immediatist argument that the Colonization Society could not Christianize Africa with poor, reluctant, uneducated blacks. Worse than encouraging false hopes for African uplift, they warned, the widespread support for African colonization indicated that America was not yet a godly country. It was not the Promised Land that would uproot heathenism throughout the world. Nor would it ever be, if the A.C.S. succeeded in forcing poor blacks out of the country. Once this was done, white Americans would never have to learn to empathize with and act toward nonwhites as gentility and Christian precepts required. "Before God," Garrison told a group of blacks, "I do not see how this nation can really be civilized and Christianized if you go. You are needed to make us Christians. . . ."[25]

Finally and most drastically the young New England immediatist rebels reserved for the A.C.S. the charge of proslavery. This was, of course, a standard claim of all early immediatists and stemmed from the failure of the Colonization Society to condemn the "peculiar institution" openly. But here, too, the mutinous New Englanders were distinguishable for the extremism of their critique. They charged that colonizationists' tolerance of slavery – the sin of sins – made understandable how the A.C.S. was perverting the American missionary spirit and ignoring its Christian egalitarian values. To be sure, colonizationists professed antislavery and noted that by removing "troublesome" free Negroes to Africa, planters would be induced to manumit their bondsmen. But this was all false and deceptive logic, the young insurgents maintained. The removal of free Negroes would actually cause slaves to lose hope of securing freedom. Moreover, the failure of the A.C.S. to attack slaveholding directly made planters more secure in the moral propriety of their "peculiar institution." Thus, colonizationists constituted a greater obstacle to the removal of slavery than did the Southern planter class. Once the deceivers who ran the A.C.S. had been exposed, truly Christian missionaries had left the society for immediatism, and the organization had been destroyed, planters would be forced to confront the perpetual existence of a free black population and the immorality of slaveholding. As Lydia Child charged, the planter's position was honorable in comparison with the colonizationist's, "for he does not add hypocrisy to wrong." "Even slavery, with its untold horrors, seems less odious than Colonization," charged Henry Wright. But Garrison put the proposition most clearly: "I look upon the overthrow of the Colonization Society as the overthrow of slavery itself – they both stand or fall together."[26]

Thus, the Colonization Society was characterized as the prime agency behind slavery, and slavery was the most insidious evil in the world. Colonizationists had allowed the spirit of slavery to promote false missionary efforts and unchristian racial animosities. Hence Wright, Child, Sewall, Garrison, and the others quickly concluded that despite their continuing desire to send missionaries to Africa, it was foolish even to offer a qualified defense of colonization. In the context of the day, colonization and proslavery had become equivalent. Thus, their plea for immediate abolition had to be made totally antithetical to colonization.

The A.C.S. and repatriation efforts had become unreformable. An agency of the devil was incapable of improvement. Since the Colonization Society was so horrendous, it naturally followed that the supportive benevolent societies – whether Missionary, Tract, Sunday School Union, or whatever – were irrevocably tainted. For the sake of true Christian morality, missionary propriety, and genuine antislavery, it was therefore imperative that truly devout missionaries disassociate from the entire benevolent society nexus, as the young insurgents had done. Anything short of that step endangered missionary piety and purity.[27]

Through these charges, the New Englanders were doing more than assaulting slavery and colonization. With their Antinomian frame of mind, they were attacking their nation for missionary hypocrisy and slavery. By cooperating with the A.C.S., they insisted, the nation's community of genteel missionary reformers was contributing to these horrendous postures. Breaking from their neighbors and even from most missionary reformers, the young insurgents were clearly propounding a far-ranging critique not only of the A.C.S. but also of the entire country. Garrison articulated this critique most fully. He initially did so very early in the 1830s and in the context of attacking the A.C.S. – not during the mid-decade antiabolitionist riots or after exposure to John Humphrey Noyes. Slavery, he proclaimed, was a spirit that tolerated the degradation of one human being by another. Thus, slavery existed well beyond the confines of Southern plantations: "I affirm that Pennsylvania is as really a slave-holding State as Georgia – that the free States are as criminal as the slave-holding States – and that the latter are merely the agents of the former." Garrison was certain that the Democratic party, dominated by Southern planters, was proslavery. But the Whig party was run by colonizationists who included Henry Clay. Therefore, it too had to be proslavery. Indeed, the spirit of slavery pervaded the nation, Garrison proclaimed; this was largely because the major parties were committed to run government to facilitate black bondage and other forms of degradation by men toward their neighbors. Slavery was the spirit of colonization, and if colonization held sway, "we had better burn our bibles, and our Declaration of Independence, and candidly acknowledge ourselves to be incorrigible tyrants and heathen."[28]

In the course of the 1830s Garrison and several of the other young New Englanders sharpened and enlarged this insurgent antislavery posture. By 1840 many of them would maintain that slavery existed wherever human institutions and human practices violated the imperatives of God's Government. By then, "slavery" clearly stood for the disparity between flawed human practices and God's flawless commands.[29]

It was, then, their increasing alienation during the early 1830s with the A.C.S. and the broader benevolent society missionary nexus that brought Garrison and other young New England insurgents to see that the problems of slavery involved more than black bondage in the South. But it is well to remember that this far-reaching metaphorical view of slavery did not originate in an intellectual vacuum. To some degree, such a social vision emerged because young reformers with Antinomian proclivities, such as Child, Rogers, and Garrison, generally had few ties with the established benevolent society movement to which the A.C.S. was intricately linked. With comparatively little stake in or taste for established benevolent reform activities, they did not feel that they had to limit the range and depth of their analysis for fear of displeasing the missionary community and its dominant organizations.

This is not to say that the young New England insurgents were untroubled as they turned to immediatism while repudiating colonization and the benevolent society movement. They had not been very active in the movement but still enjoyed personal friendships with several of its participating missionaries. Indeed, they had been particularly close to several young activists in temperance and peace societies. They watched with a pride mixed with envy as some of these friends assumed full-time, respectably funded careers in those societies while their own early immediatist organizations seemed so impoverished and unstable as to offer no real vocational alternative to unattractive local pastorates or itinerant editorships. If their vision of a morally compromised benevolent empire caused them to withdraw further than ever from association with the missionary community – to strain if not destroy the friendships that they had enjoyed with nonimmediatist missionaries – this left them with only the small number of reformers who had become immediatists for "untainted" association. But there seemed to be little choice in the matter. The very temperament of these young rebels seemed to require them to embrace undefiled piety at all costs, even at the expense of the broader social association that was also required of the diligent missionary who sought conversions for the Lord. Their profoundly Antinomian religious style – their distrust of dogma, their boredom with ritual, and their intolerance of the compromises inherent in the Christian fellowship of the benevolent societies – made them willing to walk within constricted social circles. For these reformers, the diverse community of fellows of benevolent missionary organizations that were held together by consensual dogma and moral compromise seemed far too impure and, indeed, "enslaving." The knowledge they had acquired about the sins of the Colonization Society made them more reluctant than ever to seek out morally compromising missionary fellowship. In the intensity of this reluctance, we shall see, they differed from most other early immediatists.

IV

Young Garrison, Child, Benson, Rogers, and other New England reformers with Antinomian religious proclivities had therefore launched a far-reaching attack on the Colonization Society and supportive missionary groups. Their attack was so sweeping because they had little stake in the A.C.S.–benevolent society movement. Consequently, one would expect more temperate criticisms from more Arminian immediatists who had a greater stake in the benevolent empire. This was the case. The Finneyite revivals of the 1820s and their stress on salvation through good works had prompted immediatists such as Lewis and Arthur Tappan, Elizur Wright, Jr., Joshua Leavitt, Henry Cowles, William Jay, William Goodell, Gerrit Smith, and Amos Phelps to become exceedingly busy promoters of benevolent society activities. Theodore Dwight Weld and James Gillespie Birney had been moderately busy. Arthur Tappan, for example, was almost wholly responsible for the formation of the American Tract Society and was chiefly responsible for the creation of the American Peace Society. He was also a diligent volunteer and a major donor to the American Sunday School Union, the American Bible Society, the Union Missionary Society, the American Education Society, the General Union for Promoting the Observance of the Christian Sabbath, and various New York City–based benevolent groups. Lewis Tappan assisted brother Arthur in many of these ventures. William Jay, founder of the Bible Society, remained its most active promoter for many years. In addition, Jay supported most of the other national benevolent societies and was an honorary president or vice-president of those that he assisted. Gerrit Smith played a major role in the formation of the American Home Missionary Society and the New York Temperance Society. He was also active in the American Board of Commissioners for Foreign Missions. Elizur Wright, Jr., participated in local affiliates of the Temperance, Bible, and Tract societies, served as a tract distributor in western Pennsylvania, and helped to found the Western Reserve branch of the American Education Society. Illustrations such as these of very extensive benevolent society involvement may be cited at considerable length – for Phelps, for Goodell, for Leavitt, and for other early immediatists who were more restrained in their critique than the young insurgent New Englanders. Only Weld and Birney stood out for their very modest involvement in the benevolent movement – Weld because he despised organized, institutionalized missionary activity and Birney perhaps in some measure because he resided during the 1820s and early 1830s in slaveholding regions of the South where there were few benevolent society activities.[30]

Largely because of their extensive involvement in the benevolent empire, these comparatively temperate immediatist missionaries participated much more actively in the A.C.S. during the 1820s than the more mutinous New Englanders did. Indeed, without very substantial donations from Arthur Tappan and Gerrit Smith, the Colonization Society would have been in very shaky financial condition during its formative years. Even young Elizur Wright, Jr., who was never very enthusiastic about expatriations to Africa, felt that if he did not support the A.C.S, he would disappoint his missionary colleagues in the other benevolent societies with whom he craved association. After all, the benevolent nexus had given the A.C.S. full responsibility for a moral remedy to slavery. Young Theodore Weld felt much the same way and conveyed these feelings to James Birney as he urged Birney to support Colonization Society missionary ventures.[31]

When an accumulation of misgivings about the A.C.S. caused reformers such as these to leave the organization during the early 1830s and to turn to immediatism, all of them continued to participate in other benevolent missionary societies. Moreover, they tried to operate the American Anti-Slavery Society (A.A.S.S.) precisely as the other benevolent societies operated. For example, they based the A.A.S.S. agency system upon the way missionary agents had conducted themselves as solicitors for the established benevolent societies. They also saw to it that the A.A.S.S. constitution conformed with basic provisions of benevolent society constitutions. The notion of having local and state A.A.S.S. auxiliaries derived, as well, from the benevolent missionary organizational experience. Indeed, their emphasis on winning over local ministers and the stress on making conversions in the countryside - rather than in the cities was rooted in earlier benevolent movement strategies.[32] Eventually these more temperate immediatists recognized that no matter what they said, most of their beloved benevolent missionary societies would not condemn slavery. Even then, they refused to abandon the entire benevolent empire. Rather, they participated in the free missions movement to purge the benevolent societies of their one great sin. Certain of them even founded the American Missionary Association (A.M.A.) as a result of particular dissatisfaction with the Home Missionary Society (H.M.S.). But the A.M.A. was not intended to destroy the H.M.S. Rather, it was to deplete H.M.S. income and popular support until the H.M.S. abandoned the practice of accepting slaveholding members and "Slave Power" donations.[33] Differing from the early New England insurgents, these more reticent immediatists had been so active in the benevolent societies at the beginning of their involvement in missionary work that they were never able to make a clean break with the benevolent movement. Rather, quite unlike the insurgents, they found enormous emotional and spiritual satisfaction in the community of Christian fellowship, the ritual, and the relatively Orthodox consensual dogma that the benevolent societies offered. Much more than the insurgents, they seemed almost to require the embrace of the devout in the larger missionary community, even if the piety of many in that community had been compromised through failure to repudiate the Colonization Society.

The point, then, is that the same two factors that conditioned the postures of young New England insurgents - religious styles and the degree of involvement in the benevolent movement – also determined the stance of the more temperate. Comparison of the belief systems of these two types of early immediatists during the opening years of the 1830s readily bears out this conclusion.

First, unlike the insurgent New England missionaries-turned-immediatists, the more temperate immediatists believed that effective missionary reform simply could not exist without the benevolent empire, however tainted it had become through its involvement with the A.C.S. "We love the cause of Foreign and Home Missions; we love the Tract and Bible and Education Societies. . . . We wish to see all these things done, and the work of emancipation not left undone," they proclaimed. It was necessary to "make the most direct and vigorous exertions" to assure that enemies of immediatism did not "shut us out from the pale of religious and benevolent societies." After all, even though many reformers in the benevolent missionary nexus did not see through the "colonization scheme," they were still performing salutary moral deeds. Light alone was needed to show them that the Colonization Society was anathema to the godly goals of the other missionary societies.[34]

Second, although both the early insurgents and the more temperate young immediatists attacked the A.C.S. for false missionary efforts – for sending "troublesome" free blacks to Africa with liquor, tobacco, and arms, hoping thereby to shore up Southern slavery – these "sins" only soured the New England insurgents on missionary enterprises. Their more reticent colleagues sought desperately to believe that the morality propagated by the other benevolent societies would pressure the A.C.S. to become a truly pious missionary agency. The salutary activities of Tract, Bible, Sunday School, Peace, and Foreign Missions societies in heathen lands had surely proven that even "barbaric" Africa could be Christianized without guns, tobacco, rum, and profit-hungry settlers. Rather, such profane A.C.S. practices "will stab the cause of missions to the heart." Indeed, cheap, deceptive "commerce and christianity have never yet succeeded well together." By invoking the traditions of the truly moral missionary societies, the Colonization Society might learn that Africa had to be converted with Bibles and Christian tracts. A.C.S. missionaries in Africa would discover that they needed the same deep piety as Tract and Bible Society missionaries laboring in other heathen lands.[35]

Thus, the more temperate young immediatists of the early 1830s were so deeply committed to the pious missionary tradition of the benevolent movement as to hope that this piety might reform the A.C.S. It might turn the Colonization Society from immoral proslavery deceptions into a genuine missionary body for the Christianization of Africa's heathen. If that transformation ever took place – if the A.C.S. ever became a genuinely Christian missionary venture – the benevolent

movement would be liberated of proslavery and other immoral blem-
ishes and the millennium would be close at hand. The Lord's "influences
will rush in themselves like the fluids of nature to a vacuum."[36] Quite
unlike their insurgent colleagues, then, these more mild-mannered immediatists desperately wanted to rescue the Colonization Society. The
major threat to the piety of the American missionary community would
be dissipated once the rescue was completed.

Whereas the New England rebels saw all colonizationists as agents of
Satan, the more temperate young immediatists grasped for signs that
the Colonization Society might be made into a truly pious missionary
agency. Their hope rested in sincere evangelical missionary colleagues
who continued to belong to the A.C.S. The society's constituency was
heterogeneous. Consequently, there had to be pious if uninformed
Christians as well as the ungodly: "The devoutest missionary, ready to
pour out his life on the sands of Africa, is jostled by the trafficker in
human flesh; the humbler self-denying Christian listens to the praises
of the Society from the unblushing profligate. . . ." It was unfair to
disbelieve "the sincerity of the disinterestedness of any man who up-
holds the Col. Soc." Indeed, founding fathers of the A.C.S. such as
Robert Finley were "great good men." It was hoped that the "very many
excellent citizens and devouted Christians" in the A.C.S. who abhorred
slavery as much as any abolitionist, would come to realize that the
A.C.S. repatriation program would not lead to emancipation. Indeed,
there was evidence that some of the best men in the Colonization Society were becoming aroused and would either turn the organization into
an antislavery missionary establishment or would join immediatist anti-
slavery groups.[37]

There were, then, serious hopes that truly pious missionaries within
the A.C.S. would rise up and move the society toward genuinely anti-
slavery and truly Christian goals. But by late 1833 and early 1834, most
of the more reticent young immediatists were short on faith that this
would come to pass. Rather, they were coming to feel that true Christians in the A.C.S. should leave that society and join with them in
purifying the entire benevolent movement. Together, they could replace
the A.C.S. with the American Anti-Slavery Society as the racial reform
organ within that movement. Henry Cowles of Oberlin College clearly
articulated this shifting perspective on the A.C.S.: "I have been like
most others a friend of the Colonization Society, & I am not yet prepared to condemn it altogether. The motives & wisdom of its founders I
cannot impeach." Yet Cowles found that "the selfish motive of making
slavery itself more safe," not Christian benevolence, seemed to have
drowned out the society's pious, and "I know not how this thing can be
remedied. . . ." Thus, he concluded that true Christians needed to turn
away from the A.C.S. and toward groups like the A.A.S.S., which
propounded "speedy emancipation." Cowles was echoed by other tem-

perate immediatist colleagues. They noted that the A.C.S. had gone bankrupt in its moral principles. The pious minority in the society had lost out to leaders who hated blacks and to slaveholders who felt that Africa could be used to expel "undesirable" free Negroes from America. Consequently, pious Christian missionaries were obligated to leave the A.C.S.; they were required to work to turn the A.A.S.S. into the racial organ of the benevolent empire.[38]

Thus, by 1834 the more reticent immediatists continued to endorse the benevolent society movement but felt that it could only survive internal moral decay by expunging the irrevocably tainted A.C.S. and by replacing it with a truly Christian antislavery organization. Yet it is well to note that, quite unlike the New England insurgents, confrontation and even disillusionment with the A.C.S. did not curb their hopes of Christianing heathen lands through voluntary colonization of American Negroes. In the years after 1834, William Jay advocated West Indian colonization. Lewis Tappan urged immediatists to "form an Auxiliary to the A.B.C.F. [American Board of Commissioners for Foreign] Missions" for the purpose of converting Africa. James Birney favored a plan to colonize free blacks in a buffer state between Mexico and the United States, while Gerrit Smith proclaimed that true immediatists "should delight, as much as any others, to see the whole Western coast of Africa fringed with civilization and christian communities." By 1846 several of these immediatists found themselves participating in or at least supporting the American Missionary Association as a genuine antislavery missionary organization that was intent, among other purposes, on uplifting Africa's heathen. This is all to say that more temperate immediatists arrived at a determination, early in the 1830s, to remain as close as their Christian consciences would permit to the benevolent missionary groups and the ideas that they had actively supported during the 1820s. Thus, after turning to immediatism, they remained firmly committed to more than Bible and tract distribution, Sunday schools, peace crusades, and temperance efforts. They also clung to the goal of Christianizing Africa. Had the A.C.S. assumed a position unambiguously opposing slavery, they would most certainly have continued to champion its African missionary ventures.[39]

Clearly, then, temperate immediatists of the early 1830s differed significantly from the insurgents who had totally repudiated the A.C.S., the benevolent empire, and the principle of colonization. Unlike their more Antinomian New England colleagues, they deeply and emotionally craved the benevolent community of Christian fellowship and were willing to tolerate certain "impurities" to retain social contact with nonimmediatist missionaries. Differing from the less convivial if more uncompromising insurgents, they evidenced little relish for the social marginality and unchartered personal futures that could have been the result of total withdrawal from the benevolent movement. But whereas young New England insurgents very closely resembled one another in terms of the vehemence and far-reaching nature of their criticisms of the A.C.S. and the benevolent empire, their more reticent immediatist colleagues sometimes differed in the manner in which they presented their criticisms.

Brief comparison of the thoughts of three influential but temperate early immediatists – William Jay, Gerrit Smith, and James Birney – readily demonstrates this difference. Jay, a reputable lawyer and jurist from Westchester, New York, made a critique of the A.C.S. that was unique in its balance and circumspection even among more reticent immediatists. Both immediately before and after he left the A.C.S., Jay persistently maintained that it had assets and liabilities: "It is neither a wicked conspiracy on the one hand, nor a panacea for slavery on the other." Jay noted several Colonization Society assets: support from "many wise and good men" and the potential to rescue free Negroes from oppressive and unchristian conditions in the South. But these were outweighed by the society's liabilities: "impudent management" in its Liberian colony, failure to reduce the number of slaves significantly, and refusal to oppose the "peculiar institution" on moral grounds. Thus, Jay logically concluded that the American Anti-Slavery Society, with all of the assets and none of the liabilities of the A.C.S., should simply replace it in the benevolent movement.[40] Gerrit Smith, on the other hand, refused to balance assets against liabilities. He stood unequivocally by the A.C.S. during the early 1830s when even the most reticent critics of the Colonization Society moved on to the A.A.S.S. Much more imprecise in his thinking than Jay, Smith insisted that the two organizations pursued the same benevolent antislavery ends and should cooperate. But by late 1835, when Smith finally perceived the A.C.S. equivocating on slavery and black rights, he quit, concluding that the society had no redeeming value. Moreover, unlike Jay, he began to turn against the entire benevolent missionary movement because it continued to be supportive of the A.C.S.[41] Birney illustrated still another variation among more temperate early immediatists. He was a prosperous Alabama slaveholding planter in the 1820s, but deep guilts induced him to repudiate the "peculiar institution" and to become an A.C.S. fund raiser. Disillusioned because the Colonization Society did not seem to be undercutting slavery, he resigned and went to work for the A.A.S.S. in New York City. The move to New York provided him with opportunities that he had not had in Alabama to become active in the benevolent movement. But unlike Jay and Smith, he never became very active in the benevolent empire. Unlike many other early immediatists, however, insurgent and temperate, Birney never lost enthusiasm for "truly Christian" colonization of Africa as a result of his distrust of the A.C.S.[42]

In sum, then, we see that insurgent and more reticent early imme-diatists differed over essentially two basic points. Insurgents were cer-tain that slavery involved more than black bondage in the South; the others were not. Insurgents sought to repudiate the entire benevolent missionary community; the more temperate sought to reform that community by replacing the A.C.S. with the A.A.S.S. In addition to these distinctions between insurgent and temperate immediatists, we noted certain subtle distinctions among the more temperate. Thus, although all early immediatists shared certain ideas, values, and ex-periences, attitudinal diversity was detectable from the start. In some measure, at least, these differences derived from variation in missionary temperaments. Insurgents craved undefiled piety at all costs; untainted moral associations meant more to them than the camaraderie of Chris-tian fellowship. Despite greater attitudinal variation among them, more temperate immediatists desperately desired the convivial mixing of be-nevolent missionaries even if this risked "taint" from the less than pious.

V

The range of abolitionist opinion during the early 1830s extended beyond insurgent and more reticent immediatists. Although mission-aries of both sorts broke fully with the Colonization Society, endorsed immediatism, and supported the American Anti-Slavery Society, there were other missionaries who evidenced a third view located somewhere between colonization and immediatism. Because it was espoused by reformers who were neither full-fledged immediatist abolitionists nor devout colonizationists, scholars have tended to neglect or to de-emphasize them. We know much less about their collective social traits than we know about other early 1830s abolitionists. To be sure, there is abundant data on some of them, particularly Lyman Beecher and his daughter Catharine, Ashbel Green, Leonard Bacon, Harrison Gray Otis, Horace Mann, Sarah J. Hale, David M. Reese, Joseph Tracy, and Lewis Tappan's brothers, John and Charles. But we have almost no biograph-ical detail for others, such as Ebenezer Baldwin, E. A. Andrews, D. H. Emerson, David Oliphant, George W. Benedict, and Frederick Freeman.

Only a very rough picture of certain of the common characteristics of these abolitionist-colonizationists, or "halfway abolitionists," may there-fore be drawn. They tended to be older than most insurgent and tem-perate immediatists; this may help to explain why they seemed to cling to a late eighteenth-century gradualist antislavery posture. In the main Congregationalists and staunch Calvinists, several feared that Finneyite revivalism overemphasized the potential inherent in individual good works. Sin was very difficult to eradicate – considerably more difficult than Finneyite theological "innovations" let Christians believe. Halfway abolitionists generally resided in urban areas of New England, particularly Connecticut and Massachusetts. For the most part, they enjoyed considerable wealth, and their prestige often transcended community boundaries. They became young adults during the early national period and often became involved in efforts to forge a unique cultural identity for the New Nation. All were exceedingly sympathetic to the established benevolent reform community. Indeed, Bacon, Lyman Beecher, John and Charles Tappan, and Sarah Hale became quite active in many of the benevolent societies. Moreover, all looked with great favor upon the A.C.S., and this was where they differed most significantly from both insurgent and temperate immediatists. During the 1820s insurgents had not assumed significant roles in either the A.C.S. or the larger benevolent empire. More temperate immediatists had put much more effort into Bible, Tract, Home Missionary, and Peace societies than they had devoted to the Colonization Society. But the halfway abolitionists of the early 1830s had generally concentrated most of their reform energies in the A.C.S.[43]

The broad philosophic perspective of halfway abolitionists is difficult to delineate. Like many late eighteenth-century Federalists, they ranked order, harmony, and organic Christian unity high as priorities. Indeed, most idealized a society of stable and distinctly separated ranks and orders guided by the spiritual leadership of the clergy. But they also tended to find favor with the developing Northern marketplace society of vigorously competing individuals where each entrepreneur made his separate peace with God. Like many others who became active in missionary reform causes after the War of 1812, they supported religious and philanthropic enterprises that disseminated "sound" Christian morality among the materially and spiritually "impoverished." But they also insisted that Christian reforms had to be promulgated with gentle reasonableness, the soft answer, self-control, and patient appeals. Activities for missionary uplift were useful as long as they helped to unite a community's moral sentiments. But if a missionary's reforms were advocated with harshness and bellicosity, or if those reforms diverged too drastically from the dominant values and rituals of a community, unfortunate and unnecessary social disorders and conflicts could ensue. As Lyman Beecher noted, "True wisdom consists in advocating a cause only so far as the community will sustain the reformer." Quite unlike early insurgents and even unlike many of the more temperate immediatists, these were missionaries who prized broad community accord at all costs. They perceived only distress and anxiety as the consequence of separating from consensual dogma and ritual.[44]

By the early 1830s all of these halfway abolitionists were certain that slavery was sinful and constituted a terrible moral blight upon the nation. Active in the A.C.S., they watched with great displeasure as conflict erupted between colonizationists on the one hand and immediatist abolitionists (insurgent and temperate) on the other. To this point, they had been most content with the A.C.S., for its gradualist antislavery approach had drawn together people of differing views and had averted the socially divisive sorts of controversies that the dangerous slavery question had the potential of generating. Slavery was to be tolerated as a sin and slowly eradicated, as the A.C.S. proposed, in a way that would minimize disorders or dislocation in either the North or the South. The Colonization Society policy of encouraging emancipation of bondsmen by organizing for the repatriation of free Negroes was both abolition and colonization; the two were inseparable missionary enterprises. For this reason, the young immediatists, particularly the seemingly belligerent and caustic New England insurgents, had grievously erred in attacking the A.C.S. as an agency of the slavocracy. Worse yet, in provoking conflict with colonizationists, immediatists were promoting internal social disorder that was dividing the missionary community and weakening the social fabric that held the nation together. This was the posture that Lyman and Catharine Beecher, Leonard Bacon, David Reese, Frederick Freeman, Mathew Carey, Sarah Hale, D. H. Emerson, Ashbel Green, and Horace Mann consistently assumed in the early 1830s in response to the immediatist attack upon their beloved Colonization Society – the one missionary organization they trusted to eliminate slavery without massive dislocation or civil war. Presiding over Lane Seminary, the scene of intense controversy and division between colonizationists and young immediatists, Lyman Beecher stated this halfway abolitionist posture most clearly: "I am not apprized of the ground of controversy between the Colonizationists and the Abolitionists. I am myself both, without perceiving in myself any inconsistency." The colonization approach to antislavery was better than the immediatist approach, Beecher added, because it did not "row upstream" against public opinion. Rather, while preserving social calm, it offered slaveholders "an easy, practicable way of doing their duty" and emancipating their bondsmen. Because the Colonization Society was so useful in the crusade to eradicate slavery, "the controversy likely to be introduced by an effort to put it down" would be most destructive. If immediatists continued to attack colonizationists, unnecessary social disruption and antagonistic feelings toward the antislavery cause would be the unfortunate consequences.[45]

In addition to reproaching immediatists for "misdirected" attacks on the Colonization Society, halfway abolitionists charged that the immediatists lacked understanding of the serious dilemmas facing Southern slaveholders. There were many kind Christian planters who treated their slaves well and cooperated with Southern churches to mitigate the ills of the "peculiar institution." Warm and understanding but persistent appeal to the benevolence of these planters could induce them to manumit their slaves gradually. By attempting "to sympathize with them in the existence of an evil," the missionary could help to eradicate the evil. On the other hand, by "joining in odious denunciations against our southern brethren," immediatists were incurring their resentment and were dissuading them from performing their Christian duty of manumission.[46]

Given these broad outlines of halfway abolitionist ideology, there would seem to be more cause to characterize them as antislavery colonizationists than as abolitionists. After all, they discouraged immediatist attacks upon the A.C.S. and, like many Colonization Society leaders, they sympathized with the dilemmas of the "good" slaveholder. But they differed from other missionaries who remained in the A.C.S. during the early 1830s in the sense that they sincerely sought cooperation between immediatists and colonizationists in a harmonious antislavery coalition of pious missionary brethren. To achieve this cooperation, they urged A.C.S. leaders to proclaim openly their antislavery sympathies; this action would allay the suspicions of immediatists that the Colonization Society was proslavery. At the same time, they hoped "that the Abolitionists as a body will become more calm and less denunciatory . . ." of the colonizationists. Everything good would be achieved if "the abolitionist press abolition, not seek to destroy the colonizationist, and the colonizationist, let him press still harder colonization. . . ."[47]

Unfortunately for these halfway abolitionists, immediatists and colonizationists continued vigorously to denounce one another. By late 1834 most of them had concluded that cooperation between the A.C.S. and the immediatist A.A.S.S. would not come to pass. Moreover, because A.C.S. leaders refused to heed their admonitions by issuing unambigous antislavery proclamations, several halfway abolitionists became almost as disenchanted with the Colonization Society as they were with the A.A.S.S. Neither organization seemed sensitive to their desires. Meanwhile, the clashes between the A.C.S. and the A.A.S.S. were discrediting Christian antislavery and were tearing at the social fabric of society.

In response to these distressing and disorderly conditions, halfway abolitionists from Boston's inner missionary circle of benevolent society leaders took action. Disenchanted with the local A.C.S. affiliate to which most belonged, they founded and worked to sustain the American Union for the Relief and Improvement of the Colored Race. Against neither immediatist abolitionism nor colonization, the American Union was to embrace both; it was pledged to a peaceful union of all Christian antislavery opinions. By professing "a conciliatory spirit, a Bible spirit," founders of the American Union indicated that they were intent on "securing the concurrence of slaveholders" in emancipatory measures "by an appeal to their human and Christian principles." In a program that smacked neither of colonization nor of immediatism but nonetheless was clearly of a missionary nature, the American Union announced that it was going to promote religious instruction of slaves plus education and training for free Negroes. Moreover, it would provide objective, dispassionate analysis of the "peculiar institution." It would send an agent to the South to study slavery firsthand. The Union would also compile statistics and other "reliable" data on the condition of the free blacks. It was hoped that this program would not offend immediatists, colonizationists, or slaveholders. Rather, it might slowly moderate all three. It might move them quietly and harmoniously but with a pious sense of urgency toward preparing slaves for gradual manumission and toward ameliorating the unchristian oppressions of free Negroes.[48]

The American Union never became a viable organization. It was mildly active in 1835 and 1836 but then collapsed. Yet the existence of the organization demonstrated quite tangibly that a body of antislavery opinion among missionary reformers existed along the borderlands between colonization and immediatism. It is immaterial whether we characterize this opinion as the most antislavery element of colonization or the most procolonization element of early immediatist abolitionism. What is important is that the halfway abolitionist, considered alongside the insurgent and the more temperate immediatist, demonstrated the existence of a wide range of abolitionist perspectives in the early 1830s. Where attitudes were concerned, significant differences among abolitionists were detectable from the very beginning of the immediatist crusade.

VI

Early divergence of attitudes substantially influenced social aspects of the immediatist crusade. Responding to uncomfortable feelings of moral distance from the missionaries within the benevolent empire, cravings for moral purity, and inner needs for camaraderie, young immediatists with differing attitudes began to draw together during the early and mid-1830s within small, informal intimacy circles or sanctuaries. Literally dozens of these informal groups or clusters formed, and membership composition frequently changed. Sometimes various insurgents came together to form a sanctuary such as the Boston Clique. Sometimes more temperate immediatists formed clusters of their own; Lewis Tappan's personal circle was one. On occasion, and despite their temperamental differences, a few insurgents and temperate immediatists joined hands in still another type of small intimacy group. The New York City office of the A.A.S.S. housed this sort of collectivity in the mid-1830s. Sometimes a circle was forged by immediatists who seemed to have both insurgent and temperate characteristics. By the 1850s a few halfway abolitionists even joined certain immediatist circles. Moreover, as our analysis of Elizur Wright, Jr., will reveal, an immediatist might join and leave a number of clusters or sanctuaries in the course of his life.

As we proceed in the next several chapters to investigate some of the many immediatist intimacy circles, we shall also find that group life in such a small informal collectivity often significantly modified the attitudes and temperaments of those who joined. After less than a decade in the Boston Clique, for example, Garrison, the fiery insurgent of the early 1830s, had become a more temperate, conciliatory manager of group activity. Similarly, as we shall see, the relatively mild-mannered Lewis Tappan of 1832 soon became more rebellious, daring, and distant from morally compromising missionaries in the benevolent movement in response to the increasingly militant disposition of his seemingly temperate group. There were always a number of significant differences within this first generation of immediatists, but as time transpired the differences could often be traced to the particular social dynamics of their various intimacy circles or sanctuaries.

Part II

Sanctuaries

CHAPTER 2

INSURGENTS OF
THE BOSTON CLIQUE

The young New England insurgents who rebelled against the whole benevolent empire displayed a complex religious style. The style was at once distinguishable from yet similar to that of evangelical missionaries who remained in the empire. Unlike most of the evangelicals who remained, the insurgents tended to favor Quaker and especially Unitarian devotional links. They rejected the rigidity of Orthodox Calvinism, they were suspicious of the exuberant emotionalism of Finneyite revivalism, and they occasionally even turned against the containment and dogma inherent in all formal church services. For the most part, insurgents favored the greater "mental freedom" and the emphasis upon individual piety that they perceived to exist within "liberal" religion. Liberal denominations seemed more compatible with their cravings to reform the world actively than was either Finneyite evangelicism or Orthodoxy. In particular, Quaker and Unitarian religious styles gave them a sense of direct personal responsibility for the improvement of conditions about them; there was no all-powerful benevolent movement of evangelical Christian fellows mediating their efforts. But there was also a quality to their insurgency that they shared with benevolent movement reformers – a belief that Christ's loyal agents had to struggle cooperatively against sin. Benevolent society missionaries often drew together in informal Finneyite bands embodying this evangelical premise. Similarly, insurgents believed that as missionaries for the Lord, they would have to pool their efforts somehow. Therefore, the insurgents were similar to most benevolent empire reformers in their adherence to the evangelical premise that missionary struggles were collective endeavors. They differed in the intensity of their craving for individual autonomy and in their aversion to the controls exerted by the benevolent community of Christian fellows.

We noted how estranged the insurgents felt while formulating their attacks on slavery, the Colonization Society, and the benevolent society movement generally. They sensed that they were deeply isolated not only from New Englanders generally but even from the Christian reform community. This sense of estrangement came as an unpleasant shock; few had realized that their missionary quest for personal piety could undermine the outgoing social routines of their daily existence. Among other things, they had underestimated the important bonds that New England textile and shipping interests had forged with Southern planters – bonds that the benevolent reform community refused to challenge. "It did not occur to us that nearly every religious sect, and every political party, would side with the oppressor," Garrison noted, while they stigmatized "the advocates of universal liberty as incendiaries and outlaws. . . ." "We were slow to believe," Samuel J. May recalled, "that our fellow-citizens of the New England States could be so besotted by the influence of the institution of slavery, that they would *outrage* our *persons* in its defense." Maria Weston Chapman found that when she embraced insurgency, she suddenly lost her considerable social standing and was insulted by store clerks as she walked the streets of Boston. Other insurgents made similar discoveries – how their reputations were undercut, how the religious community snubbed them, and how the "wealthy and aristocratic portions of the people give us little or no countenance. . . ."[1]

After they proclaimed their devoutness, the young New England insurgents were unwilling to regain community respect and affection by backtracking on their missionary declarations. They realized that an advocate of divinity "cannot stir *their waters* unless you are *outside*" – that he must stand alone with God if he was to continue to champion true piety. And yet they sought "a place in the hearts of my fellow men – a *kind & loving* place." Christ had admonished his followers not to satisfy their social needs by consorting with sinners but to join with Him and His Apostles. Similarly, the insurgents decided to remedy "the dispersion of the Saints" by joining with one another in their mission for the Lord. If "the world separate itself from us," Charles Follen noted, "it leads us to find a world in ourselves and in each other." There they could "look upon one another's countenances, and be glad."[2]

During the early and mid-1830s diverse insurgents in various parts of New England joined hands to forge various small "worlds in ourselves and in each other." Most of these informal groups or clusters were formed in Massachusetts – particularly in Worcester, Lynn, Hingham, Plymouth, and especially Boston. Very few small intimacy groups were forged in Connecticut, a Colonization Society stronghold. But there is evidence of early group formations in Concord, New Hampshire, in Portland, Maine, and in a few smaller communities in upper New England. A few isolated pockets of insurgency were even detectable outside of New England, namely in Indiana's Upper Whitewater Valley, in Salem, Ohio, and in Philadelphia's Quaker community. The most influential of all early insurgent intimacy groups, however, was the Boston Clique. The Clique set the editorial policy for the major insurgent newspaper, the *Liberator*. It regularly controlled the executive boards of the Massachusetts Anti-Slavery Society (initially called the New England Anti-Slavery Society) and the New England Non-Resistance Society. Clique membership was not restricted to Bostonians, and those who resided in other parts of New England regularly advised less active groups of insurgents and publicized their affairs in the *Liberator*. Moreover, by 1843 the Clique monitored the activities of the American Anti-Slavery Society. By controlling the A.A.S.S. executive board, it was even able to influence abolitionist activity outside New England. In particular, the Clique decidedly shaped the editorial policies of the *National Anti-Slavery Standard* (New York City), the *Pennsylvania Freeman* (Philadelphia), and the *Anti-Slavery Bugle* (Salem, Ohio). Thus, the Boston Clique emerged as the center for more than early New England insurgency. It came to dominate the major organizations and publications that have traditionally been labeled Garrisonian. We turn, then, to our case study of the Boston Clique both to understand the evolution of the most important segment of New England insurgency and to lodge precise meaning in the term "Garrisonian."

II

The first sign of the emergence of a Boston Clique was detectable in October 1830. Samuel Sewall and Ellis Gray Loring, two wealthy Boston Unitarian lawyers, and Samuel J. May, a Unitarian minister from Brooklyn, Connecticut, were much impressed by Garrison's public pleadings for immediate emancipation. They met privately with him in Boston, agreed to subsequent meetings, and committed themselves to help fund the launching of Garrison's *Liberator*. Over the next few years the three were joined by a diverse assortment of other New England insurgents: Arnold Buffum, George William Benson, Henry Egbert Benson, Oliver Johnson, Charles Follen, Francis Jackson, Maria Weston Chapman and her sisters Anne, Deborah, and Caroline Weston. By 1839 Buffum, Sewall, and the Benson brothers were slowly becoming disengaged from Clique activities, while Wendell Phillips, Edmund Quincy, Nathaniel Peabody Rogers, Parker Pillsbury, and Henry Wright had become central to Clique operations. Although Samuel May, Jr., had been won over to immediatism by 1837, he did not work regularly with the Clique until the early 1840s, by which time Follen had died. In 1844 Rogers and the Clique parted company. John A. Collins, David and Lydia Maria Child, Abigail Kelley, and Stephen S. Foster were good friends with several Clique members and periodically thought of themselves as members.

It is clear, then, that, although the Boston Clique was very small, it underwent some changes in membership. But from the late 1830s on, Garrison, May, May, Jr., Loring, Johnson, Chapman, the Weston sisters, Jackson, Quincy, Pillsbury, Wright, and Rogers (until 1844) were the essential figures in Clique operations. The Childs, Kelley, Foster, and

Collins were erratic if sometimes significant participants in Clique ventures.

It is very difficult to delineate common social characteristics of Boston Clique members. For some we have abundant data; for others almost none at all. We cannot determine the pervasiveness of any one social characteristic through the entire Clique with any degree of precision. At least a few members – Garrison, David Child, and Quincy – had been Federalists. But only David Child, a peripheral member or fellow traveler, ever held political office. None had a rural Finneyite evangelical background. Phillips, Pillsbury, and Wright came from orthodox Congregational homes. Several came to endorse Quakerism. But most members were reared in the cultural milieu of a rather sophisticated Boston Unitarianism and Transcendentalism. Some joined William Ellery Channing's Boston Unitarian congregation. It seems safe to conclude that a preponderance of the Clique were religious liberals and either never embraced or had at least departed from old-line Calvinist orthodoxies. Some members, especially Garrison, Johnson, and Rogers, had considerable experience as newspaper editors. After Sewall left, Loring, Rogers, and Quincy were the only lawyers in the Clique. Caroline and Deborah Weston and Charles Follen were the teachers. May and May, Jr., were lifelong ministers, while Pillsbury and Wright had been ministers for short periods. Phillips, Quincy, Chapman, the Westons, May, and Jackson had come from distinguished Massachusetts patrician families, but Garrison and Wright came from undistinguished lower-middle-class backgrounds. May and May, Jr., were first cousins, whereas Quincy was a distant cousin to May and May, Jr. Chapman served as foster mother for Phillips's wife, Ann Terry Greene. May was an intimate of the Benson household and married Helen Benson to Garrison.[3]

In general, then, there were several social characteristics that seemed to pervade the Boston Clique: liberal religion, membership in professions, friendships and family ties, and distance from party politics and officeholding. Before becoming insurgents, all members mixed freely and comfortably with the genteel New England urban middle class. When they became immediatists, relatively few members of this class would have much to do with them. Nevertheless, their Boston constituency always consisted of some professionals. A majority of these professionals were Unitarians and Quakers; several considered themselves Transcendentalists. The Boston constituency also included a few merchants and skilled artisans plus a number of free blacks.[4]

Despite the common characteristics of Boston Clique participants, each member was distinguishable in certain specific particulars from the others: Phillips for never bending from his strict Calvinist upbringing, Wright for his almost single-minded concern first with child-rearing reform and later with nonresistance, Loring for his commitment to established legal procedures, Quincy for his aristocratic mannerisms and values, Rogers for his initial extreme liking and subsequent profound distrust of organizational activities, Follen for his background as a European student activitist, and so forth.

This is all to say that there is insufficient information for precise generalization about the common social characteristics of the Boston Clique. Existing data on the apparent pervasiveness of liberal religion, professional affiliation, and urban orientation point to a sort of cosmopolitanism that would seem to have accented the strongly independent, insurgent personalities of Clique members. There were no drab conformists in the group.

Major ideological differences among Clique members underscore their strongly independent qualities. In his biography of Edmund Quincy, for example, Robert W. Tolf demonstrated that his man had a mind quite unlike that of most of Garrison's other followers. Quincy was not a radical but a latter-day Federalist whose ideas were geared toward conserving the values of a mid to late eighteenth-century deferential society. Although Ellis Gray Loring was also continually in good standing with Garrison and the Clique, his lifelong belief in the efficacy of technical legalism distinguished him from all other members. The slaveholder "has a *legal*, not a *moral* right to regard the *Emancipation* of his slaves, as the taking away of [his] *property*," Loring once explained to an astonished Garrison, insisting that the strict letter of the law had to be taken seriously. While others in the Clique vehemently objected to the formation of the Massachusetts Abolition Society as a "conservative" challenge to the Massachusetts Anti-Slavery Society in 1839, legalistic Loring wished "conservative" challengers well as long as the two rival Massachusetts organizations were legally distinguishable.[5]

More than anything else, the peace issue underscored the sharp differences in attitude within the Clique. By the late 1830s Henry Wright represented one extreme. He opposed the use of force under any and all conditions, defensive or offensive. Garrison agreed with Wright's posture, although he did not emulate Wright's adamancy. Quincy theoretically opposed violence under any conditions but also insisted that some measure of government "force" was needed to give structure and predictability to daily business transactions. Follen favored pacifism in all circumstances save where it was necessary to restrain people from interfering with the rights of others. Jackson endorsed Wright's doctrine on nonresistance, "altho' I have not been able to practice it, because of my early training. . . ." Anne Weston voiced an even less pacific posture: "I am apt to *believe* in peace & sympathize with fighting ." Samuel May, Jr., was never a pacifist, much less a nonresistant, although he helped finance the Non-Resistance Society newspaper. Wendell Phillips was at the other end of the spectrum on the peace question. He had difficulty with many brands of pacifism.[6]

There were still other important issues of the day upon which Clique members held diverse views. When Garrison took up Anti-Sabbatarianism in the 1840s, Wright, Foster, Pillsbury, Chapman, and

Jackson encouraged and often assisted him. But Quincy, May, and Phillips saw the Anti-Sabbatarian cause as secondary and possibly diversionary from more pressing problems.[7] Nor were all members of the Clique wedded to Garrison's admonitions against using the ballot box. Jackson and May, Jr., voted at least periodically throughout the pre-Civil War decades. There is some evidence that Loring voted for Liberty party candidates. Had Follen not died in 1840, he would most certainly have voted the Liberty ticket.[8] Finally, by the 1840s, Garrison, Wright, and Quincy had become vocal champions of dissolution of the federal Union. But Loring adamantly opposed disunionist doctrine, while May and Foster repeatedly voiced reservations.[9]

Clearly, members of the Boston Clique were strong-willed and independent individuals. What common social characteristics they shared did not promote overwhelmingly uniform postures on key issues of the day. "I think Garrison has done his work wisely & well," Anne Weston confided to Wendell Phillips, by defining Clique ideals so broadly that "there might honestly be differences of opinion."[10] Disagreeing over nonviolence, Anti-Sabbatarianism, voting, disunionism, and other matters, participants nonetheless constituted a group that acted as a relatively tight, cohesive unit until the mid-1860s as they directed their newspapers and their antislavery societies with fairly clear and consistent policies. How was any degree of concerted action possible? How, for example, could near anarchists like Wright and Rogers have acted with a Federalist aristocrat like Quincy and a cautious legalist like Loring? To answer this exceedingly difficult question is to understand the essential qualities of the Boston Clique's brand of New England insurgency and to lodge precise meaning in the term "Garrisonian." Unity was possible, we shall see, because of a willingness of Clique members to restrain themselves on certain particulars and to follow Garrison's directives. Social rituals also serve to unify and order members' lives. Common allegiance to the vision of a Government of God taming exploitive human institutions was still another factor drawing Clique abolitionists into concerted action. But though these diverse factors provided unified direction and satisfied needs for social rapport, they left considerable room for idiosyncratic thought and action by insurgent missionaries intent on maintaining a sense of piety through direct, unfettered, and uncompromised individual responsibility to God. Clique participants were able to image themselves as an unrestricted collectivity of Christ's followers – a devout aggregate with each member individually responsible to God for his actions.

III

Despite occasional claims by antagonists to the Boston Clique that Garrison was but a front man for Maria Chapman,[11] participants knew differently. A common loyalty, allegiance, and intense emotional warmth toward Garrison was a fundamental source of Clique cohesiveness. In large measure, this sentiment was owing to Garrison's strikingly effective leadership capacities. He constantly attempted to make each member of the Clique feel loved, respected, and even indispensable – so much so that Clique abolitionists often turned to him in moments of confusion or difficulty.

Consider, for example, Garrison's standard salutations in letters to or regarding Clique members. Unlike letters to others, "My Dear Friend" almost inevitably marked the beginning of a piece of correspondence to a Clique participant, while "Yours, with the highest regard" concluded the letter. He referred to Pillsbury as "my attached friend, and faithful anti-slavery coadjuter for the last twenty years" who possessed "the noblest attributes of a man." "The more I see of Rogers, I love him," Garrison wrote, "and his friendship for me is ardent and sincere." He acknowledged Loring's "manifold kindness since we struck hands together" and sought out information "as to the health of my dear and venerated friend, Francis Jackson, which I hope is entirely restored." Beyond greetings and expressions of admiration and concern, Garrison persistently underscored his desire to be in contact with Clique insurgents – spiritually if not physically. He always sought them out as travel companions. "My heart leaps almost wildly to see you again face to face," he told Maria Chapman. He found that the words of one of Jackson's letters "though voiceless, had a power to thrill me through and through" and hoped that he and Jackson "shall ever be found *side by side.* . . ." "How can loving, kindred spirits ever be separated?" Garrison asked Wright. He was disturbed over Samuel J. May's move from Boston to Syracuse, "yet you are as near and dear to me in spirit as though you were constantly by my side."[12]

Garrison not only wrote amiable letters and tried to accompany Clique members; he regularly sought out their advice. The leader could be the follower, giving others in the Clique a sense of self-worth and individuality. With Phillips, he could "freely unbosom myself," while Wright's views on broad matters of moral philosophy were sound and "more nearly identical with my own, than those of any other individual." Loring could be counted on for wise "counsel and generous cooperation"; May was "the strengthener of my heart." Over and over, Garrison communicated his willingness "to take the advice of my friends, and [my] desire that it may be given without reserve."[13]

Garrison's personal expressions of warmth and respect toward Clique abolitionists sprang from his perception of the Clique as familylike. He never had much of a family life himself. His father had deserted the family when he was only three. His mother then moved from place to place with his sister in search of work, leaving William and his brother James to shift for themselves. James became a naval seaman and an

alcoholic and was rarely seen. This breakup of his personal family helps
to explain Garrison's desire for a wife and a large, closely knit family of
his own. But even though his wife, Helen Benson, reversed the pattern
of his mother and stayed close to her children, Garrison remained
apprehensive about preserving the family unit. Several of his children
died as a result of premature weaning and Garrison's acceptance of
some of the more dangerous medical panaceas of the day.[14] The Clique
seemed to have been a supporting appendage to Garrison's immediate
family. It offered assurance that he would always have close familial
ties; he would break from the legacy of his father. Oliver Johnson,
Garrison's intimate friend for over forty years, was on target when he
noted that the Clique intimates and the immediate family were overlapping units: "He [Garrison] was never so happy as when surrounded
by his wife and children *and a few favored guests."* Garrison's sons Wendell
and Francis concurred with Johnson. Their father "liked nothing better"
than to have Clique intimates visit with the family in the parlor and sing
hymns with them.[15] Garrison characterized both the Clique and his
immediate family as his "little band" and named two of his children after
Clique members – Francis Jackson and Wendell Phillips. But he also
seriously considered naming children after Quincy, Wright, and May.[16]
He wrote to Johnson of "a brotherly feeling between us, which though
not of blood relationship, is of the strongest quality" and told May how
"fondly I cherish th' exuberance of a brother's glowing love. . . ."[17]
Garrison characterized Wright, who only occasionally visited his own
wife and children in Philadelphia, as one of the family and told Wright
that he "shall always find a 'home' with us, in health or sickness, in
strength or in helplessness."[18]

It is clear, then, that Garrison made no rigid distinction between his
personal family and his Clique. Like those in his blood family, he could
communicate with Clique members with familial warmth. His solici-
tations regarding the well-being of Clique abolitionists and his expressed desires to be near them and to consult with them were certainly
quite sincere. Together, Garrison's personal family and his Clique
formed a convivial social unit. Unlike his father's family, this unit would
not perish; it would withstand deaths and defections.

To understand how Garrison drew the Boston Clique together, we
must realize that by the late 1830s and early 1840s he had become a
more effective manager of consensus and harmony among his strong-
willed followers than he had been in earlier years. The family unit had
to be preserved by conciliatory fatherly management. Consequently,
while Garrison continued to castigate "sinful" outsiders much as insurgents had always done, criticisms of reformers within the Clique
became noticeably more muted. Indeed, the attacks on outsiders seemed
to imply that Clique participants stood beyond moral reproach.

One way to avoid criticizing group members was to avoid new public postures about which Clique members might hold different opinions. This tactic helps explain why Garrison's announcement in 1842 that the federal Union should be dissolved represented his last antislavery programmatic innovation. From that point on, he discouraged almost all innovative and radical ideas for their internally divisive potential.[19] Moreover, as historian James Brewer Stewart has noted, during the 1840s and 1850s Garrison coupled his role as chief arbiter of the Boston Clique with that of father-manager of the even more diverse membership of the American Anti-Slavery Society. His main focus was on diminishing personal feuds among his pious A.A.S.S. followers and mitigating ideological and tactical differences. To help achieve internal harmony and foster fellowship, he wrote and spoke of the "history" of the brave few who banded together to form the American Anti-Slavery Society. Referring specifically to Clique abolitionists as faithful heroes in this historic movement for freedom, he noted ways in which they put aside personal bickering and joined with him in the glorious struggle. This message was obviously intended to promote a sense of unity among members of the American Anti-Slavery Society in general, but especially among Clique abolitionists. Their lives had been gloriously brought together, and they were bound to "Father Garrison" in one cordial and pious unit.[20]

There can be no doubt, then, that Garrison worked assiduously to unite the devout insurgents of the Boston Clique – his much loved "family." Clique members were most responsive. In letter after letter, they told Garrison of their deep feelings of kinship and appreciation of him in words that carried deeper feelings than commonplace Victorian felicities. "It has been one of the most fortunate circumstances of my life that I was thrown so near your teaching & influence," Jackson noted. For Quincy, Garrison's friendship was "one of the chief pleasures and honors of my life. . . ." Samuel J. May noted that he was so involved with Garrison that "nothing that has affected you has been uninteresting to me." "I owe you Dear Garrison more than you would let me express," Phillips acknowledged. Johnson and Pillsbury voiced similar sentiments; the intimacy of their friendship with Garrison and his family was central to their lives. "While I have a *conscious* being," Wright explained, "my love, my devotion must cluster about you and your family." Indeed, Wright felt part of the Garrison household: "Your *Home* is my Home."[21]

Moreover, Clique activists frequently addressed Garrison in terms usually reserved for a family member. "When are you coming home – I long to see you," inquired Rogers, who was also solicitous about the health of Garrison's wife and children. "How I long to be with you," noted John Collins as part of a similar desire for familylike nearness. "If

[I] consulted my own feelings, I would have been with you 4 months since. . . ." Hoping that Garrison might stay in his home for several weeks, Samuel J. May added: "If I were a wealthy man, I would take you in my arms, or on the wings of the wind of steam – and bear you off to Egypt, Palestine, Greece, Italy, &c&c – that you might be taken out of your cares." Jackson claimed that when Garrison wrote to him, he was able to perceive Garrison physically. Wright actually lived in Garrison's home from time to time and kept personal belongings there. He cherished living in daily physical proximity to the Garrisons much as if he were a family member: "My heart and my grateful tears often bless you for the home feeling you have permitted me to cherish with you and yours."[22] Clearly the "family" that became the Boston Clique was partially forged by warm and friendly ties of intimacy between several strong-willed disciples and "Father Garrison."

Still, Clique abolitionists realized that William Lloyd Garrison was a very special sort of family member. Wright characterized him as Christlike and an "Educator of Mankind." To Johnson, Garrison's achievements "gave me a new conception of the majesty and power of a single human life. . . ." He was truly a messenger of God. Rogers described him as a faithful pioneer. Quincy called Garrison "one of those rare spirits which Heaven, at distant periods, sends upon the earth on holiest missions." Chapman claimed that he alone had commenced the chain of events that was certain to overcome Southern slavery.[23]

Thus, Garrison had no ordinary or commonplace familylike bond to other members of the Clique. He seemed to have entered their lives through God's agency, proving that their collectivity was indeed devout. For this reason, while they cared for Garrison as if he were a blood relative, they had to defer to his Christ-like commands. Such deference did not sacrifice their own individual obligations to God. Rather, by following Garrison, they acted on those obligations. Consequently, when they found themselves in difficult situations that required unfailing advice, Clique members often looked to Garrison. Johnson, for example, noted that he could not make ends meet with his $1,000 annual salary as editor of the *National Anti-Slavery Standard*. But he did not know whether it was proper to ask the financially pressed executive committee of the American Anti-Slavery Society for a raise and begged Garrison to resolve his dilemma – to tell him what was proper: "In this matter, dear Garrison, I speak to you as to my second self. . . . if you, upon consideration of all the circumstances, think I had better struggle on and do the best I can with my present salary, I will cheerfully follow your advice." Was it proper to expose Gerrit Smith for antislavery heresies, Pillsbury asked Garrison, or was it best to remain silent: "But I always defer to you, as the abler & better, as well as elder soldier, in these literally 'Wars of the Lord'. . . ." Late in 1851 Samuel J. May wrote that prior to assisting in the famous rescue of fugitive slave Jerry

McHenry in Syracuse, he felt that his spirits were "in close communion" with Garrison's, "so that you knew what I was doing or intending to do – and I know that you were consenting to it all." Five years later May felt that he could not properly interpret rumors of an affair between Henry Wright and a married woman from Ohio unless Garrison, "sensitive on such a point as a man can be," advised him on the matter. Ann Phillips insisted that Garrison, as "the leader" of the Clique, guide her husband Wendell in Washington, D.C., so that politicians there did not get the best of him. The fatherlike messiah had to direct the flock, especially during difficult moments.[24]

Because Clique members looked to Garrison as a messiah with personalized, familylike ties who could guide them during trying times, they considered him the epitome of moral worth. Thus, despite religious opinions quite different from Garrison's, Anne Weston noted that nobody could be "so good, pure & disinterested. . . ." Loring agreed, finding that any disagreements he had with Garrison were minor, inasmuch as the man had a principled "hatred of vice and wrong" and "devout reliance on God." Phillips asserted that his differences with Garrison were insignificant as against the man's almost faultless moral judgments. Jackson, Child, and Chapman echoed this point.[25]

We have, then, the beginning of an explanation of why the strongly independent personalities in the Boston Clique were able to act in concert. Garrison looked to the Clique as his beloved family. Consequently, he worked to minimize discord and to forge internal unity and cordial social bonding. Clique members responded to his efforts. Each individually loved the fatherlike messiah and was willing to follow his lead. After all, was he not like a member of one's own family?

Thus, cordial and respectful contacts between Father Garrison and Clique abolitionists promoted an overwhelming sense of unity and order. But total harmony did not prevail. It is important to note that even after the late 1830s and early 1840s, by which time Garrison had focused on eliminating internal discord, most members of the Clique were at least periodically apprehensive about their leader's "extremism" – his strong self-righteous postures that seemed to curb the group's appeal outside insurgent circles. Quincy, for example, was quite troubled by Garrison's loud pleas for women's rights, Anti-Sabbatarianism, and the Thomsonian health-care movement. Anne Weston was distressed by "Garrison's testimonies against War or plenury Inspiration" or other issues that "are nothing to us as abolitionists. . . ." May feared that Garrison's fiery language was alienating people from abolitionism. May, Jr., was apprehensive that Garrison's strong positions on issues other than slavery were diverting people from the main concern. Jackson felt that Garrison was simply "too severe" in his reform activities.[26]

Sometimes Clique criticism of Garrison became very heated, with participants lashing out at the leader for the group's failure to secure many converts. Edmund Quincy, for example, was often distressed over Garrison's supposed sloppiness, injudiciousness, and unmethodical qualities. He wondered why Garrison had to put out the *Liberator* on a rushed, last-minute basis when the rival antiinsurgent *Emancipator* was produced methodically and carefully. Nor could Quincy ever quite understand why Garrison's news coverage of antislavery society meetings was so "very badly done," why he spoke excessively at public meetings and often on extraneous matters, and why he always seemed to overextend his attack upon the American clergy and their churches. Had this "privileged character" utterly no sense of system, tact, and propriety? Parker Pillsbury was often almost as distressed as Quincy with the leader of the Clique. Because of Garrison's lack of caution, Pillsbury complained, "I still have to vindicate his general course whenever it is assailed, and that let me assure you is pretty often." Above all, Pillsbury could not understand what might have swayed Garrison to appoint Southerners as American Anti-Slavery Society lecturers. Oliver Johnson was also disturbed over his leader's sudden, impulsive qualities: "The want of arrangement, and a disposition to postpone until the last moment the performance of every duty which requires the use of his pen, I regard as his greatest faults. . . ." According to Anne Weston, "Garrison is full as much surprised that anybody can differ from him. . . ." As a result, while professing tolerance of all creeds, he was given to sudden unjustifiable attacks upon those with whom he differed. Even Samuel J. May, who was very reluctant to criticize anybody, complained that Garrison was given to unpredictable fits of rage and moments of tactlessness.[27]

Most members of the Boston Clique were apprehensive, then, about Garrison's extremism and were often very upset over the impact of his erratic, unpredictable qualities upon their collective effort. At the same time, they thought of him as a messiah and as morally impeccable. Moreover, the man occupied a central role in their everyday personal lives. The view of Garrison held by members of the Clique bears an interesting relationship to Max Weber's portrait of an effective group leader. According to Weber, the effective leader resembled a brilliant mad scientist; he had near-magical qualities but did not seem quite balanced.[28] Clique abolitionists regarded Garrison similarly. They considered him a wonderful friend and God's chosen agent to lead the nation from the sin of slaveholding – a truly extraordinary individual. He magically welded his faithful colleagues together into a united, convivial, and effective familylike social unit that directed several important antislavery organizations and publications. Yet his extremist temperament and disorderliness were an aspect of his strong and pious individuality that gave them periodic apprehensions. He surely gave order and cohesion to the Clique's reformist activities. But he was also erratic and extreme – a chronic source of disorder and unpredictability in Clique affairs.

IV

The relationship between members of the Boston Clique and Father Garrison, then, had a shaping influence on their "world in ourselves and in each other" – their sanctuary from the pervasive hostilities of the irreverent. But a regular social routine was at least equally important in shaping their refuge. Maria Chapman's house quickly became the Clique's daily meeting place. It was a short five-minute walk from the homes of Garrison, Phillips, Jackson, and Loring. Chapman's sisters – Caroline, Anne, Deborah, and Emma Weston – lived there off and on. Quincy very often made the long walk in from Dedham, while Wright and Johnson came whenever they were in town. Besides its central location, there were other reasons why Chapman's house became the central gathering place. Rarely on extended abolition travel missions or lecturing tours, Chapman and her sisters were usually at home to receive callers with a warm pot of tea. Moreover, one could always turn to Chapman for information on Clique-sponsored ventures. With a shrewd eye for managerial detail, Chapman served for eighteen years on the American Anti-Slavery Society executive committee, was counselor to the Massachusetts Anti-Slavery Society for nearly twenty-five years, served nine times on the business committee of the New England Anti-Slavery Society, ran Boston's Anti-Slavery Bazaar, organized many Massachusetts female antislavery societies, and sometimes assisted Garrison at the *Liberator* with his editorial duties. Thus, one could always count on learning the latest news concerning Clique-sponsored antislavery ventures by visiting the Chapman house. Finally Quincy pointed to the most fundamental reason why Chapman's home became the center of Clique operations. It was perhaps the only place in Boston where a Clique abolitionist could relax and lower the defensive shield of the hated if devout outsider. The Chapman house was the only place where he could go for an atmosphere that was warm and stimulating yet informal and unpretentious: "I never before found genius and talent without vanity and the thirst for display, literature without a slight tinge of pedantry or strong pervading religious feeling without some mixture of cant." For Quincy, there was no other location where like-minded insurgents could enjoy themselves without having to defend their sacred mission to the slaves or to put up with the pedantry, hypocrisy, and immorality that seemed to pervade the society about them.[29]

In a very physical sense, then, the Chapman house was a place of refuge and tranquillity for the mob-battered disciples of the Clique. It was their "other home" – the gathering ground for the larger Garrisonian family. Compared with other places, where they faced constant danger of verbal or physical abuse, it was a center of predictable calm and pleasantry. But the Chapman house was not the only gathering place for Clique abolitionists. They anxiously anticipated visits by one another – looking forward to taking another member of the Clique into their houses, especially overnight. As Quincy explained to a Dublin abolitionist in 1844: "You must know that the custom of [Clique] abolitionists of entertaining each other at their houses is still very common, arising from the closeness of the connection in the days of persecution." House visitation, Quincy noted, had a function for Clique insurgents that it did not have for most Bostonians. At base, it was a mode of affirming kindred spirits in the face of pervasive hostility. This was why members of the Clique stressed visitations in their correspondence. Pillsbury was deeply touched, for example, by Garrison's overnight visit to his house in Concord, New Hampshire: "You do not need to be told what joy your presence there gave my family. . . ." Henry Benson penned equally warm sentiments about Garrison's visit to his home. Anne Weston noted how happy she was whenever Samuel J. May came to Boston to visit: "He is such a very old friend, one who was in the cause long before we [the Weston sisters] were, that I always feel extremely delighted to meet him." Away on a trip, Garrison heard that Wright was coming to Boston and penned a note to his wife: "Tell Henry to be sure and abide under my roof."[30]

The house visitations represented a mode of warmly bonding otherwise isolated and despised Clique members and their families. So did the ritual of taking meals together; the practice became increasingly frequent as the years passed. Indeed, a common meal seemed to be the highlight of a house visitation. Over and over, members noted how much they enjoyed eating together; meals symbolized mutuality and affection in a hostile world. Like a daily stop at the Chapman house, a visit and a meal with a fellow Clique abolitionist provided visible proof that one did not have to face hostility alone – that one was not isolated in a sea of hatred.[31]

There were still other factors in the everyday ritual of Clique abolitionists that drew them together and provided structure and direction for a world peopled by hated outsiders. The patricians in the group – Jackson, Phillips, Chapman, and Quincy – were always solicitous about the financial well-being of the poorer members. Thus, through the custom of mutual assistance, no member of the Clique usually suffered for long from financial want.[32] Weddings were also deployed to give Clique participants a sense of warm comradeship and unity. Since the Clique was an association of diverse families, when any member of one of those families married, the ceremony was necessarily a group affair. Bride and groom rejoiced with all their "brothers and sisters" and with Father Garrison, who sometimes conducted the ceremony.[33] The *Liberator* itself also drew together Clique abolitionists. When Garrison felt overworked, members frequently gave a helping hand to assure that production deadlines were met and the words of the "father" were disseminated. If a member of the Clique went walking near the *Liberator* office and needed an immediate sense of comradeship, he could always stop in and count on a warm greeting from a familiar face. Members also noted that in helping to publish and distribute the *Liberator*, they sensed that their antislavery careers were purposeful. Although the paper had only 3,000 subscribers and was always in difficulty financially, the nation was somehow being enlightened by their collective efforts in insurgent antislavery journalism.[34]

The Chapman house, visits and meals, mutual financial aid, weddings, and Father Garrison's newspaper were all unifying, ordering vehicles that gave shape and reality to the Clique. These vehicles provided the members with a routine daily existence, satisfied their needs for friendship, and gave them strength to endure a hostile community. The problem was that in order to confer these needed benefits, strong-willed, independent-minded missionaries who felt individually responsible to God had to cooperate and to plan collectively. Moreover, they had to meet and to labor not only with those whose company they preferred and whose piety seemed unquestionable, but also with whichever members or periodic associates of the Clique who happened to be at the Chapman house or in the *Liberator* office. The inevitable result was bickering, disenchantment, and factionalism within the group. Thus, the very social routine that facilitated group cohesion simultaneously produced internal tensions, discord, and divisions. The practices that drew members of the Clique together, while offering some measure of comfort, also grated against their dispositions as freewheeling if pious individualists responsible only to God. The social rituals that promoted intimacy simultaneously encouraged internal discord. The same factors that drew missionary insurgents together also pulled them apart, resulting in both group cooperativeness and individual explosiveness.

V

By the late 1830s and early 1840s, signs of serious internal fragmentation within the Clique were detectable. Participants came to sense that Ellis Gray Loring, one of their founding members, was reducing his contacts with others in the group. Although Loring remained legal adviser to Garrison and Jackson and continued to be Quincy's close friend, he was becoming much more deeply involved with the private affairs of his own family. The "excitement" and "party struggles" of the Clique upset him, he noted in 1840: "I shall not be obliged to read the papers nor will it be my duty to attend the meetings."[35] By this point in time, Samuel May, Jr., had become a Clique activitist. Yet he chose to concentrate his friendship and intimacy not on Clique members generally but upon Samuel J. May, his cousin. Quickly their friendship became very deep. With the occasional exception of Garrison, others in the Clique ceased to be privy to communications between the May cousins.[36] During the late 1830s, Garrison and Wright developed an exceedingly warm friendship. It was much warmer than that which Garrison entertained with any other member of the Clique. Both men were of lower-middle-class background; both had been reared in strict Calvinism and had broken with it. Wright fully endorsed all aspects of Garrison's abolitionist posture as well as his stand on Anti-Sabbatarianism, nonresistance, temperance, and women's rights. Despite strong feelings against fugitive husbands, Garrison kept his silence over Wright's fractured marriage and regularly opened his own house to the homeless colleague, often for weeks at a time. By 1844 Garrison could confide to Wright: "There is no one on the wide earth, among the great circle of my friends, for whom I entertain greater love and respect. Your views . . . are more nearly identical with my own than those of almost any other individual." When Wright passed on in 1870, Garrison claimed that his dead friend had spoken and told him where to bury the body. In a career filled with broken friendships, Garrison was the one person whose comradeship Wright had always retained.[37]

At the same time that Loring was reducing his Clique activities, the May cousins were drawing together, and Garrison and Wright were becoming the closest of friends, Quincy, Phillips, Chapman, and the Weston sisters were cultivating their own "world in ourselves." Quincy and Phillips had much in common. They were distant cousins, their fathers had been Boston mayors, they both graduated from Harvard Phi Beta Kappa, and both entered legal practice but found few clients and lived off their large inheritances. Chapman and her sisters, the Westons, shared this leisurely aristocratic background. Moreover, Chapman had reared Phillips's wife. Quincy referred to this patrician aggregate as the inner core of the Boston Clique – "a society of educated & accomplished minds." He felt that he could only wear his ostentatious silver slippers in their company. They were the only associates with whom he could discuss high literature and attend local cultural exhibitions. Together they could all laugh and have great fun in their frequent and joyously "silly" parties and in notes to one another filled with humorous jests. In essence, Phillips, the Westons, Chapman, and Quincy could draw together in this clique-within-a-clique and enjoy some of the amenities that they had thrived on before they became insurgent immediatists. By drawing closer together, they could find some relief from less cultivated and almost perennially serious colleagues such as Johnson and Garrison.[38]

Before the first decades of the Boston Clique's existence, then, a pairing process that emphasized subgroup over common Clique comradeship was well under way. Building in some measure on blood relationships and common social background, certain members of the Clique were forging their own special intimacy groups within the larger group. Those who participated in this fragmentation process were experiencing divided loyalties – loyalty to the Clique generally, to Father Garrison, and to their closest Clique associates. The possibility that one loyalty could conflict with another loyalty was ever present. When conflict occurred, the Clique member was forced to make a distressing choice. Once made, that choice always had the potential to render misunderstanding, distrust, and general discord among other Clique insurgents. At base, then, the pairing process suggested that individual preferences were promoting internal disorders within the group. The common social rituals that drew all members of the Clique together did not always keep them together.

During and after the pairing process, short-term flare-ups between Clique members were commonplace. Johnson, Chapman, May, Jr., and Anne Weston, for example, periodically voiced apprehension about Pillsbury's "extreme" ideological postures. Some members hoped that he might be silenced. Chapman became increasingly irritated at Samuel J. May's unfailing trust in people, while Johnson, as editor of the *National Anti-Slavery Standard*, complained that Quincy never sent his articles in on time. In 1855 May, Jr., became furious with Chapman over her decision to terminate Boston's annual Anti-Slavery Bazaar. What right had she to make such a crucial decision on her own?[39] Comparatively minor disputes such as these were probably inevitable in a situation of constant and close group contact. Periodic feuds seemed endemic to social intimacy when strong-willed insurgent missionaries were involved, each of whom firmly believed in his own direct moral responsibility to God. But disenchantment with the activities of two members of the Clique – Rogers and Wright – demonstrated what the pairings and minor disputes merely suggested. Although the diverse social rituals that we have noted forged unity, orderliness, and harmony within the Clique, discord and feelings that life was in disarray were evident owing to the uncompromising sense of individual responsibility that each of the members prized.

The Nathaniel Rogers controversy of 1844 was a case in point. The debate superficially concerned the ownership of the *Herald of Freedom* newspaper. Did the publication belong to Rogers, its editor, or to the New Hampshire Anti-Slavery Society, its sponsor? Rogers had been a Clique intimate and a close friend of Garrison. But the board of managers of the New Hampshire Society was attempting to take over the paper, and it was led by Stephen Foster, an insurgent who regularly cooperated with the Clique. Foster and the board of managers were making this bid because Rogers had been moving toward an extreme "no organization" editorial policy. He had come to insist that organized antislavery activities wasted valuable time and stifled free expression; minutes, reports, agendas, and elections were to be dispensed with at antislavery society meetings everywhere. Rather, Rogers argued that anybody should be encouraged to speak on any topic whenever he felt compelled to do so. Most Clique abolitionists were not willing to carry their free speech doctrines that far. They realized that no concerted antislavery activity could survive under Roger's requirements. Consequently, they sided with Foster and the board of the New Hampshire Society. A special committee of eight insurgent immediatists (including Clique members Garrison, Phillips, and Quincy) was constituted to mediate the dispute. Predictably, it sustained Foster and the New Hampshire board of managers as owners of the *Herald of Freedom*. Rogers left the *Herald*, quit the New Hampshire Society, and commenced his own independent newspaper.[40]

Save for Henry Wright, the Clique was unanimous in its decision to rule against Rogers and for the New Hampshire Society. But it was a very difficult decision. All of the Clique abolitionists liked Rogers, and they realized that they were essentially expelling him from their group. In two letters to Dublin abolitionist Richard D. Webb, Quincy tried to articulate the ambivalent feelings that he and his colleagues felt regarding the Rogers expulsion: "As a companion we all liked him. His extravagencies & his occasional vulgarities in his paper, we were willing to make all possible allowance for." But because of Rogers's personal sensitivity to criticism, "we have always handled him like a cracked tea cup." Therefore, if Rogers had only moderated his posture a bit in the dispute, the *Herald* ownership issue might have been compromised and Rogers might have remained within the Clique: "There was never a man who threw away a more truly valuable set of friends than Rogers has done. Persons who would have done everything consistent with right, to gratify or to help him. Friendship is not a very common commodity, as I suppose you know. The genuine article, I mean. . . ."[41] Rogers subsequently tried to reforge ties with Clique members – with "those once my *lovers*" – and this added to their distress. He tried to retain close personal ties with Jackson and hoped that "Garrison will forgive my heresies about organization & committees." Indeed, in January 1845 he wrote directly to Garrison: "I lament that any thing *could* have occurred to *try* in the smallest degree our more than friendship. Perhaps it has not been tried."[42]

After the 1844 expulsion episode, Rogers kindled painful memories within the Clique. Garrison grieved but hoped "that a reconciliation may be effected, in the spirit of a noble magnanimity and unaffected charity." Quincy fretted because Rogers now seemed hostile. Johnson noted that the rift would never have happened had Rogers not suffered from a "morbid sensitiveness" due to "ill-health." After all, Rogers had been a delightful associate. In his 1869 *Recollections of Our Antislavery Conflict*, Samuel J. May admitted that whereas he had worked with Rogers, "I really have no personal recollections of him."[43] The 1844 affair was too painful to recount, and one can understand why. Rogers had been well liked by the Clique despite his opposition to private property. Moreover, even after the 1844 episode, he wanted to remain close to the other insurgents in the group. Yet efficient and harmonious organizational activity was crucial to Clique operations, and it would have been difficult to function with a man who was insisting, increasingly, on implementing extreme "no organization" policies. Hence, as Quincy put it, duty seemed to require that Garrison and his associates turn against Rogers "in the tenderest and most forbearing manner." Phillips agreed: "Let Rogers madden (good Rogers, kind Rogers, Rogers who I love and admire. . .)."[44] Although the Clique was largely built on bonds of personal intimacy among strong-willed and faithful insurgents, it was also built on cooperative and harmonious organizational efforts. Its members were making an unpleasant trade-off. They were excluding an intimate whom they all liked and who did not wish to be removed for the sake of a smoother and more harmonious collective effort. They were casting off their beloved "cracked tea cup" because he was more fiercely independent in his sense of individual obligation to God and more "disorganizing" than the rest of them – if only in degree.

Thus, the Rogers affair was not the sort of matter that intensified tensions between, say, the Quincy–Phillips–Chapman–Weston silver-slippers friendship circle and the May–May, Jr., bond. Aside from Wright, there was a consensus that Rogers had to go. The tension and distress registered within each individual member of the Clique and not between Clique subgroups. Rogers was being eliminated for more orderly and pleasant missionary activity among the devout so that they could better confront a hostile outside world. And yet the very process of disposing of Rogers left other Clique members distressed for years to come. The group may have operated more efficiently after 1844, but it did so at the expense of casting out a patently pious and dedicated reformer whose thoughts and actions had formed part of their everyday round of social existence. In opposing Rogers's removal, Henry Wright noted that once the process of internal bloodletting commenced, it could go on and on, having a chilling effect upon the desires of all members of the Clique to act independently and without fear whenever God called them for duty. At base, Clique abolitionists were upset at the way the Rogers affair concluded because, although the group's labors became more harmonious, this benefit came at the cost of the unhampered individualism that they prized and without which, they knew, there was no guarantee that a faithful missionary could always remain true to God's commands. Moreover, once any member was purged for excess piety, so might any other member of the Garrisonian "family." They were all in jeopardy.

The Henry Wright controversy was a somewhat different sort of affair. In the course of the 1840s and 1850s, Clique abolitionists periodically found serious deficiencies in Wright. Some were upset because Wright's attacks on religion went beyond criticism of the clergy. He seemed to be attacking "the religion of the Bible!" Some noted that

Wright had taken the wrong side in the Rogers case, that his intemperate columns in the *Liberator* were probably ignored by readers, and that he was counterproductive in calling for anti-Sabbath conventions. Persistent rumors that Wright was taking up with various married women provided added cause for Clique distress. So did the very close personal relationship Wright had cultivated, by the mid-1840s, with Gerrit Smith, a leader in the "anti-Garrison" Liberty party.[45] But unlike Rogers, Wright did not advocate an extreme "no organization" posture, and he did not have to be dislodged from a vital antislavery organ like the *Herald*. Moreover, his ideas were not drastically different from those of several other members of the Clique, especially Garrison. Then, too, because Clique members desperately struggled to surmount all personal propensities toward sin, they understandably tended to admire Wright's patent honesty and sincerity – his "apostlelike" qualities. And whereas Rogers had spent most of his time in New Hampshire, Wright frequently roomed at the Garrison home, dined with Jackson, and visited with Chapman, the Westons, and Quincy. Moreover, by 1847 Wright seemed to have atoned for having been the sole Clique participant who had opposed the removal of Rogers. He whispered about immediatist gatherings that Rogers, despite claims of financial hardship, had died with an estate of more than \$20,000. Finally, and most important, because Wright was Father Garrison's closest antislavery intimate, and because the two were in close ideological accord, Garrison regularly defended Wright's thoughts and actions while acknowledging that he sometimes erred in taste and judgment.[46]

Owing to all of these factors, Clique insurgents did not feel compelled to expel Wright as they had removed Rogers. Had they ever attempted to do so, Garrison would not have allowed it. So they tolerated Wright's mannerisms, and they tried not to attach excessive importance to his frequent columns in the *Liberator*. The man was a persistent irritant and source of tension within the Clique. But there was no remedy for the Wright problem, unlike the Rogers affair. Wright's irritating, disorderly, antagonizing ways simply had to be tolerated as an inextricable part of the Clique's existence. Wright survived within the group because other members were willing to put up with the inefficiencies and the disruptions in the exchanges among intimates that his activities rendered.

In some measure, Rogers and Wright posed such troublesome problems for other Clique abolitionists because the two men forced others to set limits on unfettered individuality for the devout of the Clique. Already fragmented by friendship pairings and periodic flare-ups between its members, the Clique had to arrive at a consensus on the degree to which deviations in ideology, tactics, and personal behavior could be tolerated. Unless its members could define and enforce certain limits on behavior, further fragmentation would ensue and the group would never be more than a center for bickering and ineffective action. On the other hand, once the prerogatives of a member were even vaguely restricted, the individual freedom that Clique abolitionists prized – and a member needed to be entirely *free* to obey God – was undermined. Thus, in expelling Rogers for his extreme "no organization" postures while retaining the somewhat less irritating Wright, the Clique seemed to be striking a compromise between orderly, efficient group life on the one hand and the unhampered individualism that a devout reformer required on the other. In a very rough sense, this response paralleled that to Father Garrison, leader of the Clique. Because of his conciliatory and unifying leadership and the importance they themselves attached to individual liberty for God's agents, Clique insurgents were willing to tolerate Garrison's erratic behavior.

The reconciliation of the two, then, was a balancing act of opposite forces at the heart of Clique existence. It accounted for the mixture of love and distress over Garrison's leadership, and it explained why rituals fostering group cohesion were coupled with intense bickerings among group members. Because sanctuary and good fellowship assumed at least a modestly predictable and orderly collective existence, while true faithfulness necessitated unrestrained individuality, the Clique struggled to find ways for both to exist.

VI

There is some truth, then, to the anti-Garrisonian historiography of the 1930s, 1940s, and 1950s in its characterization of Garrison and his followers as a fiercely independent and quarrelsome bunch. But there is also validity in the more favorable Garrisonian historiography of recent years, with its stress on the personal restraint, unity, and tactical shrewdness of the leader and his followers. If we equate Garrisonianism with Boston Clique insurgency, it follows that Garrisonians were freewheeling individualists who often argued among themselves, even over minor matters. At the same time, they demonstrated overwhelming concern with orderly, efficient, and socially harmonious collective effort.

Recourse to abstraction often provided Clique insurgents with the hope that they did not have to sacrifice the individual for the group. Abstract resolution of these apparent opposites was more readily effected than a resolution that was rooted in everyday social existence. Indeed, immediatists of the Clique shared and communicated a common theoretical orientation that seemed agreeably to blend individual piety with peaceful and efficient collectivity.

By the late 1830s, if not earlier, a metaphorical view of slavery had become basic to this general orientation. Clique abolitionists perceived Southern black bondage as only the worst example of American reliance on force – on man oppressing his fellow man rather than partaking in mutual love. Oppression of man by man in all its forms, not simply Southern racial bondage, made up the American slave system. Loring and Jackson, while assenting to this concept of slavery, preferred that black bondsmen constitute the principal focus; kindred oppressions did not need to be emphasized. On the other hand, Wright and Garrison went to great lengths to explore almost all manifestations of coercive "slaveholding spirits" short of class exploitations. They found the spirit of slavery in human government, in the military, jails, capital punishment, political parties, churches, voting, oath taking, officeholding, and even the man–woman relationship. Most Clique abolitionists ranged between these extremes, clinging to a broad view of slavery while differing as to the specific aspects of bondage that merited comment and action. Quincy, for example, stressed voting and elections, which men deployed to dominate their neighbors. On the other hand, May saw the spirit of slavery in the action of mobs and governments to suppress freedom of expression.[47]

All Clique insurgents felt that chaos was the result of attempts by man to dominate his neighbor – to rule others with a slaveholding spirit that was necessarily "extravagant & overbearing." Slaveholding values filled "the nation with guns, swords, and other deadly weapons and put them into the hands of gamblers, sots, swearers, vagabonds, and trained stabbers! Is this the way to secure order, virtue, and tranquility?" When God's commands were ignored and man ruled over his neighbor, society "must necessarily end in disorder, anarchy and blood." The disordering influence of slavery had created the disharmonies of poverty amid riches and degradation alongside cultivation. Slavery had fostered a chaotic legal system, as well, for it encouraged some jurisdictions to permit practices that others forbade. In sum, "anarchy prevails in all parts of the land" and would persist as long as man tried to rule over others like a slaveholder.[48]

For Clique insurgents, then, slaveholding was a spirit that caused one man to reign over another in defiance of God's laws, with chaos the inevitable result. Dominant institutions such as government, the churches, and the military were not inherently evil but were made so by the perverted, ungodly slaveholding spirit of human domination. Hence, spiritual purity required the devout man to withdraw from them. Withdrawal would demonstrate his unpolluted inner redemption. When the American people manifested spiritual regeneration by embracing abolitionism and refusing voluntary support to institutions dominated by the slaveholding spirit, the Government of God would gain hegemony over the government of man, and order would reign. Thus Clique participants stressed that the road away from slavery was through the human conscience. Institutional forms could remain and would eventually become workable if those who ran the forms were directed by God – not by power-hungry and therefore irreverent men. With this perspective, they had little sympathy with or understanding of a proposal by their former colleague, Nathaniel Rogers, for a grand alliance of Southern slaves and Northern workers – the "producing classes" – to overthrow economic exploitation. Firmly believing that the human heart and spirit had to be renovated before American institutions would ever cease to be slaveholding, Clique insurgents condemned taxpayer boycotts, labor strikes, utopian communities, and most other efforts to restructure dominant economic and political institutions as measures that placed the cart before the horse. Only inner spiritual emancipation would liberate national institutions: "Internal rather than outward reorganization . . . is needed to put away the evil that is in the world." Until this internal spiritual reorganization was achieved, it was premature and even pointless to crusade against economic exploitation in Boston, where, by 1848, the poorest 81 percent of the population owned less than 5 percent of the assessed wealth.[49]

Once individual regeneration occurred and the regenerates brought human institutions into line with God's directives, Clique abolitionists forecast that utopia would be at hand. The qualities of this utopia would be intensely individualistic. No impediments were to stand in the way of the free human spirit – not even associations of the "producing classes." God's reign would "overthrow mastery itself and slavery itself" and would make people "cherish the man who pays no homage to human authority." Under the reign of God, everybody was bound to speak as his own reason and conscience dictated. The individual mind and heart would gain hegemony over social and political organizations. Armies and police would be disbanded, special privileges would cease, and all human beings would be unfettered free agents. They would be able to roam freely over the earth without fear or restraint.[50]

Clearly, Clique insurgents conceived of God's rules as diametrically opposed to human government; the latter restrained the individual, while the former liberated him from restraint. But liberated individuals would not bring on heightened interpersonal tensions, anarchy, or disorder. Quite the opposite would occur. Under God's just reign, unfettered men would no longer want to dominate their neighbors. Rather, man would feel a brotherly love toward his neighbor; people would sacrifice for each other. A common and true allegiance to God would induce people to revere one another. The traditional conflicts between nations, between master and slave, between man and wife or parent and child, would be no more. Under God's Government, the entire earth would be harmonious and orderly.[51]

The notion that unrestrained individualism would be orderly when man ceased to tyrannize over his neighbor was therefore at the core of the ideological orientation that pervaded the Boston Clique no later than the late 1830s. It was the essence of the metaphorical view of slavery. At this point, let us recall that the everyday social and emotional life of the Clique also centered on efforts to enhance both unrestrained individualism and ordered, convivial collective life and to bring the two into some sort of stable balance. The group consisted of strong-willed and independent-minded insurgents who were intent on fulfilling their own personal responsibilities to God. At the same time, each member hoped that along with unlimited freedom, life in the Clique could afford camaraderie and effective concerted activity. Consequently, it would seem that the Clique's basic ideological orientation was deeply rooted within the everyday lives of its members. At the same time, the ideology provided hope that a permanent and stable balance was eventually to be reached between pious individuality and cordial collectivity. To some extent, then, Clique ideological orientation reflected the daily lives of its members. More basically, that orientation was a prediction of what life in the Clique might have become if unrestricted selfhood had ever been reconciled with warm collective efficiency.

VII

When Wendell Phillips spoke at the funeral of Garrison's wife, Helen Benson, in 1876, he fondly recalled life within the Boston Clique:

Some of us can recollect, only twenty years ago, the large and loving group that lived and worked together; the joy of companionship, sympathy with each other – almost our only joy. . . . The world's dislike of what we aimed at, the social frown, obliged us to be all the world to each other; and yet it was a full life. The life was worth living; the labor was its own reward; we lacked nothing.

A decade before Phillips spoke, the Clique had dissolved, owing to the deaths of certain members and a fierce dispute among the survivors concerning the dissolution of antislavery societies (discussed in Chapter 9). But like Phillips, other Clique participants stated that group life had been eminently agreeable. "If I had given up anything in becoming an Abolitionist," Edmund Quincy remarked, "I should have been amply repaid by the genuine friendships of true men & women which I have formed in consequence of it." Like others who had been Clique activists, Oliver Johnson concurred: "Never, for one moment, have I regretted the choice I made in my earliest manhood . . ., though in doing so I should be cut off from the chance of wealth or even of competence."[52]

Why had life in the Boston Clique been so desirable? Although Clique insurgents had longed for a stable and perfect balance between harmonious collective efficiency and unrestrained, pious individuality, they never secured it except as a vague ideological construct. Why had they remained loyal to the Clique and fairly content with its activities for so many decades when the tension between these two dimensions of group life persisted? The answer lies in the question. The persistent tension between cooperative collectivity and free individuality was actually the

Clique's most fundamental strength, despite the desires of its members to reconcile the two permanently somehow. Through that tension, members were able to feel that they were constantly moving back and forth between comfortable and cohesive group life, on the one hand, and unrestrained individual freedoms on the other. The tension assured a regular flow, or shift, between two poles of human need.

Consider, for example, the Clique's behavior in the Nathaniel Rogers affair. Rogers's highly individualistic "no organization" posture led to his expulsion in the interests of group preservation, harmony, and efficiency. But the process of expulsion induced surviving members to fear that each could be "swallowed up" by the collectivity and lose all feelings of selfhood. Consequently, the episode concluded with Clique insurgents temporarily deemphasizing the values of collective efficiency and vigorously endorsing notions of unrestrained individuality. Along with other factors, this shift helped Henry Wright to continue his eccentric ways without restraint from other members of the Clique. Both the succor of orderly Christian community and the freedom of pious selfhood were guaranteed because a persisting tension between the two assured that members of the group never completely lost sight of either.[53]

This is not to say that the social and emotional existence of all other abolitionist sanctuaries was structured so blatantly by tensions between the fellowship of collectivity and the piety of individuality. In two other sanctuaries that we shall now examine – the Lewis Tappan circle and the Gerrit Smith cluster – the clash between these two opposite poles of human need was much less significant. Tappan's circle cultivated a theologically based social psychology that afforded the members strong buffers against the clash. Smith's cluster formulated a concept, "the voluntary principle," which denied any incompatibility between the two poles. Thus, the missionary insurgents who forged the Boston Clique afford the clearest illustration of the tension inherent in simultaneous cravings for cordial collectivity and pious individuality – for gregarity and sainthood.

CHAPTER 3

STEWARDS OF THE LORD

As the most vigorous expression of young New England insurgency, the Boston Clique sometimes seemed to exert significant influence. Members supervised the publication of several abolitionist newspapers and helped to establish policies for a number of local and state antislavery societies. By 1843 the Clique essentially controlled the American Anti-Slavery Society. But the influence that these activities suggest was often more apparent than real. The Clique set tactical and rhetorical guidelines for first-generation insurgent immediatists, but its impact rarely extended to other spheres. Members were so preoccupied with internal Clique affairs – with establishing their own viable personal sanctuary by maintaining an internal balance between orderly, harmonious collectivity and unfettered individuality – that they sometimes seemed to lack the sustained and persistent missionary efforts necessary to enlarge their sphere of influence. Their Massachusetts Anti-Slavery Society was never able to garner more than $6,000 annually, while the income of the American Anti-Slavery Society (A.A.S.S.) declined substantially as the years progressed. All of the newspapers that the Clique supported operated in the red. Membership in the various insurgent antislavery societies reached a peak in 1837 and 1838 and then decreased; so did the number of agents who served those societies. Meanwhile, more temperate immediatists and even certain halfway abolitionists established rival organizations and publications. Certain of these immediatist rivals even tried to win over their New England insurgent following. The Boston-based Massachusetts Abolition Society and its newspaper, the *Massachusetts Abolitionist*, represented the most painful symbol, during the late 1830s, that Boston Clique territory was being "invaded" by noninsurgent immediatists. When, in 1840, certain noninsurgents bolted from the A.A.S.S. and formed the rival American and Foreign Anti-Slavery Society (A. & F.A.S.S.), Clique members mixed momentary joy with deeper apprehension. They were pleased that the A.A.S.S. had been freed of these morally suspect immediatists and that the Clique now exerted full control over the organization. On the other hand, they were distressed that a new national antislavery society had come into being intent on contesting New England missionary insurgency.

From the very beginning of the immediatist crusade in the early 1830s, an assortment of comparatively temperate abolitionists had been the principal rivals to New England insurgency in general and to Clique immediatists in particular. Despite varied backgrounds, these temperate immediatists derived deep comforts from the fellowship of missionaries within the benevolent society movement. Several of them had also been successful in organizing immediatist societies in upstate New York, in the Western Reserve of northeastern Ohio, in Cincinnati, in Philadelphia, in New York City, and as far west as Indiana and Illinois.

The differences in orientations and commitments among temperate immediatists was so substantial that no single informal collectivity could possibly have illustrated their thoughts and actions the way the Boston Clique shed light on New England insurgency. Indeed, we shall explore two different manifestations of temperate immediatism; the present chapter deals with Lewis Tappan's circle and the chapter that follows concerns Gerrit Smith's intimacy cluster. Whereas participants in the Smith cluster concentrated on Liberty party politics, members of Tappan's circle labored within the New York City Anti-Slavery Society, the Church Anti-Slavery Society, the American Reform Tract and Book Society, the Western Evangelical Missionary Association, the Union Missionary Society, the American Missionary Association, and the American and Foreign Anti-Slavery Society. In addition, the Tappan circle funded the Oberlin and Oneida Institutes – training grounds for evangelical antislavery clergy. More than any other informal aggregate, it served as abolitionism's special envoy to the benevolent empire. Finally, and most importantly, it was perhaps as reliable a register of church-centered temperate evangelical immediatism as the Boston Clique was a register of New England insurgency.

Lewis Tappan's intimacy circle included his brother Arthur, William Jay, Amos A. Phelps, Joshua Leavitt, Simeon Smith Jocelyn, Theodore Dwight Weld, and George Whipple. George Barrell Cheever worked closely if irregularly with the group. Outside the group but nonetheless supportive during the 1830s were a number of prosperous evangelical reformers in New York City – Abraham and Samuel Cox, William Green, David Leavitt, and John Rankin.

Members of Tappan's intimacy group shared certain social characteristics. To be sure, they differed sharply in financial well-being, ranging from the moderately prosperous Tappans and Jay to the chronically impoverished Joshua Leavitt, Whipple, and Weld. Almost all came from Congregational families of the Northeast (notably New England), however, and their parents had generally been supportive of the Federalist party. Jay, son of the Federalist first chief justice, was the only Episcopalian in the group. They were all influenced, in varying degrees, by Nathaniel Taylor's modifications of Calvinism along lines of greater human self-sufficiency. In revivalist leader Charles Grandison Finney, they saw the practical expression of Taylor's doctrines. Unlike members of the Boston Clique, all were quite active in the benevolent society movement and assigned highest priority to temperance, Bible and tract distribution, and Sabbatarianism. Except for Jay, all worked closely with Congregational and New School Presbyterian churches. Leavitt and Jocelyn started out as Congregational ministers, while Phelps and Cheever continued as Congregationalists of the cloth through their entire careers. All had at least some experience with religious and antislavery journalism. The Tappans were the merchants in the group, Jocelyn had worked as an engraver, and Jay was a lawyer and judge. Moreover, Whipple, Jocelyn, and Weld had had teaching experience. All had been at least modestly cordial with William Lloyd Garrison until the late 1830s. Several moved about a great deal, but New York City was usually the center for vital group activities. It is noteworthy that Phelps usually resided in Boston, while Whipple did not move from Oberlin to New York until 1847. But the Tappans, Jocelyn, and Cheever resided in New York City most of their adult lives. Jay and Weld dwelled nearby.[1]

In New York City, the men of the Tappan circle drew backing from a more varied constituency than Garrison's Clique had in Boston. Along-side active evangelical reformers and free blacks, who came most readily to their support, they found that a surprisingly large percentage of local shopkeepers and proprietors signed their diverse antislavery petitions. Certain recent English immigrants, particularly Owenites, Paineites, and Chartists, also signed petitions and even circulated some of their tracts. But the largest proportion of unexpected support came from local artisans. A number of the artisans who backed them attended evangel-ical churches. But most did not. Rather, they invoked radical Jacobin traditions and cheered for equality, democracy, and natural rights. Although these Jacobin-disposed artisans shared with the Tappan men a commitment to private property, they also favored egalitarian com-munal values over laissez-faire capitalism and were convinced that a producer class was at the heart of American society. Consequently, the Tappan men were often apprehensive as they watched these artisans campaign to send workingmen to political office so that government might halt monopoly and end special economic privilege.[2]

Despite this varied and rather unusual New York constituency, the men within Lewis Tappan's circle were unwilling to recognize problems and issues unique to the diverse classes and cultures supporting them. This inability to consider class difference and ethnic variation seriously was not unique to the Tappanites. It also characterized Boston Clique insurgents and, indeed, most first-generation white immediatists. But the limitation may have been somewhat more striking among the Tappan men. They found that they could only empathize with and work on a sustained basis alongside Finneyite Congregationalists and Presbyterians like themselves. They could only relate to like-minded evangelicals who busied themselves in local church and benevolent reform causes.

Specific biographical data on each member of the Tappan circle even make one wonder whether they were able to cooperate with each other and to constitute a working collectivity. The highly independent qualities of all except perhaps Jocelyn can be noted; most participants were as strong-willed and as fiercely independent as any members of the Boston Clique. Weld's contempt for meetings, ceremonies, and organizational activity in general is particularly suggestive evidence against a real collectivity. So is the deep hostility that arose between Lewis Tappan and Joshua Leavitt during the 1840s over the value of political antislavery. The widely divergent views that the Tappan men held on the propriety of having women officers in the American Anti-Slavery Society also induces skepticism on any cohesive collectivity. But despite their differences on specific antislavery matters, as we shall see, group participants generally enjoyed a smooth, effective, and harmonious working relationship.

One reason for the cohesiveness of the group was that members had accumulated shared experiences very early in their reform careers that forged mutual trust and some measure of empathy. Lewis Tappan's very conversion to immediatist abolition, for example, was owing to brother Arthur's "reliable" example, Weld's friendly proddings, and one of Jocelyn's early antislavery orations. For the rest of his life, Lewis felt that his own immediatism was inextricably tied to brother Arthur, Weld, and Jocelyn; all three were regarded as devout participants in a common endeavor. Cheever received similar emotional support in the mid-1830s from Lewis Tappan, Weld, and Leavitt as he moved toward a full endorsement of immediatism. Jocelyn could not have undertaken his first major civil rights venture, a black college in New Haven, without the financial and personal support of the Tappan brothers. On the basis of successful experience with the Tappans in temperance reform and religious tract distribution in the late 1820s, Leavitt joined with them and Weld in 1831 to form and to rally the Society for Promoting Manual Labor in Literary Institutions. Whipple and Weld were drawn together as students in Lane Seminary in 1834 when the trustees tried to suppress their abolitionist activities. Leavitt was visiting Lewis Tappan's home in 1834 when an antiabolition mob attacked the dwelling, and he maintained that this incident initiated his close personal comradeship with the Tappans. Support and camaraderie under trying conditions therefore helped to draw together participants in the Tappan circle. Very early in their reform careers, they came to see each other as pious stewards of the Lord amid pervasive sin and hostility.[3]

In addition to these sorts of early contacts, group members found common cause and convivial association in the 1830s as Charles Finney's supporters. Together, they defended Finney against the vocal attacks of certain conservative Calvinists on his revivalist techniques and his doctrinal emphasis upon human ability. Weld was an early member of Finney's "Holy Band," accompanied the revivalist on several of his trips, and even offered excuses for Finney's apparent antislavery "vacillations." The Tappan brothers founded "free churches" for Finney's congregations, contributed large sums to his seminaries, and built the Broadway Tabernacle in his honor. Leavitt, Jocelyn, Phelps, and Whipple quickly emerged as staunch champions of Finney. They were supportive in the church circles of Boston, northeastern Ohio, and particularly New York City.[4]

By 1839 the mutuality of interests and the frequency of contacts among the stewards of the group had reached the point where they automatically drew together during moments of crisis or at times when they sought social support. When Lewis Tappan learned of the arrest of Mendi Africans who had revolted on the slave ship *Amistad*, for example, he immediately called on Jocelyn and Leavitt to help him form a defense committee. Then he solicited the help of others in his circle.[5] In 1842 Leavitt and Weld went to Washington, D.C., to campaign against the congressional gag rule and to make Whig legislators more militantly antislavery. They spent every evening together reading, writing, and preparing for the next day. On Sundays they often worshiped together at a Negro church.[6] Positive experiences of the past also drew Jocelyn, Whipple, and Lewis Tappan together in the mid-1840s as the principal functionaries of the central office of the American Missionary Association (A.M.A.). There each mastered the other's routines and personal preferences; each became very dependent on the other. In moments of distress, the three regularly called on other pious constituents of the Tappan circle.[7]

By working together in evangelical reform activity over several decades, the stewards of the group developed mutual trusts and dependencies. By 1837 Weld felt that of all antislavery editors, only Leavitt could be depended upon to produce editorials with a personal hold upon "a multitude of persons." Lewis Tappan relied upon Jay for guidance on the legal ramifications of antislavery ventures and felt that Jay's judgment on "reform proprieties" was almost impeccable. Jay was equally trusting of Lewis: "You and I rarely differ in our anti-slavery opinions, & when we do [differ] have too much confidence in each other to think it necessary to conceal our offences." Trusting language of this sort characterized much of the correspondence between group members. Clearly, each regarded the other as dependable and impeccable – as a true comrade.[8]

Over time, the contacts, cooperative ventures, and trusts within the Tappan circle deepened to the point where members articulated strong emotional pangs for one another. Thoughts of group intimacies and friendships caused emotions to seep through the formal and disciplined exteriors of these early Victorian men. In 1869 Whipple reflected on decades of cooperation with his colleagues, particularly with Jocelyn and Lewis Tappan and concluded that his coworkers had made a life of reform worthwhile. On his deathbed, Jay wanted to see and to be remembered by all of the stewards in the group. They, in turn, grieved deeply when he departed. Whenever his children became seriously ill, Lewis Tappan eagerly sought out those in his immediate circle for sympathy and comfort, particularly Weld and Jocelyn. By the same token, Tappan was exceedingly solicitous about the dire economic condition, and later the failing health, of Phelps. When Phelps died in 1847, Tappan became very upset and promised to help out the wife and children of "a dear, dear friend."[9]

Warmth and harmony also characterized group effort because of Lewis Tappan's managerial skills. To be sure, Tappan was one of the least charismatic figures in the circle. He never evoked the near-mystical exaltations and fervor from group participants that Garrison commanded of the members of the Boston Clique. Weld once pointed out that Leavitt struck a far deeper level of emotion than Tappan ever did within the collectivity. Still, Leavitt often lacked tact and was very blunt. Worse yet, in the 1840s he deeply distressed other Tappan circle participants by vigorously championing the Liberty party over churches and benevolent societies as the proper forum for antislavery operations. Nor did Weld rival Tappan for group leadership, despite the leadership capacities which historians used to claim for him. According to Weld's two modern biographers, he neither was an unqualified evangelical abolitionist nor deeply involved himself in church and benevolent society activity. Indeed, the nature of his emphasis on individual piety was strikingly similar to that of several young New England insurgents. Thus, it comes as no surprise to find that none of the Tappan circle stewards ever regarded Weld as the group leader. Henry Wright of the Boston Clique once referred to Phelps as the leader, and Phelps did command the trust of all participants. Still, he usually lived in Boston, whereas group activities centered in New York City. Moreover, during the 1840s Phelps was too ill to coordinate the activities of any group. Although he died in 1847, group activities continued with no apparent interruption.[10]

Although Lewis Tappan had fewer qualities of dynamic leadership than Leavitt, Weld, or perhaps even Phelps, there is no doubt that he was central administrator-coordinator of most of the activities his circle undertook. During the middle and late 1830s, for example, he was a dominant figure on the New York–based executive committee of the American Anti-Slavery Society and turned that committee away from Boston Clique insurgency. He was the primary organizer of the rival American and Foreign Anti-Slavery Society in 1840 and used that body to coordinate and strengthen antislavery struggles in Northern churches. Tappan was also the central policy maker of the American Missionary Association during its early existence; because of his adamancy it remained a voice for evangelical abolitionism. Finally, he was closely connected with the publication of a dozen newspapers and periodicals in the course of his life; in this capacity he was often able to influence the writings of others in his circle. No inspiring if erratic Garrison-like messiah, Lewis Tappan was an exceedingly competent administrator, capable of an enormous workload and having a keen eye for detail. All of the stewards of his circle prized his managerial skills and deeply respected his efforts. He led the group not so much through innovations or personal charm as through his organizational competence, hard work, and persistence.[11]

One basic element in Lewis Tappan's managerial leadership style was the capacity to share policy making among appropriate group members. As long as Phelps was alive, Tappan regularly called upon him to help formulate and implement policies. Indeed, he was probably as influenced by Phelps as Phelps was influenced by him. He consulted with Jay as frequently, and his trust and respect for Jay deepened as time passed. Moreover, as Tappan once confided to James G. Birney, he had always been willing to set aside his personal preferences if most of those he trusted disagreed with him on a particular issue.[12] Tappan's managerial skill was also facilitated by his tolerant and gentle manner with the stewards in his group. For example, his reprimands of Jocelyn for tardiness in preparing an A.M.A. annual report and of Cheever for corporate membership in the "proslavery" American Board of Commissioners for Foreign Missions were mild, indirect, and cordial. Their missionary commitments were never questioned. Indeed, Tappan counseled "sweetness of disposition" and "good temper & discretion" as the way in which group members could be most effective.[13] Finally, the man's financial generosity helped him to continue over decades as the central administrator of group affairs. All group participants except the prosperous Jay were recipients of Tappan's monetary aid during times of need. He funded much of Phelps's foreign travel, provided support for Leavitt so that he could go to Washington to work with antislavery congressmen, helped Jocelyn's son out of a financial jam, and provided economic counsel and assistance to the perennially impoverished Weld.[14]

Through certain common social characteristics, cordial personal bonds, and effective managerial leadership, then, a small but united group of stewards surmounted sundry internal disagreements with no great difficulty. Indeed, from the 1830s to the Civil War, while group members were extremely active in antislavery and other benevolent reform ventures, they retained an inner calm and optimistic confidence that, in addition to bonds of intimacy and effective leadership, helped to promote stable and tranquil group operations. This calm and confidence, we shall see, often served to mitigate tension between unfettered individuality and harmonious collectivity; that tension was always less intense than it had been in the Boston Clique. Because it rarely distracted the Tappan men, they were able to work much more directly than Clique immediatists as stewards of the Lord, intent on spreading Christian truths to the unconverted. Relative calm and optimism within the group facilitated more vigorous missionary activity without.[15]

II

In his meticulous and sensitive biography of Lewis Tappan, Bertram Wyatt-Brown emphasized the outward formalism of the man and his circle of evangelical abolitionists. Lewis "seemed to wear his religion inside out, presenting its most confident aspect to the world and reserving to himself his fears and despondency."[16] Analysis of the private correspondence, diaries, and journals of Tappan, Jay, Jocelyn, and the others in the group readily validates much of Wyatt-Brown's characterization. Their formalism was largely manifested in an outward confidence that God would make earthly affairs right, and they certainly tried to keep self-doubts and gloomy moods to themselves. But outward confidence more often matched inner confidence. Faith that God would ultimately right significant wrongs caused doubts, fear, and self-questioning to occur much less frequently in the private lives of these stewards than might otherwise have been the case.

In December 1845 Lewis Tappan described the recently deceased pioneer abolitionist George Bourne as a model evangelical reformer whose trust in God resulted in inner as well as outward calm: "His disposition was cheerful, and he soared above the provocations of his enemies, trusting in God to deduce good out of seeming evil, and taking even the wrath of man to praise him." An abiding faith that God would set things right made Bourne completely tranquil.[17] This, at least, was what Tappan and his colleagues assumed should be the lot of the evangelical abolitionist. On the one hand, they espoused the Finneyite notion that man would have to rely on his own ability through good works to bring on divine assistance. On the other hand, they clung to a modified version of the Calvinist doctrine of original sin. If man was not born as an inherently depraved biological organism, he still suffered from a depraved will and a moral disinclination to obey God. Because man had persistently to struggle to overcome his depraved will and to obey God through his "natural ability" to discern and follow moral law, the Tappan men assumed that God had ultimately to control the world's affairs. Although the fallible individual was to attempt to follow moral law, God would ultimately see that the world was properly ordered. Hence, there was cause for inward as well as outward confidence that God's flawless desire would prevail over corrupt human will. Through this line of thought, Tappan's immediate circle articulated a logically inconsistent sort of "halfway Calvinism" with many of the securities yet relatively few of the terrors of orthodox Calvinism and most of the hopes yet few of the potential anxieties associated with the Finneyite stress on good works and human ability. The result was a doctrinal hodgepodge that produced confidence and resilience. Indeed, it resulted in such inner calm and assurance that it helped to block out many of life's anxieties, especially those generated by tension between group and individual interests.

This characterization of the belief system of the Tappan circle must be qualified in several particulars. For one, Weld did not always accept many of the group's basic beliefs. Consequently, he often lacked the inner calm and confidence of the others and considered himself "a quivering mass of intensities." Moreover, by the early 1840s he had become quite critical of the religious notions of other temperate evangelical abolitionists and sought to withdraw from the rough-and-tumble of their conflict with insurgent immediatists.[18] At times, too, other members of the circle were very gloomy about their personal moral deficiencies. Lewis Tappan wondered on his fiftieth birthday, for example, "How much of my life has been wasted in indolence and sin." Similarly, George Cheever warned his younger brother of the need for constant self-examination and of the persistent temptations to do evil. Not infrequently, rigorous introspection caused members of the Tappan circle to wonder whether they had ever used their abilities as their parents had formerly demanded and as God always expected. In these moments of self-doubt, confidence tended to be very low, despite the assumption that God was in supreme command.[19]

Aside from periodic remarks by Weld, no members of Lewis Tappan's circle argued for human self-sufficiency. They did not believe that man could be, in any sense, his own free agent. Therefore, they were less attracted to notions of individual piety than the members of the Boston Clique. According to Jocelyn, this was the error of Gerrit Smith's "religion" based on human reasoning and the human sense of justice: "God himself will establish justice, and his people will come to the work of salvation and the breaking of the hands of wickedness." Man performed good works only as God sought to bring on salvation. Lewis Tappan offered the same sort of critique of Unitarians and other "liberal religionists"; they did not sufficiently consider themselves "stewards of the Lord." One does rightly, Tappan noted, when with his resources he does as the Lord asks. Man's greatest danger, warned Cheever, was a false sense of self-sufficiency: "How all things teach us to rest only on God." "Hold fast to the promises of God," Whipple warned, "but trust not in man."[20]

Once delusions of self-sufficiency were dissipated, man still had to struggle to measure up to God's commands; failure to measure up could lead to severe self-doubts and despair. And yet all group members but Weld were usually confident that in even the most desperate and difficult of situations, God's intervention would ultimately merge with their own sometimes misdirected efforts or depravity of the will to make things right. Because they did not attach as much importance to self-piety as members of the Boston Clique, they fretted considerably less over curbs on individuality. Consequently, during the antiabolitionist mob outbreaks of the mid-1830s, the Tappan men were confident that despite immediate personal dangers to themselves and blatant curbs on their efforts to act on God's commands individually, there was no cause for fear or apprehension. Each member of the circle would be "safe under the protection of that great Being who will overrule all." As Jay put it, "the Supreme Lawgiver" would care for them. Rather than seek revenge against the mobsters, they had only to commit their cause to Him and could rest assured that peace and tranquillity would emerge from chaos and lawlessness. Similarly, immediately prior to the 1840 annual meeting of the American Anti-Slavery Society, Arthur Tappan was confident that although serious conflict would take place as insurgents directed by the Boston Clique tried to silence Tappanite stewards of the Lord, God would ultimately "overrule the machinations of [insurgent] disorganizers among us." Just after the 1844 election, brother Lewis noted that though President-elect Polk and most influential Democrats would attempt to silence pious opposition and to annex Texas for proslavery interests, "the Lord God Omnipotent reigneth." This made him "feel a calm belief that Texas will not be annexed to this country." Similarly, Cheever was confident that though he, his mother, and his brothers and sister were geographically separated, if they remained "partakers in his holiness," God would keep them spiritually united and would ultimately bring them together in Heaven. During the late 1850s, Jocelyn and Whipple found that financial problems, ill health, and the burden of constant policy decisions were making their work in the central office of the American Missionary Association exceedingly difficult. But through this trying period, both remained calm and unruffled, convinced that "the Lord encline [sic] us to trust in Him," that "the Lord will provide," and that "our God & Savior decideth all things well – in infinite wisdom, and often takes from us all Responsibility for his own action." The stewards of the Tappan circle faced many other specific crises – religious "deficiencies" in their relatives and their children, personal financial reversals, the deaths of loved ones, and periodic disharmonies in group life – but during the difficult times they generally remained serene. Although each steward had to strive persistently to do good, he usually assumed that God would guide him through the particular crisis and would remedy group inefficiencies and disharmonies as well. Deep inner confidence was the inevitable result.[21]

Lewis Tappan's immediate circle retained confidence in God's ultimate control over more than specific situations. Despite the small number initially enlisted in the antislavery ranks and the constant rebuffs that immediatist abolitionists often experienced, the stewards were certain that God was against human bondage and would eventually bring on emancipation. To be sure, they had to work very hard in their immediatist evangelical operations, and they had to struggle to retain their piety, but they believed God would intervene to assure victory. "Amidst all the obstacles & difficulties with which we have to contend," claimed Lewis, "we should utterly despair did we not know that the promises of the Almighty are unfailing. . . . He *will* break the rod of the oppressor, and let the oppressed go free." Antislavery would be successful, Cheever knew, because it was "depending not on man, nor man's sneaking management, but on God." "When men have done breaking God's law, they will have done with slaveholding," Phelps asserted. So long as the stewards retained "fervent prayer and living active faith on our part, he [God] will carry it [emancipation] on to a speedy and glorious issue." Because God, not man, was the ultimate guarantor of freedom, Jocelyn insisted, abolitionists should not fret about their paltry numbers: "When abolitionists become so numerous as to depend upon numbers it will be a sad day to us." Indeed, Jocelyn felt that blacks should have no long-term apprehensions, for "the Lord will hear their prayers and plea the cause." Arthur Tappan was equally certain "that God had taken our [antislavery] cause in hand, and would work it out in his own time and manner. We may stand still and witness his glorious manifestations." "Let us address ourselves to our work and leave our reputation with the Lord," Whipple insisted. Leavitt and Jay heartily concurred.[22]

Although the stewards of the Tappan circle were troubled by certain periodic reversals and occasional self-doubts, they were thus usually supremely confident men. While clinging to semi-Calvinist notions of predestination, they were committed to a life of benevolent deeds. God was inspiring them to good works, and He would ultimately assure the proper balance between unfettered individuality and orderly collective action within their group. He might sometimes appear as the old wrathful Calvinist God, as during the depression of 1857, but only to signal man to change his sinful ways. Hence, there was cause for inner calm despite tumult and reversals in the group's everyday affairs. This personal serenity and confidence allowed Lewis Tappan, for example, while extremely solicitous for the well-being of his children, to go through life relatively unruffled when one daughter suffered a severe nervous breakdown, a second daughter was confined for six months to the Philadelphia Insane Asylum, and a third made a deathbed confession to a long-term illicit sexual liaison with Henry Ward Beecher. Lewis was assured that God would ultimately make things right. So was his friend William Jay, despite persistent and serious illnesses in Jay's family ranging from dwindling eyesight to scarlet fever and cholera: "He can deliver us from Pestilence as he over daily delivers from ten thousand dangers. Put your trust in Him. . . ."[23]

Clearly, the inner calm that characterized all of the stewards in the Tappan circle except Weld tended to desensitize them from much of the anguish and unpredictability inherent in human experience. As one combs through their private correspondence, diaries, and journals, one point becomes obvious. Their supreme confidence that God would ultimately forge order and freedom operated in a way that shielded their emotions from life's daily and long-term disappointments. But before we equate desensitized reformers with human callousness, it is well to remember that the Tappan men were lifelong activists in diverse benevolent efforts, particularly antislavery. If their extreme confidence made them relatively unmoved by the illness of a loved one, it also gave them the strength to carry on in their vigorous missionary efforts for emancipation, peace, temperance, and sundry other causes, often advocating radical and unpopular positions in behalf of these causes. This was because their confidence was linked to the role model of a Christian self-made man.

III

Since the conviction by the stewards of the Tappan circle that God would eventually promote order and justice made them very confident, the role model of the energetic Christian self-made man became necessary to assure that that confidence did not lead to laziness and inaction. Intellectually, the two beliefs were related; although God would ultimately forge order and justice, the devout Christian was to struggle to implement God's will by constant self-improvement. From a psychological perspective as well the two were related. Assurance that God would dictate basic consequences provided the confidence, encouragement, and determination for reformers to have sprung into exceedingly active Christian self-help ventures. Hence, the conviction that God would eventually promote order and justice, when coupled with idealization of the Christian self-made man, became a springboard for exceedingly active lives. Combined, the two beliefs provided a basis for vigorous action as well as for personal insensitivities. Let us, then, examine this second essential element in the Tappan circle belief system – the Christian self-made man.

In 1819 Lewis Tappan proudly noted in his personal journal that he was distantly related to Benjamin Franklin, symbol of the American self-made man:

It would appear that his [Franklin's] respect for Christianity extended no farther than believing it to be a political good; and yet the religious education he had probably contributed essentially to render him so moral & useful. I have the honor to be collaterally descended from this eminent & industrious countryman.[24]

Lewis lauded Franklin's energy, perseverance, and methodical qualities in pursuit of secular good: money, inventions, and charity. But he did not separate these diligent qualities of secular self-help from religious qualities. Acknowledging that Franklin was a self-consciously secular man, Tappan was arguing that his most outstanding secular qualities had been inspired by "religious education." He was therefore characterizing Franklin as the Christian self-made man.

In his portrait of Franklin, Lewis Tappan was describing himself and his brother Arthur. Neither Lewis nor Arthur had been able to understand why their father was content to make an honest living that never exceeded $1,000 a year in his Northampton dry goods business. Refusing to follow in his footsteps, the brothers left Northampton and amassed their fortunes through their own efforts in Boston and New York. Like Franklin, they rose financially through innovative business techniques. In his New York silk import firm, Arthur broke with practice and sold goods at very low markup and only for cash or for safe short-term promissory notes. He did very well financially owing to the volume of his sales and the paucity of defaulting debtors. Lewis rose through equally innovative antebellum business techniques. In 1841 he founded the first national credit bureau – the Mercantile Agency – as a mechanism to stabilize his income despite business conditions. Even in a depressionary economy, businessmen proved willing to pay him for credit ratings on their potential customers. But though they acquired wealth, the Tappan brothers felt that their business activities reinforced basic Christian moral standards. Arthur insisted that goods-for-hard-cash was the old Christian way to trade; men were not tempted toward speculation and greed. He also settled his family in New Haven while working in New York so that the values of New England country Calvinism might stay with them. In addition, Arthur founded the *Journal of Commerce* because other commercial newspapers printed advertisements that promoted sin. Similarly, Lewis felt that his credit bureau was as much a moral agency as a profit-making venture. It assured that businessmen got only the credit that they deserved and that borrowing became an honest and reliable transaction between Christians: "It checks knavery, & purifies the mercantile air." Like Arthur, Lewis only wanted to deal with "honorable" businessmen whose ambition for profits did not diminish their Christian morality.[25]

The careers of the other members of the Tappan circle did not conform to the Franklin-like rise from rags to riches as closely as those of Arthur and Lewis Tappan did. Still, the others clearly shared their exaltation of the Christian self-made man – the person who partook in vigorous profit-making ventures along lines that fortified basic Christian morality. In *The Sabbath*, published in 1841, Amos Phelps argued that strict observance of the Sabbath simultaneously promoted business profits and morality. Allowing men a day to rest made them more efficient and successful in profit-making ventures. By affording them time for worship and religious instruction, Sabbath maintenance assured that men stayed in touch with Christian truths as they rose economically. Weld's values were identical. "Formal entrance upon *business* habits" of thrift, method, enterprise, and vigorous mental and physical activity, Weld believed, when coupled with constant reliance upon scriptural truths, led inevitably to healthful Christian living. When Christian morality was lacking, material prosperity dissipated, and one was reduced to acts of "flagrant licentiousness." Cheever also insisted that vigorous commercial activity was important for business success, but it had to be coupled with a willingness to also work hard spiritually. The soul's prosperity was as important as commercial gain. Jay, Jocelyn, and Whipple were equally convinced that the life of the Christian self-made man offered the only alternative to greed, lethargy, and sin.[26]

Although they all resided around the big cities of the Northeast, particularly New York, the stewards of the Tappan circle claimed that the Northern countryside was the only part of the nation that inspired the qualities of the Christian self-made man. The states of the slave-holding South were characterized as antithetical to these virtues. Southern sensual allurements detracted from moral business pursuits. Weld claimed that the first Southern settlers were committed to "love of domination, fiery passions, idleness, and contempt of laborious industry. . . ." They grafted onto their vice a slave system that fostered even more "contempt of labor, dissipation, sensuality, brutality, cruelty, and meanness. . . ." Because the slave South was the locus of "habits of pride, cruelty, licentiousness, and unrighteous gain," Cheever found that it defrauded whites as well as blacks of "their birthright in Christianity itself." Phelps and Lewis Tappan characterized the slave South as a center of licentiousness, sexual vice, and ruined moral reputations. Before habits of industriousness, efficient accumulation of wealth, and Christian morality could prevail, Jay insisted that the South would have to emancipate all bondsmen.[27]

Tappan circle stewards found the same vices present in the large urban centers of the North, if to a lesser degree, owing largely to big-city economic ties to the South. Lewis Tappan was fearful of "the temptations of this wicked city [New York]" and the spread of "wasteful and vicious habits" in Boston. Weld agreed that large Northern cities were too much like the South – centers of loneliness and immorality. Consequently, there was need to "let the great cities *alone*" and to turn to the virtuous Northern countryside – the villages and small towns. Cheever, too, found the greatest hope for Christian self-help virtues in the North's villages, whose inhabitants were "rejoicing in the government of God." Jay insisted that because rural Northern farmers and mechanics were untainted by aristocracy, they were the only repositories of truly moral acquisitive virtues. Whipple concurred. Although he would not ignore the cities, he found that in the countryside the missionary invariably accomplished more.[28]

In some measure, this exaltation of the rural North as the milieu where Christian self-help qualities could develop reflected group members' visions of the virtuous country Calvinism of their childhoods, where the stern moral directives of parents and clergy had held sway and the gallows had been planted in front of the schoolhouse. Then, too, the rural North was the area of the country where slothful and unchristian religious, political, and economic institutions associated with slaveholding may have had the least noticeable impact. Third, the Northern countryside provided fewer temptations toward business greed or immoral pleasures than the large urban setting. After all, cities housed the enticements that all of the Tappanites struggled to combat in themselves and in others. Finally, and most fundamentally, they seem to have perceived the Northern countryside as the one area where Christian self-help values could be exercised free of institutional restraints, whether the restraints came from the slaveholding system or from urban commercial institutions.[29]

IV

Thus, the Christian self-made man was at the core of the Tappan circle's cultural values, and members identified the Northern countryside as the area most compatible with those values. This did not distinguish them from many other evangelical missionaries active in the benevolent society movement. But their postures on the peace question and the antislavery evasions of the benevolent empire clearly set them apart. They espoused pacifism and denounced equivocal benevolent empire postures on slavery because they judged both war and slaveholding in violation of the role model of the Christian self-made man. Despite the unpopularity of their stands on these two issues, they persisted in their crusades for Christian self-help values, fully confident that God would ultimately terminate both war and slavery. Confidence that God would right basic wrongs was a springboard and source of energy for advocacy of such ideals beyond the realm of respectable benevolent reform. The goal of the self-made man gave them causes to champion and determination to pursue those causes energetically. But when self-help was combined with supreme confidence that God would right all wrong, their energy and daring moved the Tappan stewards beyond the pale of orthodox evangelical ventures. Indeed, self-help and confidence threatened to detach them from the Christian fellowship of their benevolent society colleagues and produced some of the most pertinacious reformers in antebellum America.

Let us first consider the peace question, then, to see how the Tappan stewards moved beyond evangelical respectability in their advocacy of their two basic values. Jay was president of the American Peace Society from 1848 until his death in 1858, he was an internationally recognized peace pamphleteer, and he was one of the earliest formulators of the theory of compulsory arbitration of international disputes. Named to the board of directors of the American Peace Society in 1829, Lewis Tappan served periodically as a society officer during the subsequent twenty-five years. He refused to contribute to construction costs for the Bunker Hill monument "because of my peace principles," and he circulated petitions to avert war with Britain in 1846 over the Oregon boundary dispute. Brother Arthur always sympathized with Lewis's pacifist proclivities. So did Weld, Jocelyn, and Whipple, although the entire circle became less devoted to nonviolence as sectional tensions heightened during the 1850s and certainly after the outbreak of the Civil War. Even Cheever, who had never been active in any peace society and who became one of the principal exponents of forceful resistance against the slavocracy in the 1850s, sympathized with pacifist goals during the 1830s and 1840s.[30]

It was Cheever who, while urging a nonviolent resolution of the Oregon boundary dispute, most clearly articulated the central place of pacifism in the Tappan circle belief system. He charged that war violated God's plans because it subverted the character of the Christian self-made man. Its shocking barbarities threw men off the proper course of vigorous business activity and devout piety. Under conditions of war, men let up on their daily vigor and morality, they ceased to observe the Sabbath, and they lost interest in spreading God's Gospel. War thus arrested the prudent and moral course of civilization and turned diligent Christians into brutes who sinned against God. In his 1833 *Report of the Society for Promoting Manual Labor in Literary Institutions*, Weld opposed warfare with the same line of thought. Until "fighting becomes the appropriate vocation of man, and human butchery the ordinary business of life," military activities diverted man from vigorous daily moral, literary, and business activity. They subverted the essence of Christian self-help and flew in the face of God's plans for peace on earth. Jocelyn articulated this same posture from the time of his encounter with antagonistic white youths while he tried to establish a college for blacks in the early 1830s to 1859, the year of John Brown's raid on Harpers Ferry. Lewis Tappan credited his strong pacifist proclivities to the writings of his good friend Jay. Peace, he felt, was of value first because it was mandated by God and second because peaceful conditions allowed frugal energetic business practices and sound morality to flourish. Vigorous business and moral activity would not be undermined by aristocratic or slaveholding values, "unjust monopolies," or subversion of the church to the war-making interests of the state.[31]

Clearly, Lewis Tappan's circle of stewards was as committed to peace principles as Boston Clique insurgents, even if the Tappan men were somewhat more willing to justify self-defense. Moreover, their persistent advocacy of pacifism derived from a merger of their two fundamental values – confidence that God would bring order to human affairs when his plans were implemented and the Christian self-help ideal. The two merged together nicely. Since God would ultimately bring permanent peace to earth, the stewards were not perturbed over the unpopularity of pacifist efforts amid the jingoistic, spread-eagle patriotic rhetoric that pervaded antebellum America. Although peace advocates were few in number and experienced constant setbacks, and though their societies were the weakest and most isolated within the benevolent empire, there is no evidence that Tappan circle stewards doubted that warfare would ultimately be eradicated. When God brought forth a peaceful universe, as He most certainly would, there would be no battles to throw the Christian self-made man off his proper course – vigorous business activity and religious piety. Elaborating God's plans for peace in this way, the Tappan men occasionally noted that their persistence and rigor in the face of adversity signified that they, too, were adherents of Christian self-help.[32]

Not only did the essential values of the Tappan circle – confidence in God's ordering ways and Christian self-help – provoke tensions with their missionary colleagues in the benevolent movement over the peace issue; more fundamentally, those values caused them to chastise the entire benevolent empire severely for its failure to come out strongly against black bondage in the South. Whereas their missionary associates labored vigorously to liberate and uplift heathen abroad, by the early 1830s the Tappan stewards, along with other temperate immediatists, sought to carry this crusade for Christ to domestic heathen: "Attention to foreign missions has awakened a strong desire for Salvation of men in this country." Because American slavery made it impossible for blacks to draw near to God by becoming respectable Christian self-made men, one conclusion was inescapable. The true benevolent missionary was duty bound to struggle to free the Southern slave as well as to uplift heathen abroad. Since "slavery and heathenism are, in the general, indissolubly connected," it was senseless to send Bibles and missionaries to save foreign heathen while missionaries of the benevolent empire ignored "*compulsory heathenism* in the very midst of us."[33]

To be sure, most benevolent movement missionaries were not totally ignoring "compulsory heathenism" in America. Rather, they deferred to the program of the American Colonization Society (A.C.S.) for repatriating free Afro-Americans in Africa and hoped that these repatriations would encourage Southern slaveholders to manumit their bondsmen. But by the early 1830s the Tappan stewards, like other temperate immediatists, had come to see fraud and proslavery deceit in the A.C.S. program. Unlike New England insurgents who, on the discovery of this deceit, waged war on the entire benevolent movement, the temperate immediatists demanded less. Because they deeply craved the Christian fellowship of their benevolent society colleagues, they asked only that the proslavery A.C.S. be replaced by the American Anti-Slavery Society as a benevolent empire affiliate. When benevolent society missionaries balked at this request, most of the temperate immediatists spent decades trying to persuade them. The Tappan stewards went further, however. They sharply rebuked all of the benevolent societies for vacillation on the moral question of domestic heathenism, and were particularly critical of four of the most powerful: the American Tract Society, the American Bible Society, the American Home Missionary Society, and the American Board of Commissioners for Foreign Missions. These organizations were undermining the spirit of evangelical Christianity, the stewards charged, when they sent missionaries to destroy heathenism abroad but, fearing controversy, deferred to the A.C.S. at home. Thus, the four mainstays of the benevolent movement missionary program were charged with only modest interest in replacing heathenism with Christian self-help values.[34]

The boldest stroke of the Tappan circle stewards – one that most clearly differentiated them from most other temperate immediatists – came in 1846 when they established the American Missionary Association. A merger of four patently antislavery missionary boards – the Union Missionary Society, the Western Evangelical Missionary Society, the Committee for West India Missions, and the Amistad Committee – the A.M.A. was intended *to compete* with the established benevolent societies for donations, missionaries, and heathen conversions. Quite consciously, the Tappan men concentrated A.M.A. operations in locations where the missionary organizations of the benevolent empire were most hopeful of conversions: Sierre Leone, Jamaica, Siam, Egypt, the Sandwich Islands, and among the North American Indians. But unlike those rival organizations, the A.M.A. also devoted substantial resources to emancipating and "uplifting" Southern slaves. The stewards of the Tappan circle openly advertised their interest — to survive and prosper at the expense of any benevolent movement societies that continued to vacillate on the slavery issue. They were fully confident that in time God would render one of two consequences. Either the other benevolent societies would take up their struggle against domestic as well as foreign heathenism, or those societies would lose membership and funding and would ultimately be replaced by the A.M.A. Whichever result came of their conduct, God would see to it that unambiguous antislavery morality triumphed. None doubted this ultimate result.[35]

Thus, in its relationship to the powerful benevolent empire, the Tappan circle was acting quite boldly. Men like Leavitt, Jay, Lewis Tappan, Whipple, Jocelyn, Cheever, and Phelps certainly preferred to keep the established missionary societies active and vigorous. Indeed, like other temperate immediatists, the Tappan stewards thrived on warm Christian fellowship with their missionary colleagues. But they insisted, with considerably more vigor and commitment than many other temperate immediatists, that their benevolent movement missionary colleagues had to stop wavering on slavery. Christian fellowship was only appropriate with missionaries who followed God's command and fought heathenism at home as well as abroad. The stewards would not risk personal moral contamination by consorting indefinitely with missionary colleagues who refused to take firm moral stands. Rather, by forging the A.M.A., they would force those colleagues to stop hesitating or face the demise of their benevolent societies.

What was most remarkable about this behavior by the men of the Tappan circle was their complete confidence that God would sustain their efforts. In their correspondence and their diaries, they never revealed the slightest doubt that their crusade would succeed. "It appears to me," Lewis Tappan noted, "that one hundred men even, well educated, honest, thorough, determined, filled with love & faith, spirited with zeal, could with the blessing of God, revolutionize a continent." These were hardly the words of a practical or moderate abolitionist that historians have often juxtaposed against statements by Boston Clique insurgents said to be more visionary and extreme. Rather, the words illustrated two points. First, it is difficult to argue that Tappan stewards were any more influential than Clique immediatists. As Weld candidly admitted, he and his colleagues "might rustle leaves" against the benevolent societies and even against New York City merchants dependent on slave produce, but neither their verbiage nor their deeds made many converts. Nonetheless, they continued, confident that God would ultimately let them revolutionize a continent. Second, Tappan's words illustrated how his circle of stewards regarded missionary reform as much more of a collective endeavor than Boston Clique insurgents ever had. Whereas Clique insurgents focused on the actions of the unrestrained individual reformer, the Tappan stewards (less apprehensive that collective endeavor could compromise free individuality) looked to the actions of a small band. Moreover, they were convinced that their number could grow; they could win over the many uncertain missionaries within the benevolent movement. Clique immediatists, on the other hand, had given up on those missionaries from the start.[36]

On the peace question, then, and in their efforts to prod the benevolent societies, Tappan circle men persisted in unpopular crusades because they were confident that God would ultimately render their efforts successful. The rigor of their efforts amid earthly adversities and few tangible successes confirmed their own self-image as energetic, persistent Christian self-made men. Consequently it is untenable if not irrelevant to characterize them as pragmatic conservatives or moderates in contrast to impractical Clique radicals. Directed by a man confident that he could revolutionize a continent, they were probably the least restrained and the most ambitious of all temperate immediatists.

V

Although they assumed leadership roles in the American Peace Society and the American Missionary Association while they crusaded for Christian self-help values, members of Lewis Tappan's circle considered their abolitionist ventures inextricably tied to the nation's churches. Since church life gave rise to the principal agencies that promoted morality on Earth, slavery would fall once parishioners and clergy recognized the sins of bondage. Of the entire Tappan circle, only Weld was skeptical about lodging the entire antislavery cause in the churches.[37]

Between 1837 and 1848 the Tappan group's dedication to church abolitionism was challenged on two fronts: first by growing antichurch, antiinstitutional espousals of several leading Garrisonian insurgents and then by Liberty party men who sought to move beyond the churches and into electoral politics. In the face of both challenges, the Tappan men actually deepened their commitment to church antislavery even if they did not convert their challengers. They dealt with both challenges not by taking desperate or dogmatic rearguard positions but by calmly trusting that God would set things right and by renewing their faith in the values of Christian self-help. The Tappan circle confronted its major internal abolitionist opposition just as it had dealt with the peace and missionary society issues. The period of crises concluded in the late 1840s, with the Tappan men no less committed to continue to direct their missionary crusade through the churches. Adversity invoked a two-provision belief system that held them to their traditional antislavery course even if it did not win over their adversaries or enlarge their supportive base.

Save for Weld, who refused to be influenced by the "fierce feud" with the insurgents,[38] all of the Tappan stewards participated in the group's first major conflict with other types of abolitionists. As hostilities became heated in the late 1830s, the Tappan men most often attacked Garrison, his Clique, and his other fellows for trying to attach "extraneous issues" to the functions of the American Anti-Slavery Society. Lewis Tappan stated the matter quite succinctly in his diary in June 1839:

Garrison and others have grown lukewarm on the antislavery subject & have loaded the cause with their no-government–woman's rights–non-resistant &c until we have got among breakers. Garrison told me 2½ years ago that there were subjects he considered paramount to the anti-slavery cause, to which he meant to devote his attention chiefly. It is a sad mistake to make it instrumental in carrying on other matters.[39]

On other occasions, Lewis publicly reiterated this charge. The insurgents' endorsement of women's rights, no-government, anti-Sabbatarianism, and other issues signified that they were abandoning or at least slackening their efforts in behalf of the poor slave. This was intolerable. Just as he had harshly criticized the benevolent societies and the churches for vacillation on the subject of antislavery, Lewis attacked the insurgents were turning from true Christianity, a change evident in voiced these same apprehensions. To be sure, God would ultimately eradicate slavery as he ordered human affairs. But the prospect of divine intervention was cause for intensification, not cessation, of antislavery effort. As Jay noted, this was not the time to burden the cause of abolition with various insurgent pet projects that would free no slaves.[41]

In addition to "abandoning" the slave, the Tappan men claimed that the insurgents were turning from true Christianity, a change evident in insurgent rejection of the Sabbath, the Bible, the nation's churches, and the clergy. More fundamentally, Garrison and his insurgent followers were found to be abandoning God's commands; they were becoming theologically self-sufficient. Phelps charged that the insurgents no longer met "as an assembly of Christians, with the Bible for their rule, but as an assembly of *men*, untrammelled by such rule." They had "passed the dividing line between the Christian and the infidel" because they had ceased to obey God. Lewis Tappan concurred. How could insurgents serve God when they were led by a man who had abandoned family prayer, church attendance, and the established clergy of the country? Cheever found the insurgents endorsing notions of human religious self-sufficiency that were "outrageous to the good sense of Christian feeling of the community." Jocelyn and Jay agreed. To Lewis Tappan's immediate circle, it was therefore clear why Clique insurgents and their followers were backtracking on their commitment to the slave. They were losing contact with God. Hence they were prone to steer in erroneous directions.[42]

Lewis Tappan and George Cheever found this apparent insurgent withdrawal from God's direction and consequent embrace of human self-sufficiency to be particularly dangerous. As young men, both had turned to liberal religion – Unitarianism. But during their years as Unitarians, both experienced career failures and mental torment, and both sensed that their lives lacked direction. Consequently, both returned to Orthodoxy – Cheever to Congregationalism and Tappan first to moderate Presbyterianism and then to Congregationalism. For the remainder of their lives, both men lashed out at Unitarians, Universalists, Quakers, Free Churches, "religion of reason," and other manifestations of liberal Protestantism. Others in the Tappan group joined them in this attack. They charged that liberal religion, particularly Unitarianism, destroyed the authority of the Bible, took away the sanction of divine law, and turned man into a worshiper of himself. Infidelity inevitably followed. Many of the insurgents were Unitarians, some were Quakers, and several urged total disregard for established clergy. Thus, the Tappan men were certain that if insurgency came to dominate immediatism, the slave would cease to be a first priority, and the abolitionists would break contact with true Christianity. Abolitionists would lose confidence in God and would cease to exemplify self-help virtues.[43]

At base, then, when Tappan circle participants attacked insurgency, they were defending the order-rendering God that they held most dear: a deity that would render a proper balance between collective efficiency and individual freedom rather than err, as insurgents had done, on the side of unfettered individuality. The belief that God would ultimately impose his will on earth had given them enormous confidence and energy to work as stewards of the Lord and to behave as Christian self-made men. The insurgents' apparent rejection of such a deity and embrace of self-worship therefore represented an assault on their theologies, their psychologies, and their ideals. It was an assault on the most fundamental sources of their antislavery activism. Thus, the traditional interpretation of the Tappanite–Garrisonian dispute of 1837–40 – a contest between conservative and radical abolitionists – does not take Lewis Tappan's immediate circle on its own terms. The Tappan men did not see themselves as stalwarts struggling to derail a more militant form of antislavery activism. Rather, they saw themselves as the abolitionists who remained truly committed to God, the Bible, the churches, and the emancipation of black bondsmen; their insurgent opposition had lost sight of both Christianity and the slave. Insurgents were viewed not as militants but as infidels who had abandoned the cause of Negro freedom.

During their 1837–40 confrontations with the insurgents, then, the Tappan group never questioned their fundamental values or their commitment to church-centered abolitionism. If anything, the apparent insurgent embrace of infidelity caused them to cling even more ardently to their values and church commitments. Indeed, they emerged from the conflict with insurgency having formed the American and Foreign Anti-Slavery Society – an organization directed by Lewis Tappan and fully committed to evangelical churches as the directive arm for antislavery religious missions. Between early 1839 and late 1843 they faced their second major internal abolitionist challenge – from men such as James Gillespie Birney, Alvan Stewart and, most important, their own Joshua Leavitt – to deemphasize evangelical church-centered abolitionism for a political party approach to antislavery. The episode concluded with most of the Tappan men temporarily supporting the antislavery Liberty party while continuing to rely most heavily on churches and church-linked missionary work.

To assess this third-party controversy, it is important to recognize that in 1839 Lewis Tappan's circle was active in much the same sort of political activities as the founders of the Liberty party: church prayer for better rulers, circulation of antislavery petitions, and interrogation of political candidates. Although only Leavitt took part in the formation of the Liberty party, most of the Tappan stewards voted for Liberty candidates whenever they appeared on the ballot. Thus, most Tappan circle men differed from Liberty party founders in only one particular; they fretted about moving beyond ballot box support for Liberty candidates. Only Leavitt was willing to participate in party operations and to publicly support party platforms and candidates. The Tappan brothers, Phelps, Jay, Jocelyn, Whipple, Weld, and Cheever were not initially Liberty party publicists.

If most Tappan circle abolitionists were somewhat interested in influencing party politics and voted for the new Liberty party, why did they come into a dispute with the early Liberty organizers? Their reaction to Joshua Leavitt offers the key to an explanation; it also illustrates how the inner dynamics of the Tappan circle differed from those of the Boston Clique.

In 1839 Leavitt and the Tappan brothers represented the group on the executive board of the American Anti-Slavery Society. After only minimal discussion with Lewis Tappan, Leavitt became the first member of the executive board to endorse the idea of an antislavery third party. By November of that year he used his editorship of the official A.A.S.S. newspaper, the *Emancipator*, to champion the third-party notion. This aggravated Lewis, for he had assumed that Leavitt, like the other stewards in his circle, had been irrevocably dedicated to church-centered evangelical abolitionism. Indeed, Lewis became disturbed enough over Leavitt's conduct to proclaim publicly that Leavitt did not speak for all members of the executive committee.[44]

Leavitt did not back down but turned the *Emancipator* into an organ for the emerging Liberty party. Lewis Tappan renounced him – the first time he had turned against any member of his circle – and, in the process, enunciated a critique of the Liberty party that all of the other stewards gradually came to endorse. Did Leavitt not realize the risks of third-party politics? Tappan asked. Through active participation in the Liberty party, abolitionists would become so concerned with electoral triumphs and defeats that they would become less attentive to God's directives. Abolitionists would lose their faith and their moral zeal. By mingling with politicians, the public would rightly view them not as Christian advocates for the slave but as mere seekers of public office. Indeed, "moral reformers may change the character of political partizans [sic], but political parties are not wont to effect moral revolutions." To engage in Liberty party politics was to abandon one's responsibility to "the religious and moral branches" of the crusade against slavery. When church- and mission-centered evangelical abolition drew Americans closer to the plans of God, "then the right kind of men will be elected to office of course." Most basically, Tappan charged that the party man substituted political gain for moral propriety; he lost his moral independence and thus his capacity to implement God's will consistently.[45]

This, then, became the official posture of the Tappan group, with Jay and Weld offering the fullest elaborations.[46] At base, the critique of Leavitt and his Liberty party housed the basic ideals of the Tappan stewards: God's governing role over human affairs, the moral reformer as God's agent, and the Christian self-made man epitomizing the godly reformer. When man prostituted himself to party interests, he lost sight of God, and his own independent Christian self-help capacities declined. Interestingly, Leavitt claimed that he continued to subscribe to these same Tappan circle ideals as he championed Liberty party operations. He had simply come to believe that the moral third party would be a more effective agency to pursue them than the churches, for Americans were "eminently a political people." Thus, the Liberty party was the salvation of the old Tappanite cause. For this reason, Leavitt found it difficult to understand why the Tappan stewards had joined Boston Clique insurgents in attacking the party: "I do not see but they are as prejudiced and embittered as Garrison on this score." The problem for Leavitt was that the stewards were not insurgents. They were his colleagues. He shared their ideals and missed their companionship.[47]

Thus, throughout the 1839–43 controversy, Leavitt continued to feel close affinity with the Tappan circle. Quite openly, he acknowledged that he felt much more commonality with Lewis Tappan than with Gerrit Smith, one of the Liberty party leaders. Tappan was more embittered by the controversy and feared that Liberty activity had made Leavitt "a less amiable & less spiritual man," lacking in "tender spirit" and thriving on "collision" with the stewards. Nevertheless, in early 1841 he provided financial assistance so that Leavitt could go to Washington to cover congressional sessions for the *Emancipator* and to lobby for antislavery. In the years that followed, he provided further aid to allow Leavitt to remain in the capital city. This was hardly the way a Tappan steward would treat a Boston Clique insurgent – one who had "fallen" more decidely from evangelical church-mission abolitionism. Indeed, although the stewards had essentially ousted Leavitt from their circle, Tappan seemed unwilling to make him the kind of "polluting" outsider that the Clique had made Nathaniel Rogers. Assistance to Leavitt did not threaten Tappan's circle the way aid to Rogers might have threatened the Boston Clique.[48]

The clearest evidence that the controversy between Leavitt and his former colleagues in the Tappan circle was actually a tense dialogue among stewards with roughly similar values came in mid-1843. Tappan circle men, having voted Liberty, gradually came into open and active support of Liberty party operations. In 1840 Jay had declined the Liberty party nomination for the New York governorship, characterizing the party as a compromise with morality. But by June 1843 he noted that politicians were treating abolitionists with greater respect and credited Liberty operations with having effected this change: "I begin to think that the Liberty party is effecting more than I formerly anticipated from its efforts." Moreover, Jay saw it as the only useful political base for Christian antislavery operations; the major parties seemed irrevocably committed to slavery.[49] Phelps, too, was willing to become a Liberty party spokesman because he had become convinced that party work increased church antislavery activity: "It had increased rather than diminished the amount of church action." By participating actively in Liberty ventures, Christian abolitionists were "retaining our hold on the confidence & conscience of the really religious."[50] But the major sign that the Tappan group had shed its opposition to the Liberty party came in Lewis Tappan's own conversion in the fall of 1843. Through most of that year, he saw his church and mission-centered American and Foreign Anti-Slavery Society languishing despite the most vigorous efforts of his stewards. At the same time, Tappan knew that a large portion of temperate noninsurgent abolitionists were turning to the Liberty party. Brother Arthur was among them. Insurgency and the Liberty party were therefore the realistic alternatives. Moreover, that year he had visited Joseph Sturge, the avid English evangelical reformer, and had realized that Sturge's embrace of organized political action – Free Suffrage and Chartism – did not seem to numb Sturge's Christian sensibilities. That fall Lewis Tappan publicly supported James Birney's Liberty presidential candidacy, although he was still far more comfortable with church than political antislavery: "Still I have my doubts whether abolitionists will do what they ought as political men."[51]

In the years that followed his departure from the Tappan circle, Leavitt obviously felt less inclined to think and act in concert with the stewards. His fascination with the political process deepened. By the middle and late 1840s he was working with Samuel P. Chase and Henry B. Stanton to modify the Liberty party creed so that it might appeal to discontented Whigs and Democrats, "however insensible thay may be to the motives of humanity & justice." Lewis Tappan and the other stewards saw the Free Soil party, the results of these efforts, as confirmation of their fear of immoral consequences of party politics. They felt that their early misgivings about Leavitt's fascination with the Liberty party had been validated. Consequently, while most Liberty men joined Leavitt and supported Free Soil, the Tappan stewards did not. But they never became discouraged as temperate immediatists shunned them for the Free Soil party. Rather, they remained committed to church-missionary abolitionism and the values that sustained it – to "the moral and religious aspects of the cause." The church-centered American Missionary Association, not Free Soil, was their primary reform interest in the late 1840s and early 1850s. They stuck to the less influential if more pious agency, confident that God would ultimately attend their efforts with success.[52]

Thus, the flirtation of the Tappan stewards with party politics was of short duration. In 1849 George Whipple explained why he could not vote, much less campaign, for Free Soil candidates: "I do not wish to justify voting for men who do not regard the claims of God and the rights of suffering humanity." To vote Free Soil was "to sin against God and incur his displeasure." "My heart was never in the Liberty Party instrument," Weld claimed. Anybody who had entered politics "weakened his whole moral spontaneity by the contact and appliances of a political career." "To what lengths will party men go!" Lewis Tappan lamented. Ever since the formation of the Liberty party, "attention to the political duties of Anti-Slavery men have prevented due attention to the moral & religious aspects of the cause." For George Cheever, any political party had to be deficient in "heartfelt, eternal hostility against slavery as sin, as reprobated and forbidden of God. . . ." William Jay, too, was apprehensive about ever again engaging in party politics, for none of the antebellum parties had the moral decency to endorse the principles of "the Washington School."[53]

In 1847 Boston Clique insurgent Edmund Quincy privately referred to the Tappan circle as "the religionists, who set up the [Liberty] party as a cover for their own retreat back to the world. . . ."[54] An astute observer of the social dynamics of his Clique, Quincy was far off the mark in coming to grips with the Tappan circle. The Tappan stewards were not abandoning their religious principles as they entered Liberty operations. Aside from Leavitt, they were all very apprehensive about the Liberty party as an abandonment of church-centered abolitionism and only campaigned for Liberty men by 1843 when they had been convinced otherwise. Moreover, as the Liberty party began to merge with discontented Democrats and Whigs, the stewards' apprehensions about abandoning church-centered antislavery were rekindled, and Leavitt could not draw them into the new Free Soil coalition. Whereas Leavitt himself may have been turning from the old Tappan circle brand of antislavery by the mid and late 1840s, the rest of the Tappan men held firm. Contrary to both Quincy and several modern-day historians, they were never really absorbed by the Liberty or Free Soil movements, much less by the Republican party. By the end of the 1840s they stood for the same beliefs and values that had characterized them at the end of the 1830s: supreme confidence in an order-rendering God and the Christian self-made man. They continued to perceive the old church and missionary A.M.A. approach to abolitionism as the best way to universalize God's will and Christian self-help virtues, while many of their temperate immediatist colleagues moved on to the new power centers of antislavery – the Free Soil and Republican parties.

Neither Garrisonian nor Liberty party challenges, then, had shaken the Tappan men from what they had always held most dear. It is as erroneous to call them moderates or conservatives for temporarily supporting the Liberty party as it is to assign them these labels for disagreeing with Boston Clique insurgents. In their own eyes, the men of Lewis Tappan's immediate circle were neither conservatives nor radicals but stewards of the Lord and missionaries for Christian self-help virtues. The world might change about them: The benevolent societies might vacillate on the slavery issue, the Clique insurgents might espouse ungodly doctrines and deemphasize black freedom, and colleagues like Leavitt might lose sight of God's directives through party politics. But they held firm, forever confident that God would ultimately set things right even as influence and power continued to elude them.

VI

Clearly, life within the Tappan circle differed fundamentally from activity within the Boston Clique. The Clique was led by a charismatic if erratic messiah, while the Tappan circle was administered by a steady and efficient manager. Clique immediatists felt deeply isolated and craved an extensive round of social contact and ritual to structure their "world in ourselves and in each other." Stewards of the Tappan circle never felt as isolated. They always retained at least some contacts with benevolent society missionaries. If life within the Tappan circle was less emotion-charged and less "feeling" than life in the Boston Clique, it was assuredly more stable and predictable. Leavitt's conduct did not disrupt and distress the circle the way Rogers's conduct had upset the dynamics of the Clique. Finally, whereas Clique immediatists sometimes fretted over group demise – because of either excessive individual freedoms or coercions in the name of collective efficiency – Tappan stewards were confident that God would sustain them.

This is not to say that the tensions between unfettered if devout individuality and warm collectivity, so conspicuous in the history of the Boston Clique, were undetectable within the Tappan circle. Weld clearly felt that his Tappan circle colleagues placed too high a premium on Christian fellowship at the expense of individual piety. On the other hand, stewards with strong managerial proclivities, such as Whipple, Phelps, and Lewis Tappan, occasionally fretted over the dangers of excessive individuality, especially when they watched Leavitt draw away from their circle and when they saw Clique insurgents turn to "extraneous" causes.

More often than not, however, the Tappan stewards assumed that unpolluted individual devotion and cordial collectivity were harmonious. In some measure, the assumption was due to their strong attachment to the benevolent societies where Christian fellowship and camaraderie were assumed to take place among unfettered but devout missionaries. To some degree, their sense that personal piety and fellowship were compatible derived from the very nature of daily life within their circle, where there was fundamental accord on ideals, where few squabbles took place over strategies and tactics, and where there were few perceived threats to individual freedom. More fundamentally, however, the stewards rarely felt acute tensions between the extremes of individuality and collectivity because they were staid, formal Victorians who were remarkably immune to life's apprehensions and unpredictable contingencies. They knew the kind of life they lived and the kind of world they sought – one characterized by Christian self-help values – and they were always supremely confident that God would sustain them in their missionary endeavors. They were so clear in their goals and so certain of having those goals effected that they simply had little inducement to fear stifled individuality or aborted camaraderie. Indeed, the stewards rarely even felt compelled to fret over the death of a loved one. They had constructed a thick and desensitizing sort of buffer about themselves that had immunized them from most of life's tensions and reversals.

But if the stewards of the Tappan circle were far more unfeeling than Boston Clique insurgents, it is inappropriate to characterize them as practical and moderate immediatists who judiciously applied the brakes against the excesses of their insurgent colleagues and did much to facilitate Negro freedom. Because of the buffer that the stewards built around themselves, they experienced at least as many defeats as the insurgents but were rarely thwarted or discouraged. The persisting vacillations of their benevolent movement colleagues on the slavery issue and the drift of many immediatist colleagues into the Free Soil movement underlined basic failures that rarely seemed to daunt them. Thus, the stewards confidently persisted in their clearly defined course and let nothing set them back. Sometimes they assumed roles of bold and innovative reformers, as when they formulated programs for the unpopular antebellum peace movement or when they organized the A.M.A. to challenge the benevolent empire. At other times, as in dealing with the insurgents and the Liberty party, they defended church-centered abolitionism so tenaciously that they became unresponsive to changes within the broader antislavery movement. Thus, the stewards' supreme confidence in an order-rendering God and their devotion to Christian self-help promoted insensitivities, rigidities, and ineffectualities but was also the source of remarkable pertinacity.

CHAPTER 4

VOLUNTARISTS OF THE
BURNED-OVER-DISTRICT

Tappan circle stewards had called on temperate immediatists throughout the North for support between 1837 and 1840 when they struggled for control of the American Anti-Slavery Society (A.A.S.S.). But not all temperate immediatists responded enthusiastically. Predictably, those from evangelical church circles in New York City, Philadelphia, and Boston were the most supportive. With the exception of Oberlin, however, temperate immediatists from small and medium-sized towns and rural locations beyond the Atlantic seaboard were considerably less interested in backing the Tappan men. The stewards expected more, for the hesitant temperate immediatists from more westerly locations shared with them a strong evangelical orientation, joined them in support of Finneyite revivalism, and were allied with them in the benevolent society movement of Christian fellows.

In 1840 the Tappan stewards lost control of the A.A.S.S. to the Boston Clique. But they established the American and Foreign Anti-Slavery Society (A. & F.A.S.S.) and claimed that it was the sole association within the benevolent movement that had jurisdiction in the slavery controversy. Once again, however, few temperate immediatists outside eastern urban church circles rallied behind the stewards or even joined their new society. Rather, in locations such as southwestern Ohio, southeastern Michigan, and upstate New York, temperate immediatists supported the new Liberty party as a viable abolitionist alternative to both the insurgent-controlled A.A.S.S. and the Tappanite A. & F.A.S.S.

Gerrit Smith of upstate New York was one of the many temperate immediatists who balked at rallying behind the Tappan stewards in their struggle against Boston Clique insurgents. Rather, he acknowledged that his principal interests were elsewhere.[1] Smith was very wealthy and had sponsored many benevolent reform causes. Consequently, the stewards were distressed when he hesitated to support them and felt personally rejected when he refused to hold office in the A. & F.A.S.S. They could not understand why Smith, like too many other temperate immediatists, was becoming increasing interested in

Liberty party politics amid the crucial struggle with the ungodly insurgents for control of the aboltionist crusade.

Unlike Lewis Tappan's circle of stewards, Henry Wright of the Boston Clique had some sense of Gerrit Smith's motives. He had become friendly with Smith on a lecture tour in 1839 through upstate New York. As the friendship intensified, Wright learned that Smith worked very closely with two groups. One was a cluster of Peterboro neighbors: James Barnett, Horace Brown, William Martindale, Abishai Scofield, George Klinck, and Hiram Hadden. But this small cluster usually followed the policies of a second and much more important upstate collectivity. The second group, the notable Smith circle, consisted of Smith and five other temperate evangelical immediatists: William Chaplin, William Goodell, Beriah Green, Alvan Stewart, and Myron Holley. Wright soon sensed that the new Liberty party was but an outer sign of much more fundamental differences between this group and the Tappanites.[2]

Henry Wright's perception was insightful. The difference between Tappan circle stewards and Gerrit Smith's upstate associates ran considerably deeper than preferences for church-based as against Liberty party–based abolitionism. But the difference was rooted in a similarity. Both Tappan stewards and Smith circle associates derived an orientation from their common experience as activists in the benevolent society movement. Both had come to assume that God's faithful agents worked together in harmonious collectivities. When they moved from traditional benevolent society activities to the small groups at the heart of the immediatist crusade, they retained that orientation. As they joined hands to form small and informal immediatist clusters, both the Tappan stewards and the Smith associates expected those groups to be cordial collectivities of pious fellows that would persistently struggle against slavery and for the Kingdom of God. The basic difference between Tappan stewards and Smith associates was that nothing could make the stewards cease to imagine their group as a harmonious collectivity for advocates of divinity and nothing – not even persistent defeats – could cause them to falter in their struggle against slavery. But the Smith men lacked the overwhelming steward confidence that as a faithful band they would ultimately be victorious in their battle against slavery. Rather, as their antislavery efforts on behalf of what they called the voluntary principle went down to defeat, they became discouraged, abandoned the benevolent empire tradition of harmony and goodwill among pious missionaries, and turned against one another. Consequently, whereas Tappan stewards remained a harmonious and active anti-slavery collectivity for decades, by the late 1840s the Smith group had very nearly disbanded.

We shall study Smith circle voluntarists to see how this came to pass – how the history of their group was quite different from that of the

Tappan stewards. As we proceed, let us keep in mind that Smith, Goodell, Stewart, Green, and Chaplin probably did not consciously see themselves as a group until late in 1841. By that time, Myron Holley had died and James Caleb Jackson had gained only grudging acceptance within the group. Moreover, at the very point where group self-conscience among the Smith voluntarists had developed, forces were set in motion that began to undermine collective endeavor.

II

Few data are available on the social characteristics of certain of the voluntarists in the Smith circle, particularly Chaplin and Jackson, but the information we have suggests that they were remarkably similar types of reformers, sharing certain characteristics that distinguished them, in some respects, from other abolitionists. Either they were born in New England or they had parents who had recently settled in upstate New York. They tended to be older than most Boston Clique insurgents and Tappan circle stewards. Holley was born in 1779, while Smith, Stewart, Goodell, Chaplin, and Green were born in the 1790s. But despite their age, most listened to pleas for immediate abolitionism by younger men such as Garrison and Weld for months and sometimes for years. They were not the first active immediatists of the 1830s. The Smith voluntarists also tended, generally, to be better educated than Clique insurgents or Tappan circle stewards. Holley graduated from Williams College and studied law under Chancellor James Kent. Stewart attended the University of Vermont and studied under Kent's successor, Chancellor Reuben Walworth. Smith graduated from Hamilton College and Green took a degree from Middlebury College and then studied at Andover Seminary, while Jackson had spent some time at the Manlius Academy. All were professional men. Stewart, Chaplin, and Holley practiced law early in their careers. Jackson, Holley, and Chaplin evolved into seasoned editors from sundry reform newspapers. Smith was an expert in land development. He had a keen eye for relationships between canal construction and the value of real property. Green was a professor of theology and then president of Oneida Institute. All centered their activities – professional, reformist, and personal – in central and western New York. Whereas Holley and Stewart labored for a time in the commercially active boom towns along the Erie Canal, the others usually resided in the less prosperous inland farming communities in Madison, Oneida, and Oswego counties. All except the Unitarian Holley were reared in strict Congregationalist or Presbyterian homes. Save for Goodell, all came to reject Orthodox Calvinism for a benign and tolerant God who offered salvation to all men. This disposed most of them to leave traditional denominational churches for nonsectarian churches based on a man-centered humanism. Even the Orthodox Goodell founded a church in Honeoye, New York, based on humanistic temperance and antislavery principles. Finally, all of the Smith circle voluntarists had been active in anti-Masonry or temperance reform before turning to antislavery. Two, Holley and Stewart, had also been involved in Whig party politics.[3]

Thus, the men of the Smith circle tended to be cultivated and respected central and western New York professionals with religious eccentricities linked to a Finneyite stress on human self-sufficiency. They were generally middle-aged and veterans of 1820s anti-Masonic and temperance battles when younger, less experienced men appealed to them in the early and mid-1830s to join the crusade for immediate abolition. After some hesitancy, most responded by joining the American Anti-Slavery Society. But at the same time, all save Jackson helped to found the New York State Anti-Slavery Society (N.Y.S.A.S.S.), turned it into the dominant antislavery organization in upstate New York, and devoted most of their antislavery energies to the organization. In the course of N.Y.S.A.S.S. activities, they began to recognize the similarity of their backgrounds and to assume some vague semblance of a group. Goodell edited the state society newspaper, the *Friend of Man*, while Chaplin, as the society's general agent and corresponding secretary, became the central administrative officer. Smith, Stewart, Green, and Goodell assumed leading roles on the society's executive board.[4]

Common social characteristics and shared activities in the New York State Anti-Slavery Society were, then, factors that helped to draw the Smith voluntarists together and to hold them together. A common constituency also contributed to this emerging sense of shared interests. Unlike the Boston Clique, the Smith men drew little support from urbane, cosmopolitan Unitarian and Quaker professionals, Transcendental intellectuals, and free Negroes. Unlike the Tappan stewards, few urban artisans with radical Jacobin traditions and few recent English immigrants were to be found subscribing to their newspapers or signing their petitions. Rather, the Smith circle's constituency was composed simply of a number of local mechanics, merchants, day laborers, and farmers. Coming from out of state, particularly New England, they acquired modest parcels of real property in certain almost all-white inland farm towns that were primarily situated within the fifth senatorial district of upstate New York. Although these towns rarely experienced the rapid commercial growth of communities closer to the Erie Canal, those who supported the Smith circle tended to be somewhat more prosperous than their neighbors. They also tended to subscribe to evangelical religious and cultural values more than other individuals in their towns.[5]

Given the specific men who formed the Smith circle itself, however, a common constituency and shared social characteristics were not enough to promote a sense of group unity and to thwart personal bickering. The potential for internal squabbles was very real. Whereas Stewart and

Goodell quickly became warm friends, and Chaplin and Jackson became the closest of intimates, Green held a very low opinion of Stewart. Indeed, Stewart sometimes seemed to care more for Henry B. Stanton, Samuel Lewis, Gamaliel Bailey, and Salmon P. Chase than for his fellow voluntarists. Moreover, while Smith and Goodell were usually able to tolerate Green's caustic, belligerent, suspicious ways, others in their circle often were not. Still another source of group tension derived from Jackson's early antislavery career as an insurgent supporter of the Boston Clique. Goodell, Green, and Stewart were periodically suspicious of Jackson's intentions, wondering whether his loyalties remained with Garrison[6].

Gerrit Smith had worked very hard at making the other voluntarists cooperate as a group in their N.Y.S.A.S.S. ventures. As they drew together, he also played a crucial role in blunting the sundry suspicions and antagonisms that could have destroyed the circle at its inception. His enormous wealth helped him subdue antagonisms and build group cohesion. Smith owned hundreds of thousands of acres which he used for leasing and speculative investments. His annual income averaged between $50,000 and $80,000, making him one of the wealthiest men in antebellum America. Consequently, he was able to bankroll reformers and their enterprises, perhaps donating as much as $8,000,000 in the course of his lifetime.[7] Smith gave a good portion of this money to members of his group. Goodell, for example, began a decades-long friendship and cooperative relationship with Smith when he passed through Peterboro in 1830 to solicit funds for a New York City temperance newspaper. Smith urged Goodell to tour every town in Madison County for funds, gave him a horse, and funded advance publicity. Thereafter, Smith regularly supported antislavery newspaper ventures by Goodell, Jackson, and Chaplin and even helped to fund Holley's *Rochester Freeman*. Without Smith's generous financial contributions, Green's Oneida Institute would have gone bankrupt sooner than it did. But William L. Chaplin received Smith's largest financial contribution. When Chaplin was arrested by Washington, D.C., police in 1850 for assisting the escape of two slaves, Smith asked Jackson to head a delegation to Washington to help Chaplin and underwrote all necessary expenses. Later, to secure Chaplin's release on bail, Smith served as treasurer of a fund-raising campaign and donated $12,000 of his own cash. To be sure, Smith advanced these sorts of donations more out of generosity and a desire to help friends in need than with the intentions of bankrolling a group. Nonetheless, he frequently coupled his donations with intentions that his voluntarists should cease personal squabbles and that they should learn to work cooperatively. In September 1841, for example, he used his purse to undercut ugly bickering between Jackson (who was then an insurgent) on the one hand and Chaplin and Stewart on the other. To quiet the claims of Chaplin and Stewart that Jackson had an abolitionist orientation different from their own, Smith promised Jackson funding for an antislavery newspaper in Cazenovia if Jackson publicly supported the new Liberty party, which insurgents had vehemently opposed. Jackson agreed to the condition and the dispute ceased. In essence, this was the first of a series of steps through which Smith drew Jackson into the group.[8]

In addition to largess, Smith promoted harmony by the force of his personality. He held a profound warmth and respect for all other group voluntarists. He addressed them as "my dear friend," "my much loved friend," or "my excellent friend and neighbor" and frequently boasted of their talents. Green's "intellect is not surpassed in the whole range of my acquaintance!" and Smith was proud to name his son "Green Smith." Goodell's two-volume study *The Christianity of Democracy* represented "by far the most valuable books on civil government, that I have ever read," and Goodell was "a man whom, above all others, I should love to see President." Stewart was an exceedingly effective speaker at antislavery rallies, a "man of genius" and a reformer with a "very tender Heart." Holley was a giant among men. Chaplin was "a very intellectual & well educated man – a strong writer and speaker." Jackson was "a warm hearted, affectionate impulsive man."[9]

Group members reciprocated Smith's warmth and respect. They viewed him not solely as a charismatic if erratic Father Garrison nor exclusively as an efficient administrator like Lewis Tappan. Rather, voluntarists saw both qualities in Gerrit Smith – inspiring leadership and persistent dependability. They called him "my friend" and "our captain" and they stressed how "we all love & honor you, dear brother." He was "the John Hampden of our cause" and belonged "with Wilberforce, Clarkson, Franklin, Jay, Brougham & Earl Gray & a constellation of stars, who have made their age illustrious by the greatness of their deeds in the cause of humanity." Moreover, in time of crisis, Smith was a man upon whom others in the group felt that they could usually depend. He seemed to be predictable – a leader who could always be counted on for support.[10]

Thus, Smith's wealth, plus the deep affection and respect running between him and the rest of the circle, established him as an effective, unifying leader. But his ability to respond to very specific emotional needs of particular group members also contributed. Smith perceived, for example, that Goodell desperately wanted to be consulted and to be heard. Consequently, he sought out Goodell for ideas and arguments on the merits of specific reform ventures. To the consternation of Caleb Calkins, his personal secretary, Smith frequently passed on to Goodell portions of his vast incoming correspondence so that Goodell might participate more directly in Smith's daily activities.[11] On the other hand, Smith understood that Green required expressions of personal affection mixed with open and honest dispute over ideological differences. Consequently, he publicly attacked Green's elitist preferences for "God-sent rulers" and suffrage restricted to "the righteous'" while noting that "I never loved & confided in you more. . . ." Green, in turn, was moved by Smith's open integrity and personal support.[12] Similarly, Smith understood that in their reform pursuits, Chaplin and particularly the younger Jackson looked to him for avuncular advice and sought opportunities to minister to his needs. Both felt privileged to organize Smith's speaking engagements and to disseminate his ideas.[13]

Clearly, then, Smith played a role that was basic to group cohesiveness. Similarity of social characteristics and a common constituency, plus shared responsibilities in the New York State Anti-Slavery Society and later the Liberty party, would have promoted some cooperative efforts without Smith's leadership. But without his skillful deployment of personal funds and his remarkable sensitivity to the specific needs of Goodell, Stewart, Holley, Green, Chaplin, and Jackson, it is unlikely that a cooperative circle would have come into being and operated as a harmonious collectivity of devout reformers for any length of time. Contrary to the portrait painted by his biographer, Ralph Volney Harlow, Smith was hardly a rigid, eccentric moralist. Rather, he seemed to conduct himself toward his circle with deeper human understanding and empathy than Tappan did toward his stewards or even Garrison toward his insurgents.

III

Social characteristics and group leadership are certainly important in explaining the origins and subsequent cohesion of the Smith group. But a third factor, ideology, should not be discounted. Before they had become a cooperative unit, the Smith men had become adherents of cultural voluntarism, "the voluntary principle." This was the notion that all people should be given unfettered freedom to act on God's commands but should be strongly pressured by the community of Christian fellows, by social institutions and, more generally, by the culture about them, to use their freedom "voluntarily," morally, and in a cooperative spirit. Loving the central and western New York towns and villages where they resided, the Smith men believed that the voluntary principle could only thrive in small communities where people were on intimate terms. This ideological commitment to cultural voluntarism through local activity merged with Smith's leadership skills and the commonality of members' backgrounds. Joined, these factors accounted for the increasing sense of group cohesion that the Smith voluntarists came to feel by about 1840. But as we shall see, common ideology also became a basic source of group disintegration. As time passed, the commitment to cultural voluntarism undercut the simultaneous commitment to localism, and the consequences were far-reaching.

We first need, then, a precise grasp of the voluntary principle. William Goodell's two massive volumes, *The Democracy of Christianity* and *Slavery and Anti-Slavery* contained the most comprehensive explication of the concept. Goodell postulated that the churches of primitive Christianity had encouraged "voluntaristic democracy." Through church efforts, people had been encouraged to come together and "prophesy" spontaneously. No person, however gifted, had the right to curb the time or the rights of the less gifted to communicate with God. Within this climate of unfettered freedom, individuals had been induced to behave morally, energetically, and cooperatively. The cultural and institutional pressures of early Christianity had made individuals free while inculcating them with the sense that they were obligated to obey God's commands and to join hands with their godly neighbors. Following the precedent of primitive Christianity, Goodell urged American churches, benevolent societies, and governments to promote individual freedom while encouraging individuals jointly to implement God's commands. The social, cultural, and institutional pressures that liberated all people were the very pressures that would induce them to act morally and cooperatively. When the pressures for free individuality were inspired by moral considerations, then and only then would they cause people to work peaceably as a group. On the other hand, "if expedients instead of principles be proposed as a basis of co-operation, the result will commonly be a still greater diversity of judgment. Men's sense of right and wrong are less various than their calculations of advantage and disadvantage." In essence, then, Goodell equated the voluntary principle with cultural pressures to forge free and ethical individuals who worked together harmoniously.[14]

Like Goodell, Smith elaborated on the voluntary principle where individuals could unite to build railroads, schools, and churches together and to pursue other ventures consistent with God's moral imperatives. Once cultural pressures were such that individuals simultaneously were liberated and worked with their neighbors in godly causes, Smith insisted, "then shall cease forever the spurious Christianity, which turns men into slaves." Like Goodell and Smith, Holley insisted that individuals had to be free so that they could come together and execute the "amazing responsibilities, which we *must* discharge . . . in setting up and sustaining truth, right, justice, and humanity." Indeed, Holley noted, "we here must speak of rights as moral attributes" with which to do good. He equated complete individual freedom with moral pieties such as "industry, frugality, justice, public spirit, firmness" – qualities properly executed in a cooperative spirit. Stewart enunciated similar beliefs. He even admitted that he had personally wasted too much of his freedom by failing to work sufficiently with other pious reformers in the service of God. Oneida President Green stressed that educational institutions had to use pressures that promoted individuality, morality, and collective harmony; these qualities went hand in hand. Similarly, Jackson insisted that every man had an inalienable right to the fruits of moral, industrious activity when he worked in harmony with his neighbors.[15]

Clearly, the voluntary principle was at the heart of the Smith group's belief system. It was largely a variation of the pious fellowship model for missionary activity that the Tappan stewards confidently assumed would characterize their group life and about which Clique insurgents less confidently tried to structure their collective existence. If the free individual was moral and devout, his cooperation with other missionaries would be cordial and satisfying. Indeed, the Smith men's voluntary principle differed from the Tappan stewards' and the Clique insurgents' image of convivial devotion in only one fundamental respect. The stewards and the insurgents essentially assumed that small collectivities of pious missionaries like their own were the agencies that would direct larger immediatist missionary organizations such as the American Missionary Association (A.M.A.) and the A.A.S.S. to spread God's commands and the values that they were promoting. The Smith voluntarists were not against permitting small missionary groups or clusters to work for these goals. Indeed, they conceived of their own circle as just this sort of collectivity. But they realized that pressures for cultural voluntarism would have to come from a broader supportive base than a small circle or even the entire abolitionist movement. Churches, Bible societies, schools, governments, and other agencies would also have to contribute if Americans at large were to be effectively inculcated with the voluntary principle. The Tappan stewards had confidently assumed that God would lead their small band to victory. The Boston Clique insurgents felt that once they effectively balanced the individual against the group in their small collectivity, the A.A.S.S. that they directed would take on new life, become an effective missionary agency, and secure massive conversions. Unlike stewards and insurgents, the Smith voluntarists knew that their small circle, their local constituency, and even the societies and newspapers they directed would never be enough; other nonimmediatist agencies would also be required. It was this sober realism, as we shall see, that ultimately caused the voluntarists to become dejected and their group to disintegrate.

Smith circle voluntarists differed ideologically from Tappan stewards and Clique insurgents in still another respect. Their voluntary principle linked to a corollary – condemnation of aristocracy. To be sure, less prosperous members of the Boston Clique, such as Garrison, Henry Wright, and Oliver Johnson, also attacked aristocracy. Moreover, no member of Lewis Tappan's circle had any taste for it; the Northern yeoman farmer was characterized as the backbone of society. But unlike the others, the Smith men deployed opposition to aristocracy as an indispensable component of their belief system. Because cultural voluntarism assumed that all people had to have the same freedom and opportunity to act morally, there could be no privileged class. Consequently, voluntarists opposed all distinctions of rank, all heredity transmission of authority, "heartless aristocracy," "special nobility," and any general "separation of individuals from the common lot." Equality of opportunity had to be established between "the master and the servant, the employer and the employed, the occupant of the kitchen, the owner of the field and the laborer in the field. . . ." Negro slavery represented the most invidious instance of the spirit of aristocracy, for it allowed the master to deny "the inherent right of self-ownership" in all men, upon which right all other rights were predicated. Because slavery facilitated the grossest spirit of aristocracy, the struggle against the "peculiar institution" represented the beginnings of an international battle against all forms of special privilege. Irish tenants, British workers, and Russian serfs would ultimately be freed as the spirit of aristocracy – special privilege for some at the expense of others – collapsed. The mission of the Smith voluntarists therefore embodied freedom for all downtrodden laboring classes – a goal that neither Clique insurgents nor Tappan stewards clearly or fully endorsed.[16]

All of the Smith men insisted that cultural voluntarism free of the spirit of aristocracy could readily be achieved on the local level, particularly in their own upstate New York towns and villages. There "our families, with certain very few exceptions, dwell together in peace and love; and in this there is no little proof that the religion of Jesus prevails among us." They claimed (perhaps more in hope than out of genuine belief) that in central and western New York tobacco and liquor were held in contempt and Negroes were free from invidious discriminations. The common people there were said to be blessed with "unsophisticated common sense and genuine integrity. . . ." The "hardy yeomanry of Central and Western New York are not yet become quite so refined and Athenian in their tastes as to run in feverish haste" to conform to every passing fad that emanated from the centers of special privilege. The "masses that came from the fields and shops" of the area were far more pleasant to associate with than the Eastern urbanites confused by "the soulless artificialities of the city, with its conventional, moral code!" There was nothing so thrilling as meeting with upstate New York country folk "in a beautiful grove, under God's own expansive, free sounding board!" Surely, there was no other area where individuals were so much at liberty to act out God's moral imperatives with their virtuous neighbors. It was a haven for cultural voluntarism and was resistant to the evils of special privilege. Alvan Stewart summarized the feelings of Smith circle voluntarists: "I always am discontented except when I am there."[17]

All of the men in the Smith circle, then, loved central and western New York and professed delight in mixing with the inhabitants of the vicinity, their friends and neighbors. This helps to explain why they concentrated their many reform efforts in the area, while Tappan stewards and Clique insurgents, considerably less attached to New York City and Boston, looked primarily to national and international missionary activity. Chaplin, Jackson, and Goodell spent the entire 1840s editing diverse local newspapers and organizing local antislavery rallies. Green used his own Oneida Institute in Whitesboro as a springboard for antislavery, temperance, and church reform. Stewart repeatedly urged Liberty party activists in upstate New York to focus on their own small local communities and tried to do so himself. Above all, Smith concentrated his enormous energies and funds in local activities: the Church of Peterboro, central New York stations of the Underground Railroad, a Peterboro temperance tavern, and diverse local antislavery ventures. He even donated funds to several financially pressed "friends of the slave" in the vicinity so that they might become full owners of their own homes and thus more permanent residents. "I came to the conclusion," Smith proclaimed, "that the friends of the slave had, generally speaking, better work hard, & work for triumphs in their respective locations."[18]

The clearest indication that the Smith voluntarists were deeply and emotionally committed to local reform agitation for cultural voluntarism came in the late 1830s. With considerably more vehemence than abolitionists in most other areas, they voiced outrage at the efforts of the New York City–based executive committee of the American Anti-Slavery Society to control their local efforts: "Local work cannot be done by the great central committees, whether state or national. . . . *local* effort everywhere existing, is the whole work we wish and need to have accomplished." The A.A.S.S. executive committee was charged with draining the revenues of upstate New York abolitionists while unwisely attempting to supervise their reform ventures from a distance. Stewart led the resistance, insisting that "a dollar spent at Utica is worth three spent at New York [City]." Effective reform was local and immediate – a neighborly affair. In his capacity as a principal New York State Anti-Slavery Society organizer, Chaplin was furious over the outside intervention of the national executive committee: "We constantly find our plans thwarted – the efforts of our agents defeated & the collection of funds well nigh impossible!" Chaplin insisted that true Christian reform had to be staged by local participants at the local level. Why else, he asked, were Smith circle voluntarists so successful working among their beloved fellow citizens of central and western New York? Smith, too, insisted that unless locally based antislavery societies could raise revenues for themselves and could decide vital issues on their own, the abolitionist movement would die. Intent on securing local autonomy, he introduced a resolution at the 1839 annual meeting of the American Anti-Slavery Society that would have prohibited national society agents from intervening in the states without state society consent. Goodell fully supported Smith's posture. But the two Boston Clique insurgents who knew them best, Henry Wright and Anne Weston, could not quite understand the intense determination of all Smith circle voluntarists to resist "a great central power" in New York City and to preserve local autonomy. Neither could Lewis Tappan, who provided much of the direction behind that "central power."[19]

When they commented on religious affairs, the Smith men also revealed the importance they attached to their neighbors, their local communities, and their reform ventures in upstate New York. Moreover, their comments demonstrated how their local attachments were inextricably tied to cultural voluntarism. Their villages and towns were situated in areas of central and western New York where the most intense and successful of all Finneyite revivalism had taken place during the late 1820s and early 1830s. With the occasional exception of Goodell, the Smith men agreed that those revivals had provided a salutary moral influence upon their region. Through the localistic focus of the Finneyite revivals – their concentration in specific towns until mass conversions of the local citizenry took place – the spirit of cultural voluntarism had taken hold throughout the Burned-over-District. As Finneyite revivals had been nonsectarian in their appeal and had inspired people to engage in sundry reform ventures, Smith voluntarists thought it only proper that all churches share the nonsectarian and reformist spirit.

Gerrit Smith's own Church of Peterboro exemplified the group's commitment to local, nondenominational, reform-centered religious organization. Smith had belonged to the Presbyterian Church in his town. But by the late 1830s his heavy exposure to Finneyite revivalism and immediatism had made him increasingly convinced that the "proslavery" Presbyterian General Assembly was polluting Peterboro's local Presbyterian Church. Above all the General Assembly was obstructing Abishai Scofield, the local minister who was his personal friend and an uncompromising abolitionist. Consequently, Smith urged fellow church members to secede from General Assembly control so that their local body would cease to be tainted by "foreign" controls. Unsuccessful in this effort, Smith left the Peterboro Presbyterian Church in 1843 and, with Scofield's help, organized the nondenominational Church of Peterboro. Selected minister of the new church, Smith insisted that all "true Christians" who lived in Peterboro were church members whether or not they attended services. A "true Christian" was anyone genuinely committed to cultural voluntarism. Thus, the Church of Peterboro consisted of free moral individuals cooperatively committed to God's principles of antislavery and temperance. Smith claimed that he "loved the Church of Peterboro dearly" and considered it his major reform contribution because it was genuinely local; it was free of polluting outside immoralities. He and his fellow citizens were "maintaining it on the one (but one) distinct principle, that the Christians of a place are the

Church of such a place." This principle was to hold regardless of a person's denomination or formal theology. Sectarianism was a great curse, the group maintained, for it fostered bigotry and polluted the Christian reform conscience of a local citizenry. In December 1843 Smith and twenty-seven of his Peterboro neighbors met together and resolved that their church was "a company of moral reformers" who lived happily together in the same community, who had shed old sectarian allegiances, and who embraced a new creed that was supportive of abolition, temperance, and antislavery preaching on the Sabbath. Clearly they were proclaiming themselves to be Peterboro's convivial and devout.[20]

Smith's religious commitments – to localism, against denominationalism, and to love and justice – largely paralleled those of other group members. Indeed, nondenominational "union" congregations like the Church of Peterboro were established in many of the towns of central and western New York, and they often represented centers of local reform agitation. Like Smith, Goodell seceded from his church in Honeoye, New York, in 1843 and helped to establish a local nondenominational church based on antislavery, temperance, and "pure Christianity." Goodell's 1845 pamphlet, *Come-Outerism*, defended this sort of secession and the founding of nondenominational reform churches. Righteous persons were duty bound to secede from a "corrupt church" in their community and to form a true antislavery church of their own. Justification for such action rested entirely on specific local conditions. Beriah Green, too, drew on reformers in Whitesboro to establish a temperance- and antislavery-oriented Congregational church in an effort to escape the "immoral" churches of the greater Utica vicinity. Holley had never even attended a formal denominational church. Rather, he held a simple religious service in his home for family and neighbors. Moving to Rochester in December 1840, Holley located that service in the city courthouse. Shedding formal theologies, he postulated a benign and tolerant God who encouraged the free individuals in his flock to partake cooperatively in moral reform. Although Jackson and Chaplin never participated in a revolt against a "corrupt" local denominational church and apparently never took part in formation of union congregations, both defended these secession movements for promoting the voluntary principle.[21]

Through this advocacy of local union churches, Smith circle participants were showing, in another way, how their voluntary principle caused them to differ from both Tappan stewards and Clique insurgents. With the exception of William Jay, the stewards were staunch Congregationalists and Presbyterians. Though they were willing to associate with pious reformers of other denominations in nonsectarian benevolent societies, they felt too close to Orthodox theology to install this nonsectarian spirit within their own congregations. In marked contrast, several insurgents felt so estranged from the proslavery spirit of both the nonsectarian benevolent societies and their own denominational congregations that they broke from both, sundering ties with major Protestant institutions. Like the Tappan stewards, Smith voluntarists were comfortable with the Christian fellowship of the benevolent society movement and therefore shunned an insurgentlike break from Protestant organizational affiliation. On the other hand, unlike the stewards, their love of locality and their professed respect for their upstate New York friends and neighbors made them willing to forge union churches of all virtuous citizens in a vicinity. This was better than staying within denominational congregations, where they would continue to be subjected to the "sinful" central directives of outside agencies.

Thus the commitment of Smith circle voluntarists to localism was inseparable from their allegiance to cultural voluntarism. They postulated that missionaries could readily spread the voluntary principle in local upstate communities where people were thought to be on personal terms. The problem was that not all upstate communities were the same. As Finney's revivals in the area during the late 1820s and early 1830s demonstrated, conversion techniques that worked in small, stable agricultural communities like Smithfield were not always the techniques that were effective in "boom towns" like Rochester and Utica, where grog shops, boardinghouses, and brothels testified to emerging patterns of social anonymity.

Nevertheless, it was in consequence of this intense upstate community emphasis that the voluntarists strongly opposed attempts to withdraw power from local communities and to lodge it in state and federal administrative bodies. Although a few of them had been Whigs during the 1830s, by the 1840s they all opposed Whig party proposals for federally funded internal improvements. Most voluntarists also opposed efforts to increase federal military appropriations and to centralize the structure of the United States Army in the name of efficiency. Greater centralization and efficiency in the United States Post Office Department was equally inappropriate; people in local communities were to be left to arrange the delivery of their own mails. State government sponsorship of compulsory public education and of asylums for the insane – two of the central reforms of the Jacksonian period – were also adamantly opposed. Education and care for the insane had to remain local matters. Even state ownership of canals was considered reprehensible. Smith circle voluntarists balked at all such developments that increased state or national power. But this was not so much because they were Manchester School liberals who were ideologically intent on limiting government functions to the protection of life and property. Rather, they wanted to limit state and federal actions because they believed that the "corrupt" and "proslavery" major parties dominated government at those levels. At base, then, they were profoundly distrustful of the Jacksonian national party system; they shared intense antiparty perspectives. Moreover, they wanted free individuals in local communities to be able to obey God's commands cooperatively in all of life's particulars. Central governing bodies were not inherently evil; the problem was that they thwarted citizens in localities from fulfilling the imperatives of the voluntary principle.[22]

This strong plea by the men of the Smith circle for local control was hardly new or innovative. Local loyalties had been deeply rooted in colonial society and had hardly been extinguished in the decades after the Revolution. Indeed, localism had been the cry of rather prosperous "gentlemen" who had directed antiabolitionist mobs during the mid-1830s; they had characterized immediatists themselves as outside intruders. Because the "Jacksonian persuasion" on behalf of laissez-faire government economic policies undercut various centralized directives, it, too, frequently operated in the service of localism. Nevertheless, by the middle and late 1840s it was becoming increasingly obvious throughout the North that pressures for institutional centralization emanated at both state and national levels and would surely intensify as time passed. For example, new state education boards were starting to direct new state-funded compulsory schools. Simultaneously, centralized and rationalized state-controlled asylums, almshouses, and reform schools were beginning to proliferate. Initially state medical societies were established, and then the American Medical Association was founded to eliminate the activities of certain "irregular" local community-based medical practitioners. Principles of centralization and standardization in the name of efficiency dictated the reorganization of the federal Post Office Department and the United States Army Officer Corps. Most important of all, the transportation revolution and industrialization were coming to threaten voluntaristic community-centered existence in ways that few contemporaries fully understood. By the 1840s and even more clearly by the 1850s, John Higham explains, the Northern states were experiencing a broad institutional transition toward consolidated and centralized structures. In certain quarters, the transition was beginning to render dreams of individuality and personal boundlessness obsolete. By strongly resisting this transition, Gerrit Smith and his colleagues were assuming difficult roles.[23]

To be sure, Tappan stewards and Boston Clique insurgents also prized individuality and boundlessness. But they were not as attentive as the Smith voluntarists to the kinds of structural transformations that were undermining these qualities. Indeed, the stewards focused almost entirely on individual conversions and were confident that God would attend to broader issues. Whereas the insurgents were concerned about "slaveholding" institutions of diverse sorts, they did not distinguish those that were local from those that emanated from state and national sources. Consequently, Smith circle voluntarists alone fretted over the ways in which institutional centralization threatened to undermine the power of localities.

IV

We now have a fairly comprehensive view of the elements that combined to merge the Smith men into a close, cohesive circle. They shared important social characteristics, a common constituency, and common dedication to a concept of cultural voluntarism rooted in local communities. They were also brought together because of Gerrit Smith's skillful leadership techniques that played upon their common efforts in the New York State Anti-Slavery Society and later the Liberty party. Because they cherished the upstate communities in which they resided and perceived the spread of the voluntary principle throughout the area, they became adamant opponents of centralization efforts – whether from the American Anti-Slavery Society executive committee or from the federal Post Office Department, allegedly controlled by the "Slave Power."

With this summary of the powerful sources of the Smith circle's unity, let us turn to the diverse factors that eventually undermined its existence. It is no easy task to explain why the circle began to dissolve by the late 1840s, while Clique insurgents and Tappan stewards continued their collective activities through the Civil War years. In the course of the 1840s, three factors gradually came to undercut the Smith group's adamant localism: the very logic of the voluntary principle, radical constitutional doctrine, and Liberty party affairs. As the decade progressed, these factors tended to shift the visions of the Smith voluntarists from their upstate localities to Washington, D.C., and national affairs. By the late 1840s they sought electoral victories at the national level and became disheartened because their success was limited to a few towns in the Burned-over-District. This increasing sense of dejection in men whose localistic perspective had slowly been eroded by national-level commitments was basic to group disintegration.

The logic inherent in cultural voluntarism was the most important factor that gradually caused the Smith men to look to success at the national level. Whereas the voluntary principle could and did reinforce localism, as a missionary ideology it was also capable of orienting the Smith reformers toward national concerns. For immediatists who constantly sought to demonstrate their devotion, the battle that God required them to wage collectively against heathenism knew no bounds. This was true in a very concrete way for Smith circle voluntarists. It soon became patently clear to them that the most important reforms that were required to spread the voluntary principle could not possibly have been achieved by even overwhelming success in central and western New York. The nation had to be won over to voluntarism, and the Smith men felt compelled, as God's missionaries, to struggle to accomplish that end.

This general thought process was well illustrated by that portion of William Goodell's address at the 1847 Liberty League meeting at Macedon Lock, New York, in which he pleaded the causes of antislavery and free trade. It was "a law of God," Goodell asserted, that the individual was to be free to act morally in cooperation with his neighbors. Both slavery and trade limitations impaired man's essential humanity by "counteracting the original and heaven-established laws of man's social existence and moral freedom." Neither the slave nor the laborer facing protective tariffs possessed full "self-ownership." Consequently neither could fully guide his behavior in conformity with God's moral imperatives. Goodell was, of course, espousing cultural voluntarism – the right of the individual to be free so that he could behave morally and cooperatively. But he realized that the eradication of slavery and protective tariffs were not local matters exclusively pertinent in upstate New York; abolition and free trade required action by the federal government and complementary action by governments of other nations. Goodell hoped that the Liberty League and a revitalized Liberty party would further these broad goals. Abolition and free trade were "what the country needs, AND MUST AND WILL HAVE," and once the federal government committed itself to these reforms, this would lead "to the conversion of the world."[24]

Gerrit Smith strongly endorsed Goodell's insistence on national and even international approaches to slavery and protective tariffs in similar language that derived from his commitment to the voluntary principle. So did Jackson and Green. Living in Washington, D.C., in the middle 1840s as an *Albany Patriot* correspondent, Chaplin was also quick to perceive that slavery and protectionism – impediments to cultural voluntarism – could not be eradicated without federal action. Alvan Stewart, too, came to see that more than local activity was required to eradicate slavery. Unlike the others, though, Stewart was a vociferous advocate of national protective tariffs. Yet his defense of protection was strikingly similar to advocacy of free trade by the others. Through tariffs, Stewart argued, the federal government could protect the wages of the free laborer – the worker's right to gain the true fruits of his labor. Were the nation to abolish protective tariffs, free laborers would be as impoverished as slaves. Only if the nation abolished slavery and increased tariffs could laborers be self-sufficient and capable of obeying God's moral laws.[25]

Thus, dedication to cultural voluntarism on the antislavery question and in the protectionist–free trade debate drew all of the men in the Smith cluster to look beyond their locality. They focused upon national and international avenues through which they could more reasonably

hope to secure their goals. Similarly, on other issues that vitally concerned them – the avoidance of war, the eradication of land monopolies,
and the spread of temperance – they began to appeal to "every human
being" in "our dear country" on "the earth's surface." The voluntary
principle embodied a missionary spirit – a desire to spread freedom and
morality in, but also beyond, one's immediate locality. It drove the
Smith men to embrace causes that could not entirely be achieved by
their actions in New York. Indeed, by 1854 Smith himself championed a
cause few other voluntarists, much less Clique insurgents or Tappan
stewards, were ready to support. He urged Congress to annex Canada
and Cuba so as to spread "enlightenment, civilization, and a homo-
geneousness with each other and with us."[26]

Constitutional theory emerged as a second factor that gradually modified the Smith group's localist fervor. While adamant that the federal
government should not undermine the efforts of private citizens in local
communities in education, land reform, business ventures, and most
other areas of daily existence, the Smith men became increasingly
ardent proponents of federal constitutional power to eradicate slavery
throughout the land – in the states as well as the territories and the
District of Columbia. Alvan Stewart, the most astute legal mind among
the Smith voluntarists, initiated other group members to the radical
constitutional antislavery posture. By September 1837 Stewart had
ceased to assume that the federal Constitution was "neutral" on the
slavery question. At the second annual meeting of the New York State
Anti-Slavery Society he shocked abolitionists generally, including Smith
intimates, by proclaiming that the Fifth Amendment due process clause
gave the federal government power to abolish slavery in all of the
states; federal authority was not limited to the territories and the
District of Columbia. Consequently, Congress and the federal courts
were constitutionally obligated to move against slavery wherever it
existed. Stewart made this same argument before the American Anti-
Slavery Society annual meeting in 1838. He urged the national society
to repeal an official organizational posture that conceded the states
exclusive jurisdiction over slavery. Tappan stewards and Clique insurgents successfully opposed Stewart's repeal attempt, but he persisted
elsewhere. "We have proved that certain portions of the Constitution of
the United States have been perverted to the support of slavery,"
Stewart proclaimed in 1843, whereas other portions of the document
could be turned against slavery if they were correctly interpreted.
Indeed, "if all parts of that glorious Constitution could be brought into
harmonious play . . ., this great country would be redeemed from her
present degradation, and would occupy a position among the nations of
the earth, in point of practice, as she does now in abstraction." By the
mid-1840s, Stewart's posture represented an unambiguous blend of
cultural voluntarism and radical antislavery constitutionalism. No per-

son could be constitutionally enslaved; all had the right to freedom so that they could follow God's moral imperatives in collective harmony. The federal government was legally obligated to champion individual freedom and morality. National officials were constitutionally bound to promote the voluntary principle.[27]

As Tappan stewards like Joshua Leavitt and William Jay and Clique insurgents like Ellis Gray Loring and Wendell Phillips mocked Stewart's radical constitutionalism at the 1838 American Anti-Slavery Society convention, Gerrit Smith came to Stewart's defense. By defending Stewart, Smith departed (at least in some measure) from his long-standing assumption that slavery had to be abolished by state action. In the years that followed, the writings of Lysander Spooner persuaded him further. By the mid-1840s, Smith proclaimed (with little remaining ambiguity) that the federal government was constitutionally required to abolish slavery everywhere. By simply executing the supreme law of the land, he came to insist, the federal government could secure to all American citizens the freedom to fulfill their moral obligations in co-operation with their neighbors. As early as 1839 Myron Holley also articulated this radical constitutionalism–cultural voluntarism theoretical merger, though without Alvan Stewart's precision and clarity. In 1844 James Jackson and William Chaplin jointly published William Goodell's *Views on American Constitutional Law, in Its Bearing upon American Slavery.* The book represented a wide-ranging defense of Stewart's constitutional–voluntarist stance. In addition, Goodell urged the Liberty party to endorse Stewart's views and to declare that the Constitution was unequivocally antislavery. By 1847 Chaplin editorialized in the *Albany Patriot* what had become the common position of the Smith circle; the federal Constitution was "free from pro-slaveryism" and permitted each individual to act with his neighbors as a free moral agent in God's behalf.[28]

Thus, Alvan Stewart's synthesis of radical constitutionalism and cultural voluntarism augmented what voluntarism itself had sometimes disposed the Smith men to do. They were to look beyond locality to the national scene for the promotion of free moral individualism. This is not to say that the Stewart synthesis undermined the circle's concern with local issues. Rather, Smith voluntarists continued to exalt free men working together in upstate New York and to attack many of the centralizing tendencies within antebellum society. But at the same time, they were gaining some sense of the limits of local action on questions of tariff policy, war, and especially slavery. If the national government was constitutionally required to eradicate bondage and to guarantee people the opportunity to be free moral agents, a conscientious reformer was duty bound to seek support beyond the institutions of his immediate locality.

As Smith circle participants became increasingly supportive of

Stewart's radical constitutionalism, they simultaneously became pre-occupied with the Liberty party. Indeed, Holley, Stewart, and Smith were among the founders of the party. As cultural voluntarism had helped to contour radical constitutionalism, radical constitutionalism contributed to the circle's interest in third-party activity. If, as Stewart maintained, the Constitution sanctioned federal action to remove slavery in the Southern states, Congress had to be made to follow its constitutional duty by legislating the destruction of the "peculiar institution." Once legislation was enacted, the president would have to enforce it. But as long as the Whigs and Democrats sent to Washington officials sympathetic to the Southern slavocracy, Congress would never perform its duty and the president would never execute his. Thus, independent political action was necessary to change the composition of Congress and the occupant of the White House. By the late 1830s Stewart and Holley had become convinced of the futility of a continuation by temperate immediatists of public interrogations of candidates for elected positions. The cross-examinations were not sending antislavery men to office. Instead, they concluded that an antislavery third party had to be created on a temporary basis. By voting third party, abolitionists would show major-party candidates for public office that they could only win over abolitionist support by becoming firmly antislavery. When candidates of the major parties enunciated antislavery postures to the point where at least one of the major parties became adamantly emancipationist, Stewart and Holley maintained that the third party could dissolve. Whereas Chaplin readily accepted this strategy, Smith, Goodell, and Green held out against third-party action until early 1840. Jackson continually vacillated on the issue.[29]

The assumption that the Liberty party could be temporary – that it could quickly infuse "true religion" and principled antislavery into the national political arena (as the churches were unwilling to do) and then disband – helps explain why the Smith men came to be supportive of party efforts. Through evangelical revivalism and benevolent reform, the voluntary principle had come to their Burned-over-District. If the dominant Northern wing of one of the major parties was converted to a truly moral antislavery posture (evidenced by its nomination of antislavery candidates), they felt that upstate New York cultural voluntarism could be annexed to Northern and even national political life. When this occurred, their tasks on the regional and national level would cease, their Liberty party would dissolve, and they would be able to devote more time to the concerns of upstate New York. This was how Myron Holley repeatedly justified third-partyism by mid- and late-1839. The Liberty party was to be a national venture in Bible politics – in moral reformers' collective fulfillment of their duty to God by joining religious truth to political life and thereby assuring "civil freedom." Once the national political climate had undergone moral transformation and freedom had been federally guaranteed to all people to pursue God's mandates, the political result of the evangelical moral revolution would have been sufficiently attained. Then, Holley concluded, the third party would have served its purpose. Alvan Stewart, the other early third-party proponent in the circle, fully concurred with Holley: "We use [Liberty party] politics as an instrument, by which we discharge our duty, to God." Similarly, Stewart added, once the Liberty party transformed national politics into moral Bible politics, all men of all regions would be free to discharge their own duties to God. Deeply influenced by Holley and Stewart, Goodell, Smith, Green, Jackson, and Chaplin came to outline similar postures on the goals of a temporary Liberty party. Dedicated to Bible politics, they would not allow compromise, expediency, or self-seeking to transform them. Rather, as representatives of the evangelical impulse from upstate New York, they would transform the political process so that antislavery men could win office, the federal government could, in turn, behave morally, and all men could become free moral agents. Their purpose, then, was not Liberty party electoral triumph but service as standard-bearers for the Lord. They would transform the permanent parties and thereby make the federal government a guardian of the voluntary principle.[30]

Essentially, then, the Smith men saw themselves integrating the cultural voluntarism of their localities into Northern and national political life. They naively assumed that their Liberty party activities would quickly achieve that end, leaving them to concentrate on the concerns of their beloved upstate communities. Indeed, while they turned to the Liberty party and became its major leaders in New York state, they concentrated (especially after 1842) on Liberty operations in their own communities as much as they possibly could. They equated this local emphasis with Northern and national Liberty party success. Party strength in one town or county supposedly promoted success in adjoining localities, eventually inducing New York state and then the nation to support Bible politics. "So my town continues to set a good example," they would proclaim. Once success in Madison, Oneida, or Oswego county was achieved, "not five years will pass away ere our National Government will be separated, entirely and forever, from the foul and murderous system of American slavery." The impact of Bible politics on one county would quickly set an example for all "sister counties," the state, and the nation.[31]

Clearly, the Smith men desired to spend as much of their time and energy in their upstate New York districts as possible. Smith and Green, for example, rarely consented to leave Peterboro and Whitesboro. Nevertheless, it is important to realize that they all felt compelled to justify local activism in terms of a national party strategy. The very goal of Liberty party operations was Northern, and eventually national, political transformation. As an August 1843 Liberty convention in Buffalo proclaimed, it was "a National Party" originating "in a comprehensive regard to the interests of this whole country." Like cultural voluntarism and radical constitutionalism, Liberty goals and activities required the Smith voluntarists to pay considerable attention to Northern and national issues. The Liberty party served to channel a good portion of their energies and concerns away from the professedly small, contented, upstate New York communities of free moral citizens. Indeed, it is well to note that despite their contempt for the two "ungodly" major parties imbued with the "slaveholding spirit," the Smith men were participating in a strikingly similar organizational structure. Like the Whig and Democratic parties, the Liberty leaders encouraged considerable grass-roots organizational activity: ward, town, district, and state committees. But at least in theory, all grass-roots organizational ventures were to be closely coordinated and directed by a national committee. As with the major parties, locality was explicitly designated as inferior to nationality in the context of organizational goals. Thus, although the local and largely autonomous activities that the Smith men conducted in Liberty party operations were always very substantial, national party perspectives and goals held hegemony in the formalized hierarchy of party organization.[32]

Until the mid-1840s, however, the Smith voluntarists were able to hold out the proviso that the Liberty party was temporary; once it succeeded in making national politics Bible politics, it would disappear and group members would return entirely to local central New York concerns. By 1844 and 1845, though, they were coming to sense that the party and thus their venture into national politics were going to be permanent; it would always be hazardous to retreat from politics at the national level. Foreshadowed by his suggestive letters and editorials in the *Albany Patriot*, Goodell's address to a New York state Liberty party convention in Port Byron in June 1845 provided the clearest indication of this new posture. Neither of the major parties had demonstrated a willingness to throw off Slave-Power domination, Goodell noted dejectedly. Moreover, certain Liberty men seemed desirous of replacing James Birney, a moral giant, with a more popular party presidential candidate; they even appeared willing to water down the party's firm immediatist platform in quest of votes. The task at hand, Goodell therefore concluded, was twofold. First, politically expedient calculations had to be repulsed within Liberty party ranks; the party had to be purified. Second, with their moral commitments restored, Liberty men would have to prepare to make theirs a major party that would govern the nation. Goodell concluded that this would require the party to go beyond its immediatist antislavery commitment and to take equally strong moral stands on all reform issues – on all objects of governmental power. Jackson and Chaplin had helped Goodell to formulate this Port Byron statement, and both defended it publicly. But most delegates at the state Liberty convention opposed the plea for platform stands on all reform issues.[33]

At the time of the Port Byron convention, Goodell, Jackson, and Chaplin not only were apprehensive over their failure to convert the two major parties to Bible politics but feared that because certain less-than-devout Liberty men like Gamaliel Bailey and Salmon P. Chase were desirous of expanding party influence by soft-pedaling immediatism, the Liberty party could easily be absorbed into the slavocracy-dominated major parties. Even if it was not absorbed, those Liberty men who opportunistically soft-pedaled immediatism grossly harmed the cause of Bible politics. By 1846 Green joined Goodell, Chaplin, and Jackson in opposing the apparent opportunism of many members of the Liberty party and insisting that the party assert truly moral positions on all pertinent issues of the day: "Our platform should be wide enough, to give scope to all our powers in discharging our duties as *American citizens*. Otherwise, we are not – cannot be – a National Party." Smith adopted this posture the following year. Stewart still insisted, however, that continuation of a platform restricted to the call for immediate emancipation would maximize the Liberty party's impact.[34]

In 1847 five of the Smith circle voluntarists – all but Stewart and the deceased Holley – founded and provided much of the leadership for the Liberty League. The League was to be a counterforce to impious elements in the Liberty party who might trade off antislavery militancy for votes. Through the pressure-group tactics of the League, the five voluntarists also hoped to turn the Liberty party into an institution that would take stands on all of the human rights issues of the day. Goodell hoped to draw Liberty party men into the League. He wrote a League platform calling for implementation of the Smith circle's basic goal – cultural voluntarism – through free trade, abolition of the army and navy, limitations on the size of land ownership, abolition of the federal Post Office monopoly, the inalienability of homesteads, and the exclusion of slaveholders from public office. Smith became the League's nominee for the presidency but hoped that a revitalized, moral Liberty party would ultimately absorb the League. Together with Chaplin, Jackson, Green, and Goodell, he tried to win other Liberty party leaders to the League's program. Clearly, all Smith circle voluntarists except Stewart were preparing for continuation if not intensification of activities on the national level. Because the Liberty party was to become a permanent institution and to require a long-term commitment from its supporters, the possibility of increasing involvement in local upstate New York affairs had become quite unlikely. Bible politics and programs demanded that the voluntarists remain quite attentive to national matters.[35]

As they became increasingly committed to permanent moral agitation on the national level, the Smith men actually found themselves losing what little influence they had among political abolitionists. Their Liberty

League did not rescue the Liberty party from "immoral" expediency. Quite the contrary, it demonstrated how local and limited Smith circle operations actually were within the broader structure of the Liberty party. In October 1847 most of the Smith voluntarists attended the national Liberty party convention in Buffalo. They argued against coalitions with impious nonimmediatists, insisted upon a permanent Liberty party, espoused radical constitutionalism, and argued for a wide range of reform causes consistent with their voluntary principle. But the convention delegates rejected all of their demands. Inattentive to the Smith circle at the helm of the Liberty League, moderate antislavery Liberty leaders like Salmon Chase and Gamaliel Bailey steered the Liberty party into an 1848 merger with the Free Soil party. Rebuffed by the moderately antislavery Buffalo Free Soil convention in August of 1848, the Smith circle used its Liberty League organizational base to run Gerrit Smith as the True Liberty party presidential candidate in a desperate attempt to revive the old and devout Liberty party. But the old party was dead, and Smith garnered only 2,500 votes. The voluntarists ran Goodell for president four years later, and he did even worse, securing so few votes that no state bothered to report them. In the early 1850s several ex–Liberty Leaguers, including a few Smith voluntarists, formed the National Liberty party. They held a few lackluster conventions and then merged with certain Tappan stewards and other temperate immediatists to form the American Abolition Society and the Radical Political Abolitionist party. But despite these activities during the 1850s, it was clear that their defeat in the fight to ward off Liberty party merger into Free Soil signified the end of the Smith voluntarists' influence in larger antislavery circles. On the eve of the Civil War, Gerrit Smith himself desperately persisted in his efforts to revive Bible politics, voluntarism, and the old Liberty party under the banner of the Free Constitutionalist movement. But by this time, not even old immediatist colleagues paid much attention.[36]

Thus, the broad course of Smith circle voluntarists from the late 1840s on is not difficult to chart. By 1847, if not earlier, they had abandoned the hope of quickly transforming the major parties through the Liberty party challenge and then returning to the concerns of their upstate communities. Instead, they tried desperately to head off merger of the Liberty party into the Free Soil coalition. Having failed, Smith tried to spur his group on in what he sensed was a futile attempt to resurrect the old Liberty party and the old Bible politics. The net result was the persistence of a national reform orientation among the voluntarists while they became increasingly doubtful that they would ever shape national policies. After 1847 they gave very little thought any more to reform among more friendly faces at the local level.

Unlike insurgents of the Boston Clique, then, the voluntarists did not respond to failure by pulling back for succor and reinforcement in a "world in ourselves and each other." Rather, like Tappan stewards, they persisted in the face of serious reverses. But whereas the stewards never doubted that victory would ultimately attend their efforts, by the late 1840s the voluntarists had ceased to be very confident. Consequently, their persistent efforts at the national level seemed to be the acts of desperate men who felt that they had no alternative but to continue on and face almost certain defeat. They understood the severe limitations of the immediatist power base much more clearly than the Tappan stewards, and their realism was a basic source of their discontent.

The political activities of Gerrit Smith during the 1850s illustrate this voluntarist dilemma. In 1852 he was elected to Congress through an upstate coalition of ex–Liberty men, Free Democrats, Whigs, and Democrats. Because Smith predictably went to Washington as a missionary to preach the voluntary principle rather than as a politician intent on forging legislative majorities or influencing congressional committees and caucuses, his tangible influence was minimal. He resigned in dejection before his term was up and returned to Peterboro. Yet Smith's return to his locality did not fully restore his old enthusiasm for upstate causes. To be sure, he devoted some time to the abolitionist Church of Peterboro and to temperance activities in his vicinity. But as with Goodell, Green, and the others, the combination of cultural voluntarism, radical constitutionalism, and Liberty party ventures had measurably shifted Smith's orientation away from the specifically local upstate affairs that had meant so much to him. "I confess that I would get down upon my knees for the office [of President]," Smith proclaimed in 1856, for "I have long believed that nothing short of the election of an abolition President and Congress, can save this guilty, perishing nation." Smith required considerably more, at this point in his life, than to be honored by the citizenry of upstate New York. At the same time, he realized that he could never be elected President and regretted that a handful of abolitionist friends had nominated him for the office. By the late 1850s Smith continued to seek national influence but knew that it would always elude him.[37]

V

It was ironic that as Smith circle voluntarists slowly moved along a skewed path from a decidedly localist to a heavily national orientation, any electoral success they achieved came locally and not nationally. New York was the only state with a Liberty party vote that might conceivably have decided close elections between major party candidates with any frequency. But even there the Liberty vote never exceeded 4.5 percent, and much of this paltry turnout was concentrated in the fifth senatorial district, where most of the Smith voluntarists lived. Two-sevenths of the state vote for Liberty came from Madison, Oneida, and Oswego counties – areas the voluntarists considered home base. These were the counties where the *Friend of Man*, the *Liberty Press*, and the *Albany Patriot*, newspapers they edited, had their widest circulation. Moreover, between 1840 and 1847 Smith's Madison County hometown of Smithfield led Liberty Party voting throughout the nation; 36.8 percent of the Smithfield electorate supported Liberty. But to men like Goodell, Smith, Green, and Stewart, the heavy Liberty vote in the Burned-over-District meant less as time went by. It had not caused deployment of the federal Constitution to eliminate bondage in the slave states or to promote cultural voluntarism. It had not even caused one of the major parties to take a moral posture against slavery. Indeed, local victories had even failed to halt Liberty party coalitionists who eventually merged the party into the "expedient" and "immoral" Free Soil movement. For men like Goodell, Smith, and Green, success on the local level continued to be valued, but not nearly as much as it once had been.[38]

The failures of the Smith circle participants are comparable to the failures of the "Sacred Circle" of five Old South intellectuals that have been characterized by historian Drew G. Faust. Members of the Sacred Circle worked for a South guided by men of intellect and morals like themselves, who understood the necessity of righteous government, high culture, and scientific agriculture. In time, however, Sacred Circle participants perceived that they were failing in their efforts. This weakened the foundation of their intimate association, and the collectivity began to collapse.[39] Similarly, by the mid and late 1840s, participants in the Smith circle came to sense collective failure; despite their intense concern with national affairs, the potential for success at the national level was quite remote. As the dreams of triumph that held the collectivity together began to subside, it, like the Sacred Circle, began to disintegrate.

Beriah Green was the first to turn away from the Smith circle. He had become president of Oneida Institute in Whitesboro during the period when the other voluntarists had been primarily localistic in their concerns. For this reason, he had assumed that the others would support the college in the Burned-over-District that was most fully committed to cultural voluntarism, temperance, and abolitionism. But Green quickly became discouraged. As early as February 1840 he voiced sharp criticism of the others. Much like status-conscious Southern slaveholders, his voluntarist colleagues were said to be sending their sons to more prestigious schools like Yale and Andover. Oneida Institute was forced to close for lack of funds in 1844. Green did not realize that this failure was primarily due to the school's reputation as an abolitionist stronghold; apprehensive Presbyterians had simply cut off donations. Ignoring this basic cause, Green blamed his upstate voluntarist colleagues. He charged that they were more concerned with abstract national affairs than with the preservation of his college. "If our friends do not need our services, why should we urge ourselves upon them?" he wrote bitterly to Amos Phelps. "The professed friends of Freedom have so many fruitless arrangements to maintain; among other things so many _____ ; but never mind." Green remained in Whitesboro as a pastor of a local antislavery Congregational church. But by the mid-1840s he had withdrawn from most Smith circle activities and was becoming exceedingly cynical of its crusade to alter the policies and personnel of the federal government. Personally bitter over his colleagues' failure to support Oneida and skeptical of the value of their efforts, Green broke off correspondence with all group members except Smith. He lashed out at Stewart for "prostituting his noble powers" by supporting the same objective as the "oppressive" Whig party. And he attacked Goodell for naive faith in the wisdom of the masses: "The democracy which he commends, I regard with the very deepest abhorrence." Smith tried desperately to blunt Green's attacks and to induce Green to renew his respect for the old circle of friends. But Smith's conciliatory efforts drew Green's bitter sarcasm.[40]

Because Stewart markedly differed from the others in the Smith circle in the matter of free trade, they sometimes wondered whether he was truly committed to the voluntary principle. By 1846 additional issues came to differentiate Stewart. Whereas Smith, Goodell, and even the disaffected Green insisted that true abolitionists only voted Liberty – that they never supported Whigs or Democrats – Stewart maintained that abolitionists should vote for major-party candidates who supported Negro suffrage at the state constitutional convention. By 1847 Stewart and the remainder of the Smith group also sharply disagreed about a Liberty party dedicated to "One Ideaism" (that is, antislavery as the sole party plank). Stewart felt that One Ideaism offered the Liberty party its only hope of ever gaining a wide following, while the others launched the Liberty League to force the party to take stands on all reforms consistent with cultural voluntarism. Differing over free trade, One Ideaism, and proper voting procedure during the New York Negro suffrage controversy, Stewart lashed out at the Smith circle. By September 1846 he charged that the voluntarists were shamefully lost in abstractions and were used up as effective reformers. Simultaneously, he broke off remaining working contracts with them. In subsequent years, Stewart bitterly criticized his former colleagues and singled out for attack their "foolish" Liberty League venture. By 1848 Smith noted how disheartening it was that "even my old friend, Alvan Stewart, recommends that persons like myself, be violently thrust out – be actually mobbed out – of Liberty Party meetings." "You are in a false position, my old friend," Smith warned Stewart, and urged him to "come back." But despite Smith's urgings, Stewart, who was in declining health by the late 1840s, never returned to the circle.[41]

By 1846, then, the Smith circle had been reduced from seven to four. Holley had died, Stewart had withdrawn totally from group ventures, and Green was only very rarely willing to come to Smith's assistance. Within the next few years, the group was reduced further. Poor health caused Jackson to turn his *Albany Patriot* reformist newspaper over to his close friend Chaplin in 1846. Two years later he formed a partnership with the doctors who were caring for him and established the Glen Haven Water Cure, a hygiene institute at the head of Skaneateles Lake. Jackson was so taken with this new full-time hydropathic practice that he provided only very occasional services to the Smith circle. Refusing regularly to assist the voluntarists any longer, Jackson felt free to criticize them. Smith rebuked him for this "irresponsible" conduct, and Jackson retorted that his "long-continued friendship" with the voluntarists was over.[42]

Thus, by the late 1840s the group had been reduced to Smith, Goodell, and Chaplin. But though Chaplin, the plodding antislavery administrator, was rarely one to disagree with Smith or Goodell over ideas or policies, more mundane details pulled him from them. As chief editor of the *Albany Patriot* in 1847, Chaplin protested in a very agitated tone that Goodell's written contributions had not been arriving in sufficient quantity. Goodell replied that Chaplin's real intent may have been to terminate Goodell's contributions to the *Patriot*. But Goodell would not cease writing. Henceforth, he told Chaplin, the *Patriot* would have to pay postage for his contributions. From this point on, the Chaplin–Goodell relationship showed sharp strain and distrust.[43]

Soon the Chaplin–Smith friendship also weakened. Against Smith's wishes, Chaplin had gone to Washington, D.C. In August of 1850 he was jailed by the city police for aiding fugitive slaves. He faced criminal charges in Maryland as well as in Washington. Smith posted bond to free him from both jurisdictions. Although he did not expect Chaplin to return for trial in Maryland, where he faced certain conviction, Smith had counted on him to face trial in Washington. Chaplin's failure to do so cost Smith a $12,000 bail deposit. Even for a prosperous man like Gerrit Smith, this was a considerable financial loss. The fact that Chaplin forcefully resisted arrest by the Washington police also disturbed the leader of the upstate voluntarists. It set Smith's pacifist principles upon a collision course with his desire to justify violence in behalf of antislavery. Smith was distressed as well because Chaplin had recently voted for the Free Democrats. Finally, immediately before and during the 1850 incident, Chaplin indicated that another band of reformers meant more to him than Gerrit Smith's circle – namely W. R. Smith, Joseph C. Hathaway, and ex-Smith voluntarist James C. Jackson. Thus, although Gerrit Smith lauded Chaplin for Jesus-like heroism after the arrest, the incident concluded with the old circle reduced to Smith and Goodell. Thereafter, neither man trusted nor worked closely with Chaplin.[44]

Smith and Goodell, the "remains" of the voluntarist circle, had a falling out that began in 1848 and culminated in 1860. Until then the two had been the closest of friends with the firmest of working relationships. Smith had deeply respected Goodell's ideas and had used his substantial fortune and public endorsement to give them a wider circulation. He partially funded several of Goodell's newspapers. At Goodell's urging, Smith even provided much of the money to launch the Liberty League. Goodell was deeply grateful and was most respectful of Smith – one of the few rich men who used his money to good effect. But in February 1848 the first sign of a rupture between these two friends was detectable. Goodell published a public letter to Smith in the *Albany Patriot*. In this letter, Goodell charged that he wanted to spend the rest of his life as "a free man, and exercise my little remaining strength at my discretion" rather than continue to associate actively with other reformers. He preferred unfettered individuality to cordial fellowship. Later that year Goodell refused to endorse Smith's presidential candidacy under the True Liberty party ticket and mocked Smith's flirtations with Free Soilers. In 1854 he rebuked Smith for advocating American annexation of Cuba, and in 1856 he criticized Smith's call to arm antislavery settlers in "bleeding Kansas." In the late 1850s Goodell rebuked Smith in strong language for endorsing compensation of slaveholders who emancipated their slaves, and he seemed increasingly envious of Smith's capacity to fund any reform cause at a moment's notice. By 1858 and 1859, when Smith formally proclaimed his "religion of reason" under which human reason rather than Holy Scripture became the guiding force of religious experience, Goodell refused further contact with his longtime friend. For the Orthodox Congregationalist Goodell, "nothing short of Orthodox Theology can warrant radical reforms, or lay a foundation for them." Smith's "lax theology" encouraged moral compromise. To be sure, differences between Goodell and Smith regarding religious self-sufficiency had existed for many years. But Smith's formal embrace of a religion of reason as a major reform came just when Goodell was feeling deeply discouraged over the voluntarists' other flagging reform ventures. Consequently, he saw no point in continuing his ties to Smith. In 1860 Goodell publicly repudiated Smith's presidential candidacy under the Radical Abolition party: "We are not pleased with the idea of going into a battle under the leadership of a general who tells his army, beforehand, that he has little or no hope of ultimate success in the undertaking." Weary of defeats on the national level, Goodell had repudiated his "general." The residual of the original Smith circle was gone.[45]

Clearly, the Smith voluntarists participated in a relatively short-lived collectivity. Their circle began to disintegrate in the 1840s. By 1860 it had ceased to be a meaningful social unit, although Smith continued to see old members and to hope that the group might one day be fully reconstructed. On the other hand, both Boston Clique insurgents and

Tappan circle stewards continued on through the Civil War. An important reason for the voluntarists' shorter collective longevity was their greater realism; they were more attentive to broad institutional problems. To be sure, Clique insurgents were also concerned with institutions. They perceived the spirit of slavery dominating civil government, the churches, the political parties, and other powerful agencies, and this spirit was seen to be blocking the emergence of the Government of God. But the insurgents were so deeply immersed in the inner workings of their Clique – in maintaining a proper internal balance between individual freedom and collective efficiency – that they lacked the sustained focus of the Smith voluntarists on external structural realities. Although the Tappan stewards were not as preoccupied as the insurgents with internal group social dynamics, they were not as apprehensive as the Smith men with adverse external institutional realities. Rather, the stewards were confident that whatever the shape of external institutions and events, God would ultimately see to it that their small band spread Christian self-help values everywhere. The Smith voluntarists lacked the "diversion" of intense internal group dynamics, and they lacked confidence that God would right all wrongs. Instead, they clearly perceived some of the earliest antebellum institutional shifts toward greater centralization and consolidation of power – shifts that stood to undermine their voluntary principle. Moreover, they realized that their efforts to prevail against this broad-based institutional transformation amounted to little; by the late 1840s they were even rejected by most of their Liberty party colleagues. Disillusioned be defeats, the voluntarists ultimately grew disenchanted with each other and with their collectivity. One by one, they left the Smith circle and never rallied behind Gerrit Smith when he tried to reconstruct it.

To be sure, there was a force that might conceivably have kept all of the Smith men together – a shared love of upstate New York communities as the locus of the voluntary principle. After all, they were remarkably successful in their efforts to mobilize the Burned-over-District in behalf of their voluntarist ideal. They were instrumental in the founding of numerous union churches in the vicinity, and they made upstate New York the center of Liberty party electoral strength. Moreover, they thrived as a collectivity amid local victories such as these. Signs of group disintegration were only detectable when the Smith men turned from their upstate communities and became increasingly bogged down in dismal efforts to bring cultural voluntarism to the nation. Had they not become so preoccupied with their national efforts – had they remained content with success at the local level – the Smith group might well have lasted as long as the Boston Clique and the Tappan circle. Indeed, it might have survived both of these collectivities. But there were two basic reasons why the Smith men could not have remained satisfied with victories that were limited to their upstate communities. First, like Clique insurgents and Tappan stewards, they were romantic missionaries who felt duty bound to spread moral truths beyond all previous limits and simply could not bring themselves to settle for less. Second, they were exceedingly sensitive to external structural realities. They quickly came to understand that they could not destroy black bondage or reverse the centralization of American institutions by even overwhelming success in their upstate communities. Consequently, they set out to deal with national politicians, parties, and government structures considerably earlier and with greater determination than Clique insurgents or Tappan stewards. Other factors that we shall be considering in the next three chapters – factors that affected abolitionists generally – often added to this determination of Smith circle associates to salvage their voluntary principle by centering their attention upon people and issues beyond their intimacy group and beyond the local concerns upon which their group had thrived. Consequently, it became almost impossible for the group's disintegration to halt or for Gerrit Smith to successfully reconstruct it. But the additional factors that we shall now consider also weakened the Boston Clique and the Tappan circle; neither survived Smith's group by more than a decade.

Part III

Transformations

CHAPTER 5

" DISTINCTIONS OF SEX "

It is apparent, by now, that first-generation immediatists organized their everyday lives about small unstructured sanctuaries such as the three we have examined. Each of these sanctuaries experienced significant transformations over time. The Boston Clique, for example, was not the same after Nathaniel Rogers was expelled; the episode left all remaining members guilty and apprehensive that they had undermined their dedication to free individuality. Similarly, stewards of the Tappan circle felt quite disoriented when their own colleague, Joshua Leavitt, endorsed the Liberty party as a viable alternative to church-centered abolitionism. Smith circle voluntarists, of course, experienced the most fundamental change of all – the disintegration of their sanctuary.

Despite the importance of these sorts of developments, not all basic changes among first-generation immediatists were confined entirely to specific intimacy circles or sanctuaries. Certain fundamental transformations affected immediatists in all sanctuaries, if in different degrees, owing to the social dynamics of their particular circle, their personal idiosyncrasies, and other factors. We shall explore three of these more general and fundamental changes. One concerns gender relationships (Chapter 5), another deals with race relations (Chapter 6), and a third involves deployment of violence for antislavery reform (Chapter 7). In the course of examining changes in these three areas, we shall note how they impinged on one another and upon the immediatist's sense of pious fellowship. It was no accident that the broad pattern of male–female relationships within abolitionism changed at the same time that the pattern of white–black contacts within the movement was transformed. These changes, in turn, were related to significant departures from immediatist peace principles in favor of "violent means." A number of difficult decisions were at the roots of the three general transformations – decisions that were not entirely dissimilar. In different contexts and over different specific issues, immediatists found themselves having to decide what types of reformers outside their particular intimacy circles they were to embrace as colleagues and what types they were to spurn as threats to personal piety.

The social, emotional, and ideological priorities of their intimacy groups obviously had a bearing upon the specific decisions that immediatists finally made in selecting new colleagues and rejecting others. Because of the Smith circle's early concern with national institutions, for example, even before the Mexican War members felt compelled to forge at least some sort of working relationship with more moderate antislavery men from the major national parties. Personal idiosyncratic factors of individual immediatists also influenced specific decisions, as did broader cultural currents. But once immediatists made certain particular decisions, however tentatively, these determined or at least facilitated other decisions that changed their ideals and their friendship patterns in ways that could not possibly have been anticipated. By the outbreak of the Civil War, the quality of an immediatist's ideological, social, and emotional life differed in many fundamental respects from what it had been when he had initially rebelled against the "sinful" Colonization Society. In 1861, for example, Garrison prized piety and collegiality just as strongly as he had in 1831. But his perceptions of piety had changed dramatically in the course of thirty years; so had several of the people he referred to as his colleagues.

II

The American Anti-Slavery Society (A.A.S.S.) was forged in Philadelphia in December of 1833. The organizational meeting revealed much about the pattern of gender relationships at the beginning of the crusade for immediate abolition. Arthur Tappan was substantially correct when he claimed, seven years later, that the delegates "understood, that its business should be conducted by men, *as is usual in the other benevolent societies of the age;* while at the same time, it was expected and desired, that females should form auxiliaries, in the usual way, to the parent Institution."[1] Almost all delegates in Philadelphia in 1833, male and female, were intent on forging an organization that perpetuated the gender dichotomies of tract, missionary, Bible, and other benevolent reform societies of the age. Men organized and ran the main body, while women joined affiliated societies that helped raise its funds and execute its policies. True to the pattern of the other benevolent societies of the age, most immediatists at the Philadelphia meeting expected women to hold sewing bees and bazaars and to participate in sundry activities consistent with their "natural" domestic roles supportive of the men to whom they were related by blood and marriage.[2] Consequently only men enrolled as members of the new A.A.S.S. and signed its official "Declaration of Sentiments and Purposes." Consistent with benevolent society tradition, the Philadelphia meeting closed with a resolution thanking women as the outsiders in attendance "for the deep interest they have manifested in the cause of antislavery, during the long and fatiguing sessions of the convention."[3]

One incident occurred at the Philadelphia meeting, however, that was inconsistent with the gender pratices of benevolent society gatherings. Lucretia Mott detected a specific failing in Garrison's draft of the organization's "Declaration of Sentiments." She rose to speak, as was customary at Philadelphia Quaker meetings. But then Mott hesitated, realizing that this was not a local Quaker gathering, and she turned to take her seat. At that moment, Beriah Green, chair of the convention, beckoned Mott on: "Go on mam, go on; we shall be glad to hear you." Mott spoke about the need to reword a key sentence in Garrison's "Declaration," and the convention overwhelmingly endorsed her recommendation.[4]

Decades later, first-generation immediatists referred to this incident as the point at which abolitionists began to depart from the standard gender customs of the benevolent societies. It represented the emergence of a co-missionary tradition, they insisted, and allowed male and female immediatists to labor together as devout associates in the crusade for Negro freedom.[5] This was distortive of early immediatist experience. Through the remainder of the 1830s and well into the 1840s, most immediatists carefully conformed, in most gender particulars, to benevolent society customs. Women organized separate female antislavery affiliates to support the male societies in their communities. They did no more than to provide refreshments at the gatherings of the new Liberty party. Indeed, Lucretia Mott herself later conceded that she was not really striking out for female co-missionary status at the 1833 meeting.[6]

What many immediatists in later life and at the conclusion of their antislavery crusade assuredly wanted to believe was that they had broken, at the start, from the gender customs of the benevolent empire. More fundamentally, they wanted to believe that they had always been free of certain broad antebellum social patterns that the benevolent societies reflected and that pervaded at least segments of white middle-class culture. These patterns essentially involved admonitions for women to restrict themselves to the home and dispositions of each sex to live emotionally separate from the other. Despite the abolitionists' glowing retrospective comments, the process through which these patterns eroded took many decades, the results were mixed, and the joint missionary status that emerged came more as a result of exigencies of daily antislavery operation than from abstract commitment to egalitarian principle. As Mott's good friend Mary Grew noted in 1863, it simply became more convenient and efficient for some male immediatists to treat women as colleagues: "As concert of action between men and women was important to success, so mutual counsel and discussion in the business meetings were convenient and profitable." Consequently, where male immediatists drew nearer to their female colleagues in everyday antislavery operations, the women gradually "found their work widening, their responsibility deepening at every step." Co-missionary status emerged, we shall see, as a gradual and somewhat un-anticipated result of improved day-to-day communication between the sexes.[7]

III

A primary obstacle that immediatists had to circumvent in this slow, often unconscious, and altogether undramatic movement toward co-missionary status was the pervasive concept of Woman's Sphere. This concept was articulated in innumerable novels, sermons, eulogies, schoolbooks, and behavioral manuals, as well as in private correspon-dence of the elite and the obscure. It constituted a prescriptive code to encourage middle-class women to concentrate their attentions on house-hold duties and child rearing. If she executed her duties with morality, compassion, and softness, the True Woman compensated for the im-moralities, crudities, and aggressions that characterized her father, husband, and brothers in a highly competitive commercial capitalist society.[8] Young Garrison voiced the basic tenets of this concept: "She [woman] is in truth to pass the *whole* life in softening the character, exciting the affections, and rewarding with a love beyond all prices the toils of man. . . ." Whittier as a youth similarly urged women to support their men: "And by your love of them; by every holy sympathy of your bosoms; by every mournful appeal which comes up to you from hearts whose sanctuary of actions has been made waste and desolate, you are called upon to exert it in the cause of redemption from wrong and outrage." Indeed, through the 1830s and early 1840s one finds im-mediatists of all persuasions, from the Boston Clique insurgent Henry Wright to the Tappan circle steward Amos Phelps, espousing the ele-ments of Woman's Sphere.[9] It afforded ideological justification for the separated and subordinated domain that women occupied when early immediatists decided to follow the pervasive gender pattern of the benevolent society movement.

Although early immediatists therefore deployed the concept of Woman's Sphere to build separateness and female subordination into their movement, endorsement of the concept also seems to have con-tributed to the evolution of male–female co-missionary status. By stressing women's pure and passionless domestic essence, it helped to displace a long-standing tradition of Christian distrust of women as inferior and ensnaring creatures of lust. Hence, there was less hazard for men who valued their moral purity to associate with True Women. Indeed, association with the moral supervisor of the hearth promised to enhance male purity amid the moral hazards inherent in open market capitalism and Jacksonian politics. Woman's Sphere prescriptions therefore admonished middle-class women to confine themselves to subordinate domestic roles. But they also tended to make male immediatists less apprehensive about associating with women – even in the public sphere. If male abolitionists could afford to join only with untainted colleagues, Woman's Sphere offered them certain assurances that female associates would satisfy the requirement.[10]

There was a second and perhaps even more formidable obstacle than Woman's Sphere to co-missionary status for immediatist women; it also derived from abolitionism's roots in the benevolent society movement. This was the tradition of confining all female efforts to separate if affiliated reform societies. The tradition reflected a pervasive custom within segments of middle-class culture that Woman's Sphere strongly implied; women were to associate primarily with women in hearth-centered activity and men with men in affairs outside the home. Pervasive Victorian admonitions against the exchange of sensual emotions between the sexes encouraged this separation into sorority and fraternity. Women frequently drew together in sisterhoods of emotional rapport centering on their common experience in Woman's Sphere as wives and mothers. Men tended to cultivate closer relationships as "rational" molders of the outside world of commerce and politics. To be sure, since Victorian admonitions against heterosexual emotional involvement were prescriptive and not descriptive, traditions of sorority and fraternity certainly did not extinguish many deep and loving male-female relationships within the middle class. Rather, as recent scholars have discovered, Victorian heterosexual taboos seem to have encouraged visceral and often profoundly sexual urges to manifest themselves *also* in woman–woman and man–man relationships. Margaret Fuller clearly noted these manifestations within the cultivated middle-class missionary reform circles that she saw about her:

It is so true that a woman may be in love with a woman and a man with a man. It is pleasant to be sure of it, because it is undoubtedly the same love that we shall feel when we are angels. . . . It is regulated by the same laws as that of love between persons of different sexes, only it is purely intellectual and spiritual, unprofaned by any mixture of lower instincts. . . .

Although love and cooperation between man and woman was acceptable, for Fuller it was more carnal and therefore less pure than same-sex relationships. Reform association was more devout when it involved homosocial emotional embraces.[11]

There can be little doubt that early immediatists, like their benevolent society predecessors, confined women to separate reform associations because they accepted the pervasive prescriptive literature that at least implicitly linked Woman's Sphere to sorority–fraternity divisions. Men and women tended to labor with and talk to those immediatists of their gender. Clare Taylor's published collection of 493 letters on Anglo-American abolitionism housed in the vast antislavery collection of the Boston Public Library conspicuously illustrates the acceptance of these separate male and female spheres. Regardless of the topics discussed or the abolitionists discussing them – insurgents, stewards, voluntarists, or others – male immediatists almost always corresponded with their male supporters in the British Isles, and female abolitionists wrote largely to their female counterparts. This gender-linked basis for correspondence was most noticeable during the early years of the immediatist crusade; it diminished somewhat by the 1850s. The pattern dovetailed with another characteristic of early immediatist correspondence. When a married man wrote to another man, his wife frequently attached a supplementary letter to the correspondent's wife.[12]

Although such same-sex fraternization was a pervasive middle-class cultural phenomenon involving immediatists of both genders, it was particularly conspicuous among male abolitionists during the 1830s and 1840s. Moreover, it could be detected beyond the boundaries of their particular intimacy circles. Disliked and apprehensive of violence to their persons, male immediatists often traveled and roomed together for self-defense during extensive road trips proselytizing for reform. Moreover, they enjoyed and even delighted in each other's company. Voluntarist Gerrit Smith, for example, thanked Weld of the Tappan stewards for visiting him and hoped "that God in his providence will permit me to see you frequently hereafter." He fretted that because James Birney was moving to frontier Saginaw, years could pass before the two saw each other again. Weld noted that face-to-face contact between himself and other male abolitionists was much more desirable than contact through correspondence. Temporarily alone in his house in Brooklyn, Lewis Tappan begged Amos Phelps to come and room with him: "I long to have you here." "But it would give me sincere, most unaffected pleasure, if you would make my house your home while in Boston," insurgent Ellis Gray Loring told steward John G. Whittier. Insurgent Henry Wright issued a similar appeal to steward George Cheever: "Do – dear brother – if you come to this city [Boston] – come to my boarding house. . . . Do call on me & dine & spend a night." The fervor and sense of urgency within these pleas for one another's company far exceeded Victorian literary convention.[13]

When rooming together, visiting one another's homes, or meeting at reform conventions, male abolitionists conducted other rituals of physical bonding quite different from the homosocial rituals of antebellum working-class tavern culture. During the 1830s they borrowed from early Christian custom and kissed each other on the cheek as a social greeting. They also frequently held hands. The ideal, however, was to work out some sort of arrangement where specific male immediatists could be together on a very regular basis and, in this way, they would replicate the benevolent society tradition of Christian fellowship. This is why some of them were so pleased with Mrs. Sprigg's boardinghouse in Washington, D.C., during the early 1840s. Called "Abolition House" by Southern Congressmen, it afforded missionaries like Joshua Leavitt, Theodore Weld, and Joshua Giddings a place to live together in good fellowship amid general hostility. Similarly, Elizur Wright hoped that abolitionists could emulate London's men's clubs. By establishing these clubs in the cities where they labored, they might meet happily together without "the refining influence of female society."[14]

This apprehension if not outright fear of the influence of women that fortified fraternity and stood in the way of a viable co-missionary tradition was voiced most frequently by young male immediatists facing the prospect of marriage. Because these pious young men enjoyed very cordial association with other male colleagues, they found the possibility of matrimony at once worrisome and attractive. Would they be able to consummate their marriages, as custom required, since their preoccupation with other men had made the female body a distant and potentially dangerous if somewhat alluring object? This anxiety over personal virility on the wedding night at least partially explains why Theodore Weld and John Whittier pledged not to marry until slavery was abolished. In some measure, it also accounts for young Garrison's professed attraction to "the *single life* and not trouble myself about the ladies. . . ." To be sure, as the record of the intense emotional relationship between Joshua Speed and young Abraham Lincoln suggests, the fear of successful matrimonial consummation was hardly confined to young male abolitionists. Rather, it was a more general result of Victorian cultural proscriptions against middle-class "Christian gentlemen" exploring female physical and emotional properties – proscriptions that at once reflected and augmented fraternal bonds. An older behavioral ethos stressing male sexual virility simultaneously persisted, however. This meant that the truly devoted young man was supposed to maintain a safe distance from women yet demonstrate sexual capacity from the wedding night forth. The consequence, as the experience of Speed and Lincoln as well as that of numerous young male immediatists illustrated, was a "Christian gentleman" who felt a certain vague tension between his cordial male friendships and the distance he maintained from women, on the one hand, and his personal virility on the other. The tension persisted at least until the "gentleman" consummated his marriage. It therefore operated as a restraint on the development of a co-missionary tradition where men and women worked together with ease and harmony.[15]

If male immediatists, while hardly disinterested in their female counterparts or in women generally, found enormous pleasure as well as certain apprehensions in fraternal association, it comes as no surprise that female immediatists devoted great energies to the bonds of sorority implicit in Woman's Sphere. Still, the sorority that they forged differed in important respects from the fraternity of their male counterparts. It was characterized by fewer expressions of fear and hostility toward the opposite sex, by apprehensions but little guilt over the prospect of unsuccessful marital consummation, by greater attention to abstract theoretical constructs, and by rather muted articulations of sororital bonds. Superficially, at least, antislavery sorority seemed to be constructed of less conspicuous homosocial fabric than its fraternal counterpart.

In March of 1837 the Ladies' Anti-Slavery Society of New York City defended the Grimké sisters against attacks for violating Woman's Sphere through their antislavery activism:

It is not that they love home and its sacred retirement less, but that they love the bleeding outcast slave more, that they have become voluntary exiles from the blood stained soil of Carolina, tho' it be their native one, and with a holy resolution that knows no wavering, have consecrated themselves to this pilgrimage of mercy.[16]

This defensive tone represented an effort to circumvent the prescribed middle-class mores of the day requiring women to center their lives upon hearthside domesticity. According to the Ladies' Society, the ills of slavery required the Grimkés to expand their missionary activities so that they served not only as moral guardians of the home but also as moral pilgrims dedicated to freeing the nation of sinful black bondage. Through this argument the New York women were pursuing a fundamental avenue for growth and for more diversified experience inherent within the notion of Woman's Sphere. If women, because of their moral and religious virtues, were required to take dominion over the home and to become its moral guardians, they were also required to spread their faithful qualities to the outside world that men had left in such disarray and sin.[17] Other women's antislavery groups, particularly the Philadelphia and Boston Female Anti-Slavery Societies, echoed this call to enlarge the realm of virtue by expanding the female missionary sphere.[18]

By explaining their antislavery missionary activism in this way, female immediatists were doing more than availing themselves of avenues for growth and influence implicit within prevailing notions of Woman's Sphere. By collectively championing the cause of the slave – the conspicuous underdog – they were essentially binding themselves together as underdogs. This, at least, is what several of them quickly came to sense as they justified woman's participation in the debate over slavery. As Elizabeth Cady Stanton told an annual meeting of the American Anti-Slavery Society, while the first concern of female abolitionists was "the emancipation of the Southern slave, we are, under the Divine economy, at the same time working out our own salvation. . . ." Abigail

Kelley similarly noted how female intervention for the slave had launched women upon a cooperative crusade for their own rights. "In striving to strike *his* chains off, we found most surely, that *we* were manacled ourselves." Lucy Stone explained to an early women's rights convention that female involvement in black liberation had made it clear that they were also "plunged in a degradation" and would have to come together for self-liberation.[19]

More than theoretical awareness of a common feminist interest impressed itself upon female immediatists, however. In *Beginnings of Sisterhood: The American Woman's Rights Movement, 1800–1850* (1977), a detailed study of the origins of organized agitation for female equality, historian Keith E. Melder has conclusively demonstrated what several historians had hypothesized for some years; female immediatists constructed emotional bonds of sorority while fighting initially for the slave and then for both the bondsman and themselves. To be sure, a number of urban female benevolent societies forged in the aftermath of the War of 1812 had produced important precedents for sororital cooperation in behalf of "female" causes. But *Beginnings of Sisterhood* has also proven that the rhetoric exposing underprivileged womanhood and calling for a cooperative crusade of female reformers for gender rights never assumed truly clear, concrete meaning until female immediatists gathered together in sewing circles, planned antislavery bazaars, launched antislavery petition campaigns, and organized female antislavery societies. Collective female antislavery organization proved to be most exhilarating. It provided a means for women, on a daily basis, to cast out their periodic feelings of despair and uselessness – their sense of enslavement to a somewhat less than glorious hearthside and of deprivation from the full range of life's experiences. Simultaneously, it offered channels to replace that despair. Female antislavery organizations consciously opened doors to leadership and management experience that had been closed to women in male-run institutions. Combined with new feminist ideologies, these institutions gave women a sense of collective visibility and importance. Their mission to the slaves and to the female sex assumed tangible, visible form.[20]

In essence, then, Melder's *Beginnings of Sisterhood* suggests that abolitionist sorority differed from abolitionist fraternity. Warm emotional bonds seemed to manifest themselves more readily and spontaneously among male immediatists. To be sure, one finds evidence that women such as Mary Grew reflected on companions in antislavery and women's rights such as Margaret Burleigh much as William Lloyd Garrison might have reflected on Henry Wright, his intimate in the Boston Clique: "To me it seems to have been a closer union than that of most marriages."[21] But for the most part, female abolitionists were so preoccupied with exploring the possibilities for growth and assertiveness inherent in missionary concepts of Woman's Sphere and with efforts to organize female antislavery and women's rights organizations that they did not seem to have the time or concern with hand-holding and cheek-kissing rituals or secretive personal meetings. Nor did they seem in the least concerned that close homosocial ties might inhibit sexual perform-ance with men. More explicitly, the ultimate implication of the Melder study is that female abolitionists were so intent on delineating women's deprivations, testing the limits of Woman's Sphere, and constructing sisterhood organizations – matters male abolitionists did not have to bother with – that their concerns often did not extend to the minute emotional and physical subtleties, both enriching and debilitating, that can develop within a homosocial ritual pattern.

Comparison of the relationship between Sallie Holley and Caroline Putnam to the Theodore Weld–Charles Stuart relationship helps make concrete this distinction. Holley and Putnam met in 1848 as students at Oberlin College, an institution that the Tappan circle had supported. They chose to forgo marriage and to pattern their lives around one another, with Holley the assertive leader and Putnam the caring assis-tant. Holley became an abolitionist lecturer, combining the antislavery themes of New England insurgency with a highly personalized, pious revivalist rhetorical style. Putnam often served as her travel companion, manager, adviser, researcher, and reporter. On familiar terms with leading abolitionist–women's rights activists such as Lucy Stone, Eliz-abeth Cady Stanton, and Susan B. Anthony, the two intimates began to merge antislavery arguments with theoretical justifications for women's rights. While continuing to concentrate on immediatist efforts, they supported the development of early woman suffrage organizations and arguments as seemingly logical extensions of the crusade against slav-ery. According to biographer Katherine Herbig, by the mid-1850s the Holley–Putnam relationship had evolved to the point where they were "a career couple, cooperating, sharing, occasionally feuding much like a married couple who work closely together." Sharing the same room and often the same bed, each partner to the "marriage" strived for achieve-ments that were defined as appropriate male goals. Yet there is little evidence of an intimately developed homosocial ritual pattern – kissing, touching, or even exchanging secret missives – between these life-long friends. To the contrary, their energies were absorbed in adjusting. First they had to adjust to the notion that the female missionary re-mained true to Woman's Sphere when she rallied for the slave. Second they adjusted to the requirement that women had to rally for gender rights as well as for civil rights. Finally, both adapted to the fantasied admonitions of their deceased fathers on the subject of their unortho-dox careers.[22]

The Holley–Putnam relationship was distinguishable from the rela-tionship between Theodore Weld and Charles Stuart in a number of respects. Whereas Holley was eight years older than Putnam, Stuart was twenty years Weld's senior. Moreover, Stuart spent fourteen years as a commissioner for the East India Company before he met Weld. In the early 1820s he became principal of the Utica Academy for boys. There, in 1824, the forty-one-year-old bachelor came into contact with the twenty-one-year-old recent convert to Finneyite "new measures" theology and revivalist strategy. Electricity passed between them. The friendship lasted for decades. But after 1829, when Stuart moved to England to participate in the British antislavery movement, almost all communication took the form of letters. Unlike the Holley–Putnam relationship, Stuart and Weld ceased to see each other on a regular basis. Moreover, in contrast to Holley and Putnam, who were never close to many men and who never married, Weld and Stuart experienced very troubled courtships. Although the two men remained deeply devoted to each other, Weld began to call upon Angelina Grimké, while Stuart courted Weld's sister Cornelia. After almost backing out of his engagement to Miss Grimké, Weld married her in 1838. Stuart permanently ended all contact with Weld's sister in 1834 but apparently married in the early 1850s.[23]

Whereas the Holley–Putnam relationship centered upon the intellectual and strategic adjustments that antebellum middle-class women had to make in order to live active reform lives while operating within the vague limitations of Woman's Sphere, the Weld–Stuart relationship was almost entirely personal and emotional. There is insufficient evidence to determine conclusively whether Weld ever did more, physically, with Stuart than "wept on his neck from *very love to him. . . ."* This was likely the limit, for both regarded man–man sexual consummation as Satanic pollution that would unfit them to commence, much less persist in, married life. Moreover, since most of their contact came through correspondence, the nature of the letters that ran between them was at the heart of the relationship. The substantive issue in that correspondence was neither antislavery nor women's rights but Stuart's displeasure with Weld's drift toward a nondoctrinal social Christianity theological posture. Yet this difference did not destroy the emotional bonds that drew the two men together. To the contrary, Stuart found Weld's theological shift disturbing principally because he feared that it might prevent Weld from meeting him in the next world. As he stated on one occasion: "I may approve or condemn [Weld's theology]; but I am persuaded that our love, apart from all other agreement or disagreement, is holy & eternal, in its measure, like Him, from whom it flows." Once, when Weld had temporarily broken off correspondence, Stuart mourned that "I have never forgotten our former love" and acknowledged that his affection for Weld exceeded his love for Christ. Phrases like "dearly beloved brother of my soul," "brother of my heart," "bonds which unite us," and "our mutual love" characterized Stuart's letters to Weld. Similarly, Weld acknowledged that "no one has ever filled my soul with such admiration & reverence as Charles Stuart. He alone filled out my ideal of a perfect character. For 77 [sic] years I saw more of him, & spent more time with him than with any other person & saw him at all time in manifold conditions." Weld often wrote of his "excellent friend Charles Stuart," "What a man that!" "Blessings best and ever on him!" and "Dearest soul." When Weld wrote with doubts and guilt on the eve of his wedding to Angelina Grimké that God may not have intended him to marry, it seems clear that his relationship with the still-unmarried Stuart weighed heavily in the balance.[24]

Thus, although the Weld–Stuart and the Holley–Putnam relationships were not necessarily typical or widespread among immediatists in all of their particulars, they do illustrate broad distinctions between fraternity and sorority that made gender separation a conspicuous feature of early immediatism. Fraternity centered upon a quest for free-flowing mutually spontaneous if sometimes guilt-inducing bonds of the heart. On the other hand, sorority was less private and more formalized; it was more directly oriented toward the strategic and theoretical ramifications of women's assumption of public roles in behalf of the dispossessed.

Consequently, whereas abolitionist fraternity has left us with many deeply emotional but highly idiosyncratic documents, abolitionist sorority has provided a much more substantial intellectual legacy. Application of late eighteenth-century natural rights theory to gender roles was the most conspicuous portion of this legacy; natural rights theory was deployed to justify female education, diverse legal protections, "honorable" employment, and the vote. But detailed arguments concerning the parallel positions of women and black slaves were also forged. Cogent biblical reinterpretations recognizing "neither male nor female in Christ Jesus" were invoked as well. Even the concept of overlapping spheres and dual natures – that despite extremely important gender distinctions, men and women were both human beings and citizens – derived from immediatist ventures in sorority.[25]

IV

Notwithstanding the important intellectual contribution of immediatist sorority, homosocial bonding patterns combined with Woman's Sphere prescriptions and made the early immediatist crusade a sexually segregated movement where women assumed distinctly subordinate roles. In this sense, immediatism clearly reflected its benevolent empire antecedents. Still, certain subtle forces were to be found within notions of Woman's Sphere and within homosocial bonding patterns that would eventually contribute to a more integrated and at least somewhat more egalitarian co-missionary existence among immediatists.

Both the concept of Woman's Sphere and the emergence of exclusive female antislavery societies gave female immediatists a certain sense of consequentiality and self-worth. Through Woman's Sphere, they could regard themselves as moral missionaries whose services were desperately required not only by the hearth but wherever sin had to be reversed. Separate female antislavery organizations – manifestations of sorority – gave them instrumentalities over which they could preside in fulfilling their mission to the slaves and to women's rights. Thus, although on the most obvious level both Woman's Sphere and fraternity-sorority patterns suggested that important public questions such as slavery were the exclusive province of males, in less noticeable ways they gave female immediatists means to enter the public sphere. Moreover, they entered with confidence and a sense of personal worth that made it very difficult for male abolitionists to continue to deny them joint missionary status. To be sure, during this period of female transformation, many male immediatists continued to espouse the concept of Woman's Sphere and to gravitate toward old fraternal ties, but by the late 1840s and through the 1850s it was clear that most of them were also changing. They were more fully and cordially embracing women as genuine colleagues, true associates in the mission to the slaves. Harriet Taylor Mill, the English feminist, observed this tendency in 1850. She could therefore understand why the very men who had waged the struggle against "the aristocracy of colour" in America were mingling more freely with women in "the first collective protest against the aristocracy of sex."[26] Let us explore the vital manifestations of this process which, by the 1850s and assuredly by the outbreak of the Civil War, allowed co-missionary status to become conspicuous within many abolitionist working relationships despite the continuation of older middle-class sex role stereotypes and traditions. Indeed, let us try to understand why the rigid gender dichotomies and strict female subordination evident in the 1833 organizational meeting of the A.A.S.S. had, by 1861, survived in full force only among a few unreconstructed steward and voluntarist immediatists.

Rhetorical change provided the first indication of this new departure. From at least the early 1830s, Garrison and several of his male insurgent colleagues had articulated the notion of women as moral missionaries. This view – that women gave moral testimony for and direction to society – could be traced at least as far back as late seventeenth-century gatherings of Pennsylvania Quakers. To be sure, it had always been assumed that women were to exercise their morality within their own sphere. Garrison himself fully supported this assumption. As he noted in 1834: "Nature has provided opposite spheres for the two sexes, and neither can pass over the limits of the other, without equally deviating from the beauty and decorum of their respective characters." But he and several of his Boston Clique associates came to assume a more expansive view of Woman's Sphere and greater appreciation of female capacities somewhat sooner than many other male immediatists. The proddings of Maria Chapman within the private discussions of the Clique plus the urgings of friends of the Clique such as Abigail Kelley, Lydia Maria Child, Henrietta Sargent, and Eliza Follen help to explain why. Since the men of the Clique readily admitted that women provided moral direction to society generally, this gave female insurgents crucial leverage to compel them to acknowledge that the female sphere could not be restricted to the home. The effort at persuasion was not difficult. Indeed, several male Clique insurgents quickly became quite receptive to, even enthusiastic over, female missionary activities on public issues. They were particularly pleased with female moral testimony against slavery, intemperance, and prostitution. In the late 1830s, for example, Garrison published Sarah Grimké's *Letters on the Equality of the Sexes* in the *Liberator* to broaden its circulation. He became her close colleague in antislavery and other reform ventures and was so admiring of her career and capacities that he entertained hopes of becoming her biographer. By 1850 Garrison had evolved to the point where he openly proclaimed to a women's rights meeting that each sex behaved better when in the presence of the other sex. Men would therefore be much less "outrageous" in political affairs if women entered the political arena where they could provide moral testimony.[27] Long-standing Clique insurgent Samuel J. May underwent a similar metamorphosis. As he came, increasingly, to appreciate woman as a moral leader who was needed to avert male misconduct, he associated Woman's Sphere less and less with domesticity. In 1833, for example, May had insisted that he and Arnold Buffum needed to represent Prudence Crandall at a Canterbury, Connecticut, town meeting concerning Crandall's school for black girls because "propriety forbade her appearing in person." But in time May came to conclude "that never will our governments be wisely and happily administered until we have mothers as well as fathers of the State."[28] His cousin Samuel May, Jr., evolved similarly, contending by 1844 for "the right of women to act freely, in the Antislavery field, as their conscience and sense of duty should prompt."[29] In the mid and late 1840s other Boston Clique intimates, from Oliver Johnson and Nathaniel Peabody Rogers to Henry C. Wright and Parker Pillsbury, were espousing similar opposition to rigid sexual separation; woman was within her sphere when she gave moral testimony on public issues.[30]

Not only were these Clique insurgents following Garrison's lead in propounding woman's duty, as moral missionary, to uplift the public male-dominated areas of life. They were also justifying a fact of insurgent existence; women had, in fact, come to work more closely with men during the 1840s in insurgent antislavery activities. After the 1840 schism in the American Anti-Slavery Society, insurgents generally ceased to count on the support of other male immediatists. Consequently, they felt that they could ill afford to reject totally the backing that women offered. Therefore, they came to permit the merger of male and female antislavery societies. Lydia Child, Maria Chapman, and Lucretia Mott were allowed to serve on the Clique-dominated A.A.S.S. executive committee, and for a time Child became editor of its organ, the *National Anti-Slavery Standard*, while Abigail Kelley became a major lecturer and organizer of the A.A.S.S.[31]

This drift away from nineteenth-century sex role rigidities through a more expansive and appreciative view of female moral testimony was not restricted to insurgents of the Boston Clique. Although Gerrit Smith's voluntarist circle had ceased to function as a collectivity in the 1850s, by then certain individual voluntarists could be found endorsing the new posture. Smith himself corresponded regularly with suffragettes Susan B. Anthony and Elizabeth Cady Stanton and concurred with them on most essentials. "Female modesty! Female delicacy! I would that I might never again hear such phrases. There is but one standard of modesty and delicacy for both men and women," Smith wrote to Anthony. "I believe you can make no claim for woman to which I do not respond," he told Stanton. "What woman needs to believe and man also," Smith noted, "is, that, with the exception of that physical difference, which is for the multiplication and perpetuation of the race, man is woman, and woman is man."[32] If, indeed, there was a difference in the capacity of the sexes, Smith confided to Sallie Holley, it was in women's favor. Because of their moral excellencies and personal stability, women like Holley might eventually be able to harmonize the differences between Liberty party men and Garrison's followers.[33] Two fellow upstate New York voluntarists, James Caleb Jackson and Joseph C. Hathaway, broadly concurred. Both were proud of the increasing disposition among immediatists in the area to open antislavery activities to women as well as to men. "Woman is no appendage to serve man's convenience," Jackson insisted. Hathaway wondered whether those male voluntarists who fretted over female co-missionary status actually felt inferior to women: "Are we afraid that the overflowing exuberance of her sympathizing heart will eclipse us?"[34] Elizur Wright, who had worked closely with certain Tappan stewards on the New York City executive committee of the A.A.S.S. during the 1830s, also changed markedly on women's rights once he broke off contact with them. Whereas in 1838 he, like his steward associates, had called Angelina Grimké and Abigail Kelley "male women" because they lectured before mixed audiences, by the 1840s Wright was repudiating the posture that women had to be quiescent and discreet on moral questions; after all, they were duty bound to give moral testimony against evil. By the early 1850s, Wright's expansive view of Woman's Sphere had made him an uncompromising proponent of wider opportunities for women, especially at the ballot box.[35] Even Lewis Tappan and George Whipple, who had led the steward withdrawal from the A.A.S.S. when Abigail Kelley was seated on the business committee in 1840, had modestly changed. By the late 1840s neither felt willing to go on contesting emergent patterns of cooperation between men and women in the crusade against slavery. Although both felt uncomfortable with women entering traditional "male" roles, they recognized that this trend could not be aborted.[36]

Thus, men of the Boston Clique took the lead in propagating a more liberalized and appreciative perception of Woman's Sphere; it allowed and even encouraged the female immediatist to give moral testimony beyond the hearth as a pious missionary. On the other hand, Tappan circle stewards were the most recalcitrant, as they were recalcitrant on most other apparent innovations in missionary goals and practices. Indeed, steward Amos Phelps insisted until his death in 1847 that women were unfitted physiologically and by divine command for any public role. The very year of his death, Phelps outlined a posture for the American Missionary Association schools in the West Indies that required rigid gender separation. Women teachers, being delicate and frail, were to live with missionary families and to instruct within safe, well-protected A.M.A. missions. Male teachers, on the other hand, were to work in the more dangerous, less civilized "out-stations." Nor does the data indicate that Phelps's Tappan circle colleague William Jay ever significantly modified his posture on the woman question despite increasing flexibility on other issues. Neither did John Greenleaf Whittier, a close friend of Tappan circle associates but deeply imbued in Quaker cultural traditions.[37] Finally, it is well to note that those insurgents, voluntarists, stewards, and other male abolitionists who had come to champion or at least to tolerate a wider range of female opportunities nonetheless continued to endorse the notion of woman's separate sphere as a moral missionary. New opportunities beyond the hearth were to be granted so that woman's moral testimony could be heard in all walks of life. On one level, this meant that women would be free to please God rather than the men of their households. But because female missionaries were to uplift the crude male world, it simultaneously signified that women were to help men. Thus, gender distinctions hardly became inconsequential.[38]

Although the rhetorical change that many male abolitionists evidenced by the 1840s and 1850s was certainly important, the broad significance of this change should not be exaggerated. It by no means characterized all male abolitionists, and even the most enthusiastic new proponents of expanded female opportunities were not departing, in all significant respects, from Woman's Sphere. We must even ask if the change that many male abolitionists exhibited was more than mere rhetoric. Did these men alter the way they acted toward women on a daily basis as their espousals of Woman's Sphere became more expansive and more accepting of co-missionary status within the immediatist crusade? An examination of potential alterations in the nature of abolitionists married life represents perhaps the best way of gauging whether behavior approximated rhetorical change – whether men acted any differently toward the women closest to them. Unfortunately, information regarding abolitionist marriages is quite fragmented. We lack the data to characterize husband–wife relationships and feelings in any single abolitionist marriage definitively. Highly incomplete data are available for somewhat fewer than two dozen marriages, while only small scraps of information exist for most marriages. Thus, commentaries on abolitionists' marital patterns must necessarily border on the speculative.

The seventh chapter of Blanche Hersh's important book, *The Slavery of Sex: Feminist Abolitionists in America* (1978), represents the sole scholarly investigation of marital patterns among the immediatists generally. It focuses on thirty-seven antebellum marriages. Hersh concludes that both husband and wife in at least twenty-eight of them favored gender equality and women's right to move beyond domestic duties. Liberal religion – rejection of the lowly scriptural view of women – and faith that reform could eradicate injustice emerged almost as prerequisites for these "feminist-oriented" marriages. Unfortunately, the chapter suffers from presentism. Hersh equates the abolitionist husband's sympathy for extension of Woman's Sphere beyond the hearth to a desired "partnership of equals." But in the antebellum context, as we have seen, those male abolitionists who encouraged women to enter new realms did not do so from a modern egalitarian commitment. Rather, they were endorsing variations of an older seventeenth-century Quaker missionary notion that women had to give moral testimony wherever it was needed. Hersh's chapter also suffers from a second and perhaps more serious defect. She tends to assume that abolitionist marriages began with a commitment to feminism. Consequently, she fails to consider systematically potential changes over time in the nature of her thirty-seven marriages.

To be sure, the pattern of several abolitionist marriages appears to have remained rather constant over time. Moreover, several of these seem to have reflected a trend that first became detectable within small segments of the American middle-class at the end of the eighteenth century: the decline of patriarchy and modestly affectionate cooperation between husband and wife.[39] Scraps of evidence suggest, for example, that Miller McKim, Charles Follen, James Russell Lowell, William Goodell, Oliver Johnson, Samuel J. May, Gerrit Smith, James Mott, and Elizur Wright may always have enjoyed these sorts of marriages.[40] On the other hand, overbearing manifestations of patriarchy, the absence of affection between husband and wife, or both seem to have characterized the marriages of Henry Wright, Parker Pillsbury, Calvin Philleo (Prudence Crandall Philleo), and James Swisshelm from start to finish.[41]

The overwhelming number of abolitionist marriages for which we have at least fragmentary data, however, tend to suggest a decided change over time in the quality of the relationship. The marriages usually seemed to commence with husband and wife troubled by their inability to communicate thoughts and feelings fully and freely with one another by words or by actions. Emotional and physical distance seemed to preclude much of an exchange. The marital bond therefore appeared quite frail. A number of highly particularized factors heavily contributed to this general impasse in communication, but so did hearth-centered notions of Woman's Sphere and the pervasive custom according to which men channeled intimacies toward other men and women toward women. This was true regardless of whether the couple's abolitionist allegiance was to New England insurgency, to Tappanite stewardship, to Smith circle voluntarism, to a combination of these, or to some other variation of the early immediatist impulse. Indeed, even when one or both parties to the marriage departed in some respects from Woman's Sphere or sorority–fraternity dichotomies, these two elements still seemed to exert an awesome strain upon the early years of marriage.

The commencement of Tappan circle steward Theodore Weld's marriage to insurgent Angelina Grimké is illustrative. Owing to a variety of factors – Theodore's stress on self-denial, his fear of opening his private personal self to a woman, and his strong attachment to Charles Stuart, plus Angelina's successive troubles with pregnancies, hernia, prolapsed uterus, and malaria – the fervor of equal rights and happiness of the wedding day quickly receded. Angelina withdrew from public life, sharing domestic duties and inner feelings with sister Sarah while becoming quite tense, unfulfilled, and increasingly incommunicative in her relationship with Theodore. The early years of Clique insurgent Edmund Quincy's marriage with his wife Lucilla were equally strained. Indifferent to reform causes and comfortable by the hearth, Lucilla did not attend her husband's speaking debut as an immediatist. Nor did she appear at any of his lectures for the five years that followed. Edmund, in turn, made a routine of leaving their Dedham home early each morning and returning late in the evening. When he stopped attending church, Lucilla went alone and, despite her husband's protests, insisted that the children go with her. The early years of Boston Clique intimate Wendell Phillips's marriage to insurgent Ann Terry Greene were similarly distressing. Against the wishes of his mother, Wendell quite impulsively engaged and married the Boston Female Anti-Slavery Society activist, who he assumed was dying of a nervous disorder. He had apparently hoped for a short and joyous marriage, but it did not end quickly. It soon became apparent that Ann was to be a life-long invalid who would be bedridden and troubled by headaches, fatigue, acute rheumatic pain, and regular bouts with melancholy. Wendall initially reacted to this unanticipated state of affairs with thinly veiled resentment. He realized that Ann would not die but would be so incapacitated that he himself would be required to attend to many domestic duties. Moreover, the constant bedside care that Ann required threatened to undercut his unprecedented success as an abolitionist traveling lecturer. Consequently, correspondence between the Phillipses reveals that during the first four years of marriage their passions for one another cooled markedly. Lewis Tappan's marriage to Susan Aspinwall also quickly deteriorated as Lewis insisted that his wife attend to all child-rearing and household chores while he coupled long business days with evenings in benevolent reform causes. The nadir of the relationship came when Lewis, in dire financial straits, permanently moved his family from Brookline to better business opportunities in New York City against Susan's protests. According to the guilt-stricken Lewis's somewhat ambiguous private notation, he either resorted to masturbation or partook in extramarital affairs during the move. Similarly, William Lloyd Garrison experienced sharp strains early in his marriage. Always disorderly and unpunctual, he sensed that he needed the "domestic quietude" that the methodical Helen Benson provided. She cared for his home and his children while reminding him of his speaking engagements and editorial deadlines. Nevertheless, during the first years of marriage to Helen, William sometimes wondered whether he had selected the wrong partner or even should have married. Less domestic, more reform-oriented women like Prudence Crandall and Angelina Grimké seemed more interesting even if their boldness and power left William a bit apprehensive. He was able to talk with them, as he could not with Helen, about the tactics and anxieties of insurgent immediatism – to deal with what he regarded as the primary activity of life. Discussions with these women sometimes seemed to resemble discourses with the men of the Boston Clique. Even what ultimately became perhaps the strongest and closest of abolitionist marriages – that between insurgents Abigail Kelley and Stephen Symonds Foster – commenced on a similarly fragile and worrisome basis. Before they exchanged vows, Abigail feared that marriage would curb her immediatist career: "People wish me married to get rid of me. . . ." During the early marital years, the relationship between husband and wife was strained by this apprehension. Abigail weaned her lone child at nine months and left the child in the care of husband and relatives in order to assume A.A.S.S. lecturing assignments. While attending to the child, Stephen worked his Worcester farm and wondered what was becoming of his own immediatist career, much less his marriage to a woman he rarely saw.[42]

Because only scraps of data exist for most abolitionist marriages, it is impossible to determine precisely how typical these six were – how even limited acceptance of pervasive middle-class sex role orthodoxies correlated with severe early marital distress. But in those instances where we have information on courting and marital beginnings, disappointment, strain, and distance between man and wife were far more commonplace than harmony and emotional rapport. More striking, the fragments of available data point to diminishing strain and increasing harmony between husband and wife as time elapsed. Simultaneously, the commonplace middle-class sex roles that encouraged spatial and psychological distance between the couple receded. By the eve of the Civil War (and often sooner), the abolitionist couple that had experienced serious distress in early marital life seemed to take greater pleasure in each other's company and fuller interest in one another's activities. Troubled, shallow marital relationships often evolved into deeper, caring ones.

This change is most clearly illustrated if we continue to trace the Weld, Quincy, Phillips, Tappan, Garrison, and Foster marriages after their troubled beginnings. By the early 1850s the Weld–Grimké relationship had improved decidedly; Angelina came to understand that an existence limited to domestic duties and self-effacement was not for her. She reentered public life as a history teacher at the Raritan Bay Community and as an antislavery and women's rights advocate. Theodore Weld began to share Raritan Bay teaching duties and reform ventures with his wife. Simultaneously, the couple assumed new empathy and concern for one another. The marriage became stronger as Angelina and Theodore began to take new pleasure in one another's company. As the years passed, Edmund and Lucilla Quincy also found greater enjoyment in each other. Lucilla attended some of her husband's abolitionist lectures, and Edmund began to spend more time at home. The couple also started to read French aloud to each other in the evening and enjoyed it thoroughly.[43]

By the mid-1840s the Phillips marriage also began to improve. Wendell became less resentful of Ann for her inability to perform domestic duties and for the impediments her illness placed upon his public lecturing schedule. Indeed, improvements in railway travel and telegraph communication eventually made it possible for him to increase his lecture commitments and to communicate daily with Ann while he was away. But as time transpired, Wendell came to cherish rather than resent their long hours together. Above all, husband and wife came to look forward to summers – a season when Wendell halted all reform activities and took Ann out of the Boston heat to a country house where they spent pleasurable days alone uninterrupted. Boston Clique colleagues who visited the Phillips household were amazed how much the two enjoyed each other's company and how they conversed so eagerly together on abolition, literature, and other mutual interests. After thirty years of marriage, Ann could tell her husband, "Your last sweet kiss dearest still lingers on my lips. . . ." After almost fifty years, Wendell acknowledged, "I must love her more & more as time grows shorter. . . ."[44]

Unlike the Welds, the Quincys, and the Phillipses, Lewis and Susan Tappan only modestly repaired the bruises of early married life. Susan died in 1853. A year later Lewis married Sarah Jackson who, according to a family anecdote, promptly took Susan's family heirlooms to the nearest auctioneer. Although Sarah always wanted to be the active wife of a benevolent missionary, a more domestic-centered concept of Woman's Sphere structured the first year of their marriage. But the structure soon crumbled; Sarah began to move beyond the hearth. In part, this was possible because Lewis's children had grown up and Sarah did not have Susan's considerable child-rearing responsibilities. But it was also because Sarah shared Lewis's dream of world evangelization much more avidly than Susan. By the second year of marriage, she insisted on aiding the agents of Lewis's American Missionary Association, on critiquing her husband's reports and articles for the benevolent societies, and on accompanying him on his travels in behalf of reform enterprises. Lewis found that he was rather pleased by these missionary initiatives from his new wife, despite their nondomestic character. Perhaps he had been partially motivated to marry the spinster evangelical in the hope that she would differ from Susan in this particular. "God has given me a good companion, and thus added to the great debt of gratitude I owe," he acknowledged. For the first time in his life, Lewis seemed to enjoy working alongside a woman much as he enjoyed the male comradeship of the benevolent society movement. Missionary endeavor made the couple kindred spirits.[45]

By the late 1850s and early 1860s, the Garrison marriage also showed signs of improvement. William continued to display interest in intellectual reformist-oriented women, especially Anne Weston, but he also began to regard his more domestically inclined wife, Helen, with considerably more warmth and respect. Indeed, he now saw in Helen the kindness, empathy, and warmth that his insurgent mission to the slaves was supposed to promote. "Whatever of human infirmity we may have seen in each other," he told Helen in 1861, "I believe few have enjoyed more unalloyed bliss in wedded life than ourselves." When Helen became incapacitated by a stroke in December 1863, William assumed many of the household domestic burdens without complaint or bitterness and attended to his wife's personal comforts quite as diligently as she had formerly cared for his. The Garrisons had arrived at a marriage of sharing and emotional rapport much like those of the Welds, the Quincys, the Phillipses, and the Tappans.[46]

The Abigail Kelley–Stephen Foster marriage ended along these same lines. In the first years of the relationship, we noted, Abigail acquired a salary and public recognition as an abolitionist lecturer, while Stephen unhappily attended to home and child. Gradually, however, Stephen returned to the lecture circuit, and husband and wife began to find delight in speaking publicly together. Abigail slowly ceased to regard her marriage as an ever-present threat to her reform career or to feel that Stephen's activities away from their home endangered her own. "Indeed," she confided to Wendell Phillips in 1849, "I shall govern my movements very much by his [Stephen's] as I can not think of journeying and lecturing alone any longer. . . ." The following year, Stephen told her how much their relationship had improved once they had ceased an invidious sort of competition over who could break furthest from home and family: "I *know*, now, *what* I love, & *why*." By the late 1850s the couple so deeply loved and respected one another that the marriage could adjust to difficulties: to their daughter's serious spinal deformity and to Abigail's growing physical infirmities. Husband and wife loved and cared for one another on their Worcester farm much as if they had remained full-time immediatist lecturers. Harmonious co-operation had replaced a stultifying competitiveness.[47]

Like the other five marriages we have surveyed, the evolution of the Kelley–Foster marriage certainly involved important idiosyncratic factors. Nevertheless, all six clearly fit a general pattern, and many other abolitionist marriages may be cited that did as well. Like these six, the other marriages were initially structured about domestic-centered concepts of Woman's Sphere and consequently lent themselves to some measure of homosocial bonding. In time, however, they came to evidence increasingly strong emotional attractions between husband and wife much like those that first became detectable in limited segments of the American middle class at the end of the eighteenth century. The marriages of upstate New York voluntarists such as Myron Holley and Abishai Scofield, for example, and of insurgents such as Ellis Gray Loring, Charles C. Burleigh, David Lee Child, and Sydney Howard Gay each involved a number of important idiosyncratic features while moving in the same general direction as the six we have examined.[48]

This is all to suggest that the increasing propensity of male immediatists to espouse a more expansive concept of Woman's Sphere seemed to go hand in hand with deepening emotional rapport between husband and wife. Since, as we have seen, several upstate New York voluntarists and particularly a number of New England insurgents came to voice more expansive gender ideologies than most Tappanite stewards, it is therefore understandable why we find more evidence of change within voluntarist and insurgent marriages. Indeed, within their own intimacy circle, only Theodore Weld and Lewis Tappan seemed to have allowed their wives to assume anything resembling co-missionary status. But Weld was certainly not a typical steward, and the co-missionary pattern was only allowed to emerge during Tappan's second marriage. His first, with Susan Aspinwall, was never altered significantly. As on many other issues, the staid Tappan circle stewards seemed considerably more hesitant about new words and deeds on the woman question than insurgents or voluntarists.

As several male immediatists embraced more expansive views of Woman's Sphere and as their marital relationships tended to rest on firmer and more reciprocal foundations, it was clear that they were becoming more appreciative of women's strengths as moral missionaries. By the late antebellum years, male immediatists could be found more and more frequently reaching out for female reformers as colleagues in the mission to the slaves. More important, they tried to fathom women's inner feelings and to empathize with female apprehensions. Several even tried to "absorb" or at least to emulate the morality and the inner strength in their new female colleagues – qualities that seemed peripheral to the coarse and frantic male world of open market capitalism and Jacksonian politics. Predictably, male insurgents took the lead.

Consider, for example, Boston Clique insurgent Henry Wright as he described his activities and analyzed his inner feelings within his voluminous and fascinating private journals. These journals reveal a young man who, somewhat fearful, if fascinated, by the opposite sex, firmly believed in confining females to a hearth-centered ideal of Woman's Sphere. Even as late as 1840 and 1841, he was most comfortable associating with devout male reformers, particularly Boston Clique insurgents. Beginning in 1842, however, Wright began to change. He took up a succession of secretive but nonsexual affairs with a number of reform-oriented women. By seating them on his lap and listening to their emotional discourses, Wright came to understand and to empathize with female fears of constant pregnancy and labor. He learned that many women wanted intimate, sentimental discourse with each other and even with men so long as the emotional liaison with men was accompanied by sexual forbearance. Unlike most men about him, Wright came to empathize with and even to champion this "female outlook." For him, women were truly moral missionaries; they could feel for others. Their minds were not cluttered by cold abstractions and coarsely exploitive sexual impulses.[49]

By the mid and late 1840s, James Russell Lowell, an insurgent friend of the Quincy–Phillips–Chapman aristocratic wing of the Boston Clique, experienced a similar "awakening." As he shed a constrictive view of Woman's Sphere and rigid gender dichotomies, Lowell took on deep interest in "feminine" child-rearing concerns, particularly the teething problem and nursing techniques. He came to believe that sincere and humane men like Hawthorne had something in them of "tender feminine virtues." Lowell hoped to understand and to emulate those virtues.[50] By the late 1850s Garrison, too, had taken on a special sensitivity to women and their unique qualities. In 1859, for example, he discovered that Abigail Kelley [Foster] had been deeply hurt by his charge that she had wrongly received Republican donations for abolitionist enterprises. When he learned that Kelley had construed the charge as a general distrust of female reformers, Garrison seemed more determined to make amends and correct the record than he had ever been after any of his many disputes with male immediatists. Moreover, he took special care to assuage Kelley's inner hurt. "Of all the women who have appeared on the historic stage," he confided, "I have always regarded you as peerless – the moral Joan of Arc of the world. . . . No one of my family has been nearer or dearer to me than yourself." The leader of Boston Clique insurgency was seeking strength from and rapport with this "moral" female missionary.[51]

Because stewards of Lewis Tappan's circle tended to resist the changes in Woman's Sphere that several insurgents and voluntarists were accepting, it is striking to find certain of their steward associates at Oberlin College, particularly James Fairchild, Henry Cowles, and Charles Grandison Finney, demonstrating greater understanding of female aspirations in these late antebellum years. Some historians of early Oberlin have correctly noted that by introducing coeducation, prohibiting marriage before graduation, and training female students largely in applied "domestic economy," these and other church-centered immediatist stewards who administered the college were using women to serve male interests. They were acquiring a cheap cooking, cleaning, and laundry service for their revenue-starved institution. They were also providing future wives for their male ministers-in-training; these wives would empathize with Finneyite husbands who struggled to convert the Mississippi Valley to "new measures" theology.[52] But what proponents of this characterization have failed to recognize is that the limited contacts between male and female students on the same campus created tensions that ultimately made Oberlin more than a marriage mill for steward immediatism. Owing to female dissatisfaction with education restricted to the "Ladies' course," for example, by 1850 that limitation began to erode. Female students were permitted to study the classics, including moral philosophy. Because of Antoinette Brown's keen and vocal disappointment at being barred from a theology degree, Finney allowed her to participate fully in his theology classes and even called on her to recount her religious experiences. In turn, Brown's participation provided a precedent for removal of the ban on a female theology degree. Indeed, by the time of the Civil War, and with the consent of Fairchild and Cowles as well as Finney, male and female students were taught geometry, trigonometry, botany, natural philosophy, political economy, physiology, and philosophy in the same classroom by the same instructor despite marked gender distinctions in the formal curriculum. This movement toward a richer and more varied female educational experience was coupled with less stringent "official" objection to student advocacy of feminist causes outside Oberlin's walls. By 1868, for example, Fairchild apologized in the *American Journal of Education* for three Oberlin graduates who had become prominent "lady lecturers": Lucy Stone, Sallie Holley, and Antoinette Brown. But he added that he could never repudiate these Oberlinites with "their advanced views of woman's rights and duties. While avowing a radical dissent, I can not forbear to say that they are my friends." Like Finney, Cowles, and other leading stewards at Oberlin, Fairchild had come to assume a less rigidly domestic-centered concept of Woman's Sphere. In some measure, he had come to understand and to respect some of the most "advanced" nineteenth-century feminist missionaries.[53]

Our larger point, then, is that a number of specific people and incidents may be cited to add force to what more general abolitionist rhetorical changes and marital patterns suggest: movement toward a more expansive concept of Woman's Sphere, greater appreciation of female versatility and strength, fewer apprehensions of danger in difference, and improved communication between the sexes. The trend was most conspicuous among insurgents, but as the Weld–Grimké relationship, Lewis Tappan's second marriage, and the Oberlin experience revealed, not all stewards were immune to it. This is not to say that the crusade for immediatism had also become a crusade for full gender equality. Far from it, even within insurgent circles. The notion that women were fundamentally different persisted. It had to, for increasing appreciation of female moral strength and sensitivity necessarily perpetuated perceptions of gender distinctiveness. Thus, many male immediatists obviously came to regard women as morally elevated and therefore as faithful comissionaries. Some even seem to have accepted a version of the feminist concept of overlapping spheres and dual natures that underscored gender distinctions amid similarities, but few male immediatists embraced female reformers with the same sort of warmth and the same feelings of Christian fellowship with which they embraced one another.

V

It is, of course, easier to delineate than to explain the general shift among male immediatists away from the commonplace middle-class concept of a separate and domestic Woman's Sphere that was evident in the 1833 organizational meeting of the American Anti-Slavery Society. Yet our delineation of this transformation has carried within it the underpinnings of an explanation. This explanation holds that since distinctively hearth-centered notions of Woman's Sphere tended to keep middle-class men and women apart, spatially as well as emotionally, whatever caused the different sexes to meet on a serious level, to communicate, and to cooperate would tend to promote a broadened concept of female prerogatives – a wider sense of the female missionary's moral duty. Once Woman's Sphere had become more expansive and had legitimatized female activity outside the home without deemphasizing distinctions between the sexes, a situation was at hand where male and female abolitionists could become quite appreciative of each other. Above all, men could reach out for the female moral and emotional qualities that they found so compelling. The continuing emphasis on gender distinctions promoted excitement, interest, and appreciation in the opposite sex, especially in men for women. The legitimization of a female missionary presence in most areas of antislavery endeavor allowed that interest to be pursued more actively and broadly. Male and female abolitionists could become not only more supportive, according to our explanation, but also more desirous of each other. Yet, unlike many other segments of the middle-class population, they did not have to worry a great deal about sexual improprieties as they pursued those desires. Among other factors, years of missionary reform activity for temperance, against prostitution, and especially against the allegedly promiscuous master–slave relationship, seem to have induced most immediatists to internalize Victorian admonitions against sexual license. Consequently, intellectual and emotional bonds between the sexes could intensify without causing fear of immorality.

Such an explanation for the emergence of a co-missionary tradition closely comports with the isolated nature of the early immediatist crusade. Active within a small and generally unpopular movement, immediatists could not long afford the luxury of retaining the rigid gender separations of the 1833 A.A.S.S. organizational meeting. The necessities of survival and development of a movement caused men and women to associate and to work together. Cooperative efforts by members of a hated outgroup underlined their commonalities and tended to dissipate the forces that kept the sexes apart. By working together as abolitionists, they gradually learned to work together as men and women, some more than others, depending upon the nature and extent of their cooperation. But our explanation postulates that cooperation took place between missionaries whose gender differences remained significant and thus mutually alluring but nonthreatening. Consequently, male immediatists may have felt freer to reach out for and to attempt to embrace the female moral and emotional strengths that they found so attractive.

It is noteworthy that in 1839 two leading female insurgents, Lydia Maria Child and Lucretia Mott, both provided the rough outlines of this explanation for the emergence of co-missionary status. If female immediatists simply moved themselves beyond the hearth as moral missionaries and assumed unrestricted reformist roles, Child charged, they would dissipate within the abolitionist crusade rigid and degrading limitations imposed by Woman's Sphere: "It is best not to *talk* about our rights, but simply go forward and do whatever we deem a duty." Mott fully concurred and urged that women "avail themselves of every opportunity offered them to mingle in the discussion." The more female immediatists asserted themselves, Mott maintained, and the more actively they participated in the immediatist movement, the more abolitionists of both sexes "could so lose sight of distinctions of sex as to act in public meetings on the enlightened and true ground of Christian equality."[54] Although gender distinctions were never ignored, Child's and Mott's predictions find general validation in a quick comparative review of our findings on gender relations among insurgents, voluntarists, and stewards. To the degree that women were allowed to work with men and availed themselves of the opportunity, gender limitations significantly receded. The domain for association and appreciation between different and thus mutually interesting sexes was enlarged.

Garrison and other male insurgents inside and outside the Boston Clique, we noted, were generally the least resistant to both enlarged female participation and co-missionary status. Elizabeth Cady Stanton may have exaggerated, but only somewhat, in May 1860 when she addressed the insurgent-controlled A.A.S.S.: "Yes, this is the only organization on God's footstool where the humanity of women is recognized, and these are the only men [insurgents] who have ever echoed back her cries for justice and equality." As early as the mid-1830s, Boston Clique intimates found themselves deeply attracted by the wise counsel, comforting "feminine" social graces, and emotional sensitivities of Maria Weston Chapman and her sisters. For this reason, they met at the Chapman house on a daily basis. Subsequently, Clique members as well as other insurgents encouraged and assisted the Grimké sisters during their 1837–38 lecture tours. In 1840 they supported Abigail Kelley in her controversial bid for a seat on the A.A.S.S. business committee and encouraged her, later in the decade, to assume a supervisory role over A.A.S.S. lecturers. Male insurgents similarly urged women like Lucretia Mott, Sallie Holley, and Francis Power Cobbe to become active in the full range of abolitionist ventures and supported Lydia Child as editor of the *National Anti-Slavery Standard*. They watched these women whom they had encouraged and deeply admired and were most impressed by their conduct in antislavery matters. Gradually male and female insurgents, particularly those of the Boston Clique, became warm and cordial friends. Indeed, the men of the Clique became perhaps the strongest champions of insurgent women as moral missionaries. Garrison and Phillips, for example, were pleasantly surprised by the deep inner strength and unmistakable success of the Grimké sisters as public speakers. "Our gifted friends, the Grimkés, are exerting an almost angelic influence wherever they go," Garrison noted.

"Their public lectures are thronged by both sexes, and their triumph over prejudice and error has been most signal." "I well remember," Phillips recalled, "evening after evening listening to eloquence such as never then had been heard from a woman. . . . Self poised, she [Angelina Grimké] seemed morally sufficient to herself." Samuel J. May also found himself attracted by the moral and emotional force exhibited by insurgent female missionaries in the field. He was certain that they were even capable of becoming ministers: "If you could hear, as I have heard, Lucretia Mott, or Sallie Holley, or Angelina Grimké, you would not, could not, doubt the fitness of women for this work." Similarly, although Edmund Quincy thought well of most of the female anti-slavery activitists that he and other Clique insurgents had encouraged, he was particularly impressed with Maria Chapman: "She is the most perfect creature morally, intellectually & physically that I ever knew. . . . She is a woman of genius in the true sense of the word, of the keenest sagacity surpassing Garrison himself & [of] most invincible integrity in the most exalted meaning of the term." Deeply appreciative remarks such as these became increasingly widespread among the men of the Clique as time transpired and their everyday contacts with insurgent women increased. They represented more than an acknowl-edgment of the important roles women had assumed in everyday im-mediatist operations. Men like Garrison, Phillips, May, and Quincy seemed desirous of cordially embracing devout female insurgents at a different level from that on which they embraced male colleagues – of somehow imbibing a profound female moral and emotional strength that was missing in themselves.[55]

The encouragement that voluntarists active in the Liberty party and especially church-centered stewards provided female reformers, we found, tended to be more limited. Correspondingly, we discovered considerably fewer expressions of appreciation, respect, and fascination with female immediatists. Liberty party voluntarists usually went no further than to admit women into some of their meetings. But those voluntarists who provided greater encouragement clearly cultivated deeper rapport with female abolitionists. Francis Julius LeMoyne, for example, constantly urged Lucy Caroline to join with him in antislavery work. Over the years he became quite proud of her conduct and even saw in her an inner moral power that he sought to emulate. Caroline was deeply touched. She had never before encountered a man who so warmly welcomed her misssionary efforts. "You are so near me," she wrote to him in 1848, "I repose the trust of a sister in your kindness and truth – while I feel my nature exalted by the influence of yours." Similarly, Gerrit Smith encouraged Sallie Holley to expand her anti-slavery work even though she was an insurgent. As he watched her in action, Smith took on hope that strong, intelligent, morally probing women like Holley might bridge the gulf between insurgents and voluntarists that the men of the immediatist crusade had fostered but seemed unable to repair. "He received me so cordially, so kindly, with open arms and becoming eyes," Holley wrote after visiting Smith's Peterboro estate.[56]

Because church-centered stewards such as Amos Phelps and William Jay clung tenaciously to a belief in the "God-ordained" patriarchal family where mother served as a reserve of morality, they provided even less encouragement than most voluntarists for female antislavery endeavors outside the home. Their doubts regarding female immediatists as co-missionaries were, of course, most conspicuous when they opposed the seating of Abigail Kelley on the A.A.S.S. business committee in 1840, withdrew from the A.A.S.S. annual meeting when she was seated, and made sure that women had only minor supportive roles in their rival American and Foreign Anti-Slavery Society. To be sure, several of these stewards became less adamant against expanded notions of Woman's Sphere as time transpired, particularly when they organized American Missionary Association educational ventures in the South during the 1860s. But strong reformist women rarely cultivated open cooperative relationships with them. Moreover, historian Amy Swerdloe has demonstrated that when the wives and daughters of stewards resorted to antislavery activism, they consciously attempted to harmonize with the wishes of their men folk. Open and free exchanges between male and female were generally regarded by stewards of both sexes as contrary to biblical sanction. Sometimes insurgent female abolitionists voiced open hostility to male stewards. In 1839, for example, Lydia Child asserted, "When a man advises me to withdraw from a society or convention, or not to act there according to the dictates of my own judgment, I am constrained to reply: 'Thou canst not touch the freedom of my soul.' " Similarly, in 1846 Lucy Stone attacked the male stewards who ran Oberlin: "They hate Garrison, and women's rights. I love both, and often find myself at swords' points with them. . . ."[57]

The more the open and cooperative contact that flowed between male and female immediatists, then, the more readily a constrictive view of Woman's Sphere receded, while appreciative interest in the opposite sex increased. To the extent that this interest channeled immediatists' attentions away from the members of their old intimacy circles, it weakened the emotional bonds of affection that held those circles together. But if we are to accept this outgroup cooperation thesis, we must recognize one factor that it does not explain. At the very start of the immediatist crusade in the early 1830s, before much interchange between the sexes could ensue, some male immediatists were clearly more disposed toward a cooperative co-missionary gender tradition than others. It was no accident, for example, that even before female immediatists such as the Grimkés, Mott, and Kelley began to press for co-missionary status, those male insurgents who forged the Boston Clique had brought Maria Chapman and her sisters into their intimacy circle. But the stewards who forged the Lewis Tappan intimacy group and even the voluntarists of the Smith circle never even considered inclusion of female associates. Thus, important as the increased willingness of male immediatists to cooperate with female reformers was, it did not change the essential gender composition of any of our three test clusters. Although male immediatists generally assumed new attitudes and actions toward female missionaries and drew closer to a number of them who happened to be outside their old intimacy circles, the woman question did not compel them to alter the composition of those circles.

Why had insurgents generally, and especially those of the Boston Clique, opened their inner sanctuaries to women from the very start? Why, on the other hand, had voluntarists and especially stewards held out from the beginning against female inclusion? Unfortunately, we can only suggest possible and tentative answers to these questions, which go to the heart of abolitionist gender relations. The fact that male insurgents shared decidedly more antinomian, individualistic religious proclivities than stewards or even voluntarists readily comes to mind. Because of these proclivities, they seemed more receptive to human freedom and autonomy irrespective of gender or other surface differences between people. On a deeper level, however, it would seem that male insurgents were more willing, at the start of their crusade, to come to grips with certain respects in which men were ambivalent toward women than many voluntarists and assuredly most stewards. More than most of their other male immediatist colleagues, insurgents (particularly of the Boston Clique) seemed willing to examine the subtle ways in which men feared and stood in awe of females' inner emotional and moral strength, especially the forms that appeared to be lacking in themselves. Through courageous self-exploration, their fear and awe would seem to have receded and to have been supplanted by the more earthy and humane appreciation of women that was necessary for cooperative contact between the sexes to begin in the first place. Therefore, the appreciation of female moral and emotional strength that became so apparent once cooperation between the sexes began may simply have echoed earlier and more deeply introspective insurgent probings.

Wendell Phillips's retrospective explanation of his feelings during the 1830s toward the insurgent women of the Boston Female Anti-Slavery Society in general and toward one of its members, Ann Terry Greene, lends at least a modicum of credibility to this speculation. Initially, Phillips acknowledged, he regarded these women with reverent fear. His "eyes were sealed" to their deep inner strengths. But as he came into more honest contact with his feelings, his fears dissipated, and he found that the women had certain steady inner qualities that he lacked in his own "hastiness or petulance." Phillips found himself desiring to embrace these women, particularly the young and fiery Miss Greene. Shortly thereafter, he discovered that Greene was sickly and would probably die soon, but he was so stirred by her powerful inner spirit that he rushed into marriage. Ann Greene Phillips lived a long life and, as we discovered, the initial years of marriage to Wendell were difficult. Indeed, some of Wendell Phillips's initial fears of women returned. But the discovery of an indomitable spirit in Ann that he seemed to lack stayed with Wendell. After five years of marriage, he acknowledged to his Dublin friend Richard Webb how much reformist women generally, but especially his wife, had meant to him, once he put aside his inner fears of them and realized that their example gave him strength: "Yes, my wife made an out and out Abolitionist of me, and she always preceded me in the adoption of the various causes I have advocated. . . . A sick wife though she be, I owe the little I am and do almost wholly to her mature guardian spirit."[58]

Perhaps owing to the courageous introspective efforts of male insurgents, then, a few women were initially accorded co-missionary status in the immediatist crusade. Once they and other female reformers pressed further for full responsibilities in abolitionist enterprises and once contact between the sexes increased, an abolitionist co-missionary tradition grew, and more expansive concepts of Woman's Sphere came to characterize the crusade, even at steward-dominated Oberlin College. But as we shall now discover, neither Phillips nor very many other white immediatists, male or female, from our three focal clusters or from others, were able to transcend their inner apprehensions regarding blacks. Quite the contrary. As male immediatists increasingly embraced women colleagues in the mission to the slaves, white immediatists were withdrawing from a modest co-missionary tradition with free blacks. It appeared that expansion of gender contacts required contraction of biracial contacts.

CHAPTER 6

" THE CHORD OF PREJUDICE "

Our findings in Chapter 5 suggest that fundamental transformations in first-generation immediatism involved considerably more than changes within particular clusters or sanctuaries. More fundamentally, transformations seemed to involve broad-ranging decisions concerning inclusivity and exclusivity: what people immediatists generally, as uncompromising missionaries, might befriend to enhance the morality and influence of their cause and who they had to expel or distance in the interests of avoiding impiety and ill example. Through a process of increasing association with women in antislavery ventures, male immediatists gradually came to assume that their crusade was garnering new piety and vigor through inclusion of the female moral virtues of the hearth within the rough and tumble of reform activism. Consequently, as the Civil War drew near, as women increasingly came to be accepted as devout co-missionaries, and as men often drew closer even to women outside their intimacy circles, emotional bonds between colleagues in the traditional immediatist intimacy groups sometimes became less intense. Yet women never ceased to be considered fundamentally different from male immediatists – the embodiments of a deeper and more emotionally integrated reservoir of moral strength through which males might measure the depth of their own pieties.

Although the commitment to expand Woman's Sphere beyond the hearth – to eradicate restrictions against female activity – developed only very gradually in the course of the abolitionist crusade, the ideological commitment to full opportunities for free blacks was evident from the start. Next to eradication of slavery, it represented the major professed priority of white immediatism during its early years. In an 1835 letter to voluntarist Gerrit Smith, insurgent leader William Lloyd Garrison expressed that commitment most clearly:

The first great object which I desire to accomplish is, the IMMEDIATE EMANCIPATION of two millions and a half of American SLAVES. . . . The next great object at which I aim is, the education and equalization of the colored with the white population of this country, so that the hue of the skin shall no longer be a badge of servitude and opprobrium, and the word of caste shall be consumed to ashes.[1]

Gerrit Smith fully concurred, as did almost all white immediatists, immediatist intimacy circles, and official organizations of the 1830s, whether insurgent, steward, voluntarist, or other. Next to emancipation itself, eradication of caste restrictions against Negroes was the most deeply cherished priority.

It comes as no surprise to find such a strong civil rights commitment within the early immediatist crusade. After all, young abolitionists had distinguished themselves in the late 1820s and early 1830s from other young missionary agents of the American Colonization Society (A.C.S.) in seriously considering black protestations against repatriation. Whereas most A.C.S. missionaries hastily dismissed the ideas and apprehensions of free Negroes as those of a naive and unschooled race, we discovered that white immediatists-to-be empathized with the blacks, seriously investigated black objections to A.C.S. Liberian deportations, and generally found those objections valid. They soon turned against the Colonization Society and, in varying degrees, against the broader benevolent society movement that sustained it. In some measure, this came about from the sense that the A.C.S. was proslavery. But it was also strongly rooted in an attempt to garner deeper intellectual understanding of free Negroes and to empathize with their plight. Consequently, one can understand why, next to the call for emancipation, civil rights for free blacks became the vital plank in the early immediatist crusade. Commitment to black civil rights was a major reason why a number of young missionaries with intense moral proclivities broke from colonization and became abolitionists. That commitment was vital to their sense of purpose as immediatists.

Because advocacy of the rights of free blacks did much to distinguish immediatism from its benevolent movement antecedents, one would expect to find continuing empathy with blacks and advocacy of civil rights, in word and in deed, throughout the first decade of the immediatist crusade. Indeed, whereas women generally worked at first within separate organizations and at a distance from men, black immediatists initially labored in somewhat closer proximity to whites. A cooperative biracial tradition seemed much more conspicuous during these early years than a male–female co-missionary tradition. Those white male immediatists – insurgents, stewards, and voluntarists – charged with drafting a declaration of intentions for the American Anti-Slavery Society met and labored, for example, within the home of Frederick Hinton, a Philadelphia Negro, who freely participated in the discussions. And though stewards balked at female immediatist colleagues, they were considerably more willing to work with blacks. Arthur Tappan collaborated closely with three black ministers – Theodore Wright, Peter Williams, and Samuel Cornish – in organizing the steward New York City Anti-Slavery Society. Elizur Wright, his antislavery secretary early in the 1830s, hired a black assistant and urged increased cooperation between white and black immediatists. As a student leader and antislavery activist in Lane Seminary during the early 1830s, steward Theodore Weld made a point of eating, worshiping, and laboring with Cincinnati blacks. But insurgents – the immediatists who had been most instrumental in forging a cooperative tradition with women – seemed most active in establishing contacts with Northern blacks. Boston Clique participants dined regularly with local black leaders. Ellis Gray Loring and Samuel Sewall broke precedent by taking young black apprentices into their law offices and encouraging them in insurgent reform ventures. Philadelphia insurgents Lucretia and James Mott made a point of inviting blacks to dinners in their home so that these blacks might mingle more freely with the local reform community. Even in the face of the threatening and destructive antiabolition mobs of the mid-1830s, two insurgent groups, the Philadelphia and Boston Female Anti-Slavery Societies, insisted upon holding interracial public meetings.[2]

The *Liberator* newspaper, however, most clearly illustrated how insurgents took the lead in forging a biracial tradition within early immediatism. An indispensable organ for Boston Clique operations, the *Liberator* was directed by insurgency's chief spokesman, William Lloyd Garrison. Yet it was New England blacks who kept the precariously funded publication in business and provided the preponderance of subscribers in its early years. During acute financial setbacks, when the future existence of the paper was questionable, they offered gifts, loans, and promises of additional subscribers. A few regularly followed the nonresistant Garrison home from the *Liberator* office each evening to protect him from armed assault. There were important advantages that black abolitionists perceived for New England Negroes generally by keeping the *Liberator* afloat. Because it employed young blacks like William Nell, it established an alternative to pervasive custom of excluding black apprentices from shops where whites worked. In addition, the *Liberator* provided New England black communities with an effective means of communicating among themselves. Black leaders could write essays and letters to their followers and proceedings of local black meetings could be reported fully and other gatherings advertised, while black social events and even funerals and obituaries could be listed. In perusing these black communications, white immediatists gained at least a modest measure of familiarity with the problems and aspirations of Northern blacks. The *Emancipator*, directed by New York City stewards and voluntarists, tried in time to emulate the *Liberator* and to forge a strong cooperative tradition with the city's blacks, but with considerably more modest results.[3]

If the early immediatist impulse, and particularly its insurgent manifestations, evidenced genuine empathy for free blacks and was distinguishable from its benevolent empire–colonizationist antecedents through a tradition of biracial cooperation, the obvious limitations of both empathy and biracialism must be underscored. Not one of our three central abolitionist clusters, not even the Boston Clique, ever included blacks as members (although the Clique included women). Moreover, there were sometimes racial restrictions in the membership of early immediatist antislavery societies. In locations that included Albany, Rochester, Nantucket, and Lexington (Ohio), blacks were excluded from white societies and had to form "colored" locals of their own. Indeed, the Ladies' New York City Anti-Slavery Society, relegated to auxiliary status itself by Tappan circle stewards, adamantly refused to admit black women. The Junior Anti-Slavery Society of Philadelphia did admit Negro members, but only after a tense debate and a close 19 to 17 vote. It is also noteworthy that only after the process of organizing the insurgent New England Anti-Slavery Society had been completed were blacks invited to participate.[4]

To be sure, as a result of the commitment to civil rights and biracialism, blacks were ultimately admitted to most white abolitionist societies in the course of the 1830s – voluntarist and steward dominated as well as insurgent. Nevertheless, their roles within those organizations were sharply limited from the start. They were generally excluded from significant policy making, administrative, and editorial positions. No blacks sat on the original nine-man executive committee of the American Anti-Slavery Society, although it included a coalition of insurgents, stewards, and voluntarists. When it was enlarged to a seventy-two member board of managers, six blacks were appointed members, but none was designated as an officer. Moreover, no Negro was allowed to address the A.A.S.S. annual meeting until 1839. The same pattern characterized the rival American and Foreign Anti-Slavery Society that emerged in 1840 and most state and local societies. The New England Anti-Slavery Society was one of the only immediatist groups to permit a significant black leadership role when it merged, in 1833, with the Massachusetts General Colored Association. In addition to fund-raising duties, the primary role white societies assigned to blacks was to lecture and to write pamphlets. White immediatists perceived a broad-ranging Northern interest in black orators, particularly fugitive slaves who could recount their experiences. In turn, black public speeches, "properly" edited, often became the basis of abolitionist pamphlet literature.[5]

Beyond antislavery endeavors, white immediatists of the 1830s were also reluctant to seek out blacks. While Northern free Negroes found it exceedingly difficult to secure nonmenial employment, for example, they complained that white immediatists only rarely hired them for responsible positions in their own business enterprises. The insurgent New England Anti-Slavery Society might pass resolutions calling for such employment, a steward like Simeon Jocelyn and an insurgent like Ellis Gray Loring might insist on it, and the New York City *Colored*

American might make editorial demands for jobs, but this rarely changed white immediatists' hiring propensities.[6]

Predictably, these deficiencies within the biracial experiment distressed Northern black immediatists. The egalitarian rhetoric and the cooperative professions of their white allies, particularly the insurgents, had given them hope and inspiration. Initially, they had regarded white immediatists as a breed of reformers very different from other benevolent empire missionaries. But as the 1830s progressed and blacks perceived that their white immediatist colleagues seemed to be subordinating and separating them, on the one hand, while propounding black rights and urging biracial cooperation on the other, many sensed that something had gone wrong. Continued exclusion from white intimacy groups seemed to hurt most of all; whites did not regard blacks as important enough to incorporate within their innermost circles. Consequently, a few black abolitionists began to wonder whether white immediatists were really very different on the race issue from their former Colonization Society associates. New York City black abolitionists such as Theodore Wright, Charles Ray, Thomas Van Rensselaer, and Samuel Cornish, who had participated in both integrated antislavery societies and separatist black organizations, were the sharpest critics. The seemingly low priority that the white Tappan stewards about them had assigned to expanding black rights and job opportunities, plus the stewards' intolerably heavy-handed missionary paternalism, had made these men increasingly receptive to an exclusively black "go it alone" antislavery approach. On the other hand, there were black abolitionists from Philadelphia and Boston, such as William Whipper, Robert Purvis, and William Nell, who continued to admire the *Liberator*, who found favor with certain more overtly biracial and less invidiously segregationist insurgent programs, and who were opposed in principle to participation entirely within all black organizations. But even these black leaders had become at least somewhat disillusioned with the general immediatist program of biracial cooperation. Consequently, by the late 1830s and early 1840s few black abolitionists any longer urged free Negroes to emulate their "virtuous" white antislavery colleagues as paragons of honesty, energy, and frugality. Nor were most as willing as they had been in the early years of the decade to feature white abolitionist speakers at Negro conventions or even to accord those whites honorary convention membership.[7]

Beyond specific complaints that white immediatists failed to assist the Northern free Negro community, several black abolitionists alluded to a certain attraction–repulsion pattern in the way that white immediatists purported to embrace them. Predictably, the most bitter of these blacks had received rather heavy-handed steward and voluntarist rebuffs. Samuel Ringgold Ward wrote contemptuously of white "abolitionists in *profession*" who "best loved the colored man at a distance." The *Colored*

American editorialized that "the worst feature of abolitionism" was the tendency of whites to accept blacks as theoretical equals while keeping a cool distance from them because of "inferior exhibitions of talent on the part of colored men." Theodore Wright delineated the attraction-repulsion cycle most graphically. Before the voluntarist New York State Anti-Slavery Society, he bitterly recounted how a Quaker immediatist had invited a Negro to his home but had served the Negro dinner in the kitchen and had failed to introduce him to the family.[8]

What caused such an attraction–repulsion pattern to blemish the abolitionist biracial crusade? In occasional and quite undeveloped remarks at the end of the 1830s, a few black abolitionists offered intriguing suggestions. Something – a "chord of prejudice," a "national prejudice," a "demonic" insensitivity – was preventing white immediatists from fully empathizing with the Northern free black community and from completely accepting black immediatists as fellow missionaries. This barrier was evident when Garrison publicized in the pages of his *Liberator* activities in the Boston black community of which he approved while ignoring black ventures that he disliked. It was evident that white immediatists "identified with us" when their own civil liberties were endangered but lost empathy "when their own rights are somewhat secure." Owing to this "demonic prejudice," William Whipper claimed, when white and black abolitionists "meet each other, it is for the most part under a mask, like courtiers, so that it is next to impossible, generally speaking, to divine their real meaning and intent."[9]

If, as these black abolitionists were suggesting, some "demonic" force or "chord of prejudice" precluded full white immediatist empathy toward blacks, tarnished early effort at biracial cooperation, and set the attraction–repulsion cycle in motion, what was the nature of this force as it emerged during the first decade of the immediatist crusade? Examination of the way white abolitionists characterized Northern free blacks in the 1830s affords useful clues.

II

As the decade progressed, white immediatists of all persuasions warned free blacks in rather stark and somewhat condescending tones that blacks could only help whites to demolish proslavery arguments if they resorted to impeccable middle-class living habits. Only "a specimen of free colored elevation at the north will recommend abolition principles to thousands of slave holders visiting the North." If free blacks proved that "they are susceptible of pure and exalted purposes and affections . . . and that they can rise to a high degree of social, moral and religious excellence," it would be folly to claim that the Negro was destined for bondage. "The contrast between free blacks of the North and slaves of the south ought easily be such as to burn slavery out by the roots." "The necessities of the case require not only that you should behave as well as the whites, but better than the whites," Garrison repeatedly noted when he spoke before free Negroes. An impeccable Northern black community was crucial to the crusade against slavery. These sorts of admonitions suggested that several white immediatists had constricted the earlier empathy for free blacks that they had evidenced as Colonization Society agents in the field. Instead, they seemed to be insisting that Northern blacks exemplify their own white middle-class qualities in order to facilitate a cause. Blacks were needed in the immediatist crusade because they could furnish evidence in their persons that would undermine the "peculiar institution." By subordinating empathy between the races to the success of this "noble cause," even insurgent whites seemed to be inadvertently forging barriers of formalism and emotional distance between themselves and the free Negroes to whom they appealed. To be sure, even in their days in the A.C.S., early immediatists had acknowledged that eradication of slavery was the primary racial goal; better rapport between black and white in the North as well as in the South was to follow in the wake of emancipation. But primary dedication to the war against slavery did not necessarily require white–black exchanges to become more formalized, more "cause-oriented," and less empathetic. Certain covert forces – a hidden agenda – seemed to be moving immediatist biracialism in this direction.[10]

Another sign that white immediatists of the 1830s were inadvertently cultivating emotional distance between themselves and Northern free blacks was in their constant exhortations that blacks must learn to practice self-help virtues with diligence and morality and thus rise from their lowly status. Here, too, conformity to a white middle-class standard of propriety was explicit. Dominated by stewards and voluntarists, the American Anti-Slavery Society executive committee instructed its agents that they were to instill in free Negroes "the importance of domestic order, and the performance of relative duties in families; of correct habits . . . the duty and advantages of industry and economy; promptness and fidelity in the fulfillment of contracts and obligations, whether written or verbal; and encourage them in the acquisition of property. . . ." "Establish for yourselves a character of industry, sobriety & integrity, that shall put your calumniators to silence," the insurgent New England Anti-Slavery Society proclaimed to a convention of Philadelphia blacks. Voluntarists and stewards including Gerrit Smith, Lewis Tappan, Joshua Leavitt, and Simeon Jocelyn reiterated the message. By educating themselves and working energetically but morally, blacks would "elevate themselves" to a level where cultivated whites could respect them. The clear implication was that free blacks were different from, indeed inferior to, their middle-class and devout white immediatist exhorters. In an unguarded moment, Garrison, the most vigorous champion of biracialism, made this quite clear: "Till they are equal to other people in knowledge and cultivation, they will not and cannot rank as equals." Thus, the very message that white abolitionists issued to encourage black self-improvement was simultaneously a message to themselves indicating that they, as middle-class, self-improving whites, were superior to the free blacks about them. Here, then, was another sign that white immediatists, without quite realizing it, were invoking their middle-class cultural values in a way that seemed to distance themselves from the Northern Negroes they needed for their biracial crusade. It was as if some inner "prejudice" was causing them to allow obvious differences in income, cultivation, and educational attainment to strain the biracial effort to the breaking point. As they held their own genteel white middle-class standards before blacks, they allowed class and cultural distinctions to replace the free-flowing empathy for blacks that they had felt when they left colonization for immediatism in the late 1820s and early 1830s.[11]

This is not to say that white immediatists, subconsciously, were becoming increasingly desirous of destroying their modest biracial experiment as the 1830s progressed. Rather, they wanted the relationship structured along increasingly paternalistic lines. They, the pious exemplars of cultivation and morality, were to inculcate self-help values in their black associates and thereby to furnish an example of an "elevated" free black community to counter proslavery polemicists. As Beriah Green of the Gerrit Smith circle noted, white immediatists "must raise them [free blacks] from the dust to their appropriate place – as the rational children of God, redeemed by his Son." It was this very missionary mentality that explains why, during the early 1830s, American Anti-Slavery Society agents were advised to locate some white person in every community they visited who could function as a "friend, adviser, and protector" to local blacks – as a "tried friend of the colored people." Indeed, as the 1830s progressed, white immediatists increasingly came to characterize themselves as "instructors," "Christian friends," and "elevators" of a benighted race which afforded them, in Theodore Weld's words, "excellent material to work upon."[12]

In other words, white immediatists of all varieties were not fostering distance between themselves and their black colleagues, or free Northern blacks generally, altogether from antiblack hatred or deep-seated racial contempt. They were also assuming toward those blacks the formalized role that white evangelical middle-class missionary reformers assumed toward all "debased" and "deprived" lower classes, whether those lower-class peoples were the "savages" of Sumatra, the slaves of the South, or the drunken Irish "derelicts" of Manhattan. White immediatists were the advocates of divinity, and one of their missions was to uplift the free black "heathen" of the North. The firsthand personal rapport that several young immediatists had established with the blacks they had encountered when they had been skeptical A.C.S. agents in the field was therefore being replaced by the more traditional and more abstractionist antebellum evangelical missionary pattern. "We" (the elevated white middle-class missionaries) were required to uplift a debased "them." Unfortunately, this process of abstraction seemed to be accelerating as the 1830s progressed. White immediatists seemed less and less frequently to distinguish between the majority of Northern blacks who were poorly educated, lacking formal religious training and steady employment, and the lower middle-class minority of somewhat better educated and more formally devout black abolitionists with whom they had the closest contacts. Even insurgents often failed to make the distinction. This suggests that along with the very real class and cultural differences that stood between white and black immediatists, as well as the traditional missionary mentality, white immediatists seemed to cling to certain fears that were at least somewhat rooted in race differences. As several black abolitionists had charged, a "chord of prejudice" was assuredly present.[13]

With this in mind, historians would do well to reconsider the assertions that white immediatists made during the 1830s concerning the social and sexual mixing of the races. We must no longer assume that their constant disavowals of desires for intimate interracial association solely related to expediency. By those disavowals, they were not simply trying to deflect claims that they were amalgamationists – charges that had brought on dangerous antiabolitionist mob attacks. It is important to recognize that immediatists were probably as opposed as any other segment of the Northern middle-class white population to interracial intimacies. Lydia Child was quite sincere, for example, when she declared in 1834 that "the principles of the abolitionists have been misrepresented. They have not the slightest wish to do violence to the distinctions of society by forcing the rude and illiterate [Negro] into the presence of the learned and refined [whites]." Neither was the Junior Anti-Slavery Society of Philadelphia mincing words when it resolved, "to elevate the character and condition of the free people of color" and simultaneously proclaimed that it did not seek "to encourage social intercourse between colored and white families."[14] Given their disturbingly stereotypical assumption that even the more cultivated blacks did not measure up to the white middle-class standards and conduct, and given their at least equally strong premise that women represented the moral reservoir of society, it is little wonder that white immediatists sought to avert intimate social intercourse between the races. That intercourse had, by its very nature, to be illicit and therefore subversive of female purity and of general middle-class propriety. Indeed, one reason why white immediatists of the 1830s were so outraged by the South's "peculiar institution" was that it seemed to be plagued by immoral interracial intimacies – by indulgent slaveholders who fornicated regularly with their bondswomen.[15] For all of these reasons, early immediatists were invariably vehement against amalgamation. As faithful missionaries, they had to be. Amalgamation contradicted a persisting need for an emotional gap between the white missionary reformer, whether insurgent, steward, or voluntarist, and the lower race that he sought to elevate. If that gap were ever bridged, the missionary would have to discover other peoples to uplift.

In 1842 Lydia Child told Wendell Phillips that she had recently met Charles Remond, a black immediatist who was generally supportive of Boston Clique insurgency: "He [Remond] is the first colored person I have met, who seemed to be altogether such a one as I would have him. He carries ballast enough for his sails, and that is unusual."[16] In a very real sense, this remark summarized much of the racial legacy of the first decade of immediatist biracialism – a legacy that obviously involved insurgents, if to a lesser degree than stewards and voluntarists. The free black was to be "as I would have him" with "ballast enough for his sails"; the white immediatist missionary was setting the standard for the "heathen" and determining how closely he measured up. The fact that only one of the "colored persons" Child had met approximated the standard, although she, like most friends of Garrison, came into frequent contact with rather polished black immediatists, underscored the cultural and class differences between the races as well as the missionary's need to forge and perpetuate a formal distance from his subjects of uplift. But it also underscored a certain animosity toward Negroes generally. Only one black had "ballast enough for his sails." Only one was a full, substantial human being.

Thus, it was a combination of cultural and class differences, the missionary mentality, and a covert and somewhat muted white animosity toward blacks that merged together to severely strain immediatist biracialism during its first decade. It became almost impossible for most white abolitionists, even most insurgents, to become close with their black co-laborers. To be sure, those white abolitionists who forged the biracial crusade and sought to expand black civil rights were considerably more concerned with blacks than white Northern middle-class society as a whole. At the same time, the very combination of elements that tarnished immediatist biracialism may have reflected pervasive white Northern middle-class attitudes. Immediatists may have been victimized by their class and their culture even as they tried to transcend both.

Fortunately, Ronald Takaki's essay, "The Black Child-Savage in Antebellum America" (1970), affords a cogent conceptualization of those pervasive middle-class attitudes. Most middle-class Northern whites, Takaki demonstrates, viewed the Negro as at once a carefree, impulsive, immature child and an innately untamed, uncivilized, sexually threatening savage. The two qualities blended together and forged the pervasive middle-class image of the Negro as at once child and uncivilized or savage. Whereas the black child required supervision, the savage needed to be separated from white society. Hence, middle-class Northerners generally were at once attracted to the black's childlike qualities and repulsed by his innate savagery, or at least by his deficiencies in the essentials of civility.[17]

Because they were thoroughly middle-class in their culture and values, it is not surprising that most white immediatists of the 1830s developed their own muted version of this pervasive stereotype that rejected the notion of innate black savagery. Modified in this way, the stereotype became compatible with their ethnocentric evangelical perspective through which a pious missionary (usually white) was to struggle to enlighten people of darkness, who often had swarthy complexions. Indeed, the black child-savage was the ideal subject for white immediatists to raise up to appropriate middle-class standards. His innocent childlike qualities suggested undeveloped and (in a vague romantic sense) unspoiled moral capacities. His savage features gave immediatists something against which to vent their covert racial antipathies. With diligent missionary endeavor, the immediatist could educate and uplift the innocent black child and gradually extinguish his savage crudities.

The potential for a triumphant crusade for Christ seemed, therefore, to have induced immediatists to dwell upon Negroes' childlike qualities: their "comparative simplicity" and undeveloped intellects, their "likelier" and "humbler" dispositions, their being "full of fun & frolick – in the *Zip Coon* way," their disinclination "to govern" and preference to obey, and their "instinctive" desire "to return every cruelty with kindness." To be sure, these innocent childlike qualities were sometimes cause for distress, as when immediatists found blacks unable to keep regular account of money or displaying a passion for finery. But because blacks were "more tractable than persons of like information and intelligence among the whites," humane white missionaries could anticipate eliminating their ignorance and crudities and guiding them toward moral virtue. White reformers were therefore to conduct themselves toward these uninformed and immature "woolly heads" as "our brothers' keepers" and to teach them, by good example, that "they must be industrious if they would here thrive and prosper."[18]

If immediatist missionaries felt duty bound to elevate black "children" who had the capacities for moral improvement, they were deeply distressed by barbarous qualities that blacks also seemed to exhibit. Although immediatists alluded to these savagelike qualities much less frequently and in much more muted form than their Northern white middle-class contemporaries, it is nevertheless noteworthy that they occasionally deployed the savage image. Like the dark cannibals who ate Henry Lyman in Sumatra, immediatists noted from time to time that

American blacks shared an inner barbarism. In their African milieu, these Negroes were "ignorant among savages," "barbaric," and potentially explosive. Despite "the restraints of civil law" and paternal missionary direction in America, this potential was not necessarily extinguished; a restrained child might instantly be transformed into a savage. One could spot this propensity in black partiality "toward exciting forms of religion, rather than the more quiet and rational." The uncivilized, unrestrained element of Negro personality was also evident in their "natural and enthusiastic" language, the "instinct" basis of their personality, their powers of sexual reproduction, and even in their "curly heads." It was no wonder "that intemperance, indolence, and crime prevail among them [free blacks] to a mournful extent" and that great "inconveniences" arose "from the presence of a class of degraded people" such as these.[19]

One certainly does not encounter these sorts of remarks in very many white immediatist discussions of blacks during the 1830s. Nevertheless, apparent black crudities and barbarities were obviously quite repulsive to white evangelical immediatist sensibilities. But rare and random immediatist allusions to black savagery also underscored a vast moral gap between what they perceived to be the dire state of Negro life and the cultivated level of the middle-class white society about them. This suggests that they were revealing more than a wholesale acceptance of the common middle-class Northern racial antipathies of their day. When they occasionally invoked the black savage stereotype, white immediatists were also voicing anxiety over the enormity of the task of black racial uplift that they saw before them.

As a predictable manifestation of their ethnocentric missionary perspective, then, white immediatists espoused their own peculiar version of the pervasive Northern middle-class child–savage stereotype. They emphasized black childhood but made muted and periodic references to black deficiencies in civility. In doing so, they were obviously expressing ambivalence. They wanted to associate with Negroes so as to facilitate missionary uplift. But they also experienced urges to separate themselves from blacks because of the Negro's potential for dangerous uncivilized outbursts and owing to the real possibility that efforts to enlighten the Negro might fail. This accounted for the attraction-repulsion cycle that was so evident in white immediatist conduct toward blacks through the 1830s. More fundamentally, it explained why, as they professed to befriend free Negroes, they cultivated emotional as well as spatial distance between themselves and even their rather refined black colleagues. Because they therefore emptied the deeply racist white middle-class child–savage stereotype of certain of its more vicious anti-Negro features and lodged that stereotype firmly within their we–they evangelical reform perspective, white immediatists displayed a strong missionary impulse to uplift the childlike Negro. The problem (also endemic to the missionary impulse) was that the Negro's uncivilized qualities made efforts at uplift hazardous and difficult.

III

It would be unfair to stop here in our analysis of the limitations of the immediatist biracial experiment of the 1830s. Because their ethnocentric missionary outlook was inseparable from the black child–savage stereotype, abolitionists were revealing their strong kinship to pervasive Northern white middle-class racial perspectives. But this should not obscure their striking departures from those perspectives. Unlike most Northerners about them, even unlike most benevolent movement missionaries, they repeatedly articulated a commitment to full civil rights for free Negroes, they allowed blacks into most of their antislavery societies, and they sometimes even met with blacks on a cooperative basis. This was particularly true of insurgents, but it was also evident among stewards and voluntarists. Indeed, perhaps the most remarkable feature of 1830s immediatist biracialism was that as whites separated themselves (physically and emotionally) from the blacks they professed to help and embraced the child–savage stereotype, many simultaneously questioned and attempted to throw off the racism and ethnocentrism within Northern middle-class missionary reform culture. With insurgents predictably taking the lead, immediatists struggled energetically against "the chord of prejudice" within themselves and the we–they perspective of antebellum missionary evangelicism that provided much of the form behind that prejudice. Indeed, it seemed as if several sought to rekindle somehow the empathy that they had felt for blacks during the late 1820s and early 1830s, when they had first listened to free black protestations against repatriation.

Reflection upon race relations abroad aided several immediatists in partially overcoming "the chord of prejudice," particularly the missionary ethnocentrism that did much to shape it. They were especially attentive to the Colonization Society's dreaded Liberian settlement and to race relations in the British Isles. As affairs in Texas became increasingly controversial, some immediatists also became quite attentive to Latin America. This multinational perspective allowed abolitionists of diverse perspectives to see that contrary to the claims of many former benevolent movement–Colonization Society associates, white antagonisms toward blacks were not universal. It was possible for the races to live and work together harmoniously. Strolling the streets of London, for example, Clique insurgent Wendell Phillips noted a white and a black man happily walking arm in arm: "Looking round, and seeing no appearance of a mob, gave me the most realizing sense I have had, that I was no longer in America!!" So, too, the steward-controlled *Emancipator* editorialized that, since prejudice was not "as potent on the coast of Africa, as in the United States," it could not be innate. Voluntarist James Birney similarly observed that white and black peacefully coexisted in Mexico, South America, Canada, and elsewhere where blacks had legal equality. Only where that equality was denied could one find a situation "that produces discontent." Similarly, insurgent Garrison and steward Simeon Jocelyn observed that in those areas of the globe where values of Christian morality, neighborhood, and family were most prized, racial prejudice was in ebb. Therefore, evangelical missionary values did not necessarily require animosity toward blacks.[20]

This awareness that Christian brotherhood and racial harmony were compatible helps to explain why a number of white immediatists sought to eliminate formal restrictions against Northern blacks, particularly disfranchisement, segregation in public accommodations, and inferior educational opportunities. With equal opportunities, the considerable number of blacks with ability and perseverance would become cultivated and prosperous; they could join the genteel evangelical middle class. When this transpired and black culture was "elevated," the truly refined and Christian of both races would be able to mix freely, as they could in many foreign locations. Hence, whites would allegedly be able to mix comfortably with refined middle-class black colleagues. Their relationship to these blacks would cease to be strained or "unnatural," and fears of racial amalgamation would subside.[21]

Here was the rub. If racial discriminations ceased and if blacks were given wider educational, political, and (though to a lesser degree) economic opportunity, the black child-savage stood to become an endangered species. A genteel black churchgoing middle class would supposedly have few of the incivilities that white immediatists feared. But these blacks would also appear less childlike. Thus, they would be less subject to paternalistic controls. The traditional missionary relationship through which pious and genteel white reformers uplifted the children of darkness would become unnecessary. The need to perpetuate this sort of dependency relationship may explain why immediatists often failed to recognize the cultivated middle-class qualities of black associates like Samuel Cornish and William Nell. The deep reluctance to relinquish missionary controls over even "refined" blacks also helps to explain why the *National Anti-Slavery Standard* editorially opposed separate black conventions – black abolitionists detaching themselves "from those who are your coadjutors in this great work."[22]

It is therefore striking that some white immediatists of the 1830s both within our focal Tappan steward cluster and our Boston Clique insurgent circle came to a vague sense that there was a reason why black activists sometimes drew away. Blacks did so, they grasped, because they themselves shared the prejudice of the white Northern middle class. Although immediatists were "in theory the enemies of caste," Lewis Tappan noted, "it is to be lamented that so few are its practical opponents." "We are prejudiced against the blacks; and our prejudices are indurated . . . by the secret, vague consciousness of the wrong we are doing them," Samuel J. May acknowledged in an unusually introspective moment. On a few occasions, Lydia Child admitted that she wrongly considered the Negro's color "a deformity" and that she and other missionary colleagues seemed unable to throw off their "ignoble prejudice"; it seemed to find "no intermission" within them. In unguarded moments, Garrison and Edmund Quincy of the Boston Clique and even William Jay of the Tappan circle offered similar confessions. It is noteworthy, however, that of this limited number of immediatists who owned up to their inner prejudice, none perceived how it was reinforced by an ethnocentric missionary perspective. That sort of recognition would have been debilitating, for it would have struck at the inner core of immediatist social psychology.[23]

Short of this recognition, how were the disheartening strains and disharmonies of the biracial experiment of the 1830s to be remedied? Some proposed that white immediatists generally had to associate more frequently with Northern blacks. "You [free Negroes] must be willing to mingle with us whilst we have the prejudice," Angelina Grimké pleaded, "because it is only by associating with you that we shall be able to overcome it. You must not avoid our society whilst we are in this *transition* state. . . . We entreat your aid to help us overcome it." Sister Sarah Grimké concurred, noting that inner barriers between white immediatists and blacks dissipated by "sitting with them in places of worship, by appearing with them in our streets, by giving them our countenance in steamboats and stages, by visiting them at their homes and encouraging them to visit us, receiving them as we do our white fellow citizens." Elizur Wright insisted that whites simply had to begin "stepping over the line of caste, and treating colored people precisely as if it [prejudice] did not exist." The very "sight of white humanity treating black humanity with civility" would undercut the "chord of prejudice" within whites. While favoring this solution, Beriah Green of the Smith circle of voluntarists wanted, above all, to keep prejudices away from the young: "the chord of caste will remain" unless "we bring white & black together in our schools." Garrison, Birney, Leavitt, and other immediatists of diverse perspectives and intimacy circles endorsed such proposals for interracial contact.[24]

The strategy implicit in these calls for more contacts between black and white was quite simple. Immediatist racial stereotypes and the inner fears beneath those stereotypes would disappear as white and black came into close day-to-day contact and, together, confronted the hostilities of a white Northern society antagonistic to interracial association. If our earlier finding on the changing dynamics of male–female relationships within immediatism is even roughly parallel, this was no naive strategy. Pervasive and constrictive Woman's Sphere stereotypes tend-ed to dissipate to the degree that the sexes daily worked closely in antislavery ventures. Still, there was a crucial distinction between male–female and white–black contacts within the immediatist crusade. Women with innately "superior" moral and emotional fiber were thought to be elevating men; all male missionaries desirous of retaining and deepening their moral commitments would benefit by associating with these female colleagues. But blacks, with their perceived childish and uncivilized qualities, had the potential to tarnish the cultivated moral presence of white missionaries. Thus, increased contact between white and black might eliminate prejudicial white images of blacks only to the degree that bonds of empathy and understanding between human beings of different colors could form that might conceivably weaken the white abolitionist's ethnocentric missionary perspective.

Difficult as the task was, a number of white immediatists made serious efforts during the 1830s to reach out and labor with free blacks about them. But whereas at least the insurgent Boston Clique integrated women into its daily operations, none of our three focal immediatist clusters similarly took in blacks or worked with them on a regular and sustained basis. Nonetheless, free blacks did occupy notable roles in the early immediatist crusade, and Garrison stood out, from the start, in promoting these roles. He placed blacks in positions of responsibility on the staff of the *Liberator*, stayed with local blacks during lecture tours and business trips, and frequently put up black reformers as house guests. Garrison's Clique associate, Samuel J. May, also cultivated contacts with free black activists. With the periodic cooperation of other Clique asso-ciates, Garrison and May gave black Bostonians cause to believe that there were white immediatists upon whom blacks could depend in peri-ods of distress. It was probably only because of the reticence of the culti-vated, aristocratic wing of the Clique that no Boston black reformer – not even William Nell – was integrated within the group's daily social routines and strategy sessions the way Maria Chapman and her sisters had been. The record of contact between Lewis Tappan's circle of stew-ards and free blacks was considerably more spotted. Indeed, only indi-vidual stewards in the group sought to befriend blacks at specific times; the Tappan circle never formally endorsed biracial cooperation as one of its collective endeavors. But the efforts of individual stewards were noteworthy. At Lane Seminary, for example, Theodore Weld and George Whipple defied President Lyman Beecher's admonitions, worked closely with Cincinnati free Negroes, and sometimes boarded with them. As "Lane rebels," they brought these practices with them to Oberlin Col-lege and so fostered greater camaraderie between the races in the newly integrated school on the Western Reserve. Even the formal and often aloof Lewis Tappan practiced the interracial association that he preached. While living in Boston, for example, he attended the African Sunday

School. When vacationing in upstate New York, he outraged a local congregation by placing his family within pews reserved for black communicants. The record of Gerrit Smith's circle of upstate New York voluntarists was even more limited. Unlike the Boston Clique, which looked to blacks as a major element in its local following, and unlike the Tappan circle, which included free blacks within its New York City constituency, the Smith group had no significant black following and did little, as a collectivity, to increase it. Indeed, Smith himself was the only member of his circle who sought out black reformer colleagues on a regular basis. He took special pleasure in inviting black abolitionists who were traveling in the area to dine, relax, and spend the night with him at his Peterboro estate.[25]

It is noteworthy that a number of white female immediatists, particularly insurgents, made at least equally persistent efforts to work with black colleagues. Abby Hooper Gibbons, for example, belonged to the black female Manhattan Anti-Slavery Society. Lucretia Mott and Mary Grew worked regularly and actively with Philadelphia's free black middle class. Similarly, the personal friendships that Angelina and Sarah Grimké and Lydia Child cultivated often crossed race lines. Assured of their inner moral worth by admonitions consistent with Woman's Sphere, these women may have been less apprehensive than a number of their male colleagues that contact with blacks might tarnish their claims of devotion and civility.[26]

Partly because of these efforts by such white immediatists to recognize "the chord of prejudice" within themselves and to mix with free blacks, signs of genuine empathy for the Northern Negro were detectable within abolitionism before the 1830s had elapsed. In some respects, it resembled an earlier empathy that several immediatists had felt when they discovered free black opposition to repatriation schemes. In certain quarters, at least, white immediatists were therefore discovering or perhaps rediscovering in the course of the 1830s how to probe with their emotions as well as with their intellects, to "bend back" their missionary version of the black child–savage stereotype, and to feel for "them which suffer adversity, as being yourselves also in the body." As voluntarist Beriah Green proclaimed to his colleagues, "There is no way for us to escape from guilt and corruption of heart but by cordially and joyfully yielding to our colored brethren the sympathies of our common humanity." Fellow voluntarist Gerrit Smith explained that only by acquiring empathy for the free Negro was he able to see the sin of Colonization Society repatriations: "Had I commenced with him [the Negro], instead of those who stood entirely aloof from him, I should not have been the victim of colonization delusions for so long a time; for, as soon as I came to commune with him . . . and, in a word, to make myself a colored man – I saw how crushing and murderous to all the hopes and happiness of our colored brother is the policy of expelling the colored race from this country." Boston Clique insurgent Henry Wright first felt empathy for the free Negro one cold January day in 1834 as he rode inside a stage from Newburyport to Boston. Although there was plenty of room inside the coach, a well-dressed black nearly froze to death riding atop. "Poor despised African – my heart bled for him," Wright acknowledged. "Gladly would I have exchanged seats with him & I proposed to have him get in but it was not allowed. How bitter & deep must be the feeling of revenge that broods in the hearts of the Africans among us. . . ." Similarly, after Angelina Grimké married Theodore Weld and she, together with sister Sarah, set up the Weld household, they invited their black friend Sarah Douglass for a visit. Douglass stayed but a single day. Quickly, the Grimké sisters grasped that Douglass did not feel herself a truly welcome guest in a white household. They wrote to her, explaining that she was a most "acceptable visitor" and insisting that there would be nothing strained or unnatural if Douglass spent more time with them; there was nothing significant "in receiving and treating thee as an equal. . . ." This show of empathy and understanding brought results; Douglass became a frequent household visitor – for several weeks at a time.[27]

The basic dimensions of the enormously complex 1830s abolitionist experiment in biracialism are now apparent. On the one hand, it was sharply limited by class and cultural differences between the races, by the traditional ethnocentric antebellum missionary relationship, and by the pervasive black child–savage stereotype. These were the essential elements in the immediatist "chord of prejudice." Yet the biracial experiment nevertheless survived the decade and made abolitionism an isolated island for white–black cooperative contacts in the antebellum North. Survival was possible because, apart from their prejudice and their paternalism, most white immediatists were able intellectually to perceive a world where the races could coexist as relative equals. Several immediatists went further and sensed that interracial association might ease prejudice. Some actually associated with blacks more frequently. A somewhat more limited number came to empathize deeply with blacks and, in this way, to brush aside momentarily the black child–savage image and the ethnocentric missionary perspective.

At the most fundamental level, then, 1830s immediatist biracialism was shaped by two opposite strands, or forces, that simultaneously pulled white abolitionists, if in varying degrees. First, there was the merger of an ethnocentric missionary perspective with the black child–savage stereotype, and this cultivated formal distance between the races. Second, there occurred an intellectual, and to a lesser degree emotional, embrace of a oneness between white and black. Although this second element may have had somewhat less impact upon most white immediatists than the first, it nonetheless fostered within them a disquieting tension between a paternalist–segregationalist course of conduct toward blacks on the one hand and egalitarian–integrationist propensities on the other. This tension was at the heart of what historians have too vaguely labeled "antislavery ambivalence."

IV

With our grasp of the two essential forces that shaped abolitionist biracialism in the 1830s, one basic task remains. By 1840, the year of the schism within the American Anti-Slavery Society, it was unclear which force would ultimately govern white immediatists. There was a very real danger that the paternalist–segregationist prejudice would ultimately win out over the thrust toward empathy, egalitarianism, and integration. Our present task is to determine which way the balance ultimately tilted during the 1840s and 1850s. In doing so, we shall find that because our three focal abolitionist intimacy circles continued to eschew black members, they remained fundamentally unequipped for an egalitarian resolution of the conflict.

Black immediatists during these decades perceived even more distressing displays of "the chord of prejudice" from many of their white immediatist colleagues than during the 1830s. Some, such as John Rock and William Nell, did not want to make too much of such behavior; they felt that white abolitionists were still much more sympathetic to them than white Northerners in general. In the course of the 1840s and 1850s, however, most black immediatists at least occassionally attacked the prejudice of their white colleagues. Often, their criticisms were particular: the failure of the national antislavery societies to let "black" rather than "yellow men" speak at their meetings; the continuing refusal of white abolitionists to hire black workers; the Liberty party's failure to elect black candidates for public office; the propensities of the Boston Clique to discourage New England blacks from voting; the tendency of insurgents generally to divert themselves with causes "extraneous" to black welfare.[28] But the most bitter diatribes delivered by black abolitionists centered on the paternalistic and ethnocentric missionary propensities of their white colleagues. Whenever white immediatists would consort with them – irregularly at best – they seemed to be treated like children who required parental lessons in "elevation" to alter their allegedly coarse, uncivilized propensities. According to Henry Highland Garnet, such paternalism represented no less than a "desire to sink me again to the condition of a *slave* by forcing me to think as you do." Charles Remond and Martin Delaney concurred and noted that when blacks deferred to white abolitionists, they lost confidence in their own efforts. Similarly, Frederick Douglass mocked the tendency of the whites to belittle black capacities; he cautioned, "We cannot expect to receive from those who indulge in the opinion practical recognition of our Equality." In essence, warnings such as these pointed to sharp black disappointment that white immediatists continued to be wedded to prejudice.[29]

After a decade and more, then, the white immediatist commitment to racial equality and civil rights had not been met, and black abolitionists seemed to be losing patience. "Our relations to the Anti-Slavery movement must be and are changed," Douglass proclaimed in 1855. The battle against caste and slavery "is emphatically our battle; no one else can fight it for us, and with God's help we must fight it ourselves."[30] More clearly than any other phenomenon, the changes that had taken place within the Negro convention movement between the 1830s and the 1850s illustrated this black immediatist tendency to draw away from white colleagues. In the 1830s it was commonplace for white immediatists, especially insurgents, to address these conventions as featured speakers; several whites were even accorded honorary membership. But whites were only rarely invited to the Negro conventions of the 1850s. Moreover, in a great many of these conventions, black separatist ideologies and tactics were either decidedly supplementing or entirely replacing the interracial approaches of the 1830s. At the same time, increasing talk of emigration to "black countries" was detectable, particularly after passage of the 1850 Fugitive Slave Law. As white abolitionists had at least partially separated themselves, emotionally and often even physically, from their black colleagues, black activists had begun to pull away from whites. The precise extent of this shift varied widely among Northern communities, however, and most black abolitionists never lost all hope of egalitarian biracialism.[31]

In some measure, the more decidedly separatist course of conduct during the 1840s and 1850s evidenced blacks' increasing political sophistication and maturation. Black immediatists simply needed their white colleagues less. They sensed that whites had not helped them much in the struggle against racial discrimination in the North or against slavery in the South. Moreover, by the 1850s federal government policy had become more decidedly anti-Negro in many particulars despite white immediatist efforts. Why, therefore, did black abolitionists have to continue to tolerate white immediatists' missionary paternalism, especially since many had, by then, themselves become experienced civil rights activists? In large measure blacks were changing because they perceived that their white immediatist colleagues remained the same prejudiced associates and continued to appear relatively ineffective advocates of civil rights. But as white abolitionists watched this change in blacks and perceived the more general failures of their immediatist crusade, many seemed to embrace "the chord of prejudice" even more tenaciously. There were three particularly significant manifestations of this trend.

First, the white immediatist missionary perspective was gradually modified in the course of the late antebellum decades. Perhaps owing in part to despair that was rooted in the failure of abolitionists to win over many churchmen or congregations in the course of the 1830s and early 1840s, missionary stridency outside the racial context became somewhat less intense. Even the most evangelically devout immediatists – stewards such as William Jay and George Whipple and voluntarists such as Gerrit Smith and William Goodell – were becoming less rigid generally in their views of godly and ungodly behavior. At the same time, however, most remained adamant and uncompromising on the racial front – on the right, in Whipple's words, of "our missionaries" to uplift Negroes without "compromise with the organic sin of the [Negro] people."[32] Consequently, although references to the Negro's deficiencies in civility – his coarse, savage propensities – continued to be muted and infrequent during the 1840s and 1850s, they had to become more noticeable as immediatists spoke less of reaching benighted peoples who happened to be white. There were clear if random allusions to the heathenism of the "rude African" in America, the "tropical fervor" of the "licentious" and untamed "African temper," and the "Nigger's" general absence of any sense of self-respect. "Big black wenches" were found particularly "ugly and vulgar." Because of the Negro's "frightful" qualities, "nature has fitted him," unlike the Caucasian, to "the margins of rivers flowing sluggishly under a torrid sun." Since Negroes were thought to be uncivilized as "a class," the faithful immediatist did best avoiding excessive association with them even as he struggled to enlighten these children of darkness.[33]

For an increasingly secular Northern black leadership class, it must have been painful to watch white immediatist colleagues who, while more mild-mannered and tolerant on other fronts, continued to refer to Negroes periodically as uncivilized and requiring massive if cautiously deployed techniques of missionary uplift. In addition to this retention of missionary ethnocentrism on the racial front amid relaxation elsewhere, white immediatists generally manifested a stronger acceptance of "the chord of prejudice" by channeling their energies against the Southern Slave Power at the expense of civil rights for Northern blacks. One of the earliest signs of this new priority was the decision of Liberty party immediatists (including some within Gerrit Smith's voluntarist circle) to run Ohioan Thomas Morris for vice-president in 1844. An adamant opponent of Southern slaveholders, Morris nonetheless had little use for Northern blacks and opposed Negro suffrage. The next year Alvan Stewart issued a public letter maintaining that the civil rights of free Negroes had to be subordinated to the eradication of the "peculiar institution." Opportunities for the free were only relevant as a means to "the emancipation of three millions of slaves." By 1848 other Liberty men who were rushing toward coalition with Free Soilers made even more cryptic reference to black civil rights in the crusade against slavery. Similarly, in Whittier's antislavery works of the period – poems such as "Massachusetts to Virginia" – one finds no real critique of Northern race relations. Rather, Northern blacks were to "be content to live in wretchedness and die of starvation, for the good of the cause [the attack on Southern slavery]." By the 1850s white immediatist writings and orations contained many such remarks, even among insurgents. These caused Frederick Douglass to charge that hatred of Negroes "has come to be a very common form of abolitionism." To be sure, destruction of Southern slavery had always been the primary immediatist mission; the welfare of free blacks in the North had always ranked second. But during the early years of the immediatist crusade, assistance to free blacks had nonetheless been perceived as an important simultaneous reform activity, even if the destruction of slavery itself stood to ameliorate many of the problems that free blacks faced. Only as sectional tensions intensified and as a number of abolitionists drew closer to more moderate Northern antislavery colleagues during the late antebellum years (colleagues who sought to destroy the Slave Power but cared considerably less about civil rights for free blacks) does one find many white immediatists urging black associates to "be content to live in wretchedness." Many seemed willing to downgrade their alliances with blacks in the process of improving their ties with considerably more influential white antislavery moderates.[34]

While they clung tenaciously to a race-based missionary perspective and focused more on the "crimes" of the Southern planter class, some white immediatists manifested "the chord of prejudice" in still a third new way. They began to justify repatriating free Negroes just as they had before they became immediatists – when they had supported the American Colonization Society. This was particularly true of certain immediatists who had been active in the Liberty party and who had at least modest ties or sympathies with central New York voluntarism. They were considerably closer than stewards or insurgents to the emerging Free Soil third-party political movement. Consequently they may, in part, have reembraced repatriation because of its compatibility with the Free Soil racial disposition – to keep blacks, free and slave, out of the western territories and to make those territories havens for free white labor. Like Free Soilism, colonization was racially exclusionist. Whatever the links between colonizationist proclivities among certain Liberty men and Free Soil racial dispositions, by 1852 perennial Liberty presidential candidate James Birney recommended that free blacks move to Liberia just as he had urged thirty years earlier. But now Birney had ceased to portray Liberia as a potential black utopia; it was simply "the best *retreat* they can find from the oppression of whites." Similarly, Gerrit Smith endorsed Congressman Francis Blair's bill for federal subsidization of voluntary black repatriation to Central America. By the late 1850s and early 1860s the former A.C.S. donor had come to believe that by allowing "full play to the law of nature, the blacks would move toward and the whites from the Equator." Gamaliel Bailey and Salmon Chase came to articulate similar sentiments. Sometimes these exclusionist preferences among Liberty or ex-Liberty men were even more blatant, as when Leicester King ran for governor of Ohio pledging to promote an all-white population within the state.[35]

These three developments of the 1840s and 1850s help explain why black reformers quite justifiably saw their white immediatist colleagues as more prejudiced. More conspicuous evidence, plus the failure of white immediatists to arrest increasing segregation and black economic deprivation throughout the North, indicated to many blacks that little was to be gained by continuing to labor with their white colleagues. Black displays of independence, in turn, threatened one of the most fundamental sources of white immediatist interest in white–black association – the ability to exercise missionary paternalism. Consequently, it comes as no surprise to find a New York City steward threatening to disown a black editor and to withdraw financial support from his newspaper when the editor endorsed forceful opposition to slavery while the steward administrator strongly opposed that posture. Similarly, a Boston Clique insurgent fretted because those blacks his group had supported often delivered lectures that violated insurgent principles.[36] In periods like the early 1840s, when competition between insurgents, stewards, and voluntarists for hegemony in the immediatist crusade was intense, whites seemed especially distressed at these displays of black independence. It was painful to see a young black whom one had taken into one's office and trained in moral principles now join with one's less-than-devout white rivals or move entirely into independent black reform activity. Few white immediatists fully understood that black activists were not really defecting or being disloyal or deceptive. They simply viewed racial reform in different terms. Whereas loyalty to pure missionary principles and to the untainted reformers in one's intimacy circle who supported those principles had traditionally been paramount to white immediatists, blacks, who had never even been invited into white intimacy groups, often pursued different aims. Because they faced racial discriminations and economic deprivations firsthand, they understandably concentrated on more pragmatic and survival-oriented goals, tactics, and friendship ties.[37]

A complex variety of thoughts and behaviors by both whites and blacks, often in response to one another, therefore allow us to account for much of the deterioration within immediatist biracialism during the 1840s and 1850s. Both the white paternalism inherent in the ethnocentric missionary perspective and the child–savage stereotype had forged a "chord of prejudice" that made the experiment quite vulnerable in the course of the 1830s. Other serious burdens were added as the Civil War drew nearer that often prompted white and black to think, feel, and behave in increasingly dissimilar ways. But during the 1830s, we noted,

"the chord" represented but one general strand in immediatist biracialism. It had been roughly balanced, or at least held in limbo, by a second
general strand – a vigorous white immediatist effort intellectually and
even emotionally to support the equality and oneness of the races. We
must examine this second strand during the 1840s and 1850s to determine whether some sort of balance was ultimately maintained.

Despite the exacerbated tensions between white and black abolitionists in the immediate prewar decades, there is no doubt that this second
and more positive strand remained viable. Continued and, in some
areas, expanded contacts between the races provided at least the surface
evidence of this viability. Blacks were included within the leadership of
the 1843 Liberty convention in Buffalo – an innovation in the history of
American political parties. During the 1850s they also played key roles
in the Radical Abolitionist party (largely controlled by voluntarists Gerrit Smith and William Goodell). In 1860 this party chose Frederick Douglass as one of its two electors-at-large – the first time a Negro had ever
been nominated for such a party position. The Tappan-circle-controlled
American Missionary Association responded similarly, including several
black clergymen on its executive committee. As the struggle to allow
blacks to attend Boston's public schools suggests, there may have been
even more contact between black activists and the Boston Clique during
the late 1840s and early 1850s than there had been in the 1830s. Indeed,
two Clique insurgents, Francis Jackson and Samuel J. May, increased
their cooperative activities with blacks. Moreover, whereas the vigilance
committees of the mid-1830s to aid fugitive slaves were formed and
conducted almost exclusively by black abolitionists, by the 1850s white
immediatists had become quite supportive. Finally, in his definitive
study of relationships between black reformers and John Brown, historian Benjamin Quarles has demonstrated increasing cooperation as the
1850s progressed. Brown's raid on Harpers Ferry clearly proved that
insofar as overt behavior was concerned, abolitionist biracialism had not
ceased.[38]

But the positive strand of biracialism involved more than behavior. It
also involved white immediatists in a reaching out with their minds and
emotions to understand and embrace their colleagues. In the late antebellum decades there is abundant evidence that first-generation immediatists strove with their intellects as they did during the 1830s – struggling toward reasoned justifications for supporting their black associates
as equals. Indeed, their allegiance to environmental theory – that degrading conditions rather than innate qualities explained black deficiencies in morality and economic acquisitiveness – seemed more pronounced than ever before. They appeared particularly desirous of
winning more recent converts to immediatism, such as James Freeman
Clarke and Moncure Conway, over to environmentalism. It was to be
preferred to the "romantic racialist" notion of certain new friends of the

slave that viewed the Negro as innately kind and submissive. Very eager to repudiate "romantic racialism," early immediatists like Lewis Tappan and Samuel J. May insisted, in unequivocal terms, that physical "features and tincture of the skin are nothing" – that the Negro was not innately evil or good but was entirely a product of environmental conditions. Even old immediatists such as James Birney, Gerrit Smith, and Elizur Wright, who had never entirely closed the door on cooperation with one of the two major parties, found themselves repulsed by romantic stereotypes of the Negro held by certain moderate antislavery leaders of these parties as much as they were repulsed by blatant anti-Negro hatred harbored by other party leaders. Both the stereotypes and the hatred clashed with their unreconstructed 1830s vintage environmentalism and their egalitarian intellectual commitments.[39]

But if white immediatists continued to reach out with their intellects to their black colleagues, they less frequently sought out those blacks at a deeper emotional level. To be sure, the profoundly emotional rapport and understanding that they felt with free blacks during the late 1820s and early 1830s as they left the Colonization Society and became immediatists sometimes faded at certain points in the 1830s. But it seemed considerably more difficult to recapture or reawaken by the 1840s and especially by the 1850s and the war years. Predictably, Henry Wright continued to articulate the feelings in 1861 that he had voiced twenty-five years earlier: "I am a Negro. I feel that I am in heart & soul. The scorn & hate cast on him, are cast on me." Lewis Tappan was much the same, insisting that blacks were necessarily "very sensitive on the subject of Colonization & I cannot wonder that they are so." On African colonization and on other issues, Tappan insisted, whites must demonstrate more clearly "that they sympathize with them [Negroes]." Edmund Quincy also remained the keen student of personality that he had been in the 1830s. He noted, for example, that by reading William Wells Brown's fugitive slave narrative and later visiting with Brown, he could thoroughly feel for the Negro. "It is a long time," Quincy remarked, "since I have seen a man, white or black, that I have cottoned to so much as I have to Brown. . . ." But even these men did not display empathy for free blacks as often as they had earlier in their immediatist careers. Moreover, whereas during the 1830s white immediatists such as Beriah Green, Elizur Wright, the Grimké sisters, and especially Garrison had rarely let a day go by without expressing deep feeling and understanding for black associates, during the 1840s and 1850s months often elapsed in their correspondence without empathetic expressions.[40]

In an 1844 letter to his Boston Clique colleague Wendell Phillips, Henry Wright argued that the American Anti-Slavery Society should send a white rather than a Negro agent to England:

It needs a *White* abolitionist to do the work there – a *Colored* one would not do half as well. The sympathy of Britain would flow out toward him *personally*, as a proscribed & deeply injured individual – rather than towards the Anti-Slavery cause. Sympathy with an individual, there is *here*, is of little use in our great struggle for human freedom. . . .[41]

Quite inadvertently, Wright seemed to have revealed perhaps the most basic reason why white immediatist empathy for blacks, if sometimes erratic during the 1830s, was less conspicuous in the years that followed. "Sympathy with an individual" – a free black individual – was perceived to have diminishing utility in the larger mission to free the slaves. It did not make converts to "the Anti-Slavery cause." Since that cause was foremost in the immediatist crusade, it was best not to let empathy for the black reformer (a positive good) operate as a diversion. Hence, a white abolitionist had to be sent to England.

In a very real sense, this illustrated an important shift in emphasis in first-generation immediatism in the 1840s and 1850s – away from even erratic displays of individual sympathy and toward seemingly hard-headed realism in pursuit of success – to mobilize the North against slavery. White abolitionists of all varieties sought ways to win over less ardent neighbors to the struggle against the Slave Power. Voluntarists often flirted with Free Soilers, Independent Democrats, and Republicans. Stewards concentrated on deploying their American Missionary Association to make the other benevolent societies unambiguously antislavery. Even several insurgents found themselves modestly interested in, if not supportive of, the emergence of a moderate antislavery tradition in several Northern churches, in certain Northern-based benevolent societies, and particularly within the emerging Republican party. The heightened interest of several immediatists in extinguishing the "Slave Power Conspiracy," in partially reembracing colonization, and in retaining an ethnocentric missionary perspective all testified to their craving to draw closer to more moderate antislavery Northerners. Indeed, as we shall see in the chapters that follow, first-generation immediatists of all sorts became increasingly disposed to reach out and befriend more moderate antislavery elements. Although they feared that their own purity as faithful reformers might have been "polluted" through this outreach, the spread of female moral influence in immediatist ventures may have made the risk appear less hazardous. Moreover, after many reverses, immediatists were often coming to sense that only by forging bonds with others less understanding of the old mission to the slaves could the "peculiar institution" be eradicated. Against this great goal – emancipation through a wider white middle-class antislavery coalition – the flow of sympathy between a white and a black abolitionist was not irrelevant. It simply assumed a lower priority than it had when immediatism initially separated itself from colonization and became a distinctive crusade. In part, this certainly explains why we find fewer and fewer white immediatist expressions of empathy for black colleagues as time transpired. It also helps to explain why, by the late 1840s and the early 1850s, certain immediatists seemed more willing to move beyond their cherished intimacy circles and to join socially with white antislavery moderates than to make room within their old circles for long-standing black associates.

It was this diminishing flow of empathy that made the second or positive general strand within immediatist biracialism weaker during the 1840s and 1850s than it had been in the 1830s. Without a deep if erratically deployed reserve of empathy, abstract ideological commitments to racial equality, to environmentalism, and to the common humanity of man were all that remained of the second strand. Among missionaries who imaged themselves as devout, these ideological commitments were not taken lightly. They largely explain why Boston Clique insurgents joined with local blacks in the struggle to integrate the city's public schools, why the steward American Missionary Association selected black clergymen for its executive committee, why the voluntarist Radical Abolitionist party assigned important roles to blacks, and why white immediatists generally began to cooperate with the black vigilance committees. But with diminishing empathy behind these abstract commitments, the positive strain within biracialism was offering less balance or resistance against the negative – "the chord of prejudice" – which was becoming considerably stronger. As black abolitionists knew all too well, the negative strain had secured general though not overwhelming hegemony by the outbreak of the Civil War.

This shift during the 1840s and 1850s from a rough balance to a detectable imbalance between the two general forces in the biracial experiment can be characterized in different ways. We can say that the experiment moved from bad to somewhat worse – from a very troubled white–black cooperative tradition in the 1830s to one in which the races increasingly moved along dissimilar paths in their sundry reform activities and in which difficulties between them were less likely to be surmounted. On the other hand, we can maintain that although the biracial experiment was certainly more troubled as time progressed, the abolitionist crusade remained the most conspicuous and viable island in an increasingly negrophobic antebellum North where the races could meet on at least modestly cooperative terms. Even if one prefers this second and more optimistic characterization of biracialism, it is nevertheless clear that it was considerably less viable over time than the other major immediatist cooperative experiment – between men and women. By the 1860s, women were often accepted as co-missionaries in the crusade against slavery, while blacks rarely entered into emotional bonds of Christian fellowship with their white colleagues.

I have, of course, been speaking on only the most general level of changing relationships between the races. It is also important to bear in mind that in the everyday existence of most white and black immediatists, there were diverse and even changing attitudes and actions. Daily life rarely conformed in all particulars to the general pattern of modest deterioration that has been delineated. Blacks in Syracuse, for example, found Samuel J. May more understanding of their problems in the 1850s than ever before. Then, too, a black civil rights activist in Boston, such as William Nell, found that Garrison, Phillips, and other local insurgents seemed less reclusive in the 1850s than in the 1830s in the sense that they were more willing to join with him in a campaign against public segregation. Hence, although abolitionist biracialism was of less sturdy fabric as time transpired, at any specific moment there were diverse possibilities in the white–black relationship. Frederick Douglass' dispute with the Boston Clique underscores this fluidity and complexity within the broader pattern of modest deterioration. At the same time, it provides the sort of case study that is needed to illustrate the broader pattern concretely.

V

The basic facts in the Clique's dispute with Frederick Douglass have been recounted by historians on several occasions.[42] No more than a succinct summary of them is required here.

The roots of the dispute go back to August of 1841 when Douglass, a fugitive slave living in New Bedford, met Garrison at an antislavery meeting in that town. Garrison was impressed with Douglass and invited him to become a lecturer for the insurgent Massachusetts Anti-Slavery Society. Douglass proved to be eminently successful in that capacity. Large crowds in diverse Northern locations came to hear him describe slavery from firsthand experience. During fund-raising tours to Britain in the early and middle 1840s, Douglass even seemed to outshine Garrison. He returned from his travels with funds from English antislavery friends with which to buy his freedom and to establish an antislavery newspaper of his own. Garrison and other Boston Clique insurgents urged him to continue as an insurgent lecturer. They charged that there were already too many antislavery newspapers and that Douglass was most talented as an orator. Without consulting Garrison, Douglass proceeded to make plans on his own. He moved to Rochester, where he issued the first number of his *North Star* in December 1847. Garrison and others in the Clique were resentful because their advice had been spurned, while Douglass sensed racial prejudice in their warnings against assuming editorial duties. When the British abolitionist Julia Griffith came to Rochester to assist Douglass with her funds and her considerable managerial and journalistic skills, Clique insurgents were even more displeased. They feared that a working relationship between a married black man and an unmarried white woman might prompt charges of amalgamation that would damage the immediatist cause. Moreover, by the late 1840s and early 1850s, Douglass

was drifting away from basic insurgent ideological postures: the proslavery nature of the federal Constitution, the inefficacy of a political
party approach to abolitionism, and the centrality of moral suasion antislavery appeals that eschewed electioneering. Much influenced by
Gerrit Smith, William Goodell, and other central New York voluntarists, Douglass gradually adopted basic voluntarist postures – that the
Constitution was antislavery and that third-party electoral pressure
could assure that the document was properly implemented. By 1851
Clique insurgents spoke openly of Douglass' "defection" and called him
an enemy. Garrison had Douglass' *North Star* removed from the American Anti-Slavery Society's list of approved newspapers and insisted,
"There is roguery somewhere." Douglass retorted that because the insurgents' moral suasion approach disavowed elections and voting, it
would never emancipate slaves.[43]

There are two readily apparent but insufficient explanations for the
gradual disintegration of Douglass' relationship with the most committed white immediatist participants in egalitarian biracialism – Garrison
and his fellow Clique insurgents. First, by the 1850s black abolitionists
were considerably more receptive to voting and political party electioneering tactics in the war against slavery than Clique participants or
white insurgents generally. With broad and increasing pressures in the
North to deny them the vote, blacks were understandably unwilling to
acquiesce in their own disfranchisement. Thus, certain historians have
argued that Douglass broke with the Boston Clique because Clique
insurgents were adamantly opposed to voting and party politics, while
Douglass, like many other black activists, realized that blacks could not
renounce these "tools."[44] Still, the dispute was in the making and had
become quite tense by 1847, at least two years before Douglass disavowed the Clique's particular nonvoting moral suasion approach. Disagreement over political tactics intensified the dispute and may even
have made it irreparable but could not have been the fundamental cause.

A second apparent explanation is grounded in the fact that the Boston
Clique generally (and Garrison particularly) had rather set notions of
the Negro's proper activity in the immediatist crusade – often as a
lecturer but rarely as an editor. Clique insurgents felt that blacks were
particularly suited to testify to the sins of slavery and the ills of civil
discriminations. But owing to their educationally and culturally "deficient" backgrounds, they were generally thought to lack the managerial
skills and literary talents requisite for the editor's craft. Moreover, the
inferior newspaper that came as a result of black editorial efforts might
channel black readers away from Garrison's *Liberator* and thereby en-
danger its survival. This accounts for their constant warnings to blacks
generally – not simply to Douglass – against leaving the rostrum for the
editor's craft. Indeed, it explains why Clique insurgents had felt threatened in 1838 when Benjamin Roberts, a black Bostonian, established his

Anti-Slavery Herald in their city and why they were pleased that the publication folded after only a few issues. Clearly, such an explanation for Clique opposition to Douglass' newspaper venture has the virtue of accounting for the 1847–48 period when the dispute took definitive form. It is also grounded in white perceptions of black cultural differences and in white fears of emerging patterns of black independence and separatism. Nevertheless, it does not explain enough. It does not tell us why, in the face of a number of black journalistic endeavors that did not draw many black readers away from the *Liberator*, Clique insurgents continued to insist that blacks were inherently better lecturers than editors. Nor does it explain why they never urged William Nell to become a lecturer but kept him on the *Liberator* staff for twenty years only to bypass him for the post of general agent in 1853 in favor of a journalistically inexperienced white immediatist. Finally, it fails to tell us why Gerrit Smith and other central New York voluntarists, while generally less supportive of biracialism than Clique insurgents, nonetheless sustained Douglass' journalistic venture and his quest for black editorial autonomy. In sum, we have here what verges on a successful explanation of the Clique–Douglass controversy – but does not go quite far enough.[45]

The key to a more fundamental level of explanation lies in the combination of several factors: Douglass' own awareness of certain personal needs that he felt compelled to satisfy, "the chord of prejudice" that his attempt to win satisfaction evoked in Clique insurgents, and voluntarist Gerrit Smith's capacity to empathize with Douglass. Let us analyze each of these factors and consider the way they intersected.

Even in seemingly cordial times, Douglass never felt comfortable with any Boston Clique insurgents except perhaps Wendell Phillips. From the commencement of their association in 1841 until the eruption of open hostility in 1847, Douglass' letters to them were studied, cautious responses to their sundry whims and desires. He clearly recognized that the Clique was deploying him as a public lecturer to testify to the ills of slavery and to prove that a black, once free, could be articulate and humane. Douglass also realized that he was not a Clique intimate and could not risk opening his heart and confiding to Clique members on equal terms. Even to Phillips, he acknowledged, "I cannot bring myself to approach you familiarly." In 1853, after the breach with the Clique had become irreparable, he acknowledged that he would never "have incurred the displeasure of GARRISONIANS" if he had continued to seek "their support, flattered their pride, acknowledged their claims, prophesied smooth things, withheld distasteful criticisms, shaped my course by their wishes, and basked in the sunshine of their smiles." More fundamentally, as early as 1847 Douglass grasped that Clique insurgents considered it absurd for a man "but nine years removed from slavery" and in many phases of "mental experience" only nine years old to purport to "instruct the highly civilized people of the North." Rather than let him assume an adult, independent missionary role, they pressured him to turn to Garrison for instruction – to stand in relation to Garrison as a child to a parent.[46]

What Douglass wanted was not childhood and instruction but fulfillment of a complex, even contradictory set of desires. He sought out a sense of selfhood and personal identity, and this quest set him upon two opposite paths. First, he struggled to acquire a sense of his own blackness and his personal role within the black Northern community. (This struggle culminated with the Dred Scott decision, which made it patently clear to him that he was a Negro first and then, quite secondarily, an antislavery leader.) Douglass viewed the institution of his own newspaper, independent of the Boston Clique and the *Liberator* and focusing upon the problems of the 200,000 free Northern blacks, as a crucial first step toward recognition of his racial and community identity. As he stated in an early issue of the *North Star*, if the publication could survive and prosper, this would prove that blacks could be their own representatives and advocates as they worked with whites. With the launching of this newspaper, he found himself moving, for the first time, toward meaningful rapport with blackness and black communities.[47] On the other hand, as Edmund Quincy perceptively noted in 1845, Douglass "has less of the constant sense of his color of almost any colored man I ever knew." In a brilliant and thoroughly documented analysis, historian Peter F. Walker demonstrates that Douglass knew that his father was white and hoped, more through inner emotion than outward logic, that Boston Clique insurgents would recognize this part of him. Indeed, he hoped against hope that with their contempt for positive law, they might see beyond the legal definition of blackness – that "one drop of Negro blood" did not make a Negro. They might therefore regard him much as they regarded one another. He might find a place – a real home – within the Boston Clique.[48]

Clique insurgents, however, seem to have had too high a stake in Douglass' blackness to recognize his white blood. Acknowledged as white, he would cease to offer living testimony to the immediatist claim that a Negro, once liberated, could conduct himself proficiently. Moreover, as Douglass himself observed, many in the Garrison circle seemed almost to need to regard him as a black child – an uncultivated infant who never fully matured but constantly required their paternal and uplifting guidance. To do otherwise was to curtail their roles as racial missionaries. Edmund Quincy illustrated this Clique mindset most graphically. He charged that it was unwarranted to expect that a few years of freedom would significantly transform Douglass' "undeveloped" qualities. Insurgents should try to "improve his deficiencies," Quincy maintained, but should never be under illusions that the task was completed despite Douglass' seemingly polished and articulate outward manner:

"He is one of those people with whom we must bear & forbear, for whom large allowances must be made & much credit given. . . ." It was neither proper to "spoil him" by too much forbearance nor, on the other hand, to assume that Douglass had been totally uplifted. Others in the Clique concurred in Quincy's appraisal. In their eyes Douglass was very nearly frozen in uncultivated childlike status – a "primitive" who would long require missionary uplift. This is why they fretted so when Douglass was launching the *North Star* in distant Rochester without their advice and supervision. Because he "has no *experience* in editing, nor in business affairs," the paper would certainly collapse. Great personal injury and "mortification" would result, all because Douglass was not yet capable of assuming an editorial chair. The implication of Clique insurgents was clear; he was still essentially childlike and would blunder without their supervision.[49]

Douglass vaguely sensed but never quite understood that his move to establish an independent enterprise in Rochester, a voluntarist stronghold, had tapped the Clique insurgents' "chord of prejudice" in all of its basic dimensions. If he was an uncultivated child requiring paternal missionary uplift, his defiance of insurgent guidance represented at once a case of youthful immaturity and of primitive, almost savagelike impulsiveness. Primitive childishness and savagery were but different aspects of the same general ethnocentric missionary perspective. Consequently, it was predictable that Clique members as well as many of their close insurgent associates would ultimately call Douglass, the independent black editor who had broken from them, "impulsive," "destitute of every principle of honor," "malevolent in spirit," "mercenary," and filled with "roguery"; and one noted, "His malice will have full swing." "Confidential[ly], I have always feared him," Clique confidant Abigail Kelley Foster acknowledged in late 1847 as the dispute was becoming quite heated. Richard Webb, a Dublin immediatist with very close personal ties to the Boston Clique, noted that both he and his wife found Douglass "a sort of reclaimed wild beast – & . . . it don't do to just judge him by our civilized rules." Indeed, "a strong dash of blood of the children of the burning sun in his veins" was causing all of the disruption within insurgent circles. No Clique member even reprimanded Webb for this characterization of the problem, although Maria Chapman considered it exaggerated. Like Webb, Clique insurgents sensed that they were losing control of the undeveloped black child they were required to uplift. Consequentially, they were disposed to see Douglass' quest for independent selfhood as a sign that, without proper Christian guidance, he was reverting to at least a bit of the primitive. By 1849, as the dispute grew more intense and as Douglass even started to move away from insurgent nonvoting moral suasion doctrine, Clique participants began seriously to consider separating themselves from him. Their protégé seemed to have gone too far – physically and emotionally

– beyond the boundaries for effective insurgent uplift. As Wendell Phillips, the Clique participant for whom Douglass felt the strongest attraction, acknowledged to Elizabeth Pease in 1852, "Douglass is completely estranged from us," and, unfortunately, beyond "our" influence.[50]

The changing relationship of Douglass to the Boston Clique therefore illustrated, more generally, how "the chord of prejudice" and its most essential ingredient, ethnocentric missionary paternalism, had intensified during the 1840s and 1850s to the point where it could embitter the strongest white immediatist proponents of the biracial experiment. But if this negative strain within biracialism had intensified during the late antebellum decades, another dimension to the Douglass episode revealed that the positive strain was still quite important. Gerrit Smith, a leading voluntarist, reached out to embrace Douglass intellectually and emotionally in the very years when Clique insurgents sought to separate themselves from him. The embrace was reminiscent of the first days of the immediatist crusade, when young reformers in the field felt consumed with flowing empathy for the free Negro who refused to go to Africa. At least Lewis Tappan understood it that way and urged the stewards in his circle to support the new Douglass–Smith bond of intimacy.

When Smith moved to befriend Douglass during the late 1840s and early 1850s, his intimacy group of upstate New York voluntarists had been reduced to himself and William Goodell. There is some suggestion that one of his motives for seeking out Douglass was to bring the first Negro into his all-white intimacy circle, perhaps to bring over Lewis Tappan and certain other stewards as well and in this way to revive his group somehow. Together with Goodell, he frequently conversed with Douglass and, over time, made Douglass increasingly receptive to the basic voluntarist doctrines of his old intimacy circle. Above all, Smith and Goodell convinced Douglass of the validity of two fundamental voluntarist positions that were anathema to Clique insurgents, if somewhat less objectionable to Tappanite stewards: the importance of antislavery electoral politics of the Liberty party–Liberty League variety and Alvan Steward's old voluntarist interpretation of the federal Constitution as an antislavery document. Disenchantment with Boston Clique insurgency and the persuasive arguments of Smith and Goodell contributed to Douglass' acceptance of these voluntarist positions. But so did money. Douglass' initial Rochester newspaper, the *North Star*, experienced the very financial strains that doomed most contemporary black journalistic ventures. Early in 1851 Smith proposed a remedy. He would provide a substantial subsidy, and he persuaded Lewis Tappan to supplement it, provided that Douglass allowed the *North Star* to merge with the voluntarist upstate New York *Liberty Party Paper* that Smith financed. The publication that would come of this merger, *Frederick Douglass' Paper*, was to be entirely under Douglass' control as long as Douglass opened it to local and national Liberty party news. Since Liberty party news would largely be upstate and voluntarist in orientation, Douglass would obviously find it easier to run the paper the more receptive he became to voluntarist ideas. But more than voluntarist ideas and financial support moved Smith and Douglass together with the acquiescence of Lewis Tappan. "You not only keep life in my paper but keep spirits in me," Douglass confided to his new patron. Whereas Clique insurgents had warned Douglass that he lacked editorial skills, Smith said quite the reverse, encouraging the black activist and augmenting his sense of self-worth. Indeed, whereas Clique reformers were adamant in the view that white immediatists were to be the editors and blacks confined to lecturing duties, Smith conveyed a different message which Lewis Tappan supported. He was replacing John Thomas, a white editor of the Liberty Party Paper whose journalistic skills were not excessive, with a black man as editor of the merged North Star and Liberty Party Press. Moreover, Smith was allowing that black man to name the merged publication Frederick Douglass' Paper. Finally, whereas Clique insurgents rarely welcomed blacks into their strategy sessions and social festivities at Maria Chapman's house, Gerrit Smith warmly welcomed Douglass to his Peterboro estate, urged Douglass to visit frequently, and told him that no advanced notice was ever required. Clearly, Douglass was the recipient of Smith's trust and empathetic embrace as well as of his and Lewis Tappan's money.[51]

This is not to say that Smith, much less Tappan, was free of prejudice. Like most other first-generation white immediatists in the late antebellum years, both thought increasingly about forging working alliances with more moderate antislavery whites that enlarged the audience for basic immediatist principles. Much more than shoring up biracialism, this motivated them to labor in the new American Abolition Society of the mid-1850s and, through its organ, the Radical Abolitionist party, to try to attract dissident white Republicans. Moreover, both Smith and Tappan displayed the pervasive immediatist ethnocentric missionary perspective under which pious whites felt duty bound to set standards for unenlightened blacks. Smith, for example, frequently agreed to fund missionary ventures to supervise "dwarfed" blacks so that their "undisciplined" qualities might be eradicated. By late 1856 Tappan was so upset with Douglass and other black editors for their "wrongheaded" advocacy of "brutal" slave violence against the planter class that he threatened to eliminate financial support unless they towed the mark.[52] But unlike the staid head of the steward circle, by the mid-1840s Gerrit Smith of the voluntarists had also cultivated a remarkable capacity to feel for his black immediatist colleagues – to understand how "they have come to despair of the accomplishment of this [antislavery] work by . . . even the most loud-mouthed abolitionists." Indeed, one of Smith's proudest moments was when the editor of the Ram's Horn, a black New York City reform newspaper, ventured to characterize him: "Gerrit Smith is a colored man!" "It pleased me – perhaps flattered me – to be so called," Smith acknowledged. To live up to the characterization, he felt that he had to always "show by my vote, that I am still 'a colored man.' " Smith's intense desire to empathize with the Negro – to be a colored man – helps to explain why, by the late antebellum decades, more blacks corresponded with him than with any other white abolitionist. Although most of the letters blacks wrote to Smith contained financial requests, many of them also singled him out for his unusual powers of empathy.[53]

In the years when he was moving away from the Boston Clique, Douglass' frequent letters to Smith certainly demonstrate that, like many other blacks, he sought out the Peterboro voluntarist for financial backing. They also reveal that Douglass was quite taken by the "realism" and political power that voluntarist third-party and constitutional ideas promised blacks as compared with insurgent ideas. But most importantly, Douglass' letters demonstrate that he had at last found a friend who felt for him and to whom he could reveal some of the dilemmas in his complex quest for a sense of selfhood. Smith gave him the "spirit" to struggle with these dilemmas, he acknowledged. "I do confide much in your judgment," he noted on another occasion, and "therefore solicit a few lines." Unlike Clique insurgents, and even unlike Tappan, Smith gave him confidence in himself: "You are a little more than just to me in your estimate of my ability." The more he communicated with Smith, Douglass noted, the better he was able to handle Boston Clique attacks and the more he felt "a consciousness of my own rectitude." By August 1853 Smith's empathy and eagerness to hear Douglass articulate his complex feelings had reached a new plateau. With Smith, and not with Clique insurgents, Douglass felt that he could be frank and critical without fearing repercussions. Douglass told the recently elected congressman that he would be of little use to blacks unless he became a master of parliamentary rules so that he could effectively fight for their interests in Washington. Then Douglass added: "Now just hear the impertinence of this runaway slave!! Ah! but he knows who he is talking to."[54]

With the crucial relationship between Smith and Douglass in mind, we therefore see how Frederick Douglass' controversy with the Boston Clique revealed the essential strands in abolitionist biracialism during the 1840s and 1850s as well as the fluidities within the biracial experiment. The bitter conflict between Douglass and Clique insurgents illustrated the powerful negative strand, or "chord of prejudice," in operation – fostering emotional as well as physical distance between the races. But the developing relationship between Smith and Douglass that Lewis Tappan eagerly supported illustrated how the second strand, interracial understanding, egalitarianism, and empathy, could also come into play, even between a white immediatist committed to an ethnocentric missionary perspective and a black immediatist who was torn between his blackness and his whiteness. Indeed, even as "the chord of prejudice" pulled Clique insurgents away from Douglass, it is well to recall that they drew closer to William Nell, another black leader and former Douglass associate on the *North Star* in his campaign to integrate Boston's public schools.

The Frederick Douglass controversy, and the general problem of white–black relationships that it illustrated, obviously fit within a larger set of developments that we shall examine more fully in the next three chapters. Among these developments, the tendency of first-generation immediatists to forge bonds with more moderate antislavery whites was especially important. Judging from experiences within our three focal immediatist groups and from other evidence, this tendency was serving both to reduce the importance of the abolitionists' old intimacy circles and to decrease the utility of their biracial ventures. Few immediatists considered reversing these trends by admitting blacks to white intimacy groups and by restoring the full primacy of those groups as the heart of the abolitionist social and emotional experience. It is, of course, possible that the increasingly conspicuous role of women within the abolitionist crusade eased certain white immediatists' apprehensions of moral taint as they reached out for less than devout antislavery moderates, seemed less concerned with their old if pious intimacy circles, and allowed biracialism to deteriorate. Nevertheless, we must not lose sight of the fact that strong and highly personalized white–black relationships remained quite possible under these changing general circumstances, as layers of prejudice mixed with layers of egalitarian ideology and empathy to produce widely diverse contacts between the races. Moreover, although old intimacy clusters were weakening, they did not cease to exist. Two of our focal groups – the Boston Clique and Tappan circle – survived the Civil War, and there were efforts to restore the badly disintegrating Smith circle. First-generation immediatism was transformed significantly, but old patterns did not always completely disappear as new values and new friendships emerged.

CHAPTER 7

RIGHTEOUS VIOLENCE

If historians have tended to make little of general transformations, over time, in immediatist thoughts and actions on the woman question and the biracial experiment, they have been very attentive to transformations on the "peace question." They have characterized immediatists at the beginning of their mission to the slaves as moral suasionists intent on the power of virtuous argument to persuade others of the need for emancipation. By the time the Emancipation Proclamation was promulgated, according to conventional historical wisdom, these same immediatists had left their peace principles behind and had accepted violence and coercion as necessary and appropriate means to their goal. Consequently, the preponderance of scholarship on the peace question has focused on reasons for the shift from moral suasion to violence. Some historians have seen it as a logical response to external events of the prewar period, such as the murder of Elijah Lovejoy, the enforcement of the 1850 Fugitive Slave Act, "bleeding Kansas," and John Brown's raid on Harpers Ferry. Others have characterized the accommodation as the result of immediatists' images of themselves as agents for the Lord in a noble crusade. If Americans refused to listen to their moral preachings for the peaceful eradication of slavery, they felt compelled to take "the Devil's weapons in hand" and to strike out at slavery. Still other historians have found the embrace of violence a predictable result of their support for the Union cause during the Civil War. To triumph, the Union had to deploy force and violence; to help assure that triumph, immediatists had to acquiesce in violent means.[1]

All of these explanations for immediatists' changed attitude toward violence overlap, as historians have clearly recognized. More important, all assume that an unambiguous or "pristine" immediatist commitment to moral suasion in the 1830s was transformed into an enthusiastic acceptance of violent means as the Civil War erupted. If we regard the transformation as considerably less clear-cut, the standard historical explanations become problematic. As we trace the evolution of first-generation immediatist positions on force and violence, it will become apparent that the transformation was neither clear nor direct. A dual commitment to moral suasion and violent means was evident from the start, with interesting variations among immediatists in the nature of the mix. Whereas violence became more attractive as time passed, most immediatists never relinquished their peace principles. Therefore, we are seeking explanation for a transformation not from pacifism to advocacy of force but from a rough equilibrium between moral suasion and violent means to a situation where commitment to violence gained general but never total hegemony.

As we analyze specific immediatist words and deeds from the 1830s to the 1860s, we shall have to explain why this shift occurred. Two general and complementary explanations will be offered. The first will focus upon the ethnocentric missionary perspective that set abolitionists upon their reform careers and helped to persuade them to accept women as co-missionaries while increasingly distancing blacks as heathen to uplift. We shall see how this very perspective lent itself to a Manichaean good–bad frame of mind that allowed immediatists to cultivate necessary emotional distance between themselves and those who were the subjects of their violent thoughts and actions. Our second explanation of the shift toward violent means is rooted in the immediatist quest to befriend a wider circle of associates while retaining their sense of personal piety. Increased contact with women as repositories of morality and many other variables disposed immediatists to reach out for certain less-than-pious white antislavery moderates. Much like their associations with female missionaries, working relationships with these moderates tended to loosen the emotional bonds that held together their old intimacy circles. As the intimacy circles (particularly the rapidly disintegrating Gerrit Smith circle) began to lose some of their attraction, immediatists became even more desirous of building bridges with antislavery moderates who lacked their firm commitment to biracialism and who did not share their professed peace principles in the battle against the Southern Slave Power. They made concessions to the values of the moderates in these areas – even more, we shall see, on the peace question than on the issue of biracialism. These concessions weakened their old intimacy groups further, for considerations outside group life were determining public stances. A cycle was therefore being set into motion through gender contacts, white–black relationships, and now the turn to violent means; it was altering the basic state of immediatists' social and emotional existence.

II

As we trace the changes in abolitionists' attitudes and actions on the peace question, we would be foolish to deemphasize the centrality of their early commitment to moral suasion. In 1832, for example, the New England Anti-Slavery Society pledged itself to "peaceful and lawful [antislavery] means, and that we will give no countenance to violence or insurrection." The following year, the newly organized American Anti-Slavery Society resolved that abolitionists would never resort to violence and would never "countenance the oppressed in vindicating their rights by resorting to physical force." In July of 1833 John Greenleaf Whittier observed, "All the leading abolitionists of my acquaintance are, from principle, opposed to war of all kinds, believing that the benefits of no war whatever can compensate for the sacrifice of one human life by violence." Four years later William Ladd, founder of the American Peace Society, was able to assert that "every antislavery man is a peace man; or at least I have known but two or three exceptions."[2]

There were many illustrations that Whittier and Ladd might have cited to show how pacifism seemed inseparable from the early commitment to immediatism. There was Garrison's impassioned condemnation of *David Walker's Appeal* because it advised slaves to use violence to secure their freedom. According to the leader of Boston Clique insurgency, forceful resistance was solely the prerogative of the Lord. And there was the dynamic young steward, Theodore Weld, who, while championing manual labor in literary institutions, insisted that military exercises must never become part of manual labor unless "human butchery [becomes] the ordinary business of life." In the face of heckling by white youths at his New Haven antislavery meeting and their subsequent assault upon his house, Simeon Jocelyn proudly reported that he refused to retaliate: "I have not resorted to carnal weapons of defense nor to the civil power." Occurrences during the 1830s such as these can be multiplied manyfold.[3]

Historian Robert Abzug has observed that insurgent immediatists of the 1830s may even have been more fearful of violence than they were apprehensive of the "peculiar institution"; they perceived rapid emancipation as the only way to head off bloody slave rebellions through the South. But Arthur and Lewis Tappan, Joshua Leavitt, William Jay, and others of their intimacy circle shared these perceptions, and so did many other young stewards and voluntarists. As they persistently counseled slaves against violent uprisings, they realized that it would appear absurd to veer from pacific means in their own daily activities. As Sarah Grimké warned Gerrit Smith, it was folly to urge "the poor slaves patiently to endure their afflictions and submit to a system which jeopardizes their lives every day while we resist the same kind of irresponsible and assumed power to shield our own lives from violence. We do ourselves, what we profess to think wrong for them to do."[4]

These immediatist apprehensions during the 1830s of slave rebellions pointed to much the same thing that their vivid characterizations of the bloodiness and cruelty of Southern bondage revealed. They were keenly attentive to the destructiveness and exploitation of Southern slaveholders. What Kenneth Keniston observed for the young pacifist reformer of the 1960s can be said with equal force for many a young immediatist of the 1830s:

He works toward a vague vision of a peaceful world, but he must confront more directly than most of his peers the warfare of the world. The frustrations of his work repetitively reawaken his rage, which must continually be redirected into peaceful paths. Combating destructiveness and exploitation in others, his own destructiveness and desire to exploit are inevitably aroused.[5]

It is almost impossible to turn to an early immediatist pamphlet, newspaper, sermon, or sketch of Southern slavery without sensing what their admonitions against slave rebellion made patently clear – that immediatist destructive and combative propensities were sharply aroused. One finds this feeling, for example, in Garrison's March 1837 letter to the *Boston Courier* claiming that "ours [immediatists'] will be a battle which the PRINCE OF PEACE can direct, and ours a victory which angels can applaud." And one detects it in central New York voluntarist Jabez Hammond's apprehensions early in 1836 of slave-holding states annexing Texas from Mexico: "The project ought to be resisted unto blood." Indeed, there were several occasions in the 1830s where immediatists actually prepared to draw blood – to breach their principles – if initially only in self-defense. During the 1834 antiabolitionist riots in New York City, for example, Arthur Tappan armed the clerks in his silk warehouse and ordered them to fire at the legs of all rioters who entered the building. At that moment, Elizur Wright stood at the door of his home with an axe in his hand. The following year, after a Utica mob forced members of the voluntarist New York State Anti-Slavery Society to retreat to Gerrit Smith's Peterboro estate to conclude their meeting, rumor spread that mobsters were coming to assault the voluntarists again. Consequently they "prepared their fire arms to surround the Church and to shoot down the Utica Mob. . . ." During an 1836 meeting of the Ohio Anti-Slavery Society at Granville, participants actually raised clubs and dispersed an antiabolitionist mob. That same year, James Birney thoroughly armed his home in anticipation of mob attack. It was occurrences such as these, when immediatists broke with strict moral suasion doctrine and displayed willingness to use violence (if only in self-defense), that moved Sarah Grimké toward the "painful discovery that few of those engaged in the holy cause have their hearts fixed trusting in the Lord alone, that most of them are willing to say at least that the arm of violence should be raised for their protection."[6]

Contrary to prevailing historical explanations, then, immediatists commenced their acceptance of violence at the same time that they proclaimed their commitment to moral suasion over violent means. The two went hand in hand, with avidly aggressive pacifism masking, in some measure, a willingness on the part of many to deploy force in their own defense. Perhaps this was entirely predictable. Consistent, un-ambiguous pacifism has probably always been more a reformer's ideal than a reality of social life. As Jacques Lacan observed, humans are aggressive in any sort of association with others, even in the most Samaritan of relationships and the most altruistic of crusades.[7]

In November 1837 Elijah Lovejoy, an immediatist editor from Alton, Illinois, determined to protect his fourth new printing press after local ruffians had destroyed the first three. With the permission of Alton's mayor, he and certain of his local abolitionist supporters secured pistols. When a mob formed to wreck the fourth press and launched an attack, Lovejoy raised his pistol but was quickly gunned down. Reaction to this episode more than to any other event during the early years of the immediatist crusade demonstrated how moral suasion and violent means went hand in hand.

None of the immediatists who voiced opinions about the Lovejoy episode defended the use of weapons and violence for offensive pur-poses. From a technical standpoint, the differences among them cen-tered on whether Lovejoy was justified in raising a pistol in self-defense. Yet one cannot help but sense that most immediatists regarded the distinction between offensive and defensive violence as an abstraction of altogether secondary importance. On an emotional level, what most concerned them was whether violent means were justifiable per se.

A very small minority of abolitionists, mostly insurgents, unequivo-cally condemned Lovejoy for violating the imperatives of moral suasion by deploying a weapon. The Junior Anti-Slavery Society of Philadelphia, a Quaker organization, voted to "condemn in the most decided terms, the course of our friends at Alton, in resorting to physical force." Henry Wright was frightened because Lovejoy and his Alton antislavery colleagues were "arming themselves with deadly weapons in self-defense; and . . . in so doing, they forfeited the protection of God." They had caused the immediatist campaign to be "stained with blood." Angelina Grimké concurred, charging "that there is no such thing as trusting in God and *pistols* at the same time." Sarah Grimké was even more bitter with what Lovejoy had done to abolitionism, wondering "how can we expect his [God's] blessing upon our efforts, if we take carnal weapons to fight his battles?" But beyond these few and primarily Quaker or ex-Quaker insurgent voices, the researcher is hard pressed to find abolitionists who saw nothing beneficial or even admirable in Lovejoy's resistance.[8]

A considerably larger number of immediatists (although still a mi-nority) totally opposed this posture. They lauded Lovejoy and his supporters in all particulars, even in the use of weaponry. These proponents came from diverse immediatist clusters: Wendell Phillips from the Boston Clique, Tappan circle stewards Amos Phelps and Joshua Leavitt, and young reformers such as Elizur Wright, Jr., William

H. Burleigh, and Lydia Child, who sometimes drifted between clusters. They referred to Lovejoy as a "martyr of God" who struck "for Liberty with an unwavering faith and arm of might!" No abolitionist could be truly antislavery "without employing just such measures" as Lovejoy invoked. Even when he drew his pistol, Lovejoy was acting as "the minister of God" and "a terror to evil doers." His actions had clearly demonstrated "that emancipation must come through violence." With these phrases they were able to defeat (by better than a two to one margin) a motion that Whittier had made at the 1838 annual meeting of the American Anti-Slavery Society that would have condemned Lovejoy's use of weaponry.[9]

The overwhelming number of abolitionists who commented on the Lovejoy episode mixed praise with condemnation, accurately registering the general ambivalence of the early immediatist crusade on the question of violent means. As with those who had nothing but praise for Lovejoy, the motives behind this ambivalent majority did not seem to derive from activities within informal immediatist clusters. Like the woman question and biracialism, the issue of violence often seemed to shift immediatist minds away from their clusters. A mix of praise and reprimand characterized not only stewards like Lewis Tappan and Simeon Jocelyn and Smith circle voluntarists like William Goodell but such adamant nonresistance insurgents of the Boston Clique as Garrison, Nathaniel Rogers, and Maria Weston Chapman. On the one hand, they praised Lovejoy for "the glory of martyrdom" and for acting "like our blessed Savior" and within "the spirit of 'Seventy-Six'." He had followed "the example of our revolutionary fathers" in turning back "enemies of public order, liberty, and humanity." Indeed he had sustained "the supremacy of law against anarchists and ruffians." On the other hand, Lovejoy committed a grievous sin in deploying weaponry and thereby breaking from the pious principles of moral suasion. It was "unfortunate" to learn of "that great, noble and good man's falling with a vile implement of human warfare in his hand." In all probability, "God permitted such a failure of the war principle to show abolitionists the folly of their using carnal weapons." Had Lovejoy and his followers retained a pure pacific approach, the martyr might not have been killed. But even if he and some of his supporters had been killed under those circumstances, "the spilling of the blood of defenseless men would have produced a more thrilling and abiding effect."[10]

Most immediatists were obviously unable either to condemn Lovejoy flatly or to praise him without qualification; they remained committed to moral suasion by strongly objecting to his recourse to force, even in self-defense. At the same time, they admired his willingness to defend "liberty" forcefully, as "our revolutionary fathers" had done. On the most basic level, the episode revealed that by the late 1830s most immediatists were roughly where they had been at the beginning of

their first decade – propounding peace principles while remaining receptive to violent means. There was no acceptance of violence in 1837 or
at any earlier point in time. Save for Henry Wright, the Grimké sisters,
and a few others, moral suasionists had endorsed violent means from
the beginning.

III

If immediatists subscribed to violent means as well as to peace principles
during the 1830s, the commitment to force and violence was hardly
dominant. Indeed, abolitionists rarely attempted to justify deployment
of force for more than self-defense, while they advocated pacifism as the
more general pattern of conduct. Gradually in the course of the 1840s
and 1850s, they became increasingly receptive to violent means to
remedy widely diverse problems. The balance between pacifism and
force therefore shifted from its position during the 1830s. Nevertheless,
peace principles continued to be widely held, even after John Brown's
raid on Harpers Ferry and during the Civil War. First-generation immediatist ambivalence on the peace question never ceased.

The first signs of the increasing if ambivalent receptivity to violence
were evident in the early 1840s before the outbreak of the Mexican
War. On the surface, this change appeared confined to seemingly
unrelated specifics, as when insurgent Stephen Foster urged the
governor of Massachusetts to send troops to Charleston, South Carolina, to sustain an agent of the American Anti-Slavery Society. During
this interval, steward George Cheever became a national spokesman for
capital punishment. Voluntarist Alvan Stewart began to argue that
national military necessity would require freeing the slaves and then
arming them. Anticipating what was to become a widespread position a
decade later, West Roxbury immediatist Sarah Shaw favored resistance
to any effort to return fugitive slaves to bondage.[11]

More generally, increasing receptivity to violent means was detectable
during the early 1840s in a new abolitionist posture on slave revolts.
The 1830s posture – that slaves would have to be quickly emancipated
for bloody revolts to be averted – continued to be widely voiced. But the
slave revolt itself had ceased to be perceived as an unmitigated horror.
To the contrary, the steward-dominated American and Foreign Anti-
Slavery Society lauded the bravery and humanity of the bondsmen
aboard the slaveship *Creole* who rose up and secured their freedom. The
Liberty party's 1844 platform explicitly sanctioned slave uprisings:
"When freemen unsheath the sword it should be to strike for *Liberty*, not
for despotism." Steward William Jay defended the "justifiable homicide"
of the Africans aboard the *Amistad* who fought for "the recovery of
personal liberty." Voluntarists Alvan Stewart and Gerrit Smith proclaimed that slave insurrections were entirely justifiable and recom-

mended abolitionist complicity. Even Boston Clique nonresister Nathaniel Rogers defended revolts "by force," since slavery "exterminates their [blacks'] very natures." Clearly, these departures from early 1830s apprehensions of violent uprising were not restricted to specific immediatist clusters. Indeed, few immediatists of any sort fretted over Henry Highland Garnet's widely publicized plea in 1843 at a National Colored Convention in Buffalo for slaves to "strike for your lives and liberties."[12]

This is not to say that immediatists had shed or repudiated moral suasion during the early 1840s. Few who even modestly defended peace principles in the 1830s came close to renouncing them. It was during this period that immediatists became the key figures in both the American Peace Society and the New England Non-Resistance Society. Lewis Tappan refused to contribute to Bunker Hill monument construction "because of my peace principles," while William Jay forged the concept of compulsory arbitration in disputes between nations. James Birney and Theodore Foster worked (unsuccessfully) to secure a Michigan State Anti-Slavery Society platform calling for gradual extinction of the national armed forces.[13]

Clearly, immediatists continued to favor both moral suasion and violent means during the early 1840s. Nonetheless, there were noticeable if modest shifts in their ambivalent postures. They appeared more desirous of organizational or collective support behind their peace principles and less willing to espouse them alone; moral suasion seemed less an individualistic person-to-person plea. More significant, there were clear signs that strong peace men could become receptive to force when that force appeared compatible with their missionary sense of righteousness. The balance in their mutual endorsement of pacifism and violence therefore seemed to be tilting, if only modestly.

Between the outbreak of the Mexican War in May 1846 and John Brown's raid on Harpers Ferry in October of 1859, this slight tilt became a decided shift. Acceptance of violence became much more discernible, although it never supplanted strong commitments to moral suasion. Brief perusal of first-generation immediatists' response to three events – the Mexican War, enforcement of the 1850 Fugitive Slave Act, and "bleeding Kansas" – makes this clear.

Because war with Mexico was provoked, in some measure, by Southern planter efforts to extend slavery westward with federal complicity, almost all immediatists opposed the American war effort. But this fact has caused too many historians to assume that they remained unrelenting proponents of moral suasion. This simply was not the case. Moral suasion caused them to regret deeply that America had taken up arms in defense of slavery against an "innocent" nation. But their willingness to use violent means for moral missionarylike benevolent goals made them proponents of the Mexican war effort. As combat

broke out in May 1846, for example, Clique insurgent Samuel May, Jr.,
launched an open protest, arguing that war was unjustifiable under any
conditions or for any purposes "unless it be to resist the invaders of our
hearth-stones. That exception I am not quite prepared to withhold." By
September, May was convinced that America was the invader of the
Mexican hearthstones. Therefore, he combined his pacifism with endorsement of violent means: "If there must be fighting, which I do not
desire, I hope the United States arms will be defeated." May's posture
was echoed by his good friend Garrison:

I desire to see human life at all times held sacred; but, in a struggle like this, so
horribly unjust and offensive on our part, so purely of self-defence [sic] against
lawless invaders on the part of the Mexicans, – I feel, as a matter of justice, to
desire the overwhelming defeat of the American troops, and the success of the
injured Mexicans.

Garrison's Boston Clique confidant Edmund Quincy also professed
abhorrence of the war but wished Mexico "success in her attempts to
defend her liberty against the slaveholding tyranny of the United
States." Indeed, Quincy was "heartily in hope that we shall be well *licked*
in Mexico." Abigail Kelley Foster went further. Like May, Jr., Garrison,
and Quincy, she abhorred the war as a violation of moral suasion
principles and hoped for Mexican military victory. Moreover, in May
1846 she stood up at the New England Anti-Slavery Convention to
oppose a peace resolution on the ground that Massachusetts abolitionists might soon have to take up arms to defend their homes. By the
mid-1840s, pacifist posturing seemed more obstructionist for Foster
than useful.[14]

In addition to insurgents like May, Jr., Garrison, Quincy, and Foster,
one would naturally expect to find more temperate immediatists of the
1830s, such as Henry Stanton and Elizur Wright, Jr., who had never
been terribly reticent about violent means, clamoring for the victory of
Mexican armies.[15] More than anything else, however, the reaction to
the Mexican War indicated that immediatist leaders of the New England
nonresistance movement – the strongest proponents of moral suasion
in the abolitionist crusade – were now mixing their peace principles with
hopes that virtuous Mexican arms would destroy sinful American
troops. This represented a noticeable extension of the tilt toward violence that abolitionists had generally evidenced earlier in the 1840s.
While retaining strong commitments to moral suasion, the strongest
pacifists among them found themselves endorsing more than isolated
acts of force in self-defense or even slave uprisings. In their opposition
to a slaveholder expansion westward and the federal invasion of a
foreign territory, they championed the Mexican armies in their efforts
at organized destruction of American troops. Santa Anna, the warrior,
seemed almost as great a savior as Christ, the nonresistant. Both were
missionaries for righteous causes.

Thus, within the context of their traditional endorsement of moral suasion and violent means, the Mexican War saw several first-generation immediatists unambiguously adapt to the use of violence – a decided shift from their 1830s posture, according to which pacifism was the norm and force the sometimes justifiable exception. This shift was intensified by implementation of the 1850 Fugitive Slave Law, which required public officials in Northern communities to assist Southern planters in apprehending their runaway bondsmen. The law was so invidious to all immediatists that Henry Wright, who condemned Lovejoy in 1837 and remained an unambiguous moral suasionist throughout the 1840s, finally came to justify violence. Slaves should escape bondage through whatever means or weapons happened to be necessary, Wright maintained, and Northerners were morally required to assist them, even if killing might be involved. Angelina Grimké Weld was another uncompromising moral suasionist finally driven by the sight of legally sanctioned slave catchers in Northern communities to endorse violent means: "It is clear to my mind that the Fugitive Slave Act *ought* to be, *must* be resisted even unto blood." Lewis Tappan insisted that Christians could not comply with the act. In October 1851 insurgent Samuel J. May and voluntarist Gerrit Smith were part of the vigilance committee that forcefully abducted fugitive slave Jerry McHenry from the Syracuse police, cut McHenry's shackles, and sent him to Canada. Similarly, Smith's close voluntarist associate, William Chaplin, fought with Washington, D.C., police in August of 1850 as he attempted to rescue a group of fugitive slaves. Chaplin characterized his conduct as obedience to the laws of heaven. The missionary could deploy force if the cause was moral.[16]

Despite these blatant justifications of violence, and despite their forceful defiance of the Fugitive Slave Law, first-generation immediatists had not abandoned their peace principles. Rather, they struggled to demonstrate that their conduct was compatible with those principles. Stephen Foster, for example, claimed that because he was a nonresister, he could not bring himself to oppose the infamous 1850 statute forcefully. He could only urge others to do so if their consciences would let them. Lydia Child expressed a similar posture in her critique of the Anthony Burns fugitive slave rescue in Boston. Had the rescue been planned secretly and conducted suddenly, "the poor slave might have been rescued without shedding blood." Samuel J. May agreed with Child on the Burns rescue. Just prior to the Jerry McHenry rescue, he told the vigilance group organized for the task: "If any one is to be hurt in this fray, I hope it may be one of our own party." Force and violence had become necessary as sinful slave catchers moved through Northern communities, but aid to the fugitive slave was to be as unaggressive as possible. Force had somehow to be made peaceful or at least mild and righteous if immediatists were to continue to see themselves as consistent with their divinely inspired principles of moral suasion.[17]

The outbreak of hostilities between proslavery interests and Free Soilers in Kansas in the middle 1850s also illustrated how first-generation immediatists, still exalting moral suasion, were accommodating themselves increasingly to force and violence. Most were strongly supportive of the antislavery forces in the area. Many contributed funds to the New England Emigrant Aid Company so that more antislavery men might be settled in Kansas and the settlers might be provided with rifles to defend themselves. Gerrit Smith was a major donor even though he simultaneously held office in the American Peace Society. "Much as I do abhor war," Smith proclaimed, "I nevertheless believe, that there were instances where the shedding of blood was unavoidable." It was necessary to beat "back the tide of border ruffianism and slavery." Similarly, while claiming that moral suasion was the most effective vehicle in the Kansas struggle, Wendell Phillips donated money to a rifle fund for antislavery forces in the area. While Stephen Foster acknowledged that he personally could not fight in the territory, he suspected at times that those men who fought for a free Kansas might be as loving and as virtuous as any nonresistant missionaries he knew. Sarah Grimké similarly admitted that she could not condemn the Kansas freedom fighters and wondered if this underscored a basic flaw in her character. Angelina Grimké Weld best described this ambivalence that she felt in common with her sister and with many other first-generation immediatist supporters of free Kansas: "We are compelled to choose between two evils, and all that we can do is take the *least*, and baptize liberty in blood, if it must be so."[18]

Interestingly, Lewis Tappan, Garrison, and Goodell – leading figures in our focal steward, insurgent, and voluntarist clusters – underscored the muddled, logically contradictory thinking of most of their colleagues. The rough similarity of their responses to "bleeding Kansas" suggests, of course, that factors outside immediatist intimacy circles were shaping abolitionist attitutes. The three maintained that antislavery men in Kansas would be better off shunning physical force and clinging entirely to moral suasion. Still, each of the three acknowledged that theirs was a minority posture among immediatists. As Tappan admitted, "I am almost alone in inculcating the duty & sound policy of maintaining peace. Rifles, it is said, are peace weapons." Garrison and Goodell echoed these words. But all three also strongly implied that if Sharpe's rifles were moved out of Kansas and were pointed at Southern slaveholders, there might be some justification for immediatists' funding armaments. Violence to the South was apparently more consistent with the mission to the slaves.[19]

First-generation immediatist responses to the Mexican War, the 1850 Fugitive Slave Act, and "bleeding Kansas" demonstrated a decided if muddled shift in favor of violent means. Moral suasion had clearly ceased to operate as a general governing principle for most abolitionist actions. But the situation remained fluid. In some instances, for example, reformers such as Henry Wright and Sarah Grimké still held out for consistent and uncompromising pacifism. And in certain matters, such as Kansas, Tappan, Garrison, and Goodell might claim that their colleagues were going too far along the violent path, while they reserved the option to deploy force under specific circumstances. More generally and over the long haul, however, the problem was that immediatists often had difficulty articulating their thoughts clearly and consistently because they had retained their commitment to moral suasion as an obligation of the "head" while they found themselves increasingly sympathetic to violent means as a commitment of the "heart." Anne Warren Weston noted this opposed pull in 1855: "For myself alas! I am apt to *believe* in peace & sympathize with fighting." Three years later another Boston Clique intimate, Francis Jackson, came to the same realization: "I believe that the doctrine of Non-Resistance is true; altho' I have not been able to practice it because of my early training, & long habits to the contrary. . . ."[20] Even before John Brown's raid on Harpers Ferry in fall 1859, then, the fragile basis of immediatist nonviolence – a clash between "head" and "heart," professed principle and long habits – was apparent to at least two of its proponents. So were the results of that clash.

Indeed, first-generation immediatists as pacifists had spent nearly two decades acutely attentive to the violent barbarities against the black bondsmen they sought to free. During this period, they had also experienced aggressive verbal and physical attacks on their persons from mobsters and other hostile Northerners. All the while, few came to their rescue, and their intimacy circles did not seem to protect them adequately. They felt emotionally wounded – personally fragmented. They had never been entirely pacific, and their desires to strike out at the evils they regularly confronted were bound to increase with time. Aggression held out the promise of revitalizing the wounded self and perhaps even garnering the social approval so rarely secured by men who promoted peace. Their emotions often moved along these lines when they saw younger second-generation immediatists such as Theodore Parker and Thomas Wentworth Higginson urging forceful assault on the "Slave Power Conspiracy" in apparent unison with other somewhat more moderate antislavery Northerners such as Francis Bird and Franklin Sanborn. Advocacy of violence seemed to promise to move these isolated and emotionally wounded missionaries from their station as hated outsiders into greater rapport with a number of other Northerners. But if heightened calls for violent means held out the hope of revitalizing fractured emotional lives and satisfying immediatists' convivial instincts, these calls also threatened to undermine efforts to retain and augment the devotedness of their early years. They equated that presumed piety with early 1830s moral suasion principles. To betray those pristine founding principles was to acknowledge that they had come to assume the primitive and sinful qualities of the slaveholder and the antiabolitionist mobster. Therefore, first-generation immediatists felt strongly compelled somehow to reconcile combative activity with devout, pristine 1830s missionary virtue; a warrior who fought for freedom was to be distinguished from the infidel combatant who resisted freedom. At this crucial juncture, John Brown gained notoriety for his violent assault on slavery. Was he the saintlike warrior immediatists so desperately required, or did he furnish proof that moral principle could not be reconciled with warrior virtues?

IV

John Brown led his famous raid on Harpers Ferry arsenal in Virgina late in October 1859 to secure arms with which to liberate slaves forcefully. The band was captured and Brown was executed. On the day of his execution Brown handed a statement to a jail guard that became widely publicized in abolitionist circles: "I John Brown am now quite certain that the crimes of this *guilty* land: *will* never be purged *away*; but with blood. I had *as I now think; vainly* flattered myself that without *very much* bloodshed; it might be done." Not long after the raid, it became public knowledge that two very prominent first-generation immediatists – an insurgent and a voluntarist who had espoused moral suasion principles in the 1830s – were implicated in the raid. Wendell Phillips had been intimate with the secret committee that organized the assault and knew that it was being planned in the vicinity of Harpers Ferry. Gerrit Smith's role had been even more extensive. He had been a member of the secret committee itself and gave Brown financial support and moral encouragement, and Brown freely told Smith all of the details about the raid that Smith desired to know. Thus, Phillips and Smith, two household names among immediatists, were clearly accessories before the fact. Members of major abolitionist intimacy circles that had been devoted to peace principles, they were jointly supporting a man who had blatantly disavowed pacifism for violent means. Not only did these two veteran immediatists suggest an important general ideological shift; they also demonstrated how external conditions could undermine the long-standing doctrinal postures of the old immediatist intimacy groups.[21]

Brown's raid fostered a general sense of crisis among first-generation immediatists of all sorts. It was not difficult to convince oneself that one remained true to nonviolent convictions during the 1830s and even the early 1840s. In those years pacifist posturing along with leadership in the American Peace Society and the New England Non-Resistance Society had made it possible to ignore one's own aggressive propensities. It was possible, for example, to downplay one's qualified endorsement of

Lovejoy and of sundry slave revolts. To be sure, the Mexican War, the 1850 Fugitive Slave Law, and "bleeding Kansas" made it frightfully apparent to a small number of immediatists, particularly Anne Weston and Francis Jackson, that they were indeed accepting violence. But until Brown's raid, Brown's death-day repudiation of moral suasion, and the knowledge that Phillips and Smith had aided him, most immediatists were able to believe that they remained strong pacifists, even if justice to the slaves sometimes caused them to breach their principles. The Harpers Ferry raid and the facts that were publicized in its wake changed all that. Brown, the immediatist, had repudiated moral suasion in favor of violence; two of the most respected first-generation immediatists from two leading intimacy cirles had aided him. One seemed, therefore, to have two choices – to repudiate Brown fully and retain the conviction that one still embraced the "first" principles of the 1830s, or to endorse him, move from those principles, and spend a lifetime apprehensive that one had ceased to be devout.

Very few first-generation immediatists made the first choice. Only insurgent Adin Ballou, the founder of the utopian Hopedale community and a man who had regularly cooperated with members of the Boston Clique, was able to offer an extensive critique of Brown and of other abolitionists who justified Brown's violent means. Ballou's contention was clear and to the point. Because pacifism had been a basic immediatist moral doctrine from the beginning, Brown and all who in any way justified his bloody acts had sinned and were to be condemned. Had Christ and the Apostles attempted to eradicate slavery and other evils of the Roman Empire through such force and violence, there would have been no Christian legacy of universal love and goodwill. "We deplore that this case of John Brown should have been turned so effectively against Christian non-resistance," Ballou charged, "and made so seductive an argument for bloody resistance, insurrection, and revolution." He was especially shocked that Garrison and other strong missionaries for peace had given Brown even qualified endorsement; they were allowing abolitionism to embrace heathen barbarism. Garrison retorted that his friend Ballou was "somewhat lacking in magnanimity, in tenderness of spirit, and in a philosophical view of events," and he was right. By considering abolitionism entirely as an ideological construct, Ballou had lost sight of the fact that immediatists had never been complete pacifists; they had exhibited an aggressive side from the start. In the years before Harpers Ferry, they had become increasingly disposed, emotionally, toward violent means while retaining a strong professed commitment to moral suasion. Ballou had overlooked the evolution of the immediatist "heart" and had focused entirely upon the "head." He failed to see that whereas the "head" required a sense of consistent allegiance to saintly moral suasion principles, the "heart" had craved forceful revenge against the Slave Power and friendship with

Brown and other less-than-devout antislavery Northerners who also hated the Slave Power.[22]

Indeed, in the aftermath of the Brown raid, a minority of first-generation immediatists let the "heart" have total sway and made a complete break with moral suasion. Samuel May, Jr., found this break altogether satisfying. Although he was a member of the Boston Clique, he had never been terribly comfortable with moral suasion. Since "slavery is itself a continual state of War, violence, and Bloodshed, and cruelty," May asserted, any sort of resistance to it was morally justifiable, even "physical force and bloody means. . . ." Against Ballou's strong objections, the Worcester County South Division Anti-Slavery Society "resolved, that as Abolitionists we have no disclaimers, no apologies to offer for the recent attempt of certain anti-slavery men at Harpers Ferry to break the rod of the oppressor by the same means by which our revolutionary fathers secured our national independence. . . ." Similarly, Cincinnati immediatist Nathaniel Colver found no need to apologize for Brown's violent means: "I love John Brown, I perceive him as a noble specimen of my race." Lysander Spooner had become so irrevocably committed to Brown and righteous force that he wanted to hold the governor of Virginia hostage until Brown was released from prison. Wendell Phillips joined this minority by redefining moral suasion and the "head" so that it became compatible with violence and the "heart": "I believe in moral suasion. I believe the age of bullets is over. I believe the age of ideas is come. . . . Yet, let me say, in passing, that I think you can make a better use of iron than forging it into chains. If you must have the metal, put it into Sharpe's rifles." Responsive to the charge that Brown should have used printer's type to publicize his antislavery message rather than bullets, Phillips added: "Well, he fired one gun, and has had the use of the New York *Herald* and *Tribune* to repeat its echoes for a fortnight. Has any man ever used types better?"[23]

The overwhelming number of immediatists who commented on Harpers Ferry, however, sided neither with Ballou and the "head" nor with Phillips and the "heart." Rather, they struggled to retain what they perceived to have been a pristine 1830s balance between the two – between moral suasion doctrine and aggressive propensities – not quite realizing amid their muddled thoughts that they were participating in a general transformation in immediatist feelings on the peace question. Interestingly, Garrison emerged as chief spokesman for this majority that consisted of many stewards and voluntarists as well as insurgents and of second- as well as first-generation immediatists. The binding force of early immediatist clusters, the climate of intense factional feuding, and the difference between a first generation committed to moral suasion and a second generation that was not, all seemed to recede in the face of Father Garrison's unifying and soothing reconciliation of "heart" and "head." The old immediatist small group structures of the 1830s and the old habits of intramural rivalry were certainly less significant than they had been.

In one sense, Garrison's defense of Brown resembled his defense of Lovejoy twenty-two years earlier. Like Lovejoy, Brown had acted heroically and was a great martyr to the antislavery cause, although he was morally wrong for having resorted to force and violence. But on a deeper level, Garrison's defense of Brown registered the decided shift toward violent means, toward the "heart," and toward broadened social and political contacts that the abolitionist crusade had been experiencing in the decades since the Lovejoy murder. Careful not to repudiate moral suasion, Garrison clearly noted that the kind of force against slavery that Brown had deployed at Harpers Ferry was morally legitimate and true to the old mission to the slaves: "If there is danger on the one hand, lest there be a repudiation of the doctrine of non-resistance, through the sympathy and admiration felt for John Brown, there is more danger, on the other hand, that the brutal outcry raised against him as an outlaw, traitor, and murderer . . . will lead to unmerited censure of his course." For Garrison, like the overwhelming number of first-generation immediatists in late 1859, the old balance between pacifism and violence had shifted; the greatest danger was that moral suasion might stand in the way of righteous violence and that Brown might stand condemned by wrongheaded peace men like Ballou. Indeed, Garrison went further: "Give me, as a non-resistant, Bunker Hill, and Lexington, and Concord, rather than the cowardice and servility of a southern plantation." "As a peace man," he declared on the day of Brown's execution, "I am prepared to say, 'Success to every slave insurrection in the South.' " "An advocate of peace" would prefer violence to a "cowardly and servile spirit." Because Garrison claimed to believe in "the immense superiority of spirit over carnal weapons," he could not take up weapons, as Brown had. But he saw enormous moral good coming from Brown and other antislavery Northerners who, while not moral suasionists, were nevertheless true to "the doctrine of '76" and the heroism of the Founding Fathers in taking up arms and vindicating freedom. Old-line immediatists should welcome these men as colleagues in the cause. Ballou notwithstanding, neither John Brown who took up the sword for a righteous cause nor the moral suasionist who defended him was to be equated with the coarse, heathen Southern planter who forcefully maintained black bondsmen. A holy warrior on a mission for the slaves was not to be confused with a heathen warrior.[24]

Garrison's vindication of John Brown was echoed and sustained by first-generation immediatists of all varieties. There were Boston Clique members such as Henry Wright, Samuel J. May, and Edmund Quincy, Clique supporters such as Lydia Child and Charles Burleigh, voluntarists such as William Goodell, and stewards such as Lewis Tappan, John Fee and, of course, John Greenleaf Whittier.[25] Indeed, Whittier's "Brown of Ossawatomie" may have summed up the basic meaning of the immediatist acceptance of violence even better than Garrison had. One stanza in the poem described Brown's march toward the gallows, with the great hero allegedly stopping on the way to kiss a slave mother's child:

> The shadows of his stormy life that
> moment fell apart;
> And they who blamed the bloody hand
> forgave the loving heart.
> That kiss from all its guilty means redeemed the
> good intent,
> And round 'the grisly fighter's hair the
> martyr's aureole bent!

The bloody hand was vindicated when it struck for good intent, even though Whittier concluded his poem favoring Christian sacrifice over the raid of midnight terror.[26] Most immediatists had clearly accommodated themselves to the aggressive needs of their "hearts" even as they clung tenaciously to the premise that they remained consistent with moral suasionist tradition. If anything, Harpers Ferry seemed to make it easier to ward off Anne Weston's and Francis Jackson's sense that it was hazardous "to believe in peace and sympathize with fighting." Immediatist condemnation of Brown would only gratify slaveholders, who were themselves men of violence. On the other hand, by sanctioning Brown's righteous violence, immediatists might seek to heal internal emotional wounds and frustrations by calling for aggression against evil without appearing to be violating their commitment to moral suasion. When violence was patently righteous, it was consonant with the saintly peace principles of the 1830s. Many immediatists seemed, at least, to be convincing themselves of this.

By the outbreak of the Civil War, then, the overwhelming number of first-generation immediatists had arrived at positions on questions of moral suasion and violent means that they felt comfortable espousing. Reflecting the very gradual decline in the importance that immediatists attached to their intimacy circles, these postures did not originate, in the main, from those circles. An insurgent who had derived most of his thoughts from the Boston Clique (such as Adin Ballou) and a Smith circle voluntarist (such as Beriah Green) espoused identical positions with equal comfort. Literal interpreters of moral suasion as indispensable to the devout missionary, both Ballou and Green insisted on noncoercion and nonviolence in all particulars. Their intellectual commitments to pacifism had largely contained their aggressive propensities; the "head" firmly controlled the "heart." Other immediatists such as voluntarist Gerrit Smith and Clique insurgents Samuel May, Jr., and Wendell Phillips were also at ease, for they had totally broken from moral suasion; the "heart" had gained control over the "head." Although this second posture – unqualified endorsement of righteous violence – secured additional immediatist adherents as the war progressed, it never gained the following of most first-generation immediatists. Rather, the overwhelming number remained precisely where they had been in the aftermath of Harpers Ferry, retaining the conviction that their beliefs were consistent with pristine 1830s peace principles as they found substantial good accomplished through righteous violence.

During the war Garrison continued to exemplify this middle-course taken by the majority and drew substantial support from stewards and voluntarists as well as insurgents. He continued to propound the virtuous peace principles of his "head." He voiced pride, for example, that two of his sons, William, Jr., and Wendell, were conscientious objectors and regretted that a third son, George, had enlisted. When military drill was instituted at the Boston Latin School, Garrison asked that his fourth son, Francis, be excused because it violated the pacific 1830s immediatist ideals that both he and Francis prized. At the same time, he gave vent to his convivial "heart." Once he was convinced that the Lincoln administration and the Republican party were pursuing a war of emancipation, Garrison became a vehement supporter of the president and his war policy. He cooperated with diverse nonimmediatist Republicans who supported that policy and expressed pleasure at the company of these new antislavery associates. "All my sympathies and wishes are with the [federal] government, because it is entirely in the right," he insisted, and because its military policies were intended to "stop the further ravages of death, and to extinguish the ravishes of hell." A righteous military crusade stopped the "ravages of death" and was therefore, in a rough sense, like a virtuous missionary crusade for peace. Between Sumter and Appomattox most other first-generation immediatists echoed the words of the man who, for the first time since the breach with the Colonization Society, seemed to symbolize a new if fragile and perhaps transient unity within the abolitionist crusade that appeared to transcend long-standing intimacy circles and intramural feuds. Garrison's words and deeds showed them how, through the notion of righteous missionary force and violence, immediatists might befriend a wider circle of antislavery proponents of the federal war effort while remaining broadly consistent with moral suasion principles of old. It appeared that the pacific and faithful "head" could, at least momentarily, feel at one with the cordial if aggressive "heart." In this sense, Father Garrison and righteous violence held out a hope of healing the immediatist's rather worn and fragmented sense of emotional existence.[27]

V

Thus far our primary goal has been to describe more than to explain the first-generation immediatist acceptance of violence. It has been characterized as a process that commenced in the early 1830s by which immediatists acquired a capacity "to believe in peace and sympathize with fighting." These dual commitments – to moral suasion as a professed principle and a general guide to pious conduct, on the one hand, and to aggression as an emotional need, on the other – coexisted during the first decade of the immediatist crusade. But beginning in the early 1840s, as immediatists clearly began to sanction violence for more than self-defense, the emotional needs for aggression, force, and violence gradually began to secure hegemony; the acceptance of violence commenced. The accommodation process concluded during the weeks that followed John Brown's raid on Harpers Ferry. By then the notion of righteous violence had become common currency among most immediatists and permitted most of them to give their aggressive propensities greater freedom while perpetuating the conviction that they had not essentially departed from the ideals of moral suasion.

The new attitude toward violence adopted by most first-generation American immediatists left Richard Davis Webb, a Dublin abolitionist and Boston Clique intimate, perplexed. Webb never quite understood that American abolitionists had a much more difficult task than their British counterparts. He never comprehended, for example, that the federal government did not have Parliament's firm jurisdiction over slaveholding localities or that Virginia planters would, of necessity, exercise greater influence over Congress in Washington than distant West Indian slaveholders had exerted over Parliament in London. Consequently, Webb was disturbed because his colleagues across the Atlantic, out of desperation and a sense of a failure, seemed to be departing from the eminently successful British example of nonviolent abolition. Shortly after the Civil War erupted, Webb fully articulated his long-standing apprehension. He wondered aloud why the American abolitionists, particularly the Boston Clique nonresistants whom he had come to love and respect, had decided to acquiesce in war and violence;

I wonder greatly at the unreserved exultation on the part of many out and out friends of nonresistance among the abolitionists at the opening of a long and bloody struggle. I don't wonder that they should be glad at the prospect of the overthrow of Slavery at almost any price; but I am surprised that it is [with] such unqualified gratification. . . .[28]

Webb was posing the most fundamental of questions regarding American immediatists and violent means: Why had they come to defend force and violence with exultation, even gratification? He was essentially asking what emotional benefits first-generation immediatists had derived by slowly shifting from moral suasion toward righteous violence that had made them continue so enthusiastically along this path. Our final task in this chapter is to attempt to answer Webb's question. We have been moving toward a two part answer in our delineation of the accommodation process.

The first part concerns the missionary impulse that was at the core of the immediatist crusade from the moment that it separated from the colonization movement. During the late antebellum decades as the new attitude toward violence took hold, we have noted how the immediatist missionary perspective became somewhat more relaxed, tolerant, and even relativistic – more attentive to complexities and less disposed to rigid dichotomizations. With the exception of white–black relationships and particularly the biracial experiment, the fervor and energy behind the traditional we–they immediatist missionary perspective was clearly in ebb. At the same time, abolitionists increasingly came to perceive that, contrary to their optimistic expectations of the 1830s, their mission to eradicate the "peculiar institution" was not going well. Rather, their efforts to mobilize the nation to the sins of slavery had suffered constant reverses. Consequently, the realization grew in many quarters that they lacked power and control over events – that they were not a growing dissenting minority. This sense of powerlessness became more than apparent to the men of Gerrit Smith's intimacy circle, we found, when they failed dismally in their efforts to spread the voluntary principle of upstate New York through other regions of the North through Liberty party electoral victories. Boston Clique insurgents came to a similar realization as they watched fellow immediatists who appeared to be losing moral direction and to be becoming dangerously infatuated with third-party politics. Although Tappan circle stewards doggedly assumed that with God's intervention their cause would ultimately triumph, even they became periodically discouraged over their failure to influence most of the nation's evangelical churches and benevolent societies effectively.

The violent imagination helped to renovate immediatists' somewhat lax and ebbing missionary fervor as it diminished apprehensions of powerlessness and promised to heal the accompanying sense of fragmented emotional selfhood. Thoughts of violence had this capacity because they often prompted Manichaean views of good and evil. Cravings to do violence to others necessarily tend to make us feel that our victims are bad or evil and that we are good, social psychologists maintain; otherwise the violence can become a form of self-assault. The violent imagination certainly promoted a Manichaean frame of mind among most immediatists. As such, it helped to restore fervor and rekindle ethnocentrism in what had become a feeble and and relativistic missionary perspective by encouraging immediatists to perceive themselves as the good who were on a purposeful course as they struggled to force the submission of evil proslavery interests. Through violent thoughts and the endorsement of forceful deeds, they became considerably more certain that God was behind their antislavery crusade and was firmly against their bad opponents. Consequently, despite momentary reverses and nagging feelings of personal inconsequentiality, victory now seemed to be considerably more assured. Since immediatists advocated force against evil, this force now appeared to be patently righteous and broadly consistent with virtuous peace principles of the 1830s. With this more optimistic if more dogmatic missionary cast of mind, the political and social complexities and defeats and the personal emotional confusions that abolitionists encountered in their crusade against slavery could recede. We – the good – retained spiritual purity and personal consequentiality and would triumph over the bad champions of the "peculiar institution."[29]

The concept of righteous violence, which immediatists frequently invoked as the Civil War drew near, illustrated the results of this general fusion of the violent and Manichaean perspective with the traditional immediatist missionary mentality. John Brown's "righteous actions" at Harpers Ferry, for example, gave James Redpath new confidence. To this confused and discouraged immediatist whose personal emotions and reform efforts seemed in such disarray, Brown was no crude "guerilla [sic]" who defied peace principles but "a Puritan warrior of the Lord" because he proved a simple truth. When righteous warriors struck at sinful proslavery interests, it stirred the nation to a sense of its moral responsibilities as unreformed peace principles never could. Righteous violence was therefore an appropriate revision of those principles. Similarly, by 1862 the insurgent Philadelphia Unitarian minister William Furness was so stirred by the righteous violence of federal troops engaged in charging sinful slaveholding interests that he expected "millennial splendor" to occur quickly. Whereas unmodified moral suasion doctrines had faltered and had left him with a deep sense of personal inadequacy, the violent means of devout warriors promised to secure God's kingdom on earth.[30]

To be sure, neither Redpath nor Furness were among the more learned or cosmopolitan of immediatists, and neither had assumed important roles in forging early moral suasion principles. Consequently, the restorative effect that righteous violence had upon their missionary perspective and their sense of consequentiality was not altogether unpredictable. But what of more sophisticated abolitionists who had participated in the cultivation of immediatist peace principles and who had been more receptive to a somewhat more relaxed and less dichotomized missionary perspective? Could it have served them in the same way? It certainly served Lysander Spooner, one of the most brilliant and probing intellectuals in the immediatist crusade. By the early 1850s, Spooner had tired of the petty ideological arguments, outworn moral suasion techniques, and apparent directionlessness of antislavery endeavors. Rather, he proclaimed an easy we/good-versus-they/evil missionary solution: "I hope to see freedom and slavery meet face to face, with no question between them except which shall conquer and which shall die." John Brown's raid on Harpers Ferry brought Lydia Child, the erudite woman of letters who had helped to forge early peace principles among insurgent immediatists, into the fold. For Child, the righteous violence that Brown deployed had made it pointless for abolitionists to continue debating subtleties or disputing what was and what was not consistent with old moral suasion doctrine: "All I know, or care to know, is that his example stirred me up to consecrate myself with renewed earnestness to the righteous cause for which he died so bravely." Violent means in a missionary cause had also made life's decisions much easier for Gerrit Smith: "We must not shrink from fighting for Liberty and if Federal troops fight against her, we must fight against them." But the revitalizing appeal that righteous violence and its simplistic dichotomies had for even the most subtle abolitionist thinkers was most conspicuous when, shortly after the attack on Fort Sumter, Edmund Quincy joined hands with the others. Perhaps the most cosmopolitan, learned, and prudent of all insurgent immediatists and long disposed to nonresistant principles, Quincy proclaimed that since the sins of slavery had prompted the morally degenerate South to take up the sword for ill, righteous and devout Northerners had no choice but to retaliate with "arm and sword." In this way, they would eliminate sin and sinners and effect emancipation – the goal that nonresistant immediatists had always held. If erudite abolitionists like Spooner, Child, Smith, and Quincy could endorse righteous violence because it made their complex aims and aspirations at once simple and achievable, it comes as no surprise to find less subtle immediatists partaking in the same practice. Consequently, as the acceptance of violence became more conspicuous, immediatist letters, pamphlets, and speeches increasingly came to reflect the pietistic Manichaean simplicities of the revitalized righteous missionary.[31]

Distressed enormously by these signs, Boston Clique intimate Maria Chapman charged in 1862 that "the moral sense of the great majority of even the abolitionists has been destroyed," for "they show an affinity for the dark ages." Chapman was too harsh on her colleagues. Their very need to characterize righteous violence as an efficacious modification of peace principles signified that they still did not champion warrior virtues as adamantly and unambiguously as most other late antebellum Americans. Moreover, they had accepted violence only as a last resort after others ignored their pleas to emancipate slaves peacefully. Thus, they had hardly reverted to the dark ages. Nonetheless one can understand why Chapman could be so upset. When a genteel and cosmopolitan associate such as Edmund Quincy in the refined, aristocratic segment of

the Boston Clique sounded at times like a coarse and violent fron-
tiersman, something surely must be amiss.[32]

To a large extent, then, first-generation immediatists generally became increasingly receptive to righteous violence because it seemed
consistent with their flagging missionary perspective and afforded new
optimism in the crusade against slavery while promising to order their
confused emotions and to make their lives again seem consequential.
But this, the first general explanation of the benefits immediatists derived as they moved increasingly along a violent path, must be accompanied by a second explanation because the first insufficiently considers the immediatists' insatiable longings for fellowship. My narrative
has revealed how violence repeatedly promised to satisfy the convivial
needs of the "heart" – the unending immediatist quest for greater
sociability. Unlike isolated individual warriors such as Robert Montgomery Bird's character Nathan Slaughter and Herman Melville's Ahab,
who fought largely to distance themselves from others, immediatists
seemed, in part, to endorse force and violence to secure fellowship – to
build social bridges with Northerners who were not immediatists
but who favored the sword against the Slave Power. It is crucial to
determine why immediatists saw so much benefit accruing from these
wider social contacts that, just as they had often been willing to downgrade their biracial experiment for these contacts, they were also ready
to trade off their cherished peace principles and to espouse righteous
violence.

During the first decade of the immediatist crusade, before moral
suasion began to be eclipsed by violent means, pacifism had provided
abolitionists with some degree of social and emotional sustenance. Peace
principles, like immediatism, were held in low repute throughout
Northern society. As unpopular advocates of antislavery and peace,
immediatists sought refuge in their own small intimacy circles. But
since all were hated outsiders, immediatists of different circles and
ideologies also tended at times to draw together to satisfy their longings
for society and community. In 1839 on a lecture tour of upstate New
York in behalf of the New England Non-Resistance Society, for example, Boston Clique insurgent Henry Wright found voluntarist Gerrit
Smith's town of Peterboro a haven amid pervasive hostility: "Several in
this place embrace the doctrine [nonresistance] fully and act upon it. . . .
It is good to be here." Similarly, although Clique insurgent Samuel May,
Jr., was never among the stronger proponents of peace, he offered funds
to support the major New England nonresistant periodical because he
found social associations with moral suasionists extremely pleasant.
Garrison went further, maintaining that the social instinct could only
be gratified with peace men. Among those who propounded war and
violence, "the brotherhood of mankind is forgotten or denied, good will
toward men is turned into malevolence. . . ."[33]

The problem with this early recourse to moral suasion for the gratification of social needs was that it allowed one to embrace warmly only the small number of peace men within society. Consequently, the approach simultaneously encouraged and limited social rapport. In an antebellum Northern society of warrior heroes such as Andrew Jackson, peace principles at least had to be modified if first-generation immediatists were to attain close social bonds with some of their Northern neighbors. This meant that despite their very strong missionary proclivities, they had somehow to become less intent on imposing their own pacific ideas on others and more willing to merge those ideas with conflicting notions that others prized. The moral suasionist had to become more receptive to warrior virtues if he wished to enjoy camaraderie rather than the extreme isolation of his social position in the 1830s – to move beyond the "world in ourselves and in each other" of small if sometimes cooperative immediatist intimacy circles and occasional personal friendships with abolitionists in other circles.[34]

As the Manichaean good–bad dichotomy of the violent imagination reinvigorated immediatist missionary fervor, it simultaneously helped to build the wider social ties that immediatists sought. It did this by encouraging expansion of the "we" in the traditional we–they missionary perspective so that "we" might include a diversity of Northerners: Conscience Whigs, Free Soilers, Independent Democrats, and others who were willing to join with immediatists in violent assaults upon slaveholding interests. Because they strongly opposed slavery and were willing to cooperate at least modestly with abolitionists, these nonimmediatist antislavery Northerners could be characterized as devout contributors to the immediatist mission to free the slaves. As historian James Brewer Stewart has noted, the acceptance of force in opposition to the 1850 Fugitive Slave Act and similar proslavery measures "began to submerge them [immediatists] even more completely in the broader Northern struggles against the 'slave power.' "[35] The violent imagination enlarged immediatists' conceptions of good fellow Northerners and therefore drew them closer to many of their neighbors.

Considerable evidence supports this proposition. During the 1830s many immediatists tended to equate their pacifism with small and hated communities of like-minded souls; usually these small communities did not extend far beyond their intimacy circles. But during the 1840s, 1850s, and the Civil War years, as the importance they attached to their intimacy circles seemed, at times, to be declining, immediatists came to equate their forceful opposition to slaveholding with a larger Northern collectivity of people willing to take up the sword against the "peculiar institution." Shortly after the guns of Sumter, for example, Garrison warned fellow immediatists, particularly Boston Clique insurgents, that they must never return to their 1830s roles as outsiders within the North, as that was a "needless turning of popular violence upon ourselves." Rather, "there is not a drop of blood in my veins, both as an abolitionist and a peace man, that does not flow with the Northern tide of sentiment" to forcefully defeat "barbaric and tyrannical" Southern slaveholders. Sydney Howard Gay, Garrison's insurgent editor of the *National Anti-Slavery Standard*, had made much the same point ten years earlier: If the antislavery cause expected "to sustain the weight of an armed Revolution," abolitionists would simply have to forge a rapport with many other Northerners who would join them in forceful assault against the Slave Power. During the 1850s, as he came to see that his old voluntarist circle had been reduced to himself and William Goodell, Gerrit Smith urged immediatists to join with fellow Northerners who had proved their moral virtue by fighting slaveholders; the political parties and professed philosophies of those Northerners was quite secondary. By the middle of the Civil War, Smith was so intent on preserving the unity of "men of all parties and men of no parties" behind the Northern war effort that he opposed a constitutional amendment to abolish slavery for its potentially divisive impact on the Northern pro-war coalition. In 1856 Thomas Wentworth Higginson noted that despite their peace principles of the past, insurgents "will gladly cooperate on a common platform" with all Northerners willing to repel slavery forcefully. But a Civil War development provided perhaps the clearest evidence that first-generation immediatists were enthusiastically seeking out others beyond their old intimacy circles who were intent on forceful assault against the Slave Power. Several of them, including some of the most adamant moral suasionists, insurgents as well as stewards and voluntarists, consented to support the federal war effort at public rallies. The fact that they were in great demand throughout the North during the war years illustrated how advocacy of righteous violence had helped to cultivate the larger contacts that they sought. "Never has there been a time when Abolitionists were as much respected," William Goodell happily announced at the end of 1861. "Announce the presence of a competent abolition lecturer and the house is crammed." In winter 1862 at the end of a lecture tour supportive of the Union military effort, Wendell Phillips also recognized that calls for righteous violence drew abolitionists the attention and support that 1830s moral suasion efforts launched from their small intimacy groups had never been able to capture. Roughly 50,000 fellow Northerners cheered his speeches, while another 5,000,000 read summaries of those speeches in the press. "I feel you are nearly popular *because* you have gone to the worldly men; they have not come to you," Ann Phillips wrote in despair, if accurately, to her husband at the conclusion of his lecture tour.[36]

The immediatists' accommodation to violence was, of course, taking place within the same late antebellum years during which they often deemphasized biracialism. Like the turn from biracialism, the shift toward righteous violence strengthened their rapport with other types of antislavery Northerners. But the new posture on violent means also served, in Thomas Wentworth Higginson's words, as "a connecting link between the non-resistants and the younger school of abolitionists who believed in physical opposition to the local encroachments, at least, of the slavepower." More generally, violent means made it easier for immediatists of the first generation to work with the next generation which lacked their 1830s commitment to moral suasion but which came increasingly, during the 1850s, to assert leadership roles in the abolitionist crusade. Sometimes contact with these younger immediatists provoked apprehensions of moral deficiencies. James C. Jackson warned, for example, that "the new recruits need strengthening," while Anne Warren Weston told Wendell Phillips: "I long for an infusion of *new real converts.*" At other times, as when Oliver Johnson attended a meeting with several young immediatists at Abington, there was cause for encouragement: "Well, there is comfort in thinking, as we get older, that the cause has young champions capable of carrying it on, whoever may be laid up or removed." By reducing one very serious potential source of conflict between generations – the peace issue – first-generation acceptance of righteous violence helped to assure that its members did not become estranged from the very crusade that they had launched. Old Boston Clique insurgents were able, for example, to get along better with increasingly vocal young associates of the 1850s such as Theodore Parker and Higginson, who called for "vengeance, redder yet." Lewis Tappan actually came to like youthful Henry C. Bowen, who yearned for sectional war, while the Weston sisters found Lyman Beecher's increasingly prominent children "very amiable & very likeable" despite their unfamiliarity with old peace principles. Acceptance of violence, then, helped to unify generations of abolitionists.[37]

It is clear, therefore, that first-generation immediatists, particularly those in our three focal intimacy circles, were vaguely pursuing two general categories of benefits as they slowly shifted from moral suasion to righteous violence. The first category of benefits was primarily directed toward the individual immediatist: the revitalizing, curative powers that violence seemed to offer to reverse his flagging missionary perspective. The self-confidence that would come of this revitalized sense of mission was necessary if he was ever to arrest his inner emotional turmoil and to regain a sense of control over events. But unless the immediatist succeeded in convincing himself that he was a consistent and pious reformer as he moved from moral suasion toward a concept of righteous violence – unless he fully persuaded himself that violence was righteous and saintlike – his new perspective could leave him more dispirited than ever. The second category of potential benefits from righteous violence was more social and collective. As their old immediatist intimacy circles less often seemed to be central to their lives, a great many immediatists sought to widen their social associations. New female abolitionist colleagues were not enough, and what contacts they had with blacks seemed to contribute to their sense of social isolation. As they sought to build social bridges with more moderate white antislavery Northerners and to retain harmony with the younger generation of abolitionists, they realized that old peace principles kept them isolated, but defense of righteous violence did not. Consequently, acceptance of violence held out the prospect of widening their social bonds. To the degree that this goal succeeded, it made the old immediatist intimacy circles even less crucial to their social and emotional existence.

In sum, then, immediatists sensed that the first category of desired benefits would not come to pass if, as they accommodated to violence, they made the slightest dilution of their missionary piety. But they also sensed that the second category of potential benefits – a widening circle of convivial fellows – would not come unless they made that accommodation. Consequently, their moral devotedness was actually being tested owing to their craving to expand their social circles. But this was hardly out of character. From the very commencement of their antislavery crusade, first-generation immediatists craved pious self-images as well as convivial social experiences and were never anxious to sacrifice the one for the other. They were gregarious saints before they began to accommodate decidedly to violence, and they remained gregarious saints even as they witnessed the blood and gore of the Civil War.

Part IV

Juxtaposition

CHAPTER 8

IMMEDIATISTS AND RADICALS

On a rainy and cold November day in 1837, Owen Lovejoy sat alone in a room by the body of his murdered brother, Elijah Lovejoy. The brother was killed just as he had invoked righteous violence to defend himself against an antiabolitionist mob. "I shall never forsake the cause that has been sprinkled with my brother's blood," Owen vowed beside Elijah's bier. By the late 1840s, however, Owen Lovejoy had ceased to regard himself as an immediatist. Although he continued to cooperate with his brother's immediatist colleagues and did not actually abandon the cause, he had also begun to act in concert with Conscience Whigs, Free Soilers, and diverse others who sought to resist the slave system. When Lovejoy joined other nonimmediatists and vigorously denounced the Fugitive Slave Act of 1850 as a capitulation to slavery, he found that he and his colleagues were called radicals. He wholeheartedly accepted the label. By the mid-1850s he had assumed an active role in the radical anti-slavery wing of the new Republican party.[1]

As a radical, Lovejoy won election to the House of Representatives from the third district of Illinois in 1856 with the support of imme-diatists, fellow radicals, and diverse other elements in his local con-stituency. Nominated for reelection at the third-district Republican convention in June 1858, he delivered a most revealing address. Lovejoy reiterated his love of freedom and his determination to fight slavery. Then he noted that, like his fellow radicals but unlike many immedia-tists, he would not "seek its [slavery's] extermination in unjustifiable modes." Finally, he charged that this difference between radicals and immediatists had ceased to be relevant and was best left unmentioned. Indeed, all distinctions between these two types of antislavery mis-sionaries "had to be melted in the crucible of our common cause." On the one hand, then, Lovejoy was acknowledging an important distinc-tion between radicals and immediatists. On the other hand, he belittled it and insisted that "we are all together *now*."[2]

Lovejoy's characterization of the immediatist–radical relationship evidenced mixed feelings. But this did not trouble proponents of the "peculiar institution." Neither proslavery Southerners nor their North-

ern associates felt that immediatists and radicals were essentially
distinguishable. They did not differentiate between the various types of
immediatists and those adamantly antislavery Whigs, Democrats, and
Free Soilers who came, at least by the early 1850s, to accept the radical
label. Proslavery elements referred to both categories of antislavery
missionaries sometimes as abolitionists and sometimes as antislavery
radicals. Regardless of designation, they were characterized as fanatics
who threatened the slave system and the stability of the nation.

Historians of the last two decades have not shared this bitter
contempt for either the immediatists or the radicals. A few have
assumed, quite uncritically, that immediatists of the 1830s became the
radicals of the 1850s. Other, more judicious historians, while acknowledging persisting differences between immediatists and radicals, have
delineated a cooperative tradition. For these historians, immediatists
were forerunners of the radicals, they eventually became the radicals'
closest colleagues, and an immediatist–radical alliance became the core
of the abolitionist crusade by the eve of the Civil War.[3] This second
interpretation seems to comport with a phenomenon we have noted:
the quest of first-generation immediatists to build bridges with more
moderate Northern antislavery elements. They were willing to alter
their old biracial crusade and even their peace principles to build these
bridges. A strong, united, and trusting immediatist–radical alliance
would appear to have been an inevitable result of their efforts.

The problem with this characterization of the immediatist–radical
relationship is that, while it takes full account of the importance that
first-generation immediatists assigned to expanding contacts with more
moderate antislavery reformers, it deemphasizes their loyalty to old
abolitionist principles and friendships. As we have persistently noted,
they were always hesitant about expanding their missionary contacts
for fear that their devout ideals would be compromised in the process of
mixing with the impious. To be sure, their old friendships among the
devout in their old intimacy circles (particularly the Gerrit Smith circle)
were dissipating because of specific internal group developments, the
emergence of a female co-missionary tradition, the altered state of
biracialism, and new responses to the peace issue. But these changes
encouraged them to form new types of friendships with other sorts of
abolitionists at least as much as they encouraged immediatists to join
with the radicals. Consequently, as we shall see, the evolution of the
immediatist–radical common cause was really a story of diverse types of
immediatists drawing somewhat closer together, much as they had as
they endorsed righteous violence. They made serious efforts to link
their cause with the cause of the radicals. But they discovered that they
could do so only on a limited basis because they retained much of their
old ideological and temperamental baggage, while the radicals retained
much of theirs. It is small wonder, then, that Lovejoy had such mixed

feelings about the emerging immediatist–radical cooperative tradition. Like other immediatist social and emotional undertakings, this common cause was characterized by complex and ambiguous dimensions.

II

We must note at the outset of our exploration of the immediatist–radical alliance, however, that they had a great deal in common. They shared important social and ideological characteristics that facilitated cooperation. For one, immediatists and radicals had very similar backgrounds. Both had generally been born on farms in the New England countryside. Like immediatists, radicals had frequently been inspired to oppose the "peculiar institution" and other immoralities through a Finneyite "new measures" revivalist appeal. This evangelical appeal tended to draw on a success ethic of self-help. For both, the mission to free the slaves was vaguely conceived as a mission to free man from shackles that hampered his potential for moral and financial self-improvement. Like immediatists, radicals tended either to remain in evangelical strongholds of rural and small-town New England or to move on to northern and western New York, the Ohio Western Reserve, southeastern Michigan, the "Northern Tier" counties of Pennsylvania, northern Illinois (particularly Boone and Winnebago counties), and diverse rural areas within Wisconsin. Indeed, most of the locations where the evangelical missionary impulse had helped produce immediatists in the early 1830s were centers of radical strength in the 1850s. In these diverse areas of evangelical fervor, immediatists and radicals generally labored in similar callings before they assumed either part- or full-time reform careers. Certain of them earned large profits through lumbering, leather manufacturing, flour milling, paper production, the developing iron industry of Pennsylvania and New Jersey, shoe and boot manufacture, and other relatively new areas for large-scale industrial production that operated independent of the Southern cotton staple. But most immediatists and radicals who did not have local pastorates served as legal advisers, commercial consultants, and small-town editors. Their principal patrons tended to come from within this new manufacturing elite, although there were a number of important exceptions.[4]

Partially as a result of their rural evangelical backgrounds and their economic independence of slave produce, radicals generally shared the zealous devotion to antislavery that was endemic to immediatist social psychology. Joshua Giddings, for example, warned his good friend George Julian of the grave danger that radicals would let down antislavery principles. Julian agreed, repudiating any "separation of morals from politics," although his course of action had incurred the wrath of more expedient Indiana Republicans. Similarly, Israel Washburn of Maine insisted that congressional radicals had to sacrifice voter "preferences & prejudices" for the success of their principles. Washburn's good friend Amory Battles concurred, insisting that the Republican party's adherence to its principles of freedom and humanity was low enough already and desperately required moral elevation. Three prominent Ohio radicals – Benjamin Wade, Gamaliel Bailey, and James Ashley – made much the same pleas for undaunted devotion in the struggle against the "peculiar institution": to "act boldly," to reject "trading politicians," and to acknowledge that pious principles were always paramount to party. From Wisconsin, Carl Schurz insisted that the Republican party displayed its most wholesome and devout qualities in the Western states, where it was free of "that bargaining spirit" of the East. This strong commitment to uncompromised piety can even be detected within the private writings of Samuel Chase, perhaps the most politically astute of all the radicals. Never quite realizing how he constantly reshaped his ideas to enhance his influence, Chase persistently asserted that "undefiled" and consistent adherence to antislavery principles made for good politics.[5]

Not only did immediatists and radicals share social characteristics and zealous antislavery devotedness. They viewed their antislavery activities as part of the same broad historical development – the emergence of a Northern antislavery conscience. One clear sign of this emerging conscience, they claimed, was Garrison's struggle amid pervasive hostility to sustain the *Liberator* in 1831. The process was greatly accelerated by the Free Soil movement and the formation of the Republican party. They saw it culminated in the election of an antislavery president in 1860. There were, of course, differences in the way various immediatists and diverse radicals characterized aspects of the emergence of this antislavery conscience. Charles Sumner, for example, considered national founders like Franklin and Jay to have been the initiators of the mission to the slaves. But Lewis Tappan insisted that there were no genuine abolitionists before the early 1830s. Similarly, while insurgent Samuel May, Jr., asserted that the compromising Republican party hardly represented a moral peak in the antislavery crusade, George Julian contended that the crusade floundered with no organized plan of action until the radicals and their party took the reins from the immediatists. Although disagreements such as these are noteworthy, the overriding point is that immediatists and radicals fundamentally agreed on the history of their movement: It became conspicuous with a small number of despised immediatists in the 1830s, shifted to major-party status in the 1850s, and elected Lincoln in 1860.[6]

Given these important similarities; it is understandable why immediatists and radicals frequently cooperated during the 1850s. They forged a number of close personal bonds. Joshua Giddings and George Julian, for example, were friendly with insurgents such as Garrison, Oliver Johnson, and Lucretia Mott. Charles Sumner and William

Herndon cultivated personal friendship with Wendell Phillips. Radicals Salmon Chase, Gamaliel Bailey, and Franklin Sanborn were on good terms with Gerrit Smith. Henry Wilson was always able to count on help during difficult election campaigns from his friend John Greenleaf Whittier, while Andrew White befriended Samuel J. May and deployed him as a research aid.[7] Owing to cordial personal relationships such as these, radicals and immediatists often cosponsored diverse antislavery gatherings, and some in each group attended the festivities of the other. In January 1857, for example, Francis Bird and Thomas Wentworth Higginson jointly organized a Worcester disunion convention with the explicit purpose of instituting a formal alliance between Massachusetts radicals and immediatists. Similarly, radicals such as George Julian and Henry Wilson frequently addressed immediatist conventions, while Gerrit Smith, William Goodell, and other immediatists were sometimes prompted by radicals to speak at Republican rallies. Moreover, at vigilance committee gatherings and August First celebrations commemorating emancipation in the British West Indies, radicals and immediatists either held joint sessions or sat on each other's platforms.[8]

Friendships and cooperative ventures such as these help to explain why proslavery elements could not distinguish immediatists from radicals. Moreover, the presence of warm radical colleagues made it clear to immediatists that convivial relationships could be found beyond their old intimacy circles. Nevertheless, it is well to note two very fundamental differences between immediatists, whether insurgents, stewards, or voluntarists, and most of their radical colleagues. These differences were only occasionally articulated with any clarity. Consequently, the very process of delineating them distorts them somewhat. Nonetheless, the differences placed substantial limits upon the immediatist–radical common cause and help explain why Lovejoy had such mixed feelings about the cause.

The first basic area of disagreement concerned the precise meaning of the mission to the slaves. In the fall of 1855 Henry Wright of the Boston Clique publicly chastised Salmon Chase, the radical candidate for governor of Ohio, for delivering campaign speeches that ignored slavery. According to Wright, Chase simply was not addressing himself to the most fundamental moral wrong of the day. Instead the candidate was praising the material conditions of the free laborer and was then going on to treat related issues concerning the Ohio economy. The following summer George Julian, the Indiana radical, commended Chase in a long letter for his strong antislavery postures as a gubernatorial candidate. Julian also noted that although the 1856 Republican national platform contained none of the sharp moral castigations of slavery that had marked earlier Liberty party and Free Soil platforms, both he and Chase would be able to "stand upon it" and fully articulate their reasons for opposing the "peculiar institution." The rather bland Republican platform would not circumscribe their strong antislavery attitudes. In their common references to Chase's antislavery posture, one distasteful and the other approving, Wright and Julian were revealing that they did not look upon the struggle between slavery and freedom in quite the same way.[9]

This difference in outlook was not unique to Wright, on the one hand, and Chase and Julian on the other. During the prewar decade diverse other immediatists joined Wright. They reprimanded radicals for failing to castigate slavery as a moral evil and for refusing to defend freedom. Stephen Foster and Ann Phillips, for example, insisted that the radicals' public espousal of "Free Soil, Free Speech, Free Labor, and Free Men" represented an effort to avoid speaking to the evils of the "peculiar institution." Samuel J. May charged that radicals, like their more moderate Republican colleagues, generally displayed moral cowardice by failing to speak to the righteousness of freedom and the sins of slavery. Similarly, the Western Anti-Slavery Society of Salem, Ohio, castigated the radicals for "a recklessness of principle, and a bending to the unhallowed behests of slavery and despotism." Still, like Chase and Julian, other radicals insisted that they were addressing themselves to the ills of the Southern slave labor system in a practical and organized fashion. "We shall arrest the extension of slavery, and rescue the [Federal] Government from the grasp of the Slave Power," Henry Wilson told a critical audience chiefly made up of insurgent immediatists. Charles Sumner agreed, insisting that unlike certain immediatists, radicals worked to overthrow the slave system without "vindictive, bitter, & unchristian" attacks and were therefore more apt to succeed. William S. Robinson and Samuel Gridley Howe offered similar defenses of the organized and practical radical crusade for freedom. Both chastised immediatists for failing to understand that though the radicals were often mild-mannered, they certainly were committed to the destruction of the "peculiar institution."[10]

In reality, both immediatists and radicals were determined to destroy slavery and promote freedom. Confusion developed because they placed different emphases on these terms. As we have seen in previous chapters, immediatists stressed that slavery was antithetical to the moral condition of self-ownership (freedom). It was the worst of all moral wrongs because it totally precluded individual opportunity to pursue God's command. Indeed, immediatists charged that slavery and freedom provided opposite circumstances under which individuals were to behave. Slavery prohibited individual devotedness; freedom facilitated individual devotedness. Julian, Chase, Wilson, Sumner, Robinson, Howe, and other radicals, however, usually enunciated a different perspective on the conflict between slavery and freedom. For the most part, they claimed, slavery and freedom represented different sets of economic conditions for people in the aggregate. Like a few New England

Federalists of the early national period and several antebellum labor leaders, radicals stressed that slavery was a system of economic oppression – one that denied its victims the opportunity to improve their material condition. In Wilson's words, the system forced Negroes "to toil beneath the bloody lash through a life greatly abbreviated by the severity of the unpaid tasks. . . ." In contrast, a free society blessed all laborers with economic independence and opportunities to improve themselves materially through meritorious conduct. A slave society denied laborers the possibility of upward mobility; a free society encouraged mobility by providing all laborers with the vote, public education, equal rights under the law, and freedom from distracting temptations such as liquor and prostitution. Immediatists such as Wright, Foster, and Ann Phillips emphasized that freedom was realized when an individual ex-bondsman could pursue Bible truths. Radicals like Chase, Julian, Wilson, and Sumner usually identified conditions of freedom with a collectivity of former slaves cultivating their own land with the prospect of earning profits. Immediatists tended to characterize freedom as an individual devotional experience. Radicals usually asserted that freedom was economic possibility – upward mobility – for all society.[11]

Despite their decidedly different emphases, immediatist and radical perceptions of freedom and slavery plainly converged. Like immediatists, most radicals believed that slavery was a moral outrage that stifled individual devotional experience. Men such as Charles Sumner, Francis Bird, Israel Washburn, Benjamin Wade, and Joshua Giddings were avid on the point. Second, since the mid-1830s immediatists had insisted that the survival of the slave system required the wholesale suppression of basic civil liberties in the North as well as in the South. The "peculiar institution" could not survive in the face of public criticism, they insisted; it thrived on the suppression of the traditional freedoms of speech and of the press. Radicals wholeheartedly agreed with this proposition. Indeed, a substantial number of them, particularly Salmon Chase, James Ashley, William Seward, and Charles Sumner, were probably more concerned with slavery's corrosive influence upon constitutionally guaranteed civil freedoms than upon moral freedoms. Consequently, amid the crises over the rendition of fugitive slaves, "bleeding Kansas," and the Dred Scott decision, it was actually the radicals who emerged as the leading defenders of traditional civil liberties; immediatists were usually found seconding the contentions of their more moderate antislavery associates. Third, much like radicals, immediatists contrasted the materially thriving free labor conditions of the North with the economically stagnant slave order of the South. Joshua Leavitt, for example, did so with particular vividness. Edmund Quincy regularly juxtaposed the efficiency, prosperity, and honor that the Northern free labor system permitted against the economically backward and morally deadening system of the slave states. Garrison sometimes echoed Quincy's com-

parison. These three major areas where immediatist and radical characterizations of the struggle between freedom and slavery converged
strongly suggest that the vital differences between them were not on
the level of basic conceptualization. Rather, they lay in the elements of
freedom and slavery that each group chose to underscore.[12]

An even more fundamental distinction between immediatists and
radicals concerned their temperaments. Immediatists focused on the sin
and redemption of specific individuals whom they encountered. Radicals
usually tended to be more concerned with proper economic relationships in society at large; they were more attentive to the complex
organizational efforts that would be necessary to effect their structural
goal (the spread of a free labor society to the South and West). Consequently, whereas immediatists, like most evangelical missionaries,
resorted to direct and open moral exhortation against individual sin and
consented to admit only the patently devout into their intimacy circles,
radicals needed to forge coalitions of diverse individuals and to compromise differences, or their efforts at building complex and effective
organizations would come to naught. Comparing the antislavery efforts
of Wendell Phillips, the strident immediatist, with those of Henry
Wilson, a leader within the Massachusetts radical Republican coalition,
Natick minister Jesse Jones captured this essential dissimilarity in
temperament: "Phillips is the Sheridan of the reform Army, who beats
up the enemy, draws his fire, and unmasks him; Wilson is the Thomas of
the Army, who collects the troops, organizes, brings supplies, and is
ready before he will order the attack."[13]

This clash of temperaments between a devoutly pious Sheridan out to
unmask sin and a Thomas more concerned with organizational impact is
not difficult to detect. In Chapter 4, for example, we found that Gerrit
Smith's circle of voluntarists was exceedingly suspicious of efforts by
Salmon Chase and Gamaliel Bailey to broaden the base of the Liberty
party by soft-pedaling immediatism. They were certain that the recruits
from this morally compromised organizational effort lacked devotedness. The Free Soil party that resulted was therefore an influential but
morally unreliable agency and had to be exposed. Smith and his associates would have nothing to do with it. Insurgents tended to share this
general perspective toward radicals. Abigail Kelley Foster, for example,
charged that although the Republican party platform permitted slaveholding, radicals misrepresented it as strongly antislavery. Consequently, immediatists "must convert those who think they are already
converted" before they continued "stealthily sucking the very blood
from our veins." William Furness concurred with Foster. He insisted
that "the abolitionists are but a Handful" and that owing to radical
misrepresentations, most of those won over to antislavery were "tem-
porizers." Similarly, Ann Phillips warned her husband Wendell against

taking tea with a deceptive vote-seeking radical like Salmon Chase despite the powerful antislavery political base that Chase had skillfully constructed. Such a moral compromiser "does do more harm to anti-slavery than Pierce–Douglass & Co."[14]

Although radicals were often upset over these immediatist charges of impiety, they nonetheless retorted that a broad-based antislavery co-alition was essential if slavery were to be effectively resisted – that this was not moral compromise but effective missionary organizational endeavor. Moreover, radicals sometimes turned the other cheek and urged immediatists to join their coalition. "Oh, if we could but have your voice to cheer us in our battle with the giant wrong [slavery]," Chase told Wendell Phillips. All opponents of slavery had to work to-gether if their efforts were to yield success. Joshua Giddings openly boasted of "my ability to unite men of various opinions" and insisted that he had not diluted his long-standing antislavery principles. Gamaliel Bailey concurred, noting that the statesman was needed in the battle against slavery as well as the uncompromising moralist. Similarly, William Herndon lectured immediatists that they were too critical of antislavery Republicans – that wisdom, not sin, required one to be conciliatory in politics: "To be mild but firm is not concession. . . ."[15]

Important as this temperamental contrast was between the imme-diatist and the radical, it should not be drawn too rigidly, because radicals sometimes displayed the same intense level of devotedness as immediatists. In late 1851, for example, radicals Joshua Giddings and Samuel Lewis expressed relief that Salmon Chase was leaving their Ohio Free Soil coalition and was rejoining the Democratic party. To be sure, the state Free Soil movement would miss Chase's skills as a politi-cal organizer, but Giddings and Lewis also knew that with Chase gone, the movement was less likely to trade principles for votes. Conversely, at a New England Anti-Slavery Society convention in May 1856, Stephen Foster complained that radicals like Charles Sumner should not be honored as if they were immediatists, but Wendell Phillips assumed the Thomas-like role of the conciliatory coalition builder. He retorted that radicals such as Sumner had to be honored when they acted morally. Despite their impieties, radicals who were moving toward abolitionist postures were useful in immediatist efforts.[16]

Clearly, both immediatists and radicals prized devotional piety and widening their circle of personal fellowship. Temperamentally, the essential difference between them was a matter of degrees. Immediatists became increasingly desirous, during the late antebellum years, of embracing more moderate antislavery colleagues who might assist them with righteous violence and other organized measures against the Slave Power. Nevertheless, they continued to attach greater importance than radicals to the personal piety of their associates. In measuring that piety, they accorded greater weight than radicals to an ideological perspective that stressed the moral rather than the material nature of the "peculiar institution."

III

Because the immediatist–radical common cause was burdened by basic ideological and temperamental differences, we can understand why Owen Lovejoy registered mixed feelings about it. When Democrats sought political gain at the expense of radical candidates by associating them with immediatists, the burdens on this cooperative tradition were apparent. In response to these Democratic accusations, radicals heeded James Ashley's warning and kept "cautious and judicious silence" as to their immediatist ties, or pressured the Democrats "to make the distinction between an Abolitionist and a Republican," or openly chastised the immediatists. Predictably, immediatists tended to be somewhat distressed whenever radicals deployed such tactics. Lydia Maria Child explained to Lyman Trumbull, the Illinois radical, for example, that he had placed himself in a morally difficult position by his conduct.[17]

But though radical responses to Democratic attacks did not appeal to immediatists, the strains on their common cause were more often registered in issue-oriented disputes. Owing to the fundamental differences in ideology and temperament that distinguished immediatists from radicals, they found themselves constantly disagreeing (usually in private) over three fairly specific issues: the place of permanent national political parties in the mission to the slaves, the benefits of Salmon Chase's nonextension policy, and the relationship between free soil and civil rights for Negroes. But they rarely had any sense of the fundamental shaping forces behind these disagreements. Instead of recognizing that these were really differences about the meanings of slavery and freedom and about the Sheridan versus the Thomas reform temperament, they ended in heated debate over the three specific issues. By exploring the controversy that surrounded each of these issues, we acquire a fuller, less abstract, and less abbreviated sense of the basic differences between immediatists and radicals and of the ways in which they finally dealt with these differences. We also gain a better sense of why a radical such as Lovejoy had such mixed, indeed confused, feelings about his common cause with the immediatists.

Not all immediatists were dead set against relatively permanent national parties – the first specific issue of debate. A few, such as David Child, had once been active Whigs and could understand why radicals gravitated toward major parties. Gerrit Smith's good friend Jabez Hammond refused to regard permanent parties as profane intrusions upon missionary endeavor; rather, he considered them vital to virtuous government. More generally, first-generation immediatists looked with increasing favor, during the prewar years, on alliances with various moderate antislavery reformers who identified with the major parties. But as our investigations of Gerrit Smith's upstate New York intimacy circle and Lewis Tappan's cluster have suggested, both voluntarists and stewards equated the spirit of a fairly permanent national party with the spirit of an ineradicable slave system. They were therefore at least modestly suspicious of anybody who was comfortable within a regular party. Moreover, they often felt temperamentally unable to support a regular party even indirectly; a choice between the two impious major parties was no choice at all. As William Jay warned, if immediatists ever supported "a political party striving for office & power they will be joined by a corrupt & selfish herd" and would lose "their moral feeling & moral influence." Gerrit Smith concurred, warning that true antislavery missionaries must always work as "pilots and pioneers" to uplift the major parties morally but were to stay clear of their inherently polluting natures.[18] Insurgent immediatists seemed, on one level, even more tenaciously antiparty than stewards or voluntarists, as our investigation of the Boston Clique revealed. Not only did they caution against supporting Free Soil and Republicanism; they warned abolitionists of moral contamination by supporting the professedly temporary and devoutly antislavery Liberty party. But on another level, insurgents regarded leaders of the Republican party as their erring if well-intentioned "children." If they kept up the "rub-a-dub of abolition agitation" outside the formal party structure, Republicans could sometimes be persuaded to avoid excessive moral compromises and might even render modest benefits.[19]

Radicals, too, displayed certain antiparty perspectives. Indeed, they were genuinely distressed with Republican colleagues who placed "mere party organization" above avowed principles. Moreover, most of them had bolted from the Whig and the Democratic parties; they were willing to leave the Republican party as well if it became too conservative and secular. But reflecting their satisfaction with society and its traditional institutions, satisfaction more general than that of immediatists, even rather uncompromising radicals like Israel Washburn and Francis Bird felt at home within the major parties. Indeed, radicals usually assumed that only relatively permanent parties resolved fundamental economic and institutional problems such as slavery. William Seward articulated this sentiment well in an implicit castigation of his immediatist colleagues: "All public movements are therefore undertaken, and prosecuted through the agencies, not of individuals, but of parties. . . . He who proposes means so impracticable that he can win no party to his support may be a philanthropist, but he cannot be a statesman." Similarly, Charles Sumner took issue with the immediatists. He insisted that the actions of "great" parties, not individual moral exhortation, held "men in power . . . to a just responsibility."[20]

Radicals, then, felt considerably more comfortable than immediatists operating within the more permanent parties. But as they criticized the immediatist antiparty posture and suggested that it verged on the apolitical, the radicals failed to grasp an aspect of immediatism that historian Aileen Kraditor has brilliantly demonstrated and that our early chapters have certainly corroborated. Radicals did not understand that immediatists had always been profoundly political. Indeed, immediatists had distinguished themselves from most benevolent society reformers for their intense concern with domestic politics and parties. Moreover, they had quite consciously calculated that antislavery political pressure was required outside as well as within the major parties. Because radicals did not comprehend this particular immediatist strategy, they sometimes become quite upset when immediatists appeared to substitute "mere" moral testimony for "effective" antislavery politics within the structure of a major party. As a solid Whig in 1844, George Julian felt indignant that immediatists had supposedly thrown the presidential election to proslavery candidate Polk by supporting the small and devout Liberty party over Henry Clay and the Whigs. Thirteen years later, he warned Thomas Wentworth Higginson that the slave system could only be resisted effectively if antislavery men labored within the Republican party. Similarly, in 1838 Benjamin Wade had chastised Ohio immediatists for assuring Democratic control of the state legislature; by refusing to vote Whig, "they have lent themselves to a party who are devoted soul and body to Southern dictation." Preston King, furious over a central New York voluntarist's charge that he vacillated on slavery because he identified himself as a Free Democrat, fired back that, even with moral deficiencies, the major parties would decide the success or failure of the antislavery economic and institutional mission. By the same token, Massachusetts radical W. G. Weld was dismayed that Bay State insurgents would not cast their ballots for the Republican party gubernatorial candidate, John Andrew, even though "Andrew has done everything he could for them, & the cause of John Brown."[21]

Clearly, immediatists and radicals differed sharply on the issue of relatively permanent major parties. They never quite realized that their disagreements reflected legitimate differences about appropriate antislavery political strategies. Consequently, they could not understand that the differences over strategy registered deeper ideological and temperamental differences. From an ideological standpoint, immediatists postulated that the major parties were morally compromising, if not blatantly proslavery, political institutions. But radicals believed that these parties were the only effective vehicles to destroy slavery and promote freedom; the slave labor system could only be eradicated by strong and permanent political agencies. Temperamentally, too, immediatists felt profoundly uncomfortable – morally tainted – working within major parties. On the other hand, radicals had spent most of their adult lives supporting major parties and felt few reservations about continuing to do so.

Nor did immediatists and radicals grasp these deeper differences in ideology and temperament when they quarreled about Free Soil and Republican party efforts to block the extension of slavery into the Western territories. Salmon Chase began to advocate nonextension during the 1840s. At this time, he considered himself an antislavery supporter of the Liberty party but not an immediatist. Chase was quite gratified when nonextension became a central Republican party demand during the mid-1850s, and he became a firm party loyalist. An adherent of limited federal power and states' rights, he insisted that the Constitution acknowledged "the incompetency of Congress to abolish slavery in the States." But Congress could and would abolish the slave system in the territories if antislavery activists wrestled the federal government from the control of the Slave Power by electing "virtuous men." With the "peculiar institution" confined to the South and pious antislavery officials dominating the national government, Chase assumed that "slavery will be abolished everywhere . . . by the State Governments." He regarded "argument, persuasion, remonstrance, and the like" for the eradication of slavery everywhere as the only alternative to nonextension in the crusade against black bondage. But Chase insisted that this alternative, which immediatists had deployed since the early 1830s, represented a moral rather than a political approach and consequently had very little impact. Rather, history had demonstrated that political power was always more effective than moral exhortation in rendering fundamental institutional change.[22]

Chase's elaboration of this nonextension posture struck a responsive chord among his radical colleagues and illustrated essential qualities that pervaded radical antislavery ideology and temperament. There was a zealous commitment to the mission to the slaves. But the Ohio radical perceived slavery more as a labor system than as an immoral act perpetrated by a sinful master upon a black bondsman. Unlike individual sins, immoral labor systems could be overturned only by concerted party electoral victories and effective governmental action on the part of the elected officials. Moreover, Chase felt rather content working within established parties and governmental bodies, though he was insistent that these agencies function within his perception of constitutional limitations.

Radicals predictably differed in the degree to which they emphasized the moral end of Chase's nonextension plan as against the expediency and realism of its means. Some, such as Gamaliel Bailey, Joshua Giddings, George Julian, and Thaddeus Stevens, tended to stress the moral righteousness of nonextension considerably more than Chase had. Others such as Preston King, C. S. Seldon, James Ashley, and

Benjamin Wade, dwelled on its pragmatic and politically strategic qualities somewhat more than Chase. But like Chase, all saw virtue in the
concept because it was righteous, legal, and politically effective. Nonextension would replace the evil "peculiar institution" with a morally
elevating system of free labor. The policy could be effected because its
procedures were constitutional and lay within the capabilities of the
traditional party system – a framework for reform activity in which
radicals felt rather comfortable.[23]

Chase and other radicals, then, were committed to nonextension as
the only legal and politically effective means to eradicate slavery. They
assumed that moral exhortation, the immediatist alternative, would not
command sufficient institutional pressure to crush the powerful and
complex Southern labor system. From time to time, some immediatists
voiced qualified pleasure in the radicals' nonextension policy. Indeed,
certain immediatists appeared to be more tolerant of nonextension as
time passed. In 1859, for example, Garrison told the Massachusetts
Anti-Slavery Society that, while this radical posture would not bring
down the "peculiar institution," it would at least help "to save the great
West from the encroachments of the Slave Power." Similarly, Gerrit
Smith termed it " 'full half way up the hill' of antislavery." More
generally, however, immediatists concurred with the executive committee of the American and Foreign Anti-Slavery Society that "nonextension is not abolition" – that it did not carry the mission to the
slaves far enough.[24]

Immediatist objections to Chase's nonextension program were
grounded in two different interpretations of the federal Constitution.
Voluntarists like the men of Gerrit Smith's intimacy circle considered
the Constitution a thoroughly antislavery document that authorized
Congress to abolish slavery in the states as well as in the territories.
They charged that Chase and other radicals were simply unwilling to
eradicate bondage in the South and were using false constitutional
theory to justify their immoral behavior. Although stewards were
generally less attentive to constitutional issues, a number of them
seemed disposed, by the mid-1850s, to accept the voluntarist interpretation. On the other hand, insurgent immediatists, particularly
Boston Clique activists, strongly disagreed with the voluntarists. They
insisted that the federal Constitution was thoroughly proslavery.
Consequently, they charged that it could not be cited, as the radicals had
claimed, to block slavery in the territories. Rather, disunionism was the
only way to undermine constitutional protection of the "peculiar
institution."[25]

Clearly, voluntarists and insurgents had invoked opposite constitutional interpretations that they had developed years earlier in their
intimacy circles. But in other respects their distaste for Chase's program
was remarkably similar, reflecting the general homogenization of first-

generation immediatist ideas as the intimacy circles slowly receded in significance. If antislavery elements secured control of the national government and proceeded to abolish slavery in the territories, they charged, this did not mean that the "peculiar institution" would necessarily be eliminated in the slave states. By Chase's own admission, only state legislatures had the ultimate authority to decree emancipation within their boundaries, and antislavery dominance of the federal government was no guarantee that Southern legislatures would act. Next, both voluntarists and insurgents attacked the radicals for refusing "to oppose slavery where it is [the slave states], and oppose it where it is not [the territories]." Finally, and most suggestive of a basic ideological as well as a temperamental dimension to their critique of radical non-extension policy, both insisted that slavery was not so much an economic or a political system as a moral evil. Therefore, it could not be dealt with meaningfully by the claims of Chase and other radicals concerning strategic effectiveness. The "peculiar institution" could only be decisively opposed by heartfelt expressions of moral outrage against individual slaveholders.[26]

The race issue was integrally related to the radicals' nonextension program. The program required the exclusion of black bondsmen from the Western territories but said nothing about the right of free blacks to migrate there or of Western legislatures to exclude them. Chase and other radicals had intended to cripple the entire Southern slave system by precluding its spread. But as nonextension came to be subsumed, by the late 1840s and early 1850s, by cries for "free soil, free speech, free labor, and free men," immediatists frequently wondered whether radicals and their more moderate antislavery colleagues were more interested in preserving the Western territories for whites than they were concerned with striking a death blow at slavery. Indeed, several immediatists charged that the radicals were really crusading for nonextension and free soil to exclude all Negroes from the West – free and slave. Parker Pillsbury accused Giddings and his radical associates of having no true moral commitment to black civil rights; free soil was a ruse that masked their general contempt for the Negro. Similarly, William Goodell accused radicals and Republicans generally of moral deficiency for failure "to advocate the rights and interests of other than 'white' laborers." According to John Pierpont, Charles Sumner may have been genuinely concerned with black rights. Still, the senator's radical colleagues clearly favored "the labor of the white race as against the black." The *Pennsylvania Freeman* singled out radical congressman David Wilmot as a conspicuous example of the hatred for the Negro that was to be found beneath the nonextension–free soil program. The *Freeman* insisted that Wilmot cease to "feed the popular prejudices against this outcast class."[27]

In reality, however, many radicals were as irrevocably committed to black civil rights as the immediatists, and this suggests that there were more fundamental factors at work in their dispute on the race issue. Charles Sumner, Henry Wilson, and John Andrew, for instance, regularly offered their legal services to fight discrimination against free Negroes and to defend the rights of fugitive slaves. Indeed, Andrew became known as "the Attorney General of the Negroes." Similarly, Seth Gates was revered by blacks through the North and the border states for concealing fugitive slaves in his upstate New York home and for helping them to reach Canada. Gates also worked with Gerrit Smith to eliminate racial discrimination within upstate New York communities. Similarly, after George Julian made his first contacts with Northern blacks in the early 1850s, he became their staunch ally in battles for expanded opportunities. James Ashley may never have had black friends, but he was unsurpassed in his efforts to win suffrage and the full range of civil liberties for the race.[28]

Most radicals, however, did not move beyond nonextension and free soil to support Negro civil rights as fervently as immediatists had. Although Giddings and Chase, for example, were sincerely committed to expanded black opportunities – even Negro suffrage – they often held back from taking public stands for two reasons: They feared adverse political consequences, and (like some immediatists) they doubted that white and black could live harmoniously together.[29] Several other radicals more clearly exemplified the immediatist charge that free soil was a detour from civil rights commitments and an excuse for excluding all Negroes from the Western territories. Preston King, for example, openly acknowledged that Chase's nonextension–free soil program could save the territories from "the evils of slavery and a black population." William Seward concurred: "The white man needs this continent to labor upon. . . . He must and will have it." Similarly, by the late 1850s Owen Lovejoy found himself increasingly unwilling to couple nonextension with rights for free Negroes. In 1860 he repudiated the immediatists of his home town of Princeton, Illinois, and proclaimed that the federal government belonged to the white man. A number of other radicals, particularly Benjamin Wade, Thomas Williams, Lyman Trumbull, and David Wilmot, did more than deploy free soil slogans to escape civil rights commitments. Detesting the Negro, they had few such commitments. Rather, they claimed that the Republican party and its nonextension program represented a "deliverance to the white man." It would make "white labor respectable and honorable" by keeping Negroes, free and slave, out of the West. True Republicans, they asserted, "cared nothing for the nigger."[30]

Radical attitudes such as these suggest that immediatists were considerably more committed to the free Negro. Two factors, however, tend to make this distinction between radicals and immediatists less striking – less indicative of racism on the one side and egalitarianism on the other. First, although Democrats often condemned both radicals and immediatists for "pro-Negro" proclivities, radicals more frequently pursued elective office; therefore they stood to lose more by these charges. This was particularly true in Western states such as Illinois and Indiana, where negrophobe politics was most conspicuous. Consequently, a racist electorate and a Democratic party intent on exploiting the Negro question often required radicals intent on political survival to stress nonextension rather than Negro rights. It was the safer political course. Immediatists, however, rarely sought political office. When they ran, they usually campaigned as a moral vanguard. Often they were more intent on converting individual voters on the Negro question and other issues than on winning office, controlling the federal government, and thereby destroying the slave system. Consequently, unlike many radicals, they rarely felt compelled to respond in a politically expedient fashion to a racist political climate. Second, immediatists were also victimized by the racist politics of the antebellum North. Although none ever proclaimed, as did Preston King or William Seward, that their antislavery concerns were entirely for the white man, by the 1850s the immediatists' "chord of prejudice" became more intense. Their empathy for the free Negro generally declined. Like many radicals, a number of immediatists became more concerned with overturning the Southern Slave Power than with ameliorating the lot of Northern blacks.

Thus, the differences between radical and immediatist on racial matters were not always entirely clear. What differences there were derived, in significant measure, from distinguishable temperaments and ideologies. The immediatist felt that he combated the spirit of slavery when he offered moral testimony against allowing one man to deprive another of freedom to obey God. On the other hand, the radical felt that if he made certain seemingly modest concessions to secure office, he might be able to use the federal government to promote a national system of free labor and (if he happened to believe in them) expanded civil rights for blacks as well. Even on the Negro question, then, where in reality immediatist and radical were not very far apart, different meanings of slavery and freedom and different emotional dispositions promoted heated exchanges.

IV

The reasons for Owen Lovejoy's mixed characterization of the immediatist–radical cooperative tradition are, by now, apparent. Important similarities promoted frequent cooperative efforts and conveyed the appearance of a well-unified movement. But vital differences in temperament and antislavery ideology interceded. As a result, immediatists and radicals frequently argued among themselves over the propriety of operating within relatively permanent parties, the general utility of nonextension, and the civil rights of blacks. Lovejoy's equivocation simply reflected the ambiguous nature of the immediatist–radical relationship. The place that Elizur Wright, Jr., a leading first-generation immediatist, occupied within the Bird Club of Massachusetts radicals well illustrates this ambiguity.

Wright had been an active reformer for about a decade and a half before he came into contact with Bird Club radicals. A young convert to Finneyite "new measures" theology, he was won over to a life of evangelical missionary activity during a dramatic year as an American Tract Society agent in the West. In 1832 Wright accepted a teaching post at Western Reserve College, where he cultivated friendships with two other Finneyite evangelicals: college president Charles Storrs and chaplain Beriah Green. Discovering, elaborating, and modifying points in Garrison's pamphlet, *Thoughts on African Colonization*, the three jointly endorsed immediatist abolitionism. They insisted that all Americans – not simply black bondsmen – were grievously limited in the intensity of their devotedness by the general climate of moral contamination and falsehood that Southern slaveholders and their colonizationist allies had fostered to protect the "peculiar institution." The Southern planter prevented his slave from exercising his obligations to God. The colonizationist blunted the moral sensibilities of other Americans by telling them lies about the Southern slave system so that they acquiesced in its sins. It was therefore necessary for pious missionaries like the three of them to offer moral testimony against the barbaric slaveholder and the deceptive colonizationist wherever they appeared. Like other early immediatists, then, Wright, Green, and Storrs viewed slavery as a sinful moral relationship between individuals, with the sin polluting the sensibilities of their countrymen. The duty of the immediatist was not only to free black bondsmen but to struggle to convert any individual who acquiesced in the enslavement of Africans by Southern planters.[31]

Along with Storrs and Green, young Elizur Wright therefore adopted the standard immediatist concepts of slavery and freedom and displayed the intensely devout immediatist missionary temperament. Indeed, their unequivocal stand against slavery and colonization, and their insistence upon individual repentance, turned the procolonization college trustees as well as the citizenry of Hudson, Ohio, against them. Facing dismissal, Green moved on to Oneida Institute and the supportive fellowship of Gerrit Smith's emerging circle of upstate New York voluntarists. Storrs, quite ill, set out for Braintree to die with kin. Wright gratefully accepted Arthur Tappan's offer to go to New York City and become the steward's antislavery secretary.

In December 1833, shortly after Wright arrived in New York, he accompanied Arthur Tappan to the organizational meeting of the American Anti-Slavery Society, where he was elected secretary for domestic correspondence. For the next six years, Wright dominated the central office of the A.A.S.S. in New York City. He handled official correspondence, coordinated A.A.S.S. fund-raising efforts, directed the society's agents in the field, organized its pamphleteering efforts, and directed its petition campaigns. In time, however, Wright came to feel separate from the devout steward associates in the New York City office such as the Tappans, William Green, Jr., Abraham Cox, and John Rankin. Above all, despite his strong Congregational upbringing, he found himself cooling toward the Congregational and Presbyterian church services that these men deeply cherished and referred to the services as a "fog land." By 1839, it was therefore evident to both Wright and his steward associates that he had to depart.[32]

With a house full of young children and sparse funds, Wright moved his family to Boston, where he had agreed to manage the Massachusetts Abolition Society and to edit its publication, the *Massachusetts Abolitionist*. Amos Phelps and Joshua Leavitt, members of the Tappan circle in that city, had agreed to support him financially. So had certain leaders of the Massachusetts Liberty party. Both the two stewards and the state Liberty men wanted the talented young organizer to forge a viable immediatist alternative to Garrison and Boston Clique insurgency. Both quickly became distressed, however, when they learned of Wright's disinclination toward formal church services. Still worse in Phelp's eyes was Wright's zealous support of third-party abolitionism. In Spring 1840 Wright left the Massachusetts Abolition Society with no close circle of intimates for support. He was despised by Boston Clique immediatists such as Edmund Quincy and Maria Weston Chapman, who referred to him as an "impudent varlet." Boston stewards such as Phelps and Leavitt found that they could not work with a man who mocked church services. Even local Liberty men like Henry Bowditch and Samuel Sewall fretted over Wright's apparent loss of evangelical fervor.[33]

Lacking employment and fellowship but never ceasing to believe that God's missionaries gathered strength in cooperative way stations, Elizur Wright spent the next several years at various odd jobs. In 1846 he established a Boston immediatist and general reform newspaper, the *Chronotype*. He worked day and night as publisher and editor to keep it afloat and support his family. The publication was to promote "good nature, good neighborhood, and good government" as well as antislavery principles and various other evangelical reform causes. It was to be conducted independent of any immediatist cluster or faction – unbound "to the creed or cause of any clique, association, party, sect or set of men." Although the *Chronotype* publicized and usually endorsed Bay State Liberty party positions and activities, it also backed the antislavery efforts of Stephen C. Phillips, John Gorham Palfrey, Charles Francis Adams, Henry Wilson, and other more moderate Massachusetts antislavery reformers (usually Conscience Whigs) who were coming to be called radicals. In 1848 Wright joined these radicals in support of Free

Soil presidential candidate Martin Van Buren over voluntarist Gerrit Smith. By joining with the radicals, he seemed in some measure to be seeking the sort of convivial collegiality that he had enjoyed at Western Reserve College and, for a time, at the New York office of the A.A.S.S. But he did not embrace Massachusetts radicals such as Phillips and Palfrey, who were active in the new state Free Soil movement, as fervently as he had befriended immediatist colleagues such as Storrs and Green a decade and a half earlier. Although Wright regarded the Free Soil party as the most promising antislavery missionary agency, he sensed that too many of the radicals who supported it were hesitant to offer uncompromising moral testimony against slavery. Moreover, they did not seem to grasp clearly that emancipation and freedom represented unlimited rights for all to pursue God's moral imperatives. A barrier seemed to separate Wright from these early radicals. Different temperaments and different concepts of slavery and freedom appeared to constitute its vital components.[34]

Wright, however, soon came to believe that Francis Bird, John Andrew, Henry Wilson, George Stearns, Franklin Sanborn, Charles Sumner, and Samuel Gridley Howe differed from other Bay State radicals in the intensity of their moral sensibilities. They valued his *Chronotype* as the most useful reform newspaper in Boston even though it was not a Conscience Whig or Free Soil party organ. Moreover, they provided thousands of dollars to help keep it afloat, encouraged others to subscribe, and commended Wright for his clear thoughts and uncompromising piety. As Wright began to establish a reputation during the late 1840s as a part-time technical adviser to private companies and state governments on life insurance matters, his Massachusetts radical associates urged him to draft legislation to reform this new business enterprise. When he did, they often guided the bills to final passage. Finally, as a token of their deep respect, they invited Wright to join their Saturday afternoon dining group – the Bird Club – for camaraderie and good cheer among pious Free Soil radicals in the Boston area. Socially isolated and craving convivial fellowship, Wright jumped at the opportunity.[35]

The Bird Club had come into being as an extension of the informal gatherings of Massachusetts antislavery radicals in the editorial rooms of Boston's *Daily Whig* newspaper. Francis Bird shifted the discussions to a nearby dining hall and regularized them so that they took place every Saturday afternoon around a tasteful meal. No formal membership, officers, or agenda obtained, but the seating arrangements revealed an inner circle within the club. Bird, the outgoing and much loved host, sat at the head of the table and acted as master of ceremonies. When he was absent, George Stearns substituted. Those who sat nearest to Bird – Howe and Sumner at each side and then Andrew, Wilson, Stearns, and Sanborn – were regarded as the senior members of the group. Bird functioned as the conciliator, quelling sharp disagreements at the meals and encouraging good fellowship. "Warrington" (journalist William S. Robinson) sat in as a sort of private press agent or discreet publicist of club activities and policies. Because as many as forty radicals with strong convictions sometimes attended the Saturday dinners, Bird strove, sometimes vainly, to sustain harmony. Robinson had to contour his published writings carefully so that they concealed several serious internal controversies: the appropriateness of supporting temperance and woman suffrage, the propriety of seeking out Know Nothing political backing, the validity of state aid for corporations, and the necessity of a ten-hour working day.[36]

Despite these divergencies, by the mid-1850s the Bird Club had become the organizing center of the new Massachusetts Republican party and represented its radical wing. In 1860 the club did much to help elect John Andrew, of its inner circle, governor. Through the Andrew administration it secured hegemony over state party machinery and policy and retained this dominant role until 1871. Active in years when abolitionists were feeling less attached to their old intimacy groups, the club exercised more influence than any informal circle of first-generation immediatists had ever wielded. This achievement duly impressed Elizur Wright.

In some measure, the club's tradition of effective, concerted action was possible because Francis Bird's associates shared certain general social characteristics and economic interests. A few were descendants of the old Bay State merchant aristocracy, and these men were sometimes apprehensive that they were being eclipsed by powerful cotton manufacturers who had secured control of the Massachusetts Whig party. With the diversification of the state's industrial economy during the 1840s and 1850s, other club members had been able to make substantial profits through enterprises that included paper manufacturing and boot and shoe production. Like Wright, however, most club participants served as financial and legal advisers to these new entrepreneurs or as editors who received their patronage. Because most men who attended the Saturday afternoon sessions therefore supported themselves through tasks that were independent of the slave states' cotton staple, they felt few compunctions about backing antislavery politics – first Conscience Whiggery, then Free Soil, and finally the Republican party.[37]

Clearly, the men of the Bird Club shared social traits and economic interests that were pervasive among radicals of the prewar years and evident among immediatists. Still, it would be simplistic to assume that they were no more than spokesmen for Bay State economic interests who prospered independent of the "peculiar institution." More than most other radicals, the club's inner circle and the preponderance of its members considered themselves part of an abolitionist missionary tradition – as kindred spirits with first-generation immediatists. Several regularly attended the annual meetings of the American Anti-Slavery

Society and pledged substantial contributions. A number had endorsed James Birney's Liberty party presidential candidacy in 1840 and had supported other Liberty candidates. Advocates of righteous violence against the Slave Power, they were all sympathetic to John Brown both in "bleeding Kansas" and after the Harpers Ferry raid. A few had been directly supportive. Finally, many members made concerted efforts to draw immediatists such as Gerrit Smith and Wendell Phillips into their Saturday afternoon sessions. Elizur Wright was not the only abolitionist they approached.[38]

Although they came to dominate the Republican party of a major industrial state, Bird Club radicals sometimes seemed more appreciative of the antislavery societies that had existed since the 1830s than they were of the national Republican party of the 1850s. This was particularly true of Bird and Howe. Both accused leaders of the national party of moral delinquency – of yielding to Slave Power demands. They charged that Republicans, for the most part, sought "freedom for the white man" but offered little more hope "to the earnest anti-slavery man than did the Whig party ten years ago." This was because Republican policy makers averted tackling the slavery issue head-on. Instead, they "conducted the charges into the territories" (i.e., they supported nonextensionism and free soil). Because "the republican party was not worthily asserting the anti-slavery cause," it was drifting toward its own destruction, and the moral loss would not be great. Consequently, Bird and Howe agreed with many insurgent immediatists, some stewards and voluntarists, and even a few radicals in other states that the truly devout missionary for the slaves wasted his efforts voting for the typical, morally spineless Republican.[39]

The preponderance of Bird Club members, however, did not mock voting for Republican office seekers. Indeed, while Bird and Howe had little regard for most Republican candidates, the two almost always voted Republican on the national as well as the state and local level. This differentiated club radicals from many abolitionists and may help to explain why they were not able to persuade immediatists other than Wright to attend their Saturday afternoon sessions regularly. Although Club radicals vigorously defended immediatists and their antislavery societies as reservoirs of untainted piety, and though they often debunked the compromising Republican party alternative, they were, like radicals generally, willing to settle for a less than morally impeccable antislavery party. In addition, they were able to put up with many of its vacillating and expedient members. More than most immediatists, they seemed able to enjoy good fellowship even if it meant exposure to certain blatantly flawed colleagues. More, too, than most immediatists, club associates appreciated the power that a regular national party could exert. Like radicals generally, they realized that though the Republican party was morally flawed, it had the capacity to turn the federal government against the Southern slave labor system and the extension of that system into new Western territories.[40]

This, then, was the radical Bird Club that Elizur Wright, while characterizing himself as a "renegade" immediatist and craving missionary fellowship, decided to join during the late 1840s. It is difficult to know just what transpired as he became a regular participant in the club's Saturday afternoon discussions. Neither Wright nor the group's radicals wrote very much about one another despite his presence at nearly every Bird Club gathering from the late 1840s until at least the mid-1860s. When Francis Bird romantically reminisced on the first years of the club's existence, for example, he mentioned all of the early members except Wright. When Warrington (Robinson) published his *Pen Portraits*, he provided full, loving sketches of all Republican Bird Club associates but only a sentence concerning Wright: "Elizur is a successful man of business, and the same hard-headed and perfectly honest, non-mystical old radical as ever." Similarly, James Stone made much of John Brown's participation in a club dinner in May 1859, remarking how those in attendance were thrilled by the event. But Stone failed to note that Brown came because of his schoolboy friendship with Wright. Stone, moreover, neglected to report the considerable discourse at the dinner between the two. So, too, Wright had very little to say about the Bird Club's dinner discussions. He noted that the smoking at the conclusion of every regular club meal was unpleasant and had been rare in immediatist circles. But he acknowledged that he liked and respected Sumner, Wilson, Andrew, and the other club members, and this made regular Saturday attendance worthwhile. Wright, however, confided to Nathaniel P. Banks that after about a dozen years of meals he had not received a word of comment, positive or negative, from a club colleague concerning any of his many essays on slavery and other vital public questions. Members appeared to be interested in him as an insurance reformer but not as an abolitionist or a general missionary for pious causes.[41]

Quite unlike his crucial position in the immediatist agitation at Western Reserve College and in the New York office of the American Anti-Slavery Society, then, Wright's role in the Bird Club was not central, dynamic, or even memorable. His place in the club was illustrated by a series of events that transpired between the fall of 1850 and the spring of 1852. Until the fall of 1850 Wright had great plans for his *Chronotype*; the newspaper would unite diverse reformers in behalf of the mission to the slaves and other devout causes. But at the end of the summer Wright learned that his Bird Club supporters wanted an organ that devoted itself to the activities of the Massachusetts Free Soil party. Consequently, he "felt obliged to merge my own independent paper in the new Free Soil paper," hoping that the new Boston publication that came of the merger "will soon revert to my entire control." The inner leadership circle within the Bird Club had no such intentions, however. At the instigation of Samuel Gridley Howe and with the support of other key figures in the club, a committee was formed that bought up the *Chronotype* and two other Boston antislavery newspapers. With the resources of all three publications, the committee established the *Commonwealth*. Wright was initially employed and salaried at thirty dollars a week to be a minor subeditor of sorts for the *Commonwealth*. According to Howe, he was to do office work and collect news stories but also "to have a bit in his mouth and say nothing editorially that the *Chief* does not approve." The chief was to be John Gorham Palfrey, the prudent and learned former Conscience Whig. The reasoning behind Howe's refusal to give Wright free editorial reign was obvious. While realizing that the Bird Club did not want him to "speak quite so ir-reverently and saucily" in its *Commonwealth* as he had in his *Chronotype*, Wright told his club associates that he refused to "unsay" any of his old antislavery feelings on the printed page. Palfrey's supervision of Wright's writing made Wright no less determined to persist. Eventually Howe concluded that Wright's immoderate tone was damaging to the chances of club associate Charles Sumner to win a seat in the United States Senate. Wright's ties to the Bird Club and to its new publication were seen to be turning mildly antislavery men against Sumner. In time, Howe determined to "put an end to the present embarrassing condition of things" by effectively removing Wright from his lowly position as subeditor. Francis Bird became political editor and took charge of antislavery and other reform causes. Palfrey became contrib-uting editor and wrote on topics that Bird did not cover. Wright held the title of "general editor" but was not to draft editorials. Rather, because of his mathematical and managerial skills, he was ordered to direct *Commonwealth* financial affairs. Finally, in May of 1852 the sole immediatist on the *Commonwealth* staff was entirely removed because he had proven to be wholly unreliable as a Free Soil journalist. His modest share in the ownership of the publication was to be paid off. As an aside to spare him further humiliation, club associates told Wright that he might contribute occassionally to their newspaper.[42]

Since the forging of the *Commonwealth* was a crucial Bird Club enter-prise, it demonstrated the fundamental dimensions behind Wright's long-range relationship to the group. He was trusted for managerial, financial, and sometimes even for news reporting functions. But his ideas and the manner in which they were propounded meant that his contributions had to be "screened" before they reached the printed page. Through other experiences with Wright, club leaders like Howe and Bird had come to understand the importance of placing "a bit in his mouth." They had worked with him on the Massachusetts State Texas Committee to head off American annexation of the Lone Star Republic. In this capacity, they first sensed that they did not share his perception of Southern slavery. Whereas they thought of it as a labor system that immorally blocked men's opportunities to improve their material condition, Wright considered slavery almost entirely a moral wrong that individual planters had sinfully inflicted on their bondsmen. Moreover, Bird Club associates on the Texas Committee had found Wright temperamentally imprudent in his denunciation of the impiety of clergy and editors who hedged on annexation. Their sense that Wright had a different set of priorities was reinforced in 1849 and again in 1850. Twice he ran on the Free Soil ticket for state representative from Boston without waging serious campaigns and, apparently, without any anticipation of winning. Shortly thereafter they had followed reports of his conduct at his second trial for complicity in the rescue of "Shadrach" (Frederick Jenkins), a fugitive slave, and were amazed when Wright pronounced his acquittal "a present advantage but no honor." Few Bird Club radicals comprehended why Wright publicly announced that he wished he had participated in an illegal slave rescue venture for which he had been falsely indicted. They could not understand how this sort of pronouncement could undermine the South's slave labor system. Consequently, while Bird and his associates welcomed Wright into their ranks for his "bold," "honest," and "vigorous" efforts "in the interests of humanity," they sensed increasingly that he was too "curt and caustic," too "impulsive and impracticable," and had to be watched. While they admired his bravery and uncompromised piety, they fretted over the antagonisms and political losses that this sort of temperament could produce. Because Wright's injudicious pronouncements had damaged Sumner's chance of winning a Senate seat, and because he refused to moderate his antislavery feelings in the *Commonwealth*, Bird Club radicals saw no alternative but to remove him from their publication.[43]

It is difficult to determine why Wright continued to attend Bird Club dinners after spring 1852 when he was removed from the *Commonwealth*. He never noted why he dined with the others for years after the incident, even though it clearly defined his role in the club as a very minor member. One factor that probably contributed to his regular weekly attendance at club dinners after the incident was the memory of social isolation in Boston through most of the 1840s. Despised by the Boston Clique for his efforts to forge an alternative to New England insurgency and distrusted by stewards and voluntarists because of his increasing secularism, Wright had lost the camaraderie of his old immediatist colleagues. The pains of social isolation had caused him to seek out new antislavery associates; he was pleased when men such as Bird, Howe, and Andrew responded by helping to fund his *Chronotype* and by inviting him to their Saturday afternoon dinners. To be sure, Wright was obviously humiliated when these new colleagues removed him from the *Commonwealth*. But if he had left the Bird Club in response to their action, he would only have returned to an even more socially isolated state of existence. It is true that Wright had acquired the friendship of business executives such as William Barnes and William Bryant during the late 1840s and early 1850s as he enlarged his activities in life insurance reform. But these men did not offer him the sense of convivial fellowship and intellectual stimulation among devout reformers that he had enjoyed with Charles Storrs and Beriah Green in Northeast Ohio and (if to a lesser degree) with the A.A.S.S. executive committee in New York City. If Bird Club radicals did not regard him as highly as his former immediatist colleagues, they still provided a friendly weekly gathering among sincere antislavery men whose actions during the 1850s seemed far more principled than those of other leaders of the emerging Republican party. Thus, even if Wright's role in the Bird Club was quite minor, membership still gave him some sense of the conviviality among Christian fellows that he had experienced in immediatist circles during the 1830s.

Another reason for Wright's remaining in the Bird Club after the *Commonwealth* incident related to his changing philosophic perspective. From the early 1850s until at least the mid-1860s, he held to the belief that the Free Soil party and especially Republicanism was more promising than immediatism. His disappointment with old immediatists as well as with more moderate antislavery reformers had moved him to the view that man could never be godlike but was inherently fallible regardless of the intensity of his piety. Consequently, even the actions of the most devout reformer would always be badly flawed. "I have ceased to expect to look for any outward representative of my sense of justice," Wright confided to Beriah Green. Rather, "I seek simply to have that force, whether accidental or arranged . . . do as little harm, if not as much good, as I can make it." Because of the nature of men, the Free Soil and Republican parties were "artificial bodies" capable of good and evil, as were the old antislavery societies and the Liberty party. But unlike the old immediatist agencies, the Free Soil and Republican parties seemed to have power and therefore the capacity to effect change. Because they both sought electoral victory without Southern votes, while the Democrats hoped for slaveholder support, they were likely to do less harm and more good in accomplishing the mission to the slaves. Still, the Free Soil and Republican movements had considerably less principle and "political gumption" than the old immediatist societies. Free Soilers and Republicans were generally more interested in opportunity for the white man than liberty for the black. Therefore, Wright came to believe that it was necessary for pious immediatists to become involved with Free Soil and then with the radical wing of the Republican party if both bodies were to be checked in their propensities toward moral compromise. Since his Bird Club colleagues were quite upset over the "sneaking, lily-livered" qualities of the Free Soil movement and the national Republican party, these men represented the best hope for effective antislavery action. This was true, Wright concluded, despite their compromising temperaments and their failure to understand that "slavery" represented individual moral crimes of slaveholders more than it stood for a general labor system. Moreover, he claimed that Bird and the other club radicals seemed to be somewhat more understanding of the true nature of the "peculiar institution" because he attended their Saturday sessions. He was therefore steering them toward more devout conduct. This, at least, is what Wright desperately wanted to believe if he was to justify both his continued membership in a club that had humiliated him and his endorsement of Free Soil and Republican office seekers whom he did not fully respect.[44]

In essence, Wright was acknowledging a dichotomy between his formal thoughts and his emotional sensibilities. By assuming that the quest to do good was naive – that man would always be a mix of good and evil – he had reasoned through a defense of the Free Soil and Republican parties and continuing membership in the Bird Club as the most effective course in the struggle for Negro freedom. At the same time, by acknowledging that he represented the moral missionary at Bird Club gatherings with the correct perception of slavery and freedom, Wright was revealing that his sensibilities differed from those of the radicals in attendance. Unlike his radical associates, he knew that true moral missionaries "must talk plainly, at the right time, though we may suffer for it." The "right to be righteous he [they] will never concede."[45]

In rare moments, however, Wright sensed that his old moral sensibilities contradicted his support for Bird Club radicals and the Republican party. In 1854, for example, he wrote a most revealing letter to Charles Scribner, who wanted to include Wright in an encyclopedia of American literature. Wright told Scribner that he did not belong in such a volume because he was, at heart, an immediatist: "The only interest of my life – to the world or to myself – attaches to my humblest efforts as an agitator against human slavery. My contempt for slaveholding and the miserable flunkies who govern this country in its behalf . . . is as great as any man's – and *that* I am not ashamed to have published."[46] Although a few of the radicals in the Saturday dining club may have occasionally entertained somewhat similar views, they never said so publicly and rarely acknowledged it privately. As Wright, Bird, Howe, Andrews, Sumner, and the others knew quite well, there was only one immediatist in the Bird Club.

Elizur Wright's relationship to his Bird Club associates illustrated, therefore, the ambiguous nature of the radical–immediatist cooperative tradition. Radicals and immediatists shared important social and ideological characteristics. Because of this common ground, they cooperated so frequently that others often found them indistinguishable. But fundamentally different temperaments and different concepts of slavery and freedom provoked serious personal disagreements between them that others never knew about.

By the early 1860s, this mixed relationship with the radicals had left immediatists in an awkward situation, for they found themselves considerably less attracted to their old intimacy groups than they had been at the beginning of their crusade against slavery. Indeed, of our three case studies, Gerrit Smith's intimacy group had recently dissolved and could not be reconstructed. Moreover, developments outside of the group had made life in the Boston Clique and the Tappan circle considerably less precious to several old insurgents and stewards. Consequently, we can understand why various immediatists sought out new friendship groups reflective of the immediatist–radical common cause. But as Wright's relationship with his Bird Club colleagues illustrated, major differences between immediatists and radicals very nearly precluded the development of warm and sharing intimacy circles like the old immediatist groups. Thus, for the first time since the emergence of their crusade, a good many first-generation immediatists were in a socially marginal and somewhat "homeless" position; their old friendship groups were ebbing, while no fully adequate replacements appeared in sight.

Moreover, in the course of the 1860s, immediatist piety was subjected to a rigorous test. Radical influence in the federal government soon became very substantial, especially in congressional Reconstruction policy. Constitutional amendments and Reconstruction legislation granting blacks legal emancipation, citizenship, and the vote were the most important results of their efforts. As immediatists watched radicals deploy political power decisively on behalf of Negro freedom, they began to debate among themselves whether they could withdraw from active life – whether their long-standing mission to the slaves had concluded. On the one hand, the radicals certainly had power and seemed to be wielding it to eradicate the vestiges of slavery. On the other hand, since the radicals were temperamentally disposed to compromise and did not really understand the nature of moral freedom, immediatists feared that Southern blacks could ultimately be returned to bondage unless they continued to press the radicals morally. Yet from their past experience with the radicals, immediatists knew too well that even if they remained active, the radicals would not necessarily listen to them, much less understand their promptings. Even in what seemed to be the last stages of the crusade for freedom, it therefore continued to be possible for the mission to the slaves to end in failure and for first-generation immediatists to go to their graves feeling that they had not met God's expectations of them. The old bonds of fellowship that had sustained them for decades were dissipating in these, their final years, but they had not yet become saints.

Part V

Termination

CHAPTER 9

A TROUBLED JUBILEE

In my judgment, the old anti-slavery routine is not what the cause now demands. Iconoclasm has had its day.

James Miller McKim to Oliver Johnson, January 22, 1862

Early in the spring of 1865, shortly after the fall of Richmond, William Lloyd Garrison received a telegram from the secretary of war. Along with Henry Ward Beecher, Major Gen. Robert Anderson, Theodore Tilton, and other prominent proadministration Northerners, he was invited to be the official guest of the federal government at an April 14 flag-raising ceremony at Fort Sumter. For the most part, first-generation immediatists were pleased that Garrison had been invited. Samuel May, Jr., characterized the invitation as "a recognition also of the antislavery movement of the country and a willing testimony of its essential worth. . . ." It assured Garrison "that slavery is annihilated beyond any hope of resurrection."[1]

Toward evening on April 14, after the official ceremony at Fort Sumter had taken place, Garrison went to the adjacent camp of the all Negro Fifty-fifth Massachusetts Regiment, where he met with a group of local freedmen. "Well" the editor of the *Liberator* cried to the freedmen, "you are free at last. Let us give three cheers." He led off with a first cheer, a second, and then a third, all without response. Finally, the leader of Boston Clique insurgency recognized the problem at hand. The freedmen did not understand the meaning of a commonplace cheer ritual and therefore did not know how they were supposed to respond to his promptings.[2]

In some rough sense, this episode illustrated a quandary that legal emancipation posed for first-generation immediatists. After more than three decades of arduous antislavery labor, they sensed that their active reform careers were concluding and they wanted desperately to believe that their efforts had been consequential – that they had really succeeded in freeing the slaves. But a variety of complicating factors – their suspicion of the Lincoln administration and even the radical wing of the Republican party, their distrust of the Southern planter class, and their mixed feelings about blacks in general – often tended to undercut their hopes that more than the legal formalities of emancipation had been won. Similarly, the failure of the freedmen on the outskirts of Charleston to respond to Garrison's cheers for freedom derived from a level of social and cultural isolation which he had not anticipated, and this signaled a gap between the de jure formalities of freedom and more complex social realities. Because of disparities between the legal documents of freedom and more uncertain actualities, the quest of first-generation immediatists for celebration – for clear-cut victory – became a most troublesome venture throughout the 1860s. It turned their gatherings to cheer the formal documents of emancipation into occasions for the sort of intense intramural bickering that they had not experienced since the late 1830s and early 1840s.

The bickering frequently centered on a very specific issue: Did the sundry legal guarantees of emancipation and civil rights that had been won for blacks in the 1860s (largely through the efforts of the radicals) provide ample cause for abolitionists to dissolve their old antislavery societies? On the other hand, were the old antebellum societies still needed in the struggle for de facto racial equality? Because second-generation immediatists such as Theodore Tilton and Horace White tended, more than the first generation, to look to the radicals and their party to wage that struggle for de facto equality whether antislavery societies dissolved or not, they rarely spoke out on the dissolution issue. For this reason, the active participants in the dissolution debate were almost entirely of the first generation. They struggled among themselves until the 1874 abolitionist reunion convention in Chicago. Only then were the surviving "old abolitionists" able to agree (with ambivalence) that the day of jubilee had arrived.

II

Almost all of the insurgent, steward, and voluntarist immediatists with whom we have been dealing were born between 1790 and 1810. Consequently, by the late 1850s and early 1860s some, but hardly all, could be considered old. To be sure, when the Civil War erupted Lewis Tappan had reached his seventy-third year, William Goodell was sixty-nine, Joshua Leavitt sixty-seven, and Beriah Green sixty-six. According to the perceptions of romantic writers of the time – commentators who had become keenly attentive to the aging process – these were indeed old and venerable men. But most first-generation immediatists were in their early and mid-fifties. Wendell Phillips and Abigail Kelley Foster had just turned fifty. Charles Burleigh, J. Miller McKim, and Samuel May, Jr., were fifty-one, Parker Pillsbury, Stephen Foster, and Oliver Johnson were only fifty-two, and George Cheever and John G. Whittier were fifty-four, while Garrison, George Whipple, and Henry Stanton were fifty-six.[3]

If first-generation immediatists were generally not old by Victorian standards, they nonetheless perceived themselves to be nearing the end. This is evidenced by certain set phrases in their correspondence that were invoked with increasing frequency between roughly the mid-1850s and the mid-1860s. There were constant references to "cracked voice and graying hairs," personal "wear and tear," "impaired" health, "the brink of the grave," "my little remaining strength," and "the life that is to come."[4] In part, these perceptions of personal aging were triggered by the deaths of immediatist colleagues. Whittier noted, for example, that "many" of the signers of the 1833 American Anti-Slavery Society Declaration of Sentiments "have passed away from the earth." "What havoc death is making with our scanty ranks!" Parker Pillsbury confided. Samuel May, Jr., found that deaths seemed to be decimating the families of members of the Boston Clique. More generally, he wondered, "how can we get on without" the immediatists who were being buried nearly every day.[5] Perceptions of personal aging were also prompted by the sense that the most crucial part of one's life – the period of vigorous antislavery endeavor directed by strong yet comforting immediatist clusters – was winding down and coming to an end. Oliver Johnson found, for example, that young reformers rather than the "original" missionaries who formed his Boston Clique were fast becoming the real directors of the abolitionist crusade. Similarly, Joshua Leavitt characterized antislavery colleagues, particularly those of his old Tappan circle, as belonging to "a period of life that has long passed away, never to return."[6]

By 1861, then, most first-generation immediatists, while only in their fifties, were sensing that life was passing them by. But would their crusade against slavery be successful? Were black bondsmen really to be freed? Positive answers to these questions were required to assure first-generation immediatists that the most essential part of their lives had been consequential. Negative answers, on the other hand, were to be taken as personal failure and the failure of their old immediatist clusters.

Desirous of a positive historical verdict on their antislavery agitation, immediatists had pursued two courses during the 1850s and into the war years. First, several openly acknowledged that bickering among them would not sit well with Clio. Indeed, because so many of their colleagues appeared to be dying off, factional infighting was a luxury that would have to be dispensed with. There were too few "old abolitionists" left. Maria Weston Chapman was perhaps the most cogent observer of the "strong cooperative policy" that seemed to prevail among immediatists of diverse clusters. By 1865, to be sure, fierce squabble would erupt over the questions of dissolving antislavery societies. But Chapman was able to note many efforts in the course of the 1850s to reunite "all our scattered forces from the Earliest time" and found that immediatists no longer were frightened in cooperating with other immediatists who had once struggled against them. Above all,

Chapman found that with the demise of the voluntarist Liberty party
and the steward-led American and Foreign Anti-Slavery Society, immediatists seemed to be returning to their first national organization,
the old American Anti-Slavery Society (A.A.S.S.). It was ceasing to be
the almost exclusive preserve of Boston Clique–directed insurgency.[7]

There was abundant evidence to sustain Chapman's observation.
Tappan circle steward George Cheever started to attend annual
A.A.S.S. meetings and even came to offer the prayer at opening sessions. Early during the Civil War, he opened his Church of the Puritans
in New York City for A.A.S.S. annual gatherings and fostered close
communication between that organization and his own Church Anti-
Slavery Society. Steward Theodore Weld and voluntarists Gerrit Smith
and William Goodell also renewed their support of the A.A.S.S., attended meetings, and even visited socially with members of the Boston
Clique. Henry Stanton conducted himself similarly. Lewis Tappan began
to read and to circulate the *National Anti-Slavery Standard*, the official organ
of the A.A.S.S. When Garrison invited Arthur Tappan to the A.A.S.S.
thirtieth anniversary meeting in 1863, Arthur was quite willing to
conclude their long-standing intramural feud and regretted "that any
occurrence should have estranged us from each other." From the standpoint of organizational structure, the abolitionist unity of the early
1830s seemed to have been substantially restored.[8]

First-generation immediatists realized, however, that more than an
end to antebellum factional fighting was required if they were to secure
a favorable historical verdict and with it, a sense that their lives had
been consequential. They had to help facilitate the verdict by furnishing
the proper historical materials – those that would most favorably reveal
their accomplishments. Toward that end, Wendell Phillips donated a
complete run of the *National Anti-Slavery Standard* and a three years' run of
the *Liberator* to the Library of Congress. He also provided a complete file
of the *Standard*, sundry numbers of the *Emancipator* and *Herald of Freedom*,
and several abolitionist pamphlets and reports to the Boston Public
Library. Samuel J. May gave Cornell University his enormous collection
of antislavery pamphlets and books. Voluntarist Luther Rawson Marsh
worked assiduously with Anna Weld to collect materials that would
guarantee a favorable historical place for her father. Steward William
Jay offered Wendell Phillips and other insurgents the use of his substantial library to accumulate pertinent documents on the abolitionist
crusade. Similarly, a large number of first-generation immediatists tried
to persuade Garrison to write an autobiography that would facilitate
the judgment of "the future historian of this country." The strategy
behind this flurry of activity was clear. By supplying the basic historical
materials on the antislavery crusade, immediatists could do much to
guide Clio's final judgment.[9]

The concern with antislavery history, then, at least partially reflected
immediatists' desires to be judged important, united, and consequential

as they approached the end. They proved remarkably adept at crucial and formidable last-minute historical arrangements to effect their goal. Indeed, through these arrangements, they were actually gathering together and making available materials that would publicize a tendency toward unity that had been slowly promoted, over many decades, by their efforts to forge a common cause with radicals and by the rather similar transformations that they had all experienced as they dealt with the woman question, biracialism, and violent means. As the old intramural disputes receded and, according to our three test cases, the old immediatist intimacy circles became less consequential, more and more of the abolitionist record revealed the sort of unity and celebration that Maria Chapman had described. As this evidence accumulated, and as abolitionists zealously preserved it for "the future historian," it seemed increasingly likely that Clio would smile upon them.

Unfortunately, these efforts at record preservation did not solve the most formidable problem with respect to a favorable historical judgment and a resultant sense of personal worth. Abolitionists had to consider whether the time had come to disband their old immediatist organizations and publications. If, as some had claimed as early as November 1860, they were victorious in their mission to the slaves, these were hardly needed. But could they, as pious reformers who were ultimately answerable to God, proceed to act on the premise that their mission to the slaves had been or was successful? If strong vestiges of slavery persisted as they dissolved the American Anti-Slavery Society, the *Liberator*, and the *National Anti-Slavery Standard*, shallow, worldly historians might think well of them. But God would see them as betrayers of His cause. This issue of organizational maintenance – when to dissolve – was to prove exceedingly disquieting for immediatists. No matter what they did, personal and collective distress followed. Their jubilee was a troubled one.

III

In early November 1860 Joshua Leavitt, formerly a Tappan circle steward, wrote to his radical Republican friend, Salmon Chase of Ohio, that the recent presidential election proved that antislavery principles had finally become ascendant: "Lincoln is chosen! What a growth since 1840. . . . It is a joy to have lived to this day." Garrison concurred, noting, "So far as the North is concerned, a marvellous change for the better has taken place in public sentiment, in relation to the Anti-Slavery movement." During the first year of the Civil War, first-generation immediatists of all clusters retained this sense of optimism: The Lincoln administration and the battlefield signaled the end to slavery. Voluntarist William Goodell called for the confiscation of rebel lands and their redistribution to the freedmen. Several other immediatists joined in the demand, and their expectations of success ran high.

Whittier, a steward, was sure that "the good cause goes on, and I bless God that I am permitted to see it." When General Fremont declared all slaves free within the area of his command, Garrison, the insurgent, asked Gerrit Smith, the voluntarist, "Is it not 'the beginning of the end,' and is not the end near?"[10] But when Lincoln annulled Fremont's order, a number of immediatists began to wonder whether a war to save the Union would become a war of emancipation. Insurgent Wendell Phillips and steward Simeon Jocelyn cautioned their colleagues to prepare for a long struggle; deep-seated evils like slavery and caste would be a long time in dying. By 1862 Lydia Child and Mary Grew had come to sense that even if the slaves were legally freed, their emancipators would not be peace-loving moral suasionists who "cared anything about the poor Negro." Consequently, even if emancipation came as "a 'war necessity,' everything *must* go wrong, if there is no heart or conscience on the subject."[11]

Thus, despite unmistakable and general optimism among immediatists at the beginning of the war, several quickly began to sense that Northerners had yet to be won over sufficiently to God's moral imperatives. As they warned their colleagues, immediatists generally came to assume that their antislavery organizations would have to remain active. Few dared suggest that the old mission to free the slaves had been completed.

Maria Weston Chapman of the Boston Clique was an exception. As early as fall 1861, she called for the dissolution of the American Anti-Slavery Society. The North had become antislavery, the Lincoln administration was trustworthy, and a new generation more attuned to the times would take up where "old abolitionists" left off: "All hail thou coming generation, that shall take up the work where our unqualified hands must leave it." In February 1862 Chapman elaborated, noting that her generation of immediatists was only "trained to a preparatory work" and that rising antislavery generations would destroy the vestiges of the "peculiar institution." If they wanted to continue their "preparatory" tradition, old-line immediatists could go South to areas occupied by federal troops and conduct benevolent missions to ready the blacks for freedom. Philadelphia insurgent J. Miller McKim, a friend of Boston Clique associates, concurred with Chapman. In January 1862 McKim resigned his position as corresponding secretary of the Pennsylvania Anti-Slavery Society. Since slavery would crumble under the weight of war, he insisted, there was no point in continuing old antislavery organizations. Rather, they should be supplanted by freedmen's aid associations that would send missionaries South to ready the slaves for freedom. McKim proceeded to organize several freedmen's aid missions. Chapman, diverting her financial resources from antislavery societies, became one of McKim's principal financial backers. In May 1862 Garrison himself seemed to be moving somewhat toward McKim's and

Chapman's new position. According to the leader of Boston Clique insurgency, missions to the freedmen like McKim's were *"popular* work as compared to ours" and immediatists should give it "all the incidental help in our power." Still, destruction of slavery had to remain their "special work" – at least until their radical colleagues could effect that end without their moral promptings. The other key figures in the Boston Clique strongly resisted the McKim and Chapman recommendation to shut down antislavery societies. Parker Pillsbury and Stephen and Abigail Kelley Foster voiced displeasure at Garrison's indirect and highly qualified support for McKim and Chapman. Wendell Phillips saw wisdom in the Pillsbury and Foster protests. Indeed, only Chapman's sisters, particularly Emma and Caroline Weston, defended her and McKim. The four withdrew from active support of the Boston Clique and its sundry immediatist organizations. "Their only connection with the cause now is to try and keep it quiet," Edmund Quincy sarcastically noted late in 1863.[12]

The Emancipation Proclamation added at least some plausibility to the Chapman and McKim position that the first generation's antislavery work was over and that the A.A.S.S. should disband. Although the proclamation freed no slaves within Confederate-held territory, it assured that bondsmen would be liberated when the Confederacy was defeated. Through this document, the Lincoln administration had explicitly coupled human freedom with restoration of the Union. The federal war effort was no longer officially conducted solely to save the nation. The president seemed to be listening to the immediatists and to their radical colleagues.

In December of 1863, the American Anti-Slavery Society held a special anniversary meeting in Philadelphia to celebrate the thirtieth year of its existence and to welcome the Emancipation Proclamation. Consistent with his emerging role as the embodiment of a unified abolitionist crusade, Garrison sent out a circular letter to all immediatist factions and clusters in most vicinities to effect a grand display of antislavery consensus. According to that circular, the A.A.S.S. was responsible for the Emancipation Proclamation: "The Society will have the sublime privilege to announce, as the result, primarily of its disinterested, patriotic, and Christian labors, the emancipation of Three Million Three Hundred Thousand Slaves, by the fiat of the American Government, on the lst of January last."[13]

The invitational circular characterized the tone of most pronouncements at the anniversary meeting where, for the first time, an American flag hung from the platform of an A.A.S.S. gathering. Delegates to the gathering repeatedly proclaimed that first-generation immediatists had won over the North through their organizations, their publications, and particularly their faithful missionary zeal. In 1833 "the cloud of Abolitionism was ever so big as a man's hand," McKim recalled. "Now it covers the heavens!" "We are getting near the end," charged Andrew Foss, "and I expect to see slavery abolished. I mean to be at the great jubilee. . . ." David Thurston of Maine concurred, noting that after thirty years of labor the immediatists had virtually succeeded in having their message adopted: "Behold what a great matter a little fire has kindled!" Mary Grew noted that because immediatists had always worked side by side in intimate daily cooperation, it was appropriate for them "to grasp one another's hands in fraternal congratulation" at the meeting and to express thanks "that America's Day of Jubilee had dawned. . . ." Samuel J. May fully concurred. Since fellowship – close daily association among devout reformers – had typified immediatism for so long, they should all join hands in victory, women as well as men. Clearly, a male–female co-missionary tradition seemed firmly established by 1863. This could not be said of the troubled immediatist biracial tradition.[14]

In a mood of gaiety and cheer, where aging immediatists were claiming responsibility for the Emancipation Proclamation and freely predicting the rapid death of slavery, Garrison, as presiding officer, felt compelled to bring up Maria Chapman's and J. Miller McKim's old proposal for organizational dissolution. Sensing that he had become a rallying figure among immediatists, he was not ready to be isolated from long-standing abolitionist missionaries the way McKim, Chapman, and the Weston sisters had been. "We trust that we are very near the jubilee," he stated in his introductory remarks to the convention. Next he read a letter to the gathering from Whittier, who had come around to the position of McKim and Chapman. The letter advised immediatists that personal piety required them to undertake the new mission of freedmen's aid – to "direct and educate these millions left free, indeed, but bewildered, ignorant, naked and foodless in the wild chaos of civil war." Garrison then put down Whittier's letter and offered a conditional proposal to the convention for dissolution of the A.A.S.S. If Congress abolished slavery, "I pledge the country that there shall be no more anti-slavery agitation." Since "everybody seems to desire to get rid of this kind of agitation, the shortest method is to abolish slavery, which is the sole cause of the agitation." Unlike McKim and Chapman, Garrison struck a responsive chord. Most convention delegates loudly applauded him, and one can see why. He had essentially proclaimed McKim's and Chapman's position of antislavery jubilee and immediatist redirection toward freedmen's aid missions. But unlike McKim and Chapman, he also insisted that slavery would have to be legally abolished throughout the land before the A.A.S.S. could properly disband. Of course, Garrison knew that slavery would be legally abolished on the heels of Union military victory; the Emancipation Proclamation had effectively pledged the national government to that end. Consequently, his position at the 1863 anniversary celebration would shortly allow him to credit the

A.A.S.S. with the Thirteenth Amendment and then permit him to claim, quite plausibly, that the society's mission to the slaves had been effected. He was shrewdly cultivating the soil for a recommendation that he would make in 1865.[15]

Although Garrison's skillful language garnered the support of most immediatists at the December anniversary celebration, he still encountered difficulty. Several months earlier, when he had vaguely hinted at dissolution at the annual meeting of the Massachusetts Anti-Slavery Society, he was sharply rebuked by Stephen Foster and Charles Remond. Moreover, Parker Pillsbury and Wendell Phillips of his own Boston Clique made their disapproval of Garrison's position known by boycotting the A.A.S.S. anniversary meeting. At this anniversary gathering, Foster and his wife, Abigail Kelley, warned that Garrison and other delegates were wrong even to consider the possibility of disbanding antislavery societies. The couple insisted that the mission to the slaves was far from won. Because the antislavery actions of President Lincoln were entirely motivated by political and military expediency, and because the radicals in his party had not learned what true freedom meant, neither could be counted on for sustained support. Immediatists would have to win the struggle for emancipation through their own efforts. For this reason, there could be no thought of dissolving the A.A.S.S., whatever the president or Congress did. Frederick Douglass, resentful and antagonistic toward Garrison since the late 1840s, supported the Fosters on the convention floor. He charged that the Lincoln administration and Northerners generally still regarded abolitionism as odious. They were putting down slavery to save the Union, not out of any sense of the injustice of human bondage. Until the North was morally rejuvenated, it was therefore folly to call for immediatist organizational dissolution.[16]

Garrison quickly realized what the Fosters and Douglass were doing at the December anniversary meeting to his well-disguised rendition of the McKim–Chapman plan. He struck back by defending the sincerity of Lincoln, the radicals, and antislavery Republicans generally: "It is not at all our province to undertake to determine the motives by which the people are animated, who have recently come into sympathy and cooperation with us for the abolition of slavery.. . . ." "Whoever will come up now and speak a word for freedom, I will hail as a friend and a brother," Garrison added, "and will leave his motives to God, to whom alone he is responsible." Boston Clique insurgent Oliver Johnson also moved to quell doubts about the sincerity of antislavery Republicans who were needed to defeat the South and to abolish slavery. But whereas Garrison refused to examine the possibility of impious Republican motivation, even within the party's nonradical wings, Johnson was willing to settle for Republican recognition that antislavery was "coincident with their worldly interest." "Saints – perfect people – do not travel in regiments,"

Johnson maintained. Centuries might elapse before even some radicals, to say nothing of other nonimmediatists, were "brought up to the standard of absolute justice and righteousness."[17]

The differences between the Fosters and Douglass, on the one hand, and Garrison and Johnson on the other, were clear. The former were unwilling to dissolve abolitionist organizations until the initial immediatist missionary commitment to national moral regeneration was met. The latter were ready to settle for formal legal emancipation through a broad-based coalition of pious immediatists plus radicals and other Republicans with less than pure motives. Indeed, Garrison and Johnson were apprehensive that the Foster–Douglass course could leave aging and worn-out immediatists as impotent as they had been in 1833, when the A.A.S.S. was founded. Should that transpire, they might never be able to claim victory; they would soon go to their graves without being able to feel that their lives had been significant. "Personally, I am tired of speech-making, and therefore, am glad that we are apparently so near the end of our great conflict," Garrison privately wrote to Johnson. Coalition politics with radicals and other antislavery moderates was clearly the more promising upbeat course, for it led to the end that Garrison and Johnson required.[18]

Judging from the surviving record of this 1863 anniversary meeting, Garrison and Johnson spoke for the overwhelming number of delegates. They were repeatedly cheered, whereas the Fosters and Douglass were not. But the victory was elusive. Divisions among first-generation immediatists on the question of organizational dissolution soon became more substantial.

IV

Congressional approval of the Thirteenth Amendment early in 1865 and the certainty of rapid state ratification brought out these divisions. With slavery legally abolished, it seemed quite plausible to question the ongoing responsibilities of antislavery societies. Maria Chapman and her sister, Anne Weston, raised the issue at the January meeting of the insurgent Massachusetts Anti-Slavery Society, claiming that the work of the organization had been completed. Abigail Kelley Foster quickly demanded their expulsion from the society's board of managers. Samuel May, Jr., the Boston Clique friend and associate of Chapman and Weston, skillfully headed off the expulsion effort. But the overwhelming consensus of the delegates was to retain the Massachusetts society. At the annual meeting of the steward- and Tappan circle–dominated American Church Anti-Slavery Society in May, the issue of dissolution was similarly debated but handily defeated. That same month, Garrison sought to disband the A.A.S.S. and secured the support of the board of managers. But quite uncharacteristically he miscalculated his support on the convention floor and was defeated by a lopsided vote of 118 to 48. He regarded this as a vote of no confidence and was certain, at any rate, that the A.A.S.S. had ceased to have a mission. Consequently, along with Maria Chapman, J. Miller McKim, Edmund Quincy, Oliver Johnson, Anne Weston, Samuel May, Jr., Sydney Howard Gay, and other long-standing immediatists, Garrison withdrew from the organization with which his name had so long been associated. Quincy and Johnson left the editorial office of the A.A.S.S.-sponsored *National Anti-Slavery Standard*. In turn, the victorious side of the floor vote assumed the key A.A.S.S. positions. Insurgent Phillips became president, and voluntarist Gerrit Smith and stewards George Cheever and John G. Whittier were among the vice-presidents, while insurgent Parker Pillsbury assumed editorial duties at the *Standard*. Clearly, the A.A.S.S. had ceased to be the preserve of a solidly united Boston Clique. We have noted how long-standing cluster allegiances had been weakened severely well before the dissolution controversy commenced. Now, in 1865, these allegiances seemed to have no bearing at all upon the behavior of most first-generation immediatists as insurgents, voluntarists, and stewards from diverse clusters assumed cooperative control over the A.A.S.S. The year concluded with Garrison ceasing publication of the *Liberator*.[19]

During the entire year of 1865, then, the question of dissolving long-standing immediatist societies and publications was extensively debated. It had become the foremost topic of concern for the first generation, and Garrison's position in favor of total dissolution formed the basis of most discussion. His position was clear and to the point. The Thirteenth Amendment – the supreme law of the land – outlawed slavery and all efforts at its restoration. Thus, the amendment represented "the complete triumph as well as utter termination of the Anti-Slavery struggle, as such." Consequently, Garrison claimed, "My vocation as an Abolitionist, thank God, is ended." This was a rationale not to cease missionary efforts in the freedmen's behalf but only to stop working under the abolitionist banner: "True, there will be other work to be done; but we shall then mingle with the great mass of the people, who have accepted abolition, and unite with them in carrying foward the struggle for equal political privileges." Freedmen's aid missions such as those which McKim had initiated came highly recommended as vehicles within which ex-abolitionists, radicals, and other well-intentioned Americans might unite. Indeed, Garrison seemed to take special pleasure in organizational dissolution because it meant that he would cease to be viewed as "an isolated Abolitionist, to be looked at as though I had seven heads and ten horns." Abolitionists had to break their long-standing habit of "isolation from the great mass of the people, when the reasons which compelled them to take such a position no longer exist." To remain separate was to deny the enormous victory at hand. Abolitionists had converted Americans to antislavery doctrine, and the time for

jubilance and dissolution was at hand. To remain distinctive in their
societies and publications – as the isolated if devout reformers of former
years – was to deny the enormous victory that they had achieved.
Immediatists did this at their peril, Garrison warned. At this late period
in their lives, it was far better to rejoice in their unprecedented success
than to continue "struggling against wind and tide, as I have done in the
past." After decades of effort, people now stopped Garrison in the
streets to congratulate the formerly despised insurgent for his victory.
Sixty years old and weary, he was unwilling to give that up by continuing the pious and isolated mission for the slaves.[20]

The deposed chief of the A.A.S.S. was essentially propounding two
basic and related points throughout 1865, and both followed logically
from his remarks at the December 1863 A.A.S.S. anniversary gathering.
Immediatists needed to be joyous in victory as they entered their
advanced years, and they could not really do so until they mingled with
their countrymen free of their long-standing commitment to antislavery
organization. Widened social circles, separation from the past, and
jubilee were inseparable. "Old abolitionists" such as Samuel J. May,
Theodore Weld, Marius Robinson, and Arthur and Lewis Tappan went
along with Garrison's claims without giving them very close scrutiny.
May frankly acknowledged that "our long experience of your wisdom
and sagacity forbids us to distrust the correctness of your determination." Weld, Robinson, and the Tappans thought it best to acknowledge formal victory and convert abolitionist organizations into "precious" memories. Lewis Tappan found McKim's freedman's aid
organizations too secular; he claimed that his own American Missionary
Association was better suited for the next generation of evangelical reformers who sought to aid the ex-slaves. Like the others, Henry Wright
accepted Garrison's argument for antislavery society disbandment uncritically, although he acknowledged "a feeling of isolation and loneliness"
when he ceased to hold exclusive "communion with my fellow [immedia-
tist] beings" through the columns of the Liberator. Wright was clearly un-
enthusiastic over the prospect of mixing in wider, less pious circles.[21]

Still, three long-standing members of the by now nearly defunct Boston Clique – Edmund Quincy, Oliver Johnson, and Samuel May, Jr. –
felt compelled to elaborate and buttress Garrison's case for dissolution.
They underscored the seeming illogic of maintaining antislavery organizations when slavery had ceased to be, noting that "it is an anomaly,
a solecism, an absurdity, to maintain an *anti-slavery* society after slavery
is killed." They also asserted that there was something divine in the
termination of slavery thirty-five years after the Liberator had commenced publication. God was telling immediatist missionaries that their
cause was complete with so fundamental a victory. The only thing left
for them to do in their old antislavery organizations was to engage in
"splitting of hairs," "threshing the straw after the grain was out," so

that they continued quite pointlessly in an isolated position. Rather, immediatists should break clear of their victorious but now irrelevant organizations, shed their "old clothes," and mingle with others to aid the freedmen: "It is not death, it is translation. It is not extinction, it is being swallowed up in victory."[22]

One might maintain that Garrison, Quincy, Johnson, and May, Jr., were naively zealous in accepting the legalisms of emancipation – that they were abandoning antislavery organizations before de facto freedom became a reality. But this is to demand of them unusual predictive powers. It is only in recent years that historians have fully demonstrated the perpetuation of certain slaveholder controls over blacks in the postwar years. On the other hand, these veteran abolitionists did recognize that federal military victory and the Thirteenth Amendment had significantly changed important realities – that immediatists were not confronting precisely the same issues that they had faced before the Civil War. If their insistence on disbanding old abolitionist organizations was premature, it also reflected daring and courage. It demonstrated a willingness to explore unfamiliar missionary roles by acting with a wide variety of nonimmediatists in new freedman's aid organizations – diverse new colleagues with perhaps even more questionable piety than their radical associates of the past decade and a half. To be sure, one reason why immediatists like Garrison, Quincy, Johnson, and May, Jr., supported organizational dissolution late in their reformist careers was that it allowed them to believe that those careers had been consequential and that victory had been achieved. But this should not belittle the courage involved in breaking from the old slogans, issues, societies, and publications that had become inseparable from their daily lives and endorsing a new type of missionary crusade.

In the diverse antislavery society meetings and discussions over disbandment during 1865, Garrison's position was strenuously challenged and was usually defeated whenever a floor vote was taken. As a brilliant orator, a charismatic leader, and the architect of the most fully developed antidissolution position, Clique insurgent Wendell Phillips led the opposition. He received backing from other insurgents who included Mary Grew and Lydia Child, from stewards such as Henry Cheever, from voluntarists Gerrit Smith and Beriah Green, from Elizur Wright, and from leading black immediatists Frederick Douglass, Charles Remond, Robert Purvis, and others. But Phillips's principal support came from Parker Pillsbury and Stephen and Abigail Kelley Foster – insurgents who had generally backed the Boston Clique while dwelling in more provincial parts of New England. Like Phillips, the three tended to be general social agitators as well as abolitionists. For them, antislavery often appeared to be but one aspect of a more general crusade for the rights of laborers, white and black.

In the course of 1864 and the early months of 1865, Phillips had

developed a comprehensive position against the dissolution of anti-
slavery societies. He concluded that an educated, landed, enfranchised,
yeoman-centered South would be the most formidable barrier to the
restoration of the planter class to political and economic hegemony. To
facilitate this power shift, Phillips, like the prodissolutionists, favored
education for the freedman. But he felt that education had to be accompanied by other more fundamental measures – namely confiscation
of the large plantations and dividing the land among the freedmen and
immigrants who might settle in the South. Phillips also urged the
disfranchisement of leading Confederates and the enfranchisement of
blacks through a constitutional amendment.[23] Substantial federal activity would be necessary to effect these fundamental economic and political changes, but Phillips did not think the radicals or their party would
press for it. Rather, he assumed, even with the moribund state of old
immediatist intimacy circles, abolitionists and their societies constituted
the only truly reliable pressure groups in behalf of appropriate federal
action. Unless the ex-slaves secured land and the vote, he maintained,
they would never be able to assert de facto freedom, the Thirteenth
Amendment and other emancipatory legalisms notwithstanding:

Now, to my mind, an American abolitionist, when he asks freedom for the
Negro, means effectual freedom, real freedom, something that can maintain and
vindicate itself. I do not believe in an English freedom, that trusts the welfare of
the dependent class to the good will and moral sense of the upper class.[24]

Unlike Garrison, Phillips had supported Fremont for president over
Lincoln in 1864. He was sure that a Lincoln administration that never
bothered to call upon people with thoughts like his own for advice was
neither desirous of land redistribution nor black enfranchisement – the
measures that were indispensable for de facto Negro freedom. This
meant that abolitionists could not depend upon Lincoln's good will. By
early August 1865 Phillips had also given up on Lincoln's successor,
dubbing him "Jefferson Davis Johnson." Even more than the Lincoln
presidency, Andrew Johnson's administration had to be pressured to
change its policies toward the freedmen or to be replaced through the
electoral process if it failed to rescue them from the hegemony of the
planter class. Phillips charged that Garrison's advocacy of organizational
dissolution and freedmen's aid societies drew abolitionist resources away
from this essential political task of securing a reliable federal administration. Moreover, freedmen's missions represented paternalistic
almsgiving – holding the freedmen "before the country as a chronic
pauper." This was not true abolitionism.[25]

In actuality, Phillips's justification for continuing abolitionist organizations probably represented a greater departure from antebellum
immediatist doctrines than Garrison's argument for dissolution. To be
sure, there were certain traces of themes of conflict among classes for

economic and political power in the writings of some occasional antebellum supporters of the abolitionist cause. This was particularly true
among the Jacobin-disposed artisans in the Tappan circle's New York
City constituency, with their commitments to egalitarian communal
values. Moreover, Henry Bowditch, John Collins, Nathaniel Rogers,
and a number of other rather important if iconoclastic immediatists
sometimes developed the class conflict theme quite extensively. But
judging from almost all of the members of our three focal immediatist
intimacy circles and from what historians have discovered about the
overwhelming number of other active antebellum abolitionists, most
clearly perceived the debate over the "peculiar institution" as a moral
conflict between antislavery saints and proslavery sinners for converts.
Thus, Garrison seems to have been quite right in asserting that if, by
1865, most Northerners had come to recognize the immorality of
slavery, the old mission to the slaves was properly completed. Phillips's
characterization of the antislavery crusade as a more secular struggle
against planter class hegemony was more distant from the thought of
most active antebellum immediatists and resembled, in a certain limited
sense, the ideology of a few of their radical colleagues.

The most compelling proof that Phillips was probably departing in
1865 from standard immediatist assumptions was in the pronouncements of those who supported him. Although Henry Cheever of the
Church Anti-Slavery Society, for example, was strongly disposed
toward maintaining the old antislavery organizations, he never cited
issues of class hegemony. Rather, Cheever felt that the antislavery
cause would be truly won once blacks secured the ballot "as the acknowledged right of American citizenship." Although Stephen Foster
would subsequently publicize antidissolution views much like Phillips's,
in 1865, he made only slight and fleeting references to class. Foster
underscored Negro suffrage as the paramount moral necessity and
insisted that immediatist societies were required because neither Americans generally nor the politicians they elected were truly committed to
black political equality. Parker Pillsbury, too, held back from broader
class considerations. Instead, he underscored freedman's suffrage as the
culmination of the immediatist crusade for moral rectitude. According
to Pillsbury, antislavery organizations more than freedmen's aid associations were required to direct reformers to this moral target. Although
most black abolitionists supported Phillips, they rarely ventured beyond
calls for the vote. Indeed, of all Phillips's 1865 supporters, only Gerrit
Smith was willing to publicize views that went very far beyond formal
black ballot rights. Because he had assumed for decades that the
Constitution was unambiguously antislavery, Smith was unimpressed
with the Thirteenth Amendment and other emancipatory legalities of
1865. Rather, like Phillips, Smith openly proclaimed that the power
balance in the South would determine whether de facto emancipation

occurred. But unlike Phillips, Smith saw power in racial rather than class terms. Blacks would be able to assert de facto freedom if they had ballots to elect officials who would support them against proslavery whites.[26]

It is simplistic, then, to characterize the 1865 dissolution controversy as a struggle between a Garrison camp that wanted antislavery jubilance prematurely and a Phillips camp that sought de facto emancipation. All participants in the debate wanted de facto as well as de jure Negro freedom. All, including Garrison, felt that blacks had to be rapidly franchised. And none – not even Phillips – deeply disapproved of freedmen's aid societies. After all, these societies were clearly offshoots of an antislavery missionary tradition and were pledged to uplift the freedmen. This is all to say that each participant in the 1865 debate felt that immediatists were morally bound to assist Southern blacks after emancipation was legally proclaimed. Moreover, although Edmund Quincy and Samuel Sewall strongly supported Garrison on dissolution, they came closer to accepting Phillips's class-based justification for protecting the freedmen than most of Phillips's antidissolution supporters of 1865. The real debate among immediatists was not about premature abandonment of their mission to the slaves but about whether to cut the strings to the traditional antislavery organizations much as they had cut emotional ties to the old intimacy clusters. Were they to operate with new people and new missionary agencies, or would they cling to their time-tested societies? Herein lay the quandry. Garrison, closer to traditional immediatist moral arguments, wanted to dissolve the old antislavery societies, while Phillips, departing significantly from those moral arguments with a secular and class-based analysis, struggled to perpetuate the old societies.[27]

V

The year 1865 ended with Phillips presiding over the A.A.S.S., Parker Pillsbury editing the *Standard*, the *Liberator* ceasing, the majority of antebellum antislavery societies resolved against disbanding, the Boston Clique fragmented beyond repair, the old Gerrit Smith circle making no attempt to regroup behind the former leader, and members of Lewis Tappan's cluster divided among themselves. A sorting process had taken place, with proponents of dissolution withdrawing from the old immediatist societies and working periodically within freedmen's aid agencies. In turn, those who remained within the old antislavery societies had almost invariably rallied behind Phillips. Because prodissolutionists and antidissolutionists were therefore operating, by 1866, within different organizations – either freedmen's aid agencies or the old antislavery societies – one might have predicted fewer displays of hostility. Since antagonists on the dissolution question were no longer attending the same meetings, they had no common forums in which to debate. Nevertheless, intramural conflicts remained heated.

In part, discord continued because proponents and opponents of dissolution continued to exchange sharp gibes wherever they possibly could. In January 1866, for example, Garrison appeared at the annual meeting of the Massachusetts Anti-Slavery Society to mock the delegates: "If any of you fancy that simply coming here once a year to hold a meeting is essential to the cause of freedom, you can cherish that pleasing illusion." Anne Weston made the same point. She charged that it really did not matter whether antislavery societies continued to exist in name. The reality was that abolitionists "are merged, as they should be with the great mass of their fellow citizens." Antidissolutionists responded in kind. Stephen Foster scorned "the old-time faces" who had left antislavery organizational activity before freedmen's rights were securely protected. Abigail Kelley Foster noted that it was criminal for Garrison to go to Europe "and boast there that we have had no slavery here" when blacks were "held, worked and treated as slaves" in the rural districts of the South. Parker Pillsbury even felt compelled to qualify his endorsement of a national testimonial to raise $50,000 to support Garrison. By supporting the testimonial, he was not endorsing Garrison's "false" views on antislavery society dissolution or Garrison's "false" notion of "our commingling harmoniously henceforth with the masses of the loyal North."[28]

In 1867 a very ugly fight erupted between antagonists on the dissolution question, and it centered on Francis Jackson's bequest. When Jackson, a Boston Clique intimate, died in November 1861, he left $10,000 for the antislavery cause. Garrison and Phillips were among the trustees designated to dispose of this bequest. It took more than five years to dispense with legal formalities, and the $10,000 did not become available until 1867, when the meaning of the old mission to the slaves had become a point of contention. Supported by Edmund Quincy, Maria Weston Chapman, and Samuel May, Jr., Garrison charged that the freedmen's aid societies had become the proper channel for antislavery missionary activity and therefore for the entire bequest. Phillips, backed by Pillsbury, the Fosters, and Mary Grew, strongly disagreed, insisting that the money had to support the A.A.S.S. organ, the *National Anti-Slavery Standard*, in its battle for black enfranchisement. A compromise was reached at the beginning of the year; the bequest was to be split between the A.A.S.S. and the New England branch of the American Freedmen's Union Commission (A.F.U.C.). But in May, Garrison changed his mind. A Reconstruction act was passed on March 2, and it required reconstructed state governments to permit blacks to vote. Therefore, Garrison argued, the A.A.S.S. crusade for black enfranchisement had become superfluous. Consequently, the entire bequest should go to the New England branch, which desperately required funds for missionary educational efforts among the freedmen. Phillips and his supporters were infuriated by Garrison's "betrayal" and by his charge that the A.A.S.S. had become "debris." A brief legal battle ensued. A master in chancery of the Massachusetts Supreme Court ruled for Garrison, but Phillips persuaded a majority of the trustees of the Jackson bequest to refuse to comply with the ruling. In response, the Supreme Court reconstituted the board of trustees, and all $10,000 went to the New England A.F.U.C. Phillips, the Fosters, Pillsbury, and Grew were more angry with Garrison than with the "proslavery" Supreme Court. They charged the former head of Boston Clique insurgency with betraying Jackson's intent. As they saw matters, Garrison had forgotten that Jackson had always favored unpopular causes such as the A.A.S.S. over "popular benevolent societies" such as the new freedmen's aid societies. He had lost sight of true immediatist tradition. One did better for blacks by spending money on the theater than by donating it to the A.F.U.C. Phillips's personal anger with Garrison and his prodissolution supporters over the Jackson bequest became so intense that when Samuel May, Jr., wrote a letter to the *Standard* defending Garrison's position on the controversy, Phillips would not allow it to be printed. Several years elapsed before these Boston Clique colleagues would speak to each other again.[29]

While relationships between the leading contenders in the fight over dissolution reached a nadir, discord erupted among antidissolutionists themselves on the old nemesis of organizational disbandment. Early in 1869 Congress proposed the Fifteenth Amendment and submitted it to the states for ratification. To support state ratification, the A.A.S.S. resolved at its annual meeting in May that in giving blacks the vote, the amendment represented "the capstone and completion of our movement; the fulfillment of our pledge to the Negro race." The ratification process was completed in March 1870. In April the A.A.S.S. adjourned what was clearly understood to be its final meeting *sine die*, and almost all remaining antislavery societies followed its lead at their own annual meetings. The *National Anti-Slavery Standard* changed its name to the *National Standard* – "an independent journal of Reform and Literature." For all practical purposes, abolitionism as a collective organized phenomenon – a coordinated effort of pious fellows from diverse clusters – had come to an end.[30]

Despite pervasive rhetoric of joviality and jubilance much like that of 1863 and 1865, the decision by most antidissolutionists effectively to disband provided the basis for the final intramural squabble among first-generation immediatists. Stephen Foster and Parker Pillsbury, Wendell Phillips's closest associates in the prior dissolution controversies, were the chief spokesmen for perpetuating antislavery societies throughout the 1869–70 debate. Supported by Abigail Kelley Foster, Elizur Wright, Sallie Holley, and Caroline Putnam, they turned against Phillips,

Charles Burleigh, Gerrit Smith, Frederick Douglass, and most of their other colleagues who had defied Garrison and had remained in antislavery societies after 1865. In essence, Foster and Pillsbury maintained that passage of the Fifteenth Amendment completed the process through which the freedmen had been vested with formal legal rights. But they still had "none of the capacities to use those rights." They now had, for example, the formal right to cast ballots. But they did not have the means to deal with efforts by the Southern planter class to force them away from the voting booth or to punish them if they voted against planter interests. Therefore, antislavery societies were still needed to assure that de jure rights of Southern freedmen became de facto rights. More specifically, the A.A.S.S. and other antislavery societies were needed as agencies to pressure the federal government and Southern state legislatures to redistribute land – to take it from the planter class and transfer it to the freedmen. For blacks to cast uncoerced ballots and thereby become capable of asserting and preserving de facto freedom, they had to own their own homesteads. Land ownership would make them economically independent of the planter aristocracy, and this independence would allow them to resist political intimidation by the planters. Thus, land redistribution was required before the mission to the slaves could terminate.[31]

Although Foster and Pillsbury had not characterized the struggle for freedmen's rights quite as comprehensively in terms of class conflict in 1869 and 1870 as Phillips had in 1865, their argument against dissolution was nevertheless strikingly similar to the argument that Phillips had deployed that year against Garrison and his supporters. Between 1865 and 1869, however, the leading figure in the A.A.S.S. had changed.

By early 1869 Wendell Phillips was propounding a prodissolution position. His attitude somewhat paralleled that which had prompted Garrison openly to support dissolution four years earlier. As Garrison's prodissolution posture of 1865 had partially reflected a desire to move on from abolitionism to freedmen's aid projects, Phillips's acceptance of dissolution in 1869–70 was at least modestly rooted in his desire to move on to the emerging Massachusetts Labor party and its campaign for a shorter work day and a state bureau of labor statistics. Indeed, in 1870 Phillips became the Labor party's gubernatorial candidate and narrowly missed being nominated by the National Labor Union for the presidency in 1872. To be sure, unlike Garrison in 1865, Phillips in 1869 and 1870 conceded Foster's and Pillsbury's point that formal rights would not necessarily evolve into de facto rights. Also unlike Garrison, Phillips perceived the struggle for Negro freedom as part of a larger struggle of laborers against capital and aristocratic privilege. But though Phillips remained more the general agitator against class privilege than Garrison, by 1869 and 1870 he too counseled his fellow immediatists to overlook Foster and Pillsbury and to become more temperate and tolerant of their fellow citizens – to mellow and to recognize that most of their associates were necessarily somewhat less than pious. He urged abolitionists to mingle with people of goodwill outside of the old immediatist agencies, for with the Fifteenth Amendment their antislavery views had at last been entirely accepted by their countrymen: "We don't disband: she (the nation) takes us on board. We have no constitution left under which to exist. The Constitution of the United States has absorbed it all." With intelligent use of the ballot and a national consensus supportive of his rights, the freedman should be able to fend for his own needs: "He holds at last his sufficient shield [the vote] in his hands; that which has always sufficed, in the long run, for the protection of an oppressed class. Thwarted at one moment, bullied or starved at another, the voter, if true to himself, always conquers and dictates his own fate and position in the end. . . ." With the freedman finally able to fend for himself effectively, Phillips concluded, abolitionists had accomplished "all that the friends of freedom have ever asked the nation," and the time for jubilation was at hand: "Our long work is sealed at last." Antislavery societies could finally disband, never having to regroup again save for "some unexpected emergency."[32]

Historian Richard Curry has correctly noted that Wendell Phillips's ideas were in extreme flux during the late 1860s and that it may be impossible to fathom all of his objectives.[33] But the promulgation of the Fifteenth Amendment seems crucial in understanding his new posture on the dissolution issue. It may have given him a rationale for traveling beyond old immediatist agencies and becoming more supportive of his Labor party and National Labor Union colleagues in labor's struggle against capital. At any rate, by 1869 and 1870 we find Phillips detailing a class-based analysis in his discussions of workingmen's agitation while he propounded a Garrison-like moral suasion posture when he spoke of the old mission to the slaves. While defending the specific material interests of the laboring population, he repeated Garrison's moral and legal testimonials concerning the end of Negro slavery (deemphasizing the actual material condition of black bondsmen). With the realization that blacks could legally vote, Phillips had actually invoked the same essential argument for dissolution that Garrison had enunciated four years earlier – that there was cause for jubilation because the nation had granted all of the immediatists' traditional demands. Other "old abolitionists" of diverse antebellum backgrounds and intimacy groups who had balked at calls for dissolution in 1865 now echoed Phillips. Delegates to the 1869 annual meeting of the A.A.S.S. were only willing to support a version of Foster's and Pillsbury's call for land redistribution in the South that was watered down to the point of being almost meaningless. By 1870 first-generation immediatists as committed as Gerrit Smith, John G. Whittier, Charles Burleigh, David and Lydia Child, Lucretia Mott, Mary Grew, and Edward Davis had left the old antislavery societies and periodicals with Wendell Phillips's words on their lips – that their immediatist organization "ceases because its work is done." They had moved "from the small and apparently hopeless beginning of the Anti-Slavery movement nearly forty years ago, to the hour when not only Slavery but prejudice of color and distinctions of caste are forever prohibited by the amended constitution of the country." The Fifteenth Amendment had fully guaranteed that "master and slave have become equal fellow-citizens. Thus is accomplished the work for which the Anti-Slavery Societies of this country were organized." But immediatists must never become overconfident. Now and then they were required to look southward at "the country of the old enemy, to see and proclaim what is going on there." They might also work in behalf of the laboring man, women's rights, and other egalitarian causes, for the devout reformer was always in demand. But they could rejoice that their mission to the slaves had ended and that, like their old intimacy circles, their antislavery societies were no longer needed.[34]

One can, of course, maintain that Foster and Pillsbury and their supporters were left in a minority position in 1869 and 1870 because most of the antidissolutionists of 1865 felt that antislavery societies should exist until blacks secured ballot rights. The Fifteenth Amendment insured freedmen the franchise, making disbandment feasible. But this explanation hardly reveals why Gerrit Smith, Wendell Phillips, and others who had focused on de facto power realities in 1865 and had made little of franchise formalities seemed willing to settle for those formalities a few years later. Nor does it indicate why the franchise was such an important legal formality to the overwhelming number of the antidissolutionists of 1865. Finally, the explanation fails to inform us why antidissolutionists including Pillsbury, the Fosters, Elizur Wright, Sallie Holley, and Caroline Putnam continued to be unimpressed with de jure voting rights and wanted to press on in 1870 with the old antislavery societies.

If our exploration of first-generation immediatists has, by now, made one point clear, it is that we only superficially account for intramural divisions and behavioral changes by looking at their ideas devoid of the specific social and psychological context. We miss the crucial hidden issues of the dissolution debates of the 1860s if we restrict ourselves to ideological probing. To be sure, Phillips, Pillsbury, and Stephen Foster had espoused class-oriented social philosophies throughout the 1870s and had participated in labor reform movements of the decade. But during the prior decade – the period of the dissolution debates – their general social ideas and ultimate goals were less clear; not even Phillips had consistently expounded a class analysis. The value of ideological analysis is also limited if we note that none of the participants in the 1860s dissolution debates differed fundamentally on specific policies in behalf of the freedmen – not even Phillips, Pillsbury, and Foster. All participants in the debates sought de facto as well as de jure Negro rights. All believed that whether the old antislavery agencies existed or not, immediatists had to remain concerned with de facto freedom. They had to keep a "telescope" on the South and regroup in the unlikely event of "some unexpected emergency." The divisions and angry disputes that followed the Emancipation Proclamation, the Thirteenth Amendment, and the Fifteenth Amendment all focused on disbanding antislavery societies. Therefore, they essentially concerned the continuation or alteration of the institutional structure of immediatists' reform careers. In debating dissolution, immediatists were asking themselves whether, with their old intimacy circles nearly extinct, they still wanted to remain in prewar organizations, to publish and read antislavery literature, and to work until their dying days for full Negro freedom. They were deciding whether to continue to center their efforts in the old societies of pious fellows that had been formed when they had been a hated minority or whether the time had come for them truly to mix in common cause with other reformers with different backgrounds, values, and interests. In some measure, they were even deciding whether, as elderly people, they could begin to devote time to private personal cares that did not missionize or uplift society. At base, then, they were trying to determine the basic directions of their lives in the years that remained to them.

Eventually, all but a very small handful of first-generation immediatists arrived at the same general responses to these issues. They decided to complete the break with their antebellum immediatist past. But some, like J. Miller McKim and Maria Chapman, came to a decision very early in the 1860s, while others, such as Wendell Phillips and Gerrit Smith, did not make a final decision until the Fifteenth Amendment was ratified nearly a decade later. The different amounts of time that immediatists took to reach a final decision were at the roots of the dissolution squabbles of the 1860s. Various abolitionists were essentially insisting that their own particular timing accorded with God's dictates for the completion of the mission to the slaves.

Perceptions of external racial realities contributed significantly to the differences in timing. The outbreak of the Civil War was sufficient to assure McKim and Chapman that the immediatist mission was secure, Garrison required the Emancipation Proclamation, and Quincy, Johnson, and May, Jr., needed the Thirteenth Amendment, while Phillips, Smith, and most other "old abolitionists" had to have the Fifteenth Amendment. But the sense that one was aging and drawing near the grave may have affected the timing of an immediatist at least as much as his perception of racial realities. Indeed, in the course of the 1860s one constantly notes private references by first-generation immediatists to being "too worn and weary for active labor," and "too old to engage anew in controversy." "My age & infirmities unfit me for conflict," wrote one. "I am growing old, and am disposed to ask for peace in my day," noted another. Indeed, Stephen and Abigail Kelley Foster accused several of their fellow immediatists of proclaiming victory and calling for dissolution of antislavery societies because they felt too tired to continue on in the strenuous mission to the slaves. A subtler truth, however, is that jubilance was indispensable if an abolitionist was to sense, as he neared the grave, that his life had been important. Lydia Child was sixty-eight and her husband, David, was seventy-six when, too feeble to attend the final meeting of the A.A.S.S. in 1870, they coauthored a letter to the delegates. It was well to cheer for victory and dissolve, they wrote, for "soul-stirring experiences" such as the immediatist mission "come but once in a lifetime; but when the chariot of fire ascends, it drops upon the earth a mantle for succeeding prophets." It was too late in life for abolitionists to experience again the enthusiasm that they had felt in the antislavery cause, but they could rest content that their lives had been rich and their success grand.[35]

Unfortunately for the Childs and for the peace of mind of most other first-generation immediatists who happened to be alive in 1870, there were still old colleagues such as the Fosters and Pillsbury around, who charged that the cause was being abandoned before the slaves were truly free. In part this concern explains why, even as they approached the grave, most "old abolitionists" continued to watch for suspicious developments in the South and to worry about them.

VI

With the dissolution issue finally resolved in 1870 and with first-generation immediatists aging and lacking the stamina to wage intramural wars over other differences, it was predictable that the bitterness among them would gradually subside. The personal reconciliation between Garrison and Phillips in the early 1870s highlighted this process. They visited and corresponded as if former divisions had never existed, attended one another's birthdays, and spoke at the funerals of departed abolitionists. "It is too late now to dwell on these [former] differences," Whittier insisted. Even Parker Pillsbury, one of the last to hold out against dissolution, made little of past differences in his history of the movement, *Acts of the Anti-Slavery Apostles*: "With all these questions or quibbles, the abolitionists made short shrift and went on with their work." To be sure, noteworthy differences continued to exist among them regarding the merits of presidential candidates, the value of the Liberal Republican movement, and even the benefits of federal intervention in Southern affairs. But these never provoked sharp emotional hostilities, as the dissolution debates of the 1860s had done. First-generation immediatists were determined to spend their remaining years in peace with untarnished memories of the Great Jubilee – the fulfillment of the mission to the slaves.[36]

This new harmony is best illustrated by a reunion convention of abolitionists in Chicago in 1874, four years after the dissolution debate had concluded. In January of that year, a group of old immediatists living in the Midwest agreed to stage a three-day gathering in Chicago to review "the period of self-sacrifice, when Anti-Slavery principles were advocated in faith and hope; the progress of the reform and its growth in public opinion; and its final triumph; with congratulations at the success which we have been permitted to realize. . . ."[37] Headed by Zebina Eastman, the former immediatist editor, the organizing committee consciously tried to avoid appearances of favoring any old immediatist cluster or faction or of slighting the immediatists' common cause with the radicals. It sent invitations to all abolitionists for whom it could secure addresses and even to several radicals. Perhaps because Illinois immediatists tended to favor Liberty party and Free Soil approaches, voluntarists and other types of political abolitionists composed a majority of the delegates in attendance, much to the consternation of insurgent Oliver Johnson. Aside from Johnson, no member of the defunct Boston Clique had the strength or desire to travel to Chicago, and none from Lewis Tappan's old circle of stewards showed up. Only William Goodell represented Gerrit Smith's upstate New York circle of former intimates. Nor were many black or female delegates in attendance. Perhaps owing to the patently unrepresentative character of the immediatists who did go to Chicago, considerable convention time was set aside to read letters from insurgents, stewards, blacks, and women from the Northeast. Clearly, the intent was to make this a fair, free, and open gathering. The organizing committee did not want charges of factional favoritism to disrupt the harmony of the occasion.[38]

For the most part, the committee succeeded in effecting the kind of convention that it wanted. A tone of harmony and celebration prevailed. Letter after letter from absent immediatists and speech after speech by delegates in attendance recalled the heroic abolitionist deeds of the past and explained how these deeds contributed to the success of the mission to the slaves. In a letter of greeting, Frederick Douglass told how the abolitionists had accomplished *the* great work of the century and might rest during the last years of life with enormous satisfaction. Whittier sent much the same message. Michigan immediatist Giles Stebbins advised that "the high lessons of fidelity, justice, and persistent courage learned in the memorable Anti-Slavery struggle" might also bring success to woman suffrage and other benevolent movements. Consistent with this spirit of jubilation, goodwill, and optimism, desires were expressed to "extend the right hand of fellowship and kinship to all the brotherhood," to "grasp the hand of those old veterans that remain," and to "look you in your faces and feel the pressure of your hands." Old and pious missionaries wished to celebrate victory with conviviality and Christian fellowship, so as to commemorate the presumed closeness of their antebellum intimacy circles and annual meetings.[39]

Perhaps the most convincing proof of how intent immediatists were, after the stormy dissolution debates of the 1860s, to have harmony in their final years lay in the way potential controversies were quickly smoothed. Consider two examples. To honor the immediatist co-missionary tradition, one delegate to the Chicago meeting proclaimed that abolitionists were the first reformers who took their wives and daughters to political meetings, and he was almost unanimously applauded. But the remark irritated Austin Willey, the Maine immediatist and no ally of the co-missionary tradition. Willey proclaimed that both the old woman question of 1840 and the new woman suffrage issue were extraneous to the antislavery purposes of the Chicago reunion. He, too, was applauded by almost everyone.[40]

A second and even more revealing example of how those in attendance would not allow discord to erupt came when a delegate presented a series of resolutions. These resolutions asserted that as long as the freedmen were excluded from public schools and from equal accommodations in railroad cars, hotels, churches, and public amusements, the spirit of slavery persisted and work remained to be done. The delegate urged the convention first to endorse his resolutions and then to petition Congress to make the freedmen secure in "the political and civil rights of American citizens." As convention chairman, Zebina Eastman intruded and announced that the gathering was intended to review the past and to celebrate the jubilee – not to offer resolutions or calls to action; it was a reunion and not an antislavery society meeting. But the overwhelming majority of delegates was intent on avoiding displays of "gag rule" repression. They referred the resolutions to a committee that very cleverly modified them and reported them back to the convention. The delegates overwhelmingly approved the committee's version, and it consisted of two statements: (1) that freedmen were to be secure in their civil and social rights and (2) that the freedmen required educational and religious uplift. The first statement implicitly endorsed the Phillips–Foster–Pillsbury position that freedmen had to be protected in the exercise of their legal rights. The second represented approval of the Garrison–McKim–Chapman advocacy of freedmen's aid societies. Clearly, the Chicago convention was intent on accommodating all major immediatist viewpoints and all values. The strife of the 1860s was not to be renewed.[41]

If the Chicago convention delegates generally succeeded in burying intramural squabbles and proclaiming jubilee, they could not always keep the underlying question of the 1860s from resurfacing – whether the mission to the slaves had truly ended. Indeed, this question was apparent in the resolution for civil and social rights for the freedmen. But it was even more blatant in the comments of certain delegates and the letters of a few immediatists who could not attend. Garrison's letter noted that "the siren cry of 'conciliation' " between North and South was often promoting "the old dragon spirit of slavery, and perpetuating caste distinctions by law." John Fee and Amos Dresser warned the convention that neither the spirit of bondage nor that of caste discrimination had been eradicated and that the abolitionists' tasks did not end until these ills were finally buried. But letters by Sallie Holley and Amasa Walker most strikingly raised the issue of a continuing immediatist mission. Holley told how in her school for blacks in Virginia she was engaged in a "hand to hand conflict with the remains of the Old Slave Power" so intense that she had no time for "congratulation or review of the past triumphs of the Anti-Slavery cause." Walker detailed his recent trip to "the late Slave States" and underscored the need for "continued efforts in their [freedmen's] behalf." If they now failed to assist the former slaves, Walker warned, "Anti-Slavery men had better have done nothing."[42]

The Chicago convention was not an antislavery society gathering. Since the Pennsylvania Society for Promoting the Abolition of Slavery was the only antislavery organization that maintained even a feeble existence at the time, the old dissolution controversy could not surface in 1874. But the inner personal distress beneath the dissolution debate had not ceased. This was because those immediatists who were alive in the mid-1870s remained ambivalent about continuing the old mission to the slaves. To be sure, they had dissolved their old antislavery societies with the hope that they could finally celebrate jubilee, and they maintained, increasingly, that a new generation of missionaries was required to uplift "shiftless" Appalachian whites as they themselves had aided black bondsmen.[43] But they were simply unable to shed their ambivalent feelings about the propriety of antislavery celebration – in 1874 as in 1865, 1869, and 1870. Consequently, they listened in silence to the words of Garrison, Fee, Dresser, Holley, and Walker, no longer ready to argue as they had been in the 1860s. Like missionaries everywhere, they wanted to die with the knowledge that their lives had been important – that they had achieved significant feats. But as devout reformers, they also sensed that there were still more battles to be fought in the mission for the slaves. Although most in the first generation had retired from an active role in those battles, it was literally impossible to remain unconcerned. The quest for jubilee would remain troubled as long as immediatists sought sainthood in this world rather than in the next.

NOTES

1 Betty Fladeland, *Men and Brothers: Anglo-American Antislavery Cooperation* (Urbana: University of Illinois Press, 1972), p. xii.
2 George Whipple in the *American Missionary*, IV, no. 5 (March 1850); Parker Pillsbury to George B. Cheever, October 21, 1856, Cheever Family Papers, American Antiquarian Society.

CHAPTER 1. YOUNG MISSIONARIES: VARIETIES OF EARLY IMMEDIATISM

1 Robert B. Berkhofer, Jr., *Salvation and the Savage: An Analysis of Protestant Missions and American Indian Response, 1787–1862* (Lexington: University of Kentucky Press, 1965), pp. 1–2, 167; Lois W. Banner, "The Protestant Crusade: Religious Missions, Benevolence, and Reform in the United States, 1790–1840" (Ph.D. dissertation, Columbia University, 1970), pp. 8, 9, 307–9; Carroll Smith-Rosenberg, *Religion and the Rise of the American City: The New York City Mission Movement, 1812–1870* (Ithaca, N.Y., and London: Cornell University Press, 1971), p. 49; Charles I. Foster, *An Errand of Mercy: The Evangelical United Front, 1790–1837* (Chapel Hill: University of North Carolina Press, 1960), pp. 132–3; John R. Bodo, *The Protestant Clergy and Public Issues, 1812–1848* (Princeton, N.J.: Princeton University Press, 1954), p. 18.
2 For good recent analyses of this transformation of the Northern middle class, see Paul E. Johnson, *A Shopkeeper's Millennium: Society and Revivals in Rochester, New York, 1815–1837* (New York: Hill and Wang, 1978), especially pp. 8, 115, 136–41, and Paul Boyer, *Urban Masses and Moral Order in America, 1820–1920*, part 1 (Cambridge, Mass.: Harvard University Press, 1978).
3 Foster, *Errand of Mercy*, pp. 143–4; Charles C. Cole, Jr., *The Social Ideas of the Northern Evangelists, 1826–1860* (New York: Columbia University Press, 1954), p. 103; Joshua Leavitt in the *Evangelist* (New York), May 5, 1832.
4 John Raymond McKivigan, "Abolitionists and the Churches, 1830–1865: A Study of Attitudes and Tactics" (Ph.D. dissertation, Ohio State University, 1977), pp. 270–1; Lois W. Banner, "Religious Benevolence as Social Control: A Critique of an Interpretation," *Journal of American History*, LX, no. 1 (July 1973), 27; Banner, "Protestant Crusade," pp. 336–7, 355–7; Bertram Wyatt-Brown, "Prelude to Abolitionism: Sabbatarian Politics and the Rise of the Second Party System," *Journal of American History*, LVIII, no. 2 (September 1971), 334.
5 See, e.g., Smith-Rosenberg, *Religion and the Rise of the City*, especially pp. 7–9, 272; Banner, "Religious Benevolence"; Ronald G. Walters, *American Reformers, 1815–1860* (New York: Hill and Wang, 1978), pp. 34–5; Boyer, *Urban Masses*, pp. 14, 59; Lewis Perry, *Radical Abolitionism: Anarchy and the Government of God in Antislavery Thought* (Ithaca, N.Y.: Cornell University Press, 1973), pp. 40–1; Robert H. Abzug, "Theodore Weld: A Biography" (Ph.D. dissertation, University of California, Berkeley, 1977), p. 60.

6   T. Scott Miyakawa, *Protestants and Pioneers: Individualism and Conformity on the American Frontier* (Chicago and London: University of Chicago Press, 1964), particularly p. 214.

7   See, e.g. [Miss Lyman], *The Martyr of Sumatra: A Memoir of Henry Lyman* (New York, 1857); Leonard Wood, *A Sermon Delivered in the Chapel of the Theological Seminary, Andover, February 1, 1835, on the Death of Henry Lyman and Samuel Munson, Missionaries . . .* (Andover, Mass.: Gould and Newman, 1835); Joseph P. Thompson, *Memoir of Rev. David Tappan Stoddard, Missionary to the Nestorians* (New York, 1859); Ralph R. Gurley, *Life of Jehudi Ashmun, Late Colonial Agent in Liberia . . .* (Washington, D.C., 1835); Bela B. Edwards, *Memoir of Elias Cornelius* (Boston, 1834); "Memoir of Mrs. E. H. Jones, Late Missionary to Burmah," *American Baptist Magazine*, XII (April 1832); E. P. Barrow, Jr., *Memoir of Everton Judson* (Boston, 1852); Gardiner Spring, *Memoirs of Rev. Samuel J. Mills, Late Missionary to the South Western Section of the United States . . .* (New York, 1820).

8   Gurley, *Life of Jehudi Ashmun*, pp. 1–92; Bertram Wyatt-Brown, "The Missionary Impulse in the Old Republic: The Psychology of Commitment to a Noble Cause," manuscript (Cleveland: Case-Western Reserve University, 1971), pp. 20–1.

9   For analyses of the following of the A.C.S. and its varied interests, see George M. Fredrickson, *The Black Image in the White Mind: The Debate on Afro-American Character and Destiny, 1817–1914* (New York: Harper and Row, 1971), pp. 6–30; Alice Dana Adams, *The Neglected Period of Anti-Slavery in America* (rpt., Gloucester, Mass.: Peter Smith, 1964), pp. 104, 205–6; Penelope Campbell, *Maryland in Africa: The Maryland State Colonization Society, 1831–1857* (Urbana: University of Illinois Press, 1971), pp. 9–10; *Abolitionist*, I, no. 3 (March 1833), 44; *Ohio Observer* (Hudson), July 23, 1835.

10 Chandler in *Genius of Universal Emancipation*, IV, no. 11, n.s. (November 20, 1829), 84; Simeon S. Jocelyn to R. R. Gurley, February 20, October 5, 1829, Joshua Leavitt to Gurley, October 20, 1829, American Colonization Society Papers, Library Of Congress [L.C.]; P. J. Staudenraus, *The African Colonization Movement, 1816–1865* (New York: Columbia University Press, 1961), pp. 126, 128, 130, 131; Ralph Volney Harlow, *Gerrit Smith, Philanthropist and Reformer* (New York: Henry Holt, 1939), pp. 62–63; Betty Fladeland, *James Gillespie Birney: Slave-holder to Abolitionist* (Ithaca, N.Y.: Cornell University Press, 1955), pp. 51–4; Phelps and the Tappans in John L. Myers, "The Agency System of the Anti-Slavery Movement, 1832–1837, and Its Antecedents in Other Benevolent and Reform Societies" (Ph.D. dissertation, University of Michigan, 1960), pp. 120–1, 129; Benjamin P. Thomas, *Theodore Weld: Crusader for Freedom* (New Brunswick, N.J.: Rutgers University Press, 1950), p. 33; Walter M. Merrill and Louis Ruchames, eds., *The Letters of William Lloyd Garrison*, 6 vols. (Cambridge, Mass.: Harvard University Press, Belknap Press, 1971–81), 1, p. 86 *n*. 2 (vol. 1, *I Will Be Heard! 1822–1835*; vol. 2, *A House Dividing against Itself, 1836–1840*; vol. 3, *No Union with Slaveholders, 1841–1849*; vol. 4, *From Disunionism to the Brink of War, 1850–1860*; vol. 5, *Let the Oppressed Go Free, 1861–1867*; vol. 6, *To Rouse the Slumbering Land, 1868–1879*; individual volumes are cited as *Letters of Garrison* with the volume number). John L. Thomas, *The Liberator: William Lloyd Garrison* (Boston: Little, Brown, 1963), pp. 89, 92.

11 Thomas, *The Liberator*, p. 101; Merton L. Dillon, *Benjamin Lundy and the Struggle for Negro Freedom* (Urbana: University of Illinois Press, 1966), pp. 145–63; Bruce Rosen, "Abolition and Colonization, the Years of Conflict: 1829–1834." *Phylon*, XXXIII, no. 2 (second quarter, 1972), 177–92; Lawrence J. Friedman, *Inventors of the Promised Land* (New York: Alfred A. Knopf, 1975), pp. 224–41.

12 Bertram Wyatt-Brown, *Lewis Tappan and the Evangelical War against Slavery* (Cleveland, Ohio: Press of Case Western Reserve University, 1969), pp. 13–14; Carleton Mabee, *Black Freedom: The Nonviolent Abolitionists from 1830 through the Civil War* (New York: Macmillan, 1970), p. 195, on the Smith brothers; Abzug, "Weld," p. 24.

13 For data relating to immediatists-to-be listening to free blacks about the ills of the A.C.S. colony in Liberia and about Afro-American disinclination to seek repatriation, see, e.g., Eugene P. Southall, "Arthur Tappan and the Anti-Slavery Movement,"

Journal of Negro History, XV, no. 2 (April 1930), 169-71; Louis R. Mehlinger, "The Attitude of the Free Negro toward African Colonization," *Journal of Negro History*, I, no. 3 (June 1916), 276-301; Phyllis Mary Bannan, "Arthur and Lewis Tappan: A Study in New York Religious and Reform Movements" (Ph.D. dissertation, Columbia University, 1950), pp. 78-9; David K. Sullivan, "William Lloyd Garrison in Baltimore, 1829-1830," *Maryland Historical Magazine*, LXVIII, no. 1 (spring 1973), 65; Elizur Wright, Jr., to Amos A. Phelps, August 8, 1834. Boston Public Library [B.P.L.]. For colonizationists who refused to take black opposition to repatriation seriously, see, e.g., M. L. Fullerton to R. R. Gurley, September 6, 1830, David I. Burr to R. R. Gurley, November 5, 1833, American Colonization Society Papers, L. C.; *African Repository*, XIII, no. 1 (January 1837), 29; XVI, no. 23 (December 1, 1840), 353.

14   Lyman in Wood, *A Sermon Delivered in the Chapel* . . . especially pp. 28-32; Phelps in *Anti-Slavery, Religion and Reform: Essays in Memory of Roger Anstey*, ed. Christine Bolt and Seymour Drescher (Folkestone, England: Dawson, 1980), p. 197.

15   Wyatt-Brown, "Prelude to Abolitionism," pp. 339-41, intelligently discusses and documents this point.

16   Donald M. Scott, *From Office to Profession: The New England Ministry, 1750-1850* (Philadelphia: University of Pennsylvania Press, 1978), pp. 76-94; Abzug, "Weld," pp. 145-6; Daniel H. Calhoun, *Professional Lives in America, Structure and Aspiration, 1750-1850* (Cambridge, Mass.: Harvard University Press, 1965), pp. 115-71; Bertram Wyatt-Brown, "New Leftists and Abolitionists: A Comparison of American Radical Styles," *Wisconsin Magazine of History*, LIII, no. 4 (summer 1970), 256-68; J. Auping, *The Relative Efficiency of Evangelical Nonviolence: The Influence of a Revival of Religion on the Abolition of Slavery in North America, 1740-1865* (Rome: Pontificia Universitas Gregoriana, 1977).

17   Berkhofer, Jr., *Salvation and the Savage*, p. 9.

18   Quoted in Harriet Beecher Stowe, *The Lives and Deeds of Our Self-Made Men* (Hartford: Worthington, Dustin, 1872), pp. 160-1. See also Lyman Beecher Stowe, *Saints, Sinners, and Beechers* (Indianapolis: Bobbs-Merrill, 1934), p. 60.

19   See, e.g., Rosen, "Abolition and Colonization," pp. 177-92; Fredrickson, *Black Image*, pp. 27-42; Lorman Ratner, *Pre-Civil War Reform: The Variety of Principles and Programs* (Englewood Cliffs, N.J.: Prentice-Hall, 1967), pp. 4-5; John L. Thomas, "Romantic Reform in America, 1815-1865," *American Quarterly*, XVII, no. 4 (winter 1965), 661; Clifford Griffin, "The Abolitionists and the Benevolent Societies, 1831-1861," *Journal of Negro History*, XLIV, no. 3 (July 1959), 195-216.

20   For examples of the widespread support of Garrison's *Thoughts on African Colonization*, see Goodell in the *Genius of Temperance* (New York), October 3, 1832; Roman J. Zorn, "Garrisonian Abolitionism, 1828-1839" (Ph.D. dissertation, University of Wisconsin, 1953), p. 84. For instances of immediatists apologizing for having been deceived by the A.C.S., see, e.g., *Abolitionist*, I, no. 5 (May 1833), 77; *African Repository*, IX, no. 3 (May 1833), 65-66; Merrill and Ruchames, eds., *Letters of Garrison*, 1, 122-3; Lewis Tappan, *The Life of Arthur Tappan* (New York: Hurd and Houghton, 1870), p. 129; James G. Birney to Gerrit Smith, November 14, 1834, James G. Birney Papers, L.C.; Gerrit Smith, *Letter of Gerrit Smith to Hon. Henry Clay* (New York: American Anti-Slavery Society, 1839), p. 33. Immediatist comments on the illogic and impracticality of African colonization are exemplified in *Emancipator* (New York), January 14, 1834 (Denison), March 14, 1839 (Goodell); *Liberator* (Boston), October 4, 1834 (Birney); Bannan, "Arthur and Lewis Tappan," pp. 78-9; Thomas, *Liberator* (Boston), p. 116. On blacks' unwillingness to be repatriated to Africa, see, e.g., Elizur Wright, Jr., to A. A. Phelps, August 8, 1834, B. P. L.; *Herald of Freedom* (Concord), July 21, 1838; October 27, 1837. For immediatist claims of colonizationists accepting perpetual black degradation, see Leavitt in the *Evangelist* (New York), March 15, 1834; Goodell in *Genius of Temperance* (New York), September 7, 1831; Garrison in *Genius of Universal Emancipation* II, no. 6, 3d ser. (October 1831), 93; Elizur Wright, Jr., to Beriah Green, May 6, 1833, Elizur Wright, Jr., Papers, L.C.; Arthur Tappan to W. L. Garrison, January 21,

1832, B.P.L. For a sampling of attacks on the A.C.S. for its failure to condemn slavery, see the *Emancipator* (New York), April 15, 1834 (Jay), February 3, 1835 (Birney); *African Repository*, XVI, no. 20 (October 15, 1840), 315; *Genius of Universal Emancipation*, IV, no. 26, n.s. (March 5, 1830), 202; Smith, *Letter of Gerrit Smith to Henry Clay*, p. 33; James G. Birney, *Letter on Colonization, Addressed to Rev. Thornton J. Mills, Corresponding Secretary of the Kentucky Colonization Society* (New York, 1834), pp. 10–12; William Jay, *Miscellaneous Writings on Slavery* (Boston: John P. Jewett, 1853), p. 20.

21 The liberal religion common to most of these young New Englanders is noted in William H. Pease and Jane H. Pease, *Bound with Them in Chains: A Biographical History of the Antislavery Movement* (Westport, Conn.: Greenwood Press, 1972), pp. 32, 311–12, while William L. Van Deburg, "William Lloyd Garrison and the 'Pro-Slavery Priesthood': The Changing Beliefs of an Evangelical Reformer, 1830–1840," *Journal of the American Academy of Religion*, XLIII (June 1975), 225–6, n. 2, deals with young Garrison the Baptist. For Henry Wright's affiliations with the benevolent empire, see Henry C. Wright, *Human Life: Illustrated in My Individual Experience as a Child, a Youth, and a Man* (Boston: Bella Marsh, 1849), pp. 327, 332, 342; Jayme A. Sokolow, "Henry Clarke Wright: Antebellum Crusader," *Essex Institute Historical Collections*, III, no. 2 (April 1975), 127–8. Garrison's association with the benevolent movement is noted in Walter M. Merrill, "Prologue to Reform – Garrison's Early Career," *Essex Institute Historical Collections*, XCII, no. 2 (April 1956), 153–70; Van Deburg, "Garrison and 'Pro-Slavery Priesthood'," 226; Oliver Johnson, *William Lloyd Garrison and His Times* (Boston: B. B. Russell, 1880), pp. 45–6; Staudenraus, *African Colonization*, pp. 131, 193–4. The connections of Samuel J. May and George Benson are noted in Pease and Pease, "Freedom and Peace: A Nineteenth Century Dilemma," *Midwest Quarterly*, IX, no. 1 (October 1967), 25–6, and Pease and Pease, *Bound with Them in Chains*, p. 281. For useful discussions of pro–Federalist party dispositions of these New England reformers, see Robert H. Abzug, "The Influence of Garrisonian Abolitionists' Fear of Slave Violence on the Antislavery Argument, 1829–1840," *Journal of Negro History*, LV, no. 1 (January 1970), 17, and Robert W. Tolf, "Edmund Quincy: Aristocrat Abolitionist" (Ph.D. dissertation, University of Rochester, 1957), pp. 213–16.

22 Staudenraus, *African Colonization*, p. 194; Zorn, "Garrisonian Abolitionism," p. 130.

23 Records of the New England Anti-Slavery Society, 1831–3, B.P.L.; *National Anti-Slavery Standard* (New York), July 15, 1841, May 26, 1842; Nathaniel Peabody Rogers, *A Collection from the Miscellaneous Writings of Nathaniel Peabody Rogers* (Boston: Benjamin B. Mussey, 1849), pp. 24, 50, 54.

24 William Lloyd Garrison, *Thoughts on African Colonization*, pt. 1 (rpt., New York: Arno Press, 1968), p. 7; Samuel J. May, *Some Recollections of Our Anti-Slavery Conflict* (Boston: Fields, Osgood, 1869), p. 76; Amasa Walker in *First Annual Report of the New England Anti-Slavery Society* (Boston, 1833), pp. 6–7. L. Maria Child, *An Appeal in Favor of That Class of Americans Called Africans* (New York: John S. Taylor, 1836), p. 142.

25 See, e.g., Garrison, *Thoughts on Colonization*, pt. 1, pp. 24–5; *Abolitionist*, 1, no. 8 (August 1833), 113; Samuel J. May, *A Discourse on Slavery in the United States, Delivered in Brooklyn, July 3, 1831* (Boston, 1832); *Liberator* (Boston), June 23, 1832, August 9, 1861; N. P. Rogers, *Collection*, pp. 22, 48; Henry C. Wright Journal, XVII, May 20, 1835, Houghton Library, Harvard University; Garrison, *The Maryland Scheme of Expatriation Examined* (Boston: Garrison and Knapp, 1834), p. 19; Child, *An Appeal*, p. 133; Garrison to Henry Benson, July 30, 1831, B.P.L.; Henry C. Wright, "Notes on Non-Resistance and Christian Attitude toward War and Use of Physical Force," unpublished manuscript, 1830–7, III, pp. 61–4 (B.P.L.).

26 Although Child had articulated this position a decade earlier, she stated it most clearly in the *National Anti-Slavery Standard* (New York), July 28, 1842; Wright in the *Liberator* (Boston), May 19, 1837; Garrison to Henry E. Benson, July 21, 1832, B.P.L. See also Garrison in the *Liberator* (Boston), April 23, 1831; Henry C. Wright Journal,

XVII, May 20, 1835, Houghton Library; Child, *An Appeal*, p. 130; May, *Recollections*, pp. 9–10, 18–19; Merrill and Ruchames, eds., *Letters of Garrison*, 1, p. 194; *Herald of Freedom* (Concord), December 15, 1838.

27 See, e.g., Henry C. Wright Journal, XVII, May 20, 22, 1835, Houghton Library; Garrison, *Maryland Scheme of Expatriation*, pp. 14–15; the *Liberator* (Boston), September 22, August 30, 1839, April 10, 1840; *Herald of Freedom* (Concord), August 18, 1838; H. Wright, *Human Life*, p. 344.

28 Merrill and Ruchames, eds., *Letters of Garrison*, 1, pp. 124, 248–9; *Liberator* (Boston), December 20, 1834; Garrison to George Benson, March 13, 1834, B.P.L.; Garrison, *A Brief Sketch of the Trial of William Lloyd Garrison, for an Alleged Libel on Francis Todd of Newburyport, Mass.* (Boston: Garrison and Knapp, 1834), p. iii.

29 Perry, *Radical Abolitionism*, provides the most cogent analysis of this larger concept of slavery.

30 See, e.g., Clifford Griffin, *Their Brothers' Keepers: Moral Stewardship in the United States, 1800–1865* (New Brunswick, N.J.: Rutgers University Press, 1960), pp. 41, 63–4; Southall, "Arthur Tappan," p. 163; Wyatt-Brown, *Lewis Tappan*, pp. 51–2; Clifton Herman Johnson, "The American Missionary Association, 1846–1861: A Study of Christian Abolitionism" (Ph.D. dissertation, University of North Carolina, 1958), p. 30; Gilbert H. Barnes and Dwight L. Dumond, eds., *Letters of Theodore Dwight Weld, Angelina Grimké Weld, and Sarah Grimké, 1822–1844*, 2 vols. (New York and London: D. Appleton-Century, 1934), 1, p. 209 *n.* 5; Harlow, *Gerrit Smith*, pp. 58, 68–9; Jeremiah Everts to Gerrit Smith, September 3, 1830, Gerrit Smith Papers, Syracuse University; David French, "Elizur Wright, Jr., and the Emergence of Anti-Colonization Sentiments on the Connecticut Western Reserve," *Ohio History*, LXXXV, no. 1 (winter 1976), 51–2; John L. Myers, "The Agency System," p. 132.

31 Bannan, "Arthur and Lewis Tappan," p. 78; Gerald Sorin, *The New York Abolitionists: A Case Study of Political Radicalism* (Westport, Conn.: Greenwood Publishing, 1971), pp. 30–1; French, "Elizur Wright, Jr., and Emergence of Anti-Colonization," p. 54; Pease and Pease, *Bound with Them in Chains*, pp. 219–20; Fladeland, *Birney*, pp. 38, 42, 51–4; Friedman, *Inventors of Promised Land*, p. 237.

32. Myers, "The Agency System," describes most comprehensively how these more temperate immediatists structured abolitionist organization and activities along benevolent society patterns. See also Wyatt-Brown, *Lewis Tappan*, pp. 113–14; Barnes and Dumond, eds., *Weld-Grimké Letters*, 1, p. 122; Griffin, "Abolitionists and Benevolent Societies," p. 199; A. A. Phelps to Elizur Wright, Jr., August 2, 1838, Elizur Wright, Jr., Papers, L.C.

33 Johnson, "American Missionary Association," pp. 50, 90–1, 159–60; Griffin, "Abolitionists and Benevolent Societies," p. 204; Gerald Sorin, *Abolitionism: A New Perspective* (New York: Praeger, 1972), p. 72.

34 *Liberator* (Boston), August 11, 1837; Elizur Wright, Jr., to A. A. Phelps, January 22, 1835, to Susan C. Wright, April 9, 1833, Elizur Wright, Jr., Papers, L.C.; Weld to James G. Birney, May 28, 1834, in Dwight L. Dumond, ed., *Letters of James Gillespie Birney, 1831–1857*, 2 vols. (New York: D. Appleton-Century, 1938), 1, p. 113; Amos Phelps, *Lectures on Slavery and Its Remedy* (Boston: New England Anti-Slavery Society, 1834); William Jay, *Inquiry into the Character and Tendency of the American Colonization, and American Anti-Slavery Societies* (New York: R. G. Williams, 1838), pp. 61, 96–7; Foster, *Errand of Mercy*, p. 201; *Fourth Annual Report of the Board of Managers of the Massachusetts Anti-Slavery Society* (Boston, 1836), p. 59; *Emancipator* (New York), May 26, 1835.

35 Amos A. Phelps to Rev. R. Anderson, March 9, 1835, B.P.L.; *Emancipator* (New York), June 22, 1833; Jay, *Miscellaneous Writings*, pp. 64, 121; Jay, *Inquiry*, p. 121; Leavitt in the *Evangelist* (New York), April 27, May 25, 1833; January 18, February 15, 1834; April 18, May 9, August 1, 1835; August 6, 1836; John G. Whittier, *Justice or Expediency* (New York: American Anti-Slavery Society, 1833), p. 61; Jay in the *Abolitionist*, I, no. 8

(August 1833), 119; H. H. Davis, "Leavitt," pp. 132, 136; Barnes and Dumond, eds., *Weld-Grimké Letters*, 1, pp. 103–4, 161; Elizur Wright, Jr., to A. A. Phelps, June 10, 1834, Elizur Wright, Jr., Papers, L.C.; Southall, "Arthur Tappan," 167.

36 *Emancipator* (New York), May 26, 1835.

37 Jay, *Inquiry*, p. 12; Joshua Leavitt to Gerrit Smith, March 31, 1834, Gerrit Smith Papers, Syracuse University; Arthur Tappan to R. R. Gurley in the *Emancipator* (New York), June 29, 1833; Jay in the *Evangelist* (New York), April 5, 1834; Jay, *Miscellaneous Writings*, p. 121; Bayard Tuckerman, *William Jay and the Constitutional Movement for the Abolition of Slavery* (rpt., New York: Negro Universities Press, 1893), p. 45; Theodore D. Weld to Elizur Wright, Jr., Janaury 10, 1833, Elizur Wright, Jr., Papers, L.C.; Barnes and Dumond, eds., *Weld-Grimké Letters*, 1, p. 225; Elizur Wright, Jr., to Gerrit Smith, August 6, 1834, Smith Papers, Syracuse University.

38 Henry Cowles to Elizur Wright, Jr., January 19, 1833, Elizur Wright, Jr., Papers, L.C.; Elizur Wright, Jr., to Beriah Green, June 7, 1833; to _____, January 30, 1834; to A. A. Phelps, February 20 and September 13, 1834; all in Elizur Wright, Jr., Papers, L.C.; Wright in the *Evangelist* (New York), June 8, 1833; *Anti-Slavery Reporter*, I, no. 2 (July 1833), 29; Leavitt in the *Evangelist* (New York), March 8, 1834; *Emancipator* (New York), June 1, 25, 1833; Dumond, ed., *Letters of Birney*, 1, pp. 116–17; Phelps, *Lectures on Slavery*, p. 166.

39 Jay, *Inquiry*, p. 74; Lewis Tappan to Gerrit Smith, February 15, 1836, Smith Papers, Syracuse University; James G. Birney to Mexican Legation, April 1, 1840, Birney Papers, Clements Library, University of Michigan; Gerrit Smith to John H. Cocke, December 11, 1840, 1827–43 Letterbook, Smith Papers, Syracuse University; Johnson, "American Missionary Association," p. 297.

40 *Abolitionist*, I, no 8 (August 1833), 119; *Emancipator* (New York), June 22, 25, 1833; Jay, *Miscellaneous Writings*, p. 9; Jay, *Inquiry*, p. 73.

41 Gerrit Smith to R. R. Gurley, October 10, 1827, February 8, 1831, October 7, 1833, American Colonization Society Papers, L.C.; *African Colonization, Proceedings of the Formation of the New-York State Colonization Society; together with an Address to the Public, from the Managers Thereof* (Albany, N.Y.: Websters and Skinners, 1829), pp. 19–21; Smith to William Goodell, October 5, 1833, Smith Papers, Syracuse University; *African Repository*, IX, no. 12 (February 1834), 358–9; Harlow, *Smith*, p. 64; Octavius Brooks Frothingham, *Gerrit Smith: A Biography* (New York: G. P. Putnam, 1878), pp. 163–4; Smith to R. R. Gurley, November 24, 1835, American Colonization Society Papers, L.C.; *Emancipator* (New York), May 25, 1837; *Liberator* (Boston), July 13, 1838; Smith to William Ellery Channing, August 17, 1841, Smith Papers, Syracuse University.

42 Dumond, ed., *Letters of Birney*, 1, pp. xii–xiii, 5–6, 20–3, 51–2, 72, 88–90, 97, 147–8, 150; 2, pp. 945–6; Fladeland, *Birney*, pp. 38, 42, 51–4, 73–4, 81–2; Birney, *Letters on Colonization, Addressed to Rev. Thornton J. Mills, Corresponding Secretary of the Kentucky Colonization Society* (New York, 1834), especially pp. 7, 10–12, 16–19, 28, 43–5; Friedman, *Inventors of the Promised Land*, pp. 236–41.

43 Much of the biographical data on these halfway abolitionists comes from the two standard studies of the A.C.S., Staudenraus's *African Colonization Movement*, and Early Lee Fox, *The American Colonization Society, 1817–1840* (Baltimore, Md.; Johns Hopkins University Press, 1919). See also Timothy J. Sehr, "Leonard Bacon and the Myth of the Good Slaveholder," *New England Quarterly*, XLIX, no. 2 (June 1976), 194–213; Barbara M. Cross, *Horace Bushnell: Minister to a Changing America* (Chicago: University of Chicago Press, 1958); Wyatt-Brown, "Missionary Impulse"; Wyatt-Brown, *Lewis Tappan*; Barbara M. Cross, ed., *The Autobiography of Lyman Beecher* (Cambridge, Mass.: Harvard University Press, Belknap Press, 1961); Isabelle Webb Entrikin, *Sarah Josepha Hale and Godey's Lady's Book* (Philadelphia: Lancaster Press, 1946); Jonathan Meserli, *Horace Mann: A Biography* (New York: Alfred A. Knopf, 1972).

44 Beecher is quoted in Ralph Korngold, *Two Friends of Man: The Story of William Lloyd Garrison and Wendell Phillips and Their Relationship with Abraham Lincoln* (Boston: Little,

Brown, 1950), p. 43. See also Kathryn Kish Sklar, *Catharine Beecher: A Study in American Domesticity* (New Haven: Yale University Press, 1973), p. 12.

45 Lyman Beecher's statement is quoted in Cross, ed., *Autobiography of Lyman Beecher*, 2, pp. 242–3, and in Bodo, *Protestant Clergy*, p. 142. See also *Christian Examiner and General Review*, XIII (1833), 108, 308; Catharine E. Beecher, *An Essay on Slavery and Abolitionism, with Reference to the Duty of American Females*, 2d ed. (Philadelphia: Henry Perkins, 1837), pp. 135–6; Lorman Ratner, *Powder Keg: Northern Opposition to the Antislavery Movement, 1831–1840* (New York: Basic Books, 1968), p. 61; Frederick Freeman, *Yardee: A Plea for Africa, in Familiar Conversations on the Subject of Slavery and Colonization* (Philadelphia: J. Whetham, 1836), pp. 181, 204, 297–9; Mathew Carey, *Letters on the Colonization Society, with a View of Its Probable Results . . .* (Philadelphia, 1830), pp. iii–iv, 17; *Report of the Executive Committee [for the American Union for the Relief and Improvement of the Colored Race] at the Annual Meeting of the Society, May 25, 1836* (Boston, 1836); Leonard Bacon, *Slavery Discussed in Occasional Essays, 1833–1846* (New York: Baker and Scribner, 1846), pp. 74–5; Hale in *American Ladies' Magazine*, V, no. 9 (September 1832), 429; Green in *Christian Advocate*, XI (1834), 568; Gilbert Hobbs Barnes, *The Antislavery Impulse, 1830–1844* (New York: Harcourt, Brace and World, Harbinger, 1964), pp. 45–6; D. H. Emerson to A. A. Phelps, February 25, 1839, Elizur Wright, Jr., Papers, L.C.; "Report of the Committee on the Subject of Slavery as Connected with the Seminary, August 1834," Lane Seminary Manuscripts, McCormick Theological Seminary.

46 See, e.g., Sehr, "Leonard Bacon," pp. 196–9; Bacon, *Slavery Discussed*, p. 87; Ebenezer Baldwin, *Observations on the Physical, Intellectual, and Moral Qualities of Our Colored Population: With Remarks on the Subject of Emancipation and Colonization* (New Haven: L. H. Young, 1834), p. 43; Catharine E. Beecher, *Essay on Slavery and Abolitionism*, pp. 12–14, 35–6, 82–3; Ratner, *Powder Keg*, p. 99; Robert C. Senior, "New England Congregationalists and the Anti-Slavery Movement, 1830–1860" (Ph.D. dissertation, Yale University, 1954), pp. 88–9, 106.

47 Leonard W. Bacon, *The Services of Leonard Bacon to African Colonization* (Washington, D.C., 1900), pp. 23–4; Freeman, *Yardee*, pp. 298–9; *African Repository*, X (November 1834), 282; Barnes, *Antislavery Impulse*, pp. 44–5; David Oliphant to R. R. Gurley, November 13, 1833, American Colonization Society Papers, L.C.; Cross, ed., *Autobiography of Lyman Beecher*, 2, pp. 259–60.

48 Useful data on the founding and operations of the American Union can be found in James R. Stirn, "Urgent Gradualism: The Case of the American Union for the Relief and Improvement of the Colored Race," *Civil War History*, XXV, no. 4 (December 1979), 309–28; Wyatt-Brown, *Lewis Tappan*, pp. 138–42; Henry C. Wright, diary fragment, January 11, 1835, Houghton Library; *Report of the Executive Committee of the American Union . . ., May 25, 1836*.

CHAPTER 2. INSURGENTS OF THE BOSTON CLIQUE

1 Garrison in the *Liberator* (Boston), December 8, 1837. Samuel J. May, *Some Recollections of Our Antislavery Conflict* (Boston: Fields, Osgood, 1869), pp. 36–7. Mitchell Snay, "A World in Themselves and Each Other: Leadership in the New England Anti-Slavery Society," seminar paper (Waltham, Mass.: Brandeis University, 1976), p. 29, reports on Chapman. See also the *Non-Resistant* (Boston), August 17, September 7, 1839; Parker Pillsbury, *Acts of the Anti-Slavery Apostles* (Concord, N.H., 1883), p. 104; Caroline Weston to Samuel May, Jr., December 2, 1848, Boston Public Library [B.P.L.]; Anne Warren Weston to J. B. Estlin, 27, 1850 October, B.P.L.; William Lloyd Garrison to Ann Phillips, January 1, 1854, Blagden Collection, Houghton Library, Harvard University; Josiah P. Quincy, "Memoir of Edmund Quincy," *Proceedings of the Massachusetts Historical Society*, 2d ser., XVIII (October 1904), 407–9.

2 Ann Phillips to Wendell Phillips, n.d.; Henry C. Wright to Wendell Phillips, September 25, 1842; Edmund Quincy to Wendell Phillips, November 5, 1848; all in the

Blagden Collection, Houghton Library. *The Works of Charles Follen, With a Memoir of His Life*, 5 vols. (Boston: Hilliard, Gray, 1841-2), 1, p. 383. (vol. 1, *The Life of Charles Follen*; vol. 2, *Sermons*; vol. 3, *Lectures on Moral Philosophy. Fragment of a Work on Psychology*; vol. 4, *On Schiller's Life and Dramas*; vol.5, *Miscellaneous Writings*; individual volumes are cited as *Works of Follen* with the volume number). *Non-Resistant* (Boston), August 17, 1839 (Edmund Quincy).

3   Thousands of letters by Clique members in the vast Garrisonian holdings of the Boston Public Library and the Blagden Collection at Harvard's Houghton Library supplied most of the information on social characteristics. There were also several very helpful printed sources, particularly Wendell Phillips Garrison and Francis Jackson Garrison, *William Lloyd Garrison, 1805-1879: The Story of His Life as told by His Children*, 4 vols. (New York: Century, 1885-9): vol. 1, *1805-1835*; vol. 2, *1835-1840*; vol. 3, *1841-1860*; vol. 4, *1861-1879* (individual volumes are cited as *Garrison* with the volume number); Walter M. Merrill and Louis Ruchames, eds., *The Letters of William Lloyd Garrison*, 6 vols. (Cambridge, Mass.: Harvard University Press, Belknap Press, 1971-81): vol. 1, *I Will Be Heard! 1822-1835*; vol. 2, *A House Dividing against Itself, 1836-1840*; vol. 3, *No Union with Slaveholders, 1841-1849*; vol. 4, *From Disunionism to the Brink of War, 1850-1860*; vol. 5, *Let the Oppressed Go Free, 1861-1867*; vol. 6, *To Rouse the Slumbering Land, 1868-1879* (individual volumes are cited as *Letters of Garrison* with the volume number); Walter M. Merrill, *Against Wind and Tide: A Biography of William Lloyd Garrison* (Cambridge, Mass.: Harvard University Press, 1963); and the two Clique controlled newspapers, the *Liberator* (Boston), and the *National Anti-Slavery Standard* (New York). Snay, "A World in Themselves and Each Other," is the most systematic effort at delineating "Garrisonian" social characteristics, although it is restricted to the leaders of the New England Anti-Slavery Society.

4   For information on the Clique's Boston constituency, see Snay, "A World in Themselves and Each Other," pp. 7-12; Theodore M. Hammet, "Two Mobs of Jacksonian Boston: Ideology and Interest," *Journal of American History*, LXII, no. 4 (March 1976), 864-65; Patsy S. and Billy Ledbetter, "The Agitator and the Intellectuals: William Lloyd Garrison and the New England Transcendentalists," *Mid-America*, LXII, no. 3 (October 1980), 173-85; and James O. Horton and Lois E. Horton, *Black Bostonians: Family Life and Community Struggle in the Antebellum North* (New York: Holmes and Meier, 1979), pp. 48, 50, 61-6.

5   Robert W. Tolf, "Edmund Quincy: Aristocrat Abolitionist" (Ph.D. dissertation, University of Rochester, 1957), especially pp. 394-5; Ellis Gray Loring to William Lloyd Garrison, December 5, 1835, B.P.L.; Loring to William Jay, March 15, 1838, Ellis Gray Loring Letterbook, Houghton Library; Loring to A. A. Phelps and Elizur Wright, Jr., May 28, 1839, Elizur Wright, Jr., Papers, Library of Congress [L.C.].

6   Jayme A. Sokolow, "Henry Clarke Wright: Antebellum Crusader," *Essex Institute Historical Collections*, III, no. 2 (April 1975), 128; Garrison and Garrison, *Garrison*, 2, pp. 234-36, treats Quincy; *Works of Charles Follen*, 5, p. 359; Francis Jackson to Lysander Spooner, December 3, 1858, B.P.L.; Anne Warren Weston to Mary A. Estlin, February 5, 1855, B.P.L.; Samuel May, Jr., to Edmund Quincy, July 9, 1842, Edmund Quincy Papers, Massachusetts Historical Society; John White Chadwick, "Samuel May of Leicester," *New England Magazine* (April 1899), 213-14; Irving H. Bartlett, *Wendell Phillips: Brahmin Radical* (Boston: Beacon Press, 1961), p. 66

7   Russel B. Nye, *William Lloyd Garrison and the Humanitarian Reformers* (Boston: Little, Brown, 1955), pp. 139-40; Garrison and Garrison, *Garrison*, 3, pp. 218-20; Samuel J. May to William Lloyd Garrison, January 15, 1848, B.P.L.

8   Francis Jackson to Samuel Hubbard, November 3, 1837, B.P.L.; Samuel May, Jr., to George Davis, June 29, 1840, B.P.L.; Richard H. Sewell, *Ballots for Freedom: Antislavery Politics in the United States, 1837-1860* (New York: Oxford University Press, 1976), p. 111; Douglas C. Stange, "The Making of an Abolitionist Martyr: Harvard Professor Charles Theodore Christian Follen," *Harvard Library Bulletin*, XXIV, no. 1 (January 1976), 23.

9 Larry Wertheim, "Garrisonian Abolitionists and the Republican Party, 1854–1861," seminar paper (Madison: University of Wisconsin, 1972), p. 2; Anne Warren Weston to Deborah Weston, May 11, 1842, B.P.L.; Ellis Gray Loring to "Dear Friend" [Anne Warren Weston?], September 9, 1853, B.P.L.; William H. Pease and Jane H. Pease, "Freedom and Peace: A Nineteenth Century Dilemma," *Midwest Quarterly*, IX, no. 1 (October 1967), 28–9.

10 Anne Warren Weston to Wendell Phillips, February 20, 1852, Blagden Collection, Houghton Library.

11 See, e.g., Lewis Tappan to Gamaliel Bailey, October 26, 1843, Letterbook, Lewis Tappan Papers, L.C.; N. P. Rogers to R. D. Webb, August 12, 1845, B.P.L.

12 For Garrison's greetings and expressions of concern for Clique members, see Merrill and Ruchames, eds., *Letters of Garrison*, 4, p. 290 (regarding Pillsbury); 2, pp. 617–18 (on Rogers); 4, p. 263 (on Jackson); Garrison to Louisa Loring, March 19, 1843, Ellis Gray Loring Family Papers, Ratcliffe College. Evidence of Garrison's desires for close contacts with Clique abolitionists abounds. Samuel J. May to R. D. Webb, May 6, 1860, B.P.L., notes Garrison's hesitancy to travel without a Clique friend. Garrison's remarks on Chapman are in Merrill and Ruchames, eds., *Letters of Garrison*, 4, pp. 353, 369. Ibid., 4, pp. 354, 604–05, for Garrison's letters to Jackson. For Garrison on Wright, see ibid., 4, pp. 24–28; 4, pp. 2–3, 461; and 3, p. 302, for Garrison on May; Garrison to May, June 8, 1869, B.P.L.

13 Merrill and Ruchames, eds., *Letters of Garrison*, 4, pp. 45–6 (Garrison to Phillips); 3, pp. 262–3 (Garrison to Wright); 3, pp. 530–1 (Garrison to Louisa Loring); 4, pp. 389, 483 (Garrison to May); Garrison to Samuel J. May, September 12, 1864, Garrison Papers, Massachusetts Historical Society. For the remark about willingness "to take the advice of my friends," see Garrison to Samuel E. Sewall, October 24, 1835 (typescript), Garrison Papers, Massachusetts Historical Society.

14 For useful data on Garrison's childhood and on his family life as an adult, see the two standard Garrison biographies: Merrill, *Against Wind and Tide*, and John L. Thomas, *The Liberator: William Lloyd Garrison* (Boston: Little, Brown, 1963). See also William Lloyd Garrison, *Helen Eliza Garrison, A Memorial* (Cambridge, 1876); Merrill and Ruchames, eds., *Letters of Garrison*, 1, p. 3; 3, p. 28.

15 Oliver Johnson, *William Lloyd Garrison and His Times* (Boston: B. B. Russell, 1880), pp. 397–8 (emphasis added); Garrison and Garrison, *Garrison*, 4, p. 313.

16 Johnson, *Garrison*, p. 399; Merrill and Ruchames, eds., *Letters of Garrison*, 3, pp. 599–600; Garrison to Francis Jackson, November 5, 1848, Garrison Papers, Massachusetts Historical Society.

17 Merrill and Ruchames, eds., *Letters of Garrison*, 4, p. 686, on Johnson; Garrison and Garrison, *Garrison*, 1, pp. 273–4, on May.

18 Merrill and Ruchames, eds., *Letters of Garrison*, 4, p. 634.

19 Bertram Wyatt-Brown, "William Lloyd Garrison and Antislavery Unity: A Reappraisal," *Civil War History*, XIII, no. 1 (March 1967), 5–24, provides an excellent analysis of Garrison's adoption of consensus antislavery politics.

20 James Brewer Stewart, "Garrison Again, and Again, and Again, and Again . . ." *Reviews in American History*, IV, no. 4 (December 1976), 539–45; Merrill and Ruchames, eds., *Letters of Garrison*, 4, pp. 290, 350, 604–5; Garrison and Garrison, *Garrison*, 3, p. 299 n. 2; 4, p. 126; Garrison to Louisa Loring, May 24, 1858, Ellis Gray Loring Family Papers, Ratcliffe College.

21 Francis Jackson to William Lloyd Garrison, November 3, 1855, B.P.L.; Edmund Quincy to Editor of the *Transcript*, September 5, 1850 (clipping), Edmund Quincy Papers, Massachusetts Historical Society; Samuel J. May to William Lloyd Garrison, January 18, 1841, B.P.L.; Wendell Phillips to William Lloyd Garrison, January 6, 1846, B.P.L.; Oliver Johnson to W. L. Garrison, March 4, 1841, B.P.L.; Parker Pillsbury to W. L. Garrison, April 7, 1861, B.P.L.; Henry C. Wright to W. L. Garrison, September 5, 1861, B.P.L.

22 Nathaniel Peabody Rogers to W. L. Garrison, September 14, 1843, July 16, 1841,

B.P.L.; John A. Collins to W. L. Garrison, April 3, 1841, B.P.L.; Samuel J. May to W. L. Garrison, September 25, 1860, B.P.L.; Francis Jackson to W. L. Garrison, July 26, 1843, B.P.L.; Henry C. Wright to William and Helen Garrison, January 19, 1858, in Garrison and Garrison, *Garrison*, 4, p. 328.

23 Henry C. Wright to W. L. Garrison, September 3, 1846; February 3, 1860, B.P.L.; Johnson, *Garrison*, p. 52; Oliver Johnson, untitled manuscript, June 10, 1838, Album, Western Antislavery Society Manuscripts, L.C.; Rogers in the *Herald of Freedom* (Concord), February 23, 1839; Qunicy in *Sixth Annual Report of the Board of Managers of the Massachusetts Anti-Slavery Society* (Boston, 1838); Maria W. Chapman to Mary A. Estlin, November 15, 1858, B.P.L.

24 Oliver Johnson to W. L. Garrison, March 3, 1859, B.P.L.; Parker Pillsbury to W. L. Garrison, January 7, 1859, B.P.L.; Samuel J. May to W. L. Garrison, November 23, 1851, February 8, 1857, B.P.L.; Ann G. Phillips to W. L. Garrison, March 24, 1862, B.P.L.

25 Anne Warren Weston to J. B. Estlin, February 3, 1850, B.P.L.; Ellis Gray Loring, "To the Friends of the Liberator," January 3, 1842, Edmund Quincy Papers, Massachusetts Historical Society; Bartlett, *Phillips*, pp. 104–5; Jackson in Garrison and Garrison, *Garrison*, 2, p. 252; David Lee Child in ibid., 2, p. 1; Maria W. Chapman to A. G. Chapman, July [?] 21, 1862, B.P.L.

26 Tolf, "Quincy," pp. 197–9; Anne Warren Weston to Wendell Phillips, February 11, ____, Blagden Collection, Houghton Library; Samuel J. May, *Some Recollections of Our Antislavery Conflict*, pp. 36–7; May, Jr., in Clare Taylor, ed., *British and American Abolitionists: An Episode in Transatlantic Understanding* (Edinburgh: Edinburgh University Press, 1974), p. 362; Francis Jackson to Samuel Osgood, June 1, 1839, B.P.L.

27 Quincy in Garrison and Garrison, *Garrison*, 3, pp. 84–7, 91; Edmund Quincy to R. D. Webb, January 29, 1843; December 13, 1845, Quincy–Webb Correspondence, B.P.L.; Edmund Quincy Journal, May 4, 10, 1842, Edmund Quincy Papers, Massachusetts Historical Society; Edmund Quincy to Wendell Phillips, December 9, 1846, September 7, 1851, Blagden Collection, Houghton Library. Parker Pillsbury to John A. Collins, November 18, 1839; Pillsbury to Samuel May, Jr., December 21, 1855; both in B.P.L. See also Louis Filler, "Parker Pillsbury: An Anti-Slavery Apostle," *New England Quarterly*, XIX, no. 3 (September 1946), 332. Oliver Johnson to Gerrit Smith, October 11, 1839, Gerrit Smith Papers, Syracuse University. Anne Warren Weston to Mary A. Estlin, November 11, 1851, October 26, 1852, B.P.L. Samuel J. May to W. L. Garrison, January 18, 1841, January 15, 1848, B.P.L.

28 S. N. Eisenstadt, ed., *Max Weber on Charisma and Institution Building* (Chicago: University of Chicago Press, 1968), pp. 22–5, 253–5. See also Philip E. Slater, *Microcosm: Structural, Psychological, and Religious Evolution in Groups* (New York: John Wiley, 1966), p. 15, for the same point.

29 Bartlett, *Phillips*, p. 82, and Tolf, "Quincy," p. 99, on the location of the Chapman house. The eight Edmund Quincy Journals at the Massachusetts Historical Society provide an exacting and almost day-by-day account of those who visited the Chapman house. Data on Maria Chapman are provided in Jane H. Pease and William H. Pease, "The Role of Women in the Antislavery Movement," *Historical Papers of the Canadian Historical Society* (June 7–10, 1967), 174; Lawrence Ladner, *The Bold Brahmins: New England's War against Slavery, 1831–1863* (New York: E. P. Dutton, 1961), p. 59. Edmund Quincy to Maria Weston Chapman, April 26, 1840, B.P.L.; Quincy to R. D. Webb, March 9, October 3, 1848, Quincy–Webb Correspondence, B.P.L.; Tolf, "Quincy," p. 100; Robert V. Sparks, "Abolition in Silver Slippers: A Biography of Edmund Quincy" (Ph.D. dissertation, Boston College, 1978), pp. 113–14.

30 Edmund Quincy to R. D. Webb, September 22, 1844, Quincy–Webb Correspondence, B.P.L.; Parker Pillsbury to William L. Garrison, December 28, 1859, B.P.L.; Garrison and Garrison, *Garrison*, 1, p. 338 (Benson); Anne Warren Weston to Mary A. Estlin, April 4, 1852, B.P.L.; Merrill and Ruchames, eds., *Letters of Garrison*, 4, p. 423 (Garrison).

31   See, e.g., Edmund Quincy Journal, July 3, December 30, 1841, Edmund Quincy
      Papers, Massachusetts Historical Society; Henry C. Wright to John A. Collins, April
      23, 1840, B.P.L.; Ellis Gray Loring to Lydia M. Child, February 22, 1839, Ellis Gray
      Loring Letterbook, Houghton Library.

32   See, e.g., Will of Francis Jackson, January 28, 1861, B.P.L.; Francis Jackson and
      Wendell Phillips to Thomas Davis, December 13, 1847, Garrison Papers, Massachu-
      setts Historical Society; Donors to W. L. Garrison Fund, November 27, 1847, Garri-
      son Papers, Massachusetts Historical Society; John White Chadwick, ed., *A Life for
      Liberty: Anti-Slavery and Other Letters of Sallie Holley* (New York and London: G. P. Putnam,
      1899), p. 77; Nye, *Garrison*, pp. 160–1; Bartlett, *Phillips*, p. 280; Merrill, *Against Wind and
      Tide*, p. 284; Oliver Johnson to Wendell Phillips, February 4, 1860, Blagden Collection,
      Houghton Library.

33   Edmund Quincy to R. D. Webb, March 29, 1845, Quincy–Webb Papers, B.P.L.; Mer-
      rill and Ruchames, eds., *Letters of Garrison*, 1, p. 370; 2, p. 269; Samuel J. May to Samuel
      E. Sewall, December 21, 1865, Robie–Sewall Papers, Massachusetts Historical Soci-
      ety; Edmund Quincy to Wendell Phillips, January 7, 1864, Blagden Collection, Hough-
      ton Library.

34   Garrison and Garrison, *Garrison*, 3, pp. 228, 313–14; Nathaniel Peabody Rogers, *A
      Collection from the Miscellaneous Writings of Nathaniel Peabody Rogers* (Boston: Benjamin B.
      Mussey, 1849), p. 60; Samuel May, Jr., to J. B. Estlin, March 30, 1846, B.P.L.; Parker
      Pillsbury to John A. Collins, November 18, 1839, B.P.L.; Jane H. Pease and William H.
      Pease, *Bound with Them in Chains: A Biographical History of the Antislavery Movement* (West-
      port, Conn.: Greenwood Press, 1972), p. 40.

35   Ellis Gray Loring to Louisa Loring, May 14, 1840, Ellis Gray Loring Family Papers,
      Ratcliffe College. See also Loring to William H. Blake, September 25, 1838, and
      Loring to Lydia M. Child, February 22, 1839, Loring Letterbook, Houghton Library;
      Francis Jackson to Louisa Loring, May 27, 1858, Loring Family Papers, Ratcliffe
      College; Tolf, "Quincy," pp. 81–2.

36   Chadwick, "May of Leicester," 205–6; Samuel J. May to Henry G. Chapman, No-
      vember 10, 1840, B.P.L.; Samuel May, Jr., to J. B. Estlin, February 26, 1846, B.P.L.;
      Samuel May, Jr., to R. D. Webb, November 7, 1858, B.P.L.

37   Lewis Perry, *Childhood, Marriage, and Reform: Henry Clarke Wright, 1797–1870* (Chicago:
      University of Chicago Press, 1980), p. 222; William Lloyd Garrison to Henry C.
      Wright, October 1, 1844, B.P.L.; Garrison and Garrison, *Garrison*, 4, pp. 253 *n*. 1, 328;
      Merrill, *Against Wind and Tide*, pp. 185–6; Merrill and Ruchames, eds., *Letters of Garrison*,
      3, pp. 16, 376, 540; Thomas, *The Liberator*, p. 241; Henry C. Wright to W. L. Garrison,
      February 6, 1860, B.P.L.

38   Sparks, "Abolition in Silver Slippers," particularly pp. 113–14, 209–12, provides the
      best characterization of this patrician clique within the Boston Clique. See also Tolf,
      "Quincy," p. 95; Bartlett, *Phillips*, p. 102; Maria W. Chapman to William L. Garrison,
      May 20, 1877, B.P.L.; Edmund Quincy Journal, August 30, 1841, October 13, 1842,
      and Quincy to R. D. Webb, January 29, 1843, Quincy Papers, Massachusetts Histori-
      cal Society.

39   For objections to Pillsbury, see Oliver Johnson to Harriet Martineau, May 7, 1859,
      B.P.L.; Johnson to Maria W. Chapman, August 18, 1859, B.P.L.; Maria W. Chapman
      to Samuel May, Jr., March 15, 1857, B.P.L.; Anne Weston to Mary A. Estlin, February
      23, 1853, B.P.L.; Maria W. Chapman to William L. Garrison, n.d. [August 1861],
      B.P.L. The complaint by Chapman against Samuel J. May is quoted in Margaret
      Munsterberg, "The Weston Sisters and 'The Boston Controversy,'" *Boston Public Library
      Quarterly*, X, no. 1 (January 1958), 49. Oliver Johnson to William L. Garrison, July 13,
      1853, B.P.L. (about Quincy). Samuel May, Jr., to R. D. Webb, January 12, March 30,
      June 6, November 7, 1858, B.P.L., on Chapman.

40   For the basic facts in the Rogers controversy, see Steven Cox, "Nathaniel P. Rogers
      and the Rogers Collection," *Historical New Hampshire*, XXXIII, no. 1 (spring 1978), 52–7;
      Filler, "Pillsbury," pp. 325–6; Bartlett, *Phillips*, p. 109. For a clear example of Rogers's

1844 "no organization" position, see Rogers to R. D. Webb, January 29, 1844, B.P.L.

41   Quincy to R. D. Webb, December 14, 1844, in Garrison and Garrison, *Garrison*, 3, pp. 125–6; Quincy to R. D. Webb, March 29, 1845, Quincy–Webb Correspondence, B.P.L. See also Sparks, "Abolition in Silver Slippers," pp. 239–40.

42   W. P. Garrison, *Garrison*, 3, p. 127; Nathaniel P. Rogers to Francis Jackson, October 30, December 11, 1844, B.P.L.; Rogers to William L. Garrison, January 3, 1845, B.P.L.

43   Garrison in the *Liberator* (Boston), January 10, 1845; Quincy in Sparks, "Abolition in Silver Slippers," pp. 239–40; Johnson, *Garrison*, pp. 301–2; May, *Recollections*, p. 405.

44   Quincy in Garrison and Garrison, *Garrison*, 3, pp. 125–6; Phillips in Eleanor Lewis, ed., "Letters of Wendell Phillips to Lydia Maria Child," *New England Quarterly*, V (February 1892), 732.

45   Anne W. Weston to Mary A. Estlin, September 7, 1850, B.P.L.; Samuel May, Jr., to R. D. Webb, April 15, 1860, B.P.L.; Edmund Quincy to R. D. Webb, March 28, 1847, March 9, 1848, January 18, 1853, B.P.L.; Samuel May, Jr., to R. D. Webb, February 8, 1857, B.P.L.

46   Merrill and Ruchames, eds., *Letters of Garrison*, 4, p. 63, includes one of Garrison's strongest defenses of Wright. For other expressions of admiration for Wright by Clique members, see, e.g., Edmund Quincy to Henry C. Wright, December 31, 1838, B.P.L.; Quincy to R. D. Webb, January 29, March 26, 1843, B.P.L.; Samuel May, Jr., to J. B. Estlin, February 26, 1846, B.P.L.; *Non-Resistant* (Boston), October 14, 1840. *Chronotype* (Boston), January 6, 1848, reports on Wright unknowingly misrepresenting Rogers's estate. Although Rogers had left $20,000, after liabilities were deducted the estate totaled only $6,320.

47   See, e.g., Quincy in the *Non-Resistant* (Boston), June 15, 1839, and *Emancipator* (New York), May 31, 1838; N. P. Rogers, *Miscellaneous Writings*, pp. 13, 88; May in the *Non-Resistant* (Boston), October 5, 1839; Wright quoted in Lewis Perry, *Radical Abolitionism: Anarchy and the Government of God in Antislavery Thought* (Ithaca, N.Y.: Cornell University Press, 1973), p. 52.

48   *Liberator* (Boston), December 1, 1837, June 29, 1838, May 24, 1839, May 23, 1851; *Works of Follen*, 5, pp. 198, 213; Merrill and Ruchames, eds., *Letters of Garrison*, 2, pp. 286, 436; Samuel May, Jr., to R. D. Webb, October 5, 1856, B.P.L.; Henry C. Wright, "Human Government," May 4, 1839, Album, Western Anti-Slavery Society, L.C.; John A. Collins to Maria W. Chapman, February 28, 1843, B.P.L.; *National Anti-Slavery Standard* (New York), December 10, 1840.

49   Quincy in the *Non-Resistant* (Boston), May 12, 1841; Wright in the *Liberator* (Boston), May 24, 1839, and Henry C. Wright, *Human Life: Illustrated in My Individual Experience as a Child, a Youth, and a Man* (Boston: Bela Marsh, 1849), p. 391; Phillips in Merton Dillon, *The Abolitionists: The Growth of a Dissenting Minority* (Dekalb: Northern Illinois University Press, 1974), p. 59; Garrison and Garrison, *Garrison*, 3, pp. 94–5 n. 1; Thomas, *The Liberator*, p. 298; Nye, *Garrison*, p. 140. Figures for assessed wealth in Boston are given in Edward Pessen, *Riches, Class, and Power before the Civil War* (Lexington, Mass.: D. C. Heath, 1973), p. 39.

50   Rogers in *National Anti-Slavery Standard* (New York), December 24, 1840, and Rogers, *Miscellaneous Writings*, p. 62; Chapman in the *Non-Resistant* (Boston), June 15, 1839; May in *Proceedings of the Pennsylvania Yearly Meeting of Progressive Friends, Held at Old Kennett, Chester County, Fifth Month, 1853* (New York, 1853), pp. 49–50; Henry C. Wright Journal, XXXV, November 9, 1845, B.P.L., and Wright in the *Liberator* (Boston), July 21, 1837; Merrill and Ruchames, eds., *Letters of Garrison*, 2, pp. 402, 529, 632–3, and Garrison in the *Liberator* (Boston), December 15, 1837.

51   See, e.g., Henry C. Wright Journal, XXXV, November 9, 1845, B.P.L., Samuel J. May in Pease and Pease, "Freedom and Peace," pp. 24–5; Garrison in the *Liberator* (Boston), December 15, 1837; *A Letter on the Political Obligations of Abolitionists by James G. Birney: with a reply by William Lloyd Garrison* (Boston, 1839), p. 16; Merrill and Ruchames, eds., *Letters of Garrison*, 2, pp. 632–3.

52 *Tributes to William Lloyd Garrison, at the Funeral Services, May 28, 1879* (Boston: Houghton, Osborn, 1879), p. 53, quoting Phillips. Edmund Quincy to Wendell Phillips, May 20, 1845, Oliver Johnson to Wendell Phillips, February 4, 1860, both in Blagden Collection, Houghton Library.

53 See Slater, *Microcosm*, p. 86; Graham S. Gibbard, John H. Hartmann, Richard D. Mann, eds., *Analysis of Groups* (San Francisco: Jossey-Bass, 1974), p. 90; and Erving Goffman, *Asylums: Essays on the Social Situation of Mental Patients and Other Inmates* (Garden City, N.Y.: Doubleday, Anchor, 1961), p. 320, for excellent theoretical discussions of this pull between symbiosis and individuation and how it tends to provide durable group existence.

CHAPTER 3. STEWARDS OF THE LORD

1 The most fruitful sources for data on social characteristics of the Tappan circle are: the Lewis Tappan Papers in the Library of Congress [L.C.], the American Missionary Association Archives of the Amistad Research Center, Dillard University [A.M.A. Papers]; Gilbert H. Barnes and Dwight L. Dumond, eds., *Letters of Theodore Dwight Weld, Angelina Grimké Weld, and Sarah Grimké, 1822–1844*, 2 vols. (New York and London: D. Appleton-Century, 1934); Gerald Sorin, *The New York Abolitionists: A Case Study of Political Radicalism* (Westport, Conn.: Greenwood Publishing, 1971); Bertram Wyatt-Brown, *Lewis Tappan and the Evangelical War against Slavery* (Cleveland: Press of Case Western Reserve University, 1969); Clifton H. Johnson, "The American Missionary Association, 1846–1861: A Study of Christian Abolitionism" (Ph.D. dissertation, University of North Carolina, 1958).

2 For a comprehensive analysis of this Tappan circle constituency, see John B. Jentz, "Artisans, Evangelicals, and the City: A Social History of Abolition and Labor Reform in Jacksonian New York" (Ph.D. dissertation, City University of New York, 1977), and Jentz, "The Antislavery Constituency in Jacksonian New York City," *Civil War History*, XXVII, no. 2 (June 1981), 101–22.

3 Wyatt-Brown, *Lewis Tappan*, p. 102, on Lewis's conversion. Robert M. York, "George B. Cheever, Religious and Social Reformer, 1807–1890," *University of Maine Bulletin*, LVII, no. 12 (April 1, 1955), 86–9, on the supportive role played by Tappan, Weld, and Leavitt while Cheever was embracing immediatism. William Louis Lang, "Black Bootstraps: The Abolitionist Educators' Ideology and the Education of the Northern Free Negro, 1828–1860" (Ph.D. dissertation, University of Delaware, 1974), pp. 90–1, and Johnson, "The American Missionary Association," p. 110, note Jocelyn's Negro college venture. The founding of the Manual Labor Society is discussed in Hugh Houck Davis, "The Reform Career of Joshua Leavitt" (Ph.D. dissertation, Ohio State University, 1969), pp. 74–5; Gilbert Hobbs Barnes, *The Antislavery Impulse, 1830–1844* (New York: Harcourt, Brace and World, Harbinger, 1964), p. 38; Walter M. Merrill, *Against Wind and Tide: A Biography of William Lloyd Garrison* (Cambridge, Mass.: Harvard University Press, 1963), p. 117. Thomas, *Weld*, p. 72, on Whipple and Weld at Lane Seminary. Leavitt's visit to Lewis's house when the mob struck is cited in Joshua Leavitt to Mr. and Mrs. Roger Leavitt, July 12, 1834, Joshua Leavitt Papers, L.C., and in Louis Filler, "Liberalism, Antislavery, and the Founders of the Independent," *New England Quarterly*, XXVII, no. 3 (September 1954), 300.

4 Thomas, *Weld*, pp. 10–11, 14; Barnes and Dumond, eds., *Weld-Grimké Letters*, 1, p. 243; Russel B. Nye, *William Lloyd Garrison and the Humanitarian Reformers* (Boston: Little, Brown, 1955), p. 59; Sorin, *New York Abolitionists*, p. 73; H. Davis, "Leavitt," p. 100; Joshua Leavitt to Chloe Leavitt, January 17, 1835, Leavitt Papers, L.C.; S. S. Jocelyn to Lewis Tappan, April 11, 1857, and A. A. Phelps to Lewis Tappan, March 8, 1842, both in the Lewis Tappan Papers, L.C.

5 Wyatt-Brown, *Lewis Tappan*, p. 206; Austin Willey, *The History of the Anti-Slavery Cause in State and Nation* (Portland, Me.: Brown Thurston, 1886), p. 127; H. Davis, "Leavitt," p. 201.

6   James M. McPherson, "The Fight against the Gag Rule: Joshua Leavitt and Antislavery Insurgency in the Whig Party, 1839–1842," *Journal of Negro History*, XLVIII, no. 3 (July 1963), 188.

7   Wyatt-Brown, *Lewis Tappan*, pp. 293, 325, n. 22; S. S. Jocelyn to George Whipple, July 2, 20, 1857, and William Jay to Lewis Tappan, April 3, 1856, both in A.M.A. Papers, Dillard University; George Whipple to Gerrit Smith, November 4, 1869, Gerrit Smith Papers, Syracuse University; Lewis Tappan Journal, December 11, 1856, and S. S. Jocelyn to Lewis Tappan, August 25, 1857, both in the Lewis Tappan Papers, L.C.; H. Davis, "Leavitt," pp. 294–5.

8   Weld on Leavitt in Dwight L. Dumond, ed., *Letters of James Gillespie Birney, 1831–1857*, 2 vols. (New York: D. Appleton-Century, 1938), 1, p. 390. *New York Tribune*, October 21, 1858, and Lewis Tappan to L. S. Chamesovozow, April 3, 1855, Lewis Tappan Papers, L.C., indicate Lewis's attitude toward Jay. William Jay to Lewis Tappan, September 20, 1851, Lewis Tappan Papers, L.C., contains Jay's statement about Lewis.

9   George Whipple to Gerrit Smith, November 4, 1869, Smith Papers, Syracuse University. About the dying William Jay, see Jay to S. S. Jocelyn, July 1, 1858, A.M.A. Papers, Dillard University; Jay to Lewis Tappan, September 6, 1858, Lewis Tappan to William Jay, July 26, 1857, Tappan Letterbook, and Lewis Tappan Journal, March 30, 1858, all in the Lewis Tappan Papers, L.C. Lewis Tappan notes in his journal the comfort that he received from group members when his children took ill or died; see Journal, July 16, 1838, May 8, 1841, Lewis Tappan Papers, L.C. Lewis Tappan comments on Phelps in Tappan to A. A. Phelps, May 17, 1844, September 10, 1844, Boston Public Library [B.P.L.]; Tappan to Mrs. L. T. Phelps, August 19, 1847, Lewis Tappan Papers, L.C.

10 Dumond, ed., *Letters of Birney*, 1, p. 390, contains Weld's comment on Leavitt's leadership, while Charles C. Cole, Jr., *The Social Ideas of the Northern Evangelists, 1826–1860* (New York: Columbia University Press, 1954), p. 202, notes Leavitt's tactical shortcomings. For analyses of Weld as leader, see Thomas, *Weld*, and Robert H. Abzug, *Passionate Liberator: Theodore Dwight Weld and the Dilemma of Reform* (New York: Oxford University Press, 1980). Henry C. Wright's Journal, XLVIII, May 27, 1842, Houghton Library, cites Phelps as leader of the Tappan group. Phelps's chronic ill health during the 1840s is perhaps best revealed in A. A. Phelps to Lewis Tappan, March 8, 1842, Lewis Tappan Papers, L.C.

11 Wyatt-Brown, *Lewis Tappan*, pp. 100–2, 143–4, 197–8, 293; Nye, *Garrison*, pp. 130–1; Phyllis Mary Bannan, "Arthur and Lewis Tappan: A Study in New York Religious and Reform Movements" (Ph.D. dissertation, Columbia University, 1950), pp. 182–3; William Jay to Lewis Tappan, June 11, 1849, Lewis Tappan Papers, L.C.; Lewis Tappan to George Whipple and S. S. Jocelyn, January 4, 1855, A.M.A. Papers, Dillard University.

12 For examples of Lewis Tappan's use of consultation, see Lewis Tappan to Benjamin Tappan, January 2, 1840, Lewis Tappan to William Jay, June 11, 1841, and A. A. Phelps to Lewis Tappan, April 23, 1845, all in the Lewis Tappan Papers, L.C.; Lewis Tappan to A. A. Phelps, November 16, 1833, B.P.L. See Dumond, ed., *Letters of Birney*, 2, pp. 1006–7, for Tappan's confidential comment to Birney.

13 Lewis Tappan to S. S. Jocelyn, January 20, 1846, Lewis Tappan Papers, L.C.; Tappan to George B. Cheever, February 24, 1856, Cheever Family Papers, American Antiquarian Society [A.A.S.]; Tappan to Joshua Leavitt, October 12, 1843, January 8, 1848, Lewis Tappan Papers, L.C.; Tappan to George Whipple, October 8, 1852, A.M.A. Papers, Dillard University; Tappan to A. A. Phelps, May 19, 1840 (copy), Elizur Wright, Jr., Papers, L.C.

14 Lewis Tappan to A. A. Phelps, October 6, 1843, May 17, 1844, September 11, 1846, B.P.L.; Barnes, *Anti-Slavery Impulse*, p. 291 n. 20; Tappan to S. S. Jocelyn, January 5, 1859 (Tappan Letterbook), Tappan to Weld, March 12, 1840 (Tappan Letterbook), Lewis Tappan Journal, July 7, 1836, all in Lewis Tappan Papers, L.C.

15 In his book *Optimism: The Biology of Hope* (New York: Simon and Schuster, 1979),

anthropologist Lionel Tiger maintains that when optimistic confidence in the future is shared by a group, it tends to override individual differences that can cause unending friction. Optimistic confidence is particularly cohesive, Tiger finds, when it is tied to a shared religious faith.

16 Wyatt-Brown, *Lewis Tappan*, pp. xii, 261.

17 Quoted in the *Emancipator* (Boston), December 10, 1845.

18 Thomas, *Weld*, p. 154; Wyatt-Brown, *Lewis Tappan*, pp. 248-9; John White Chadwick, ed., *A Life for Liberty: Anti-Slavery and Other Letters of Sallie Holley* (New York and London: G. P. Putnam, 1899), pp. 107-8.

19 Lewis Tappan Journal, May 22, 1838, Lewis Tappan Papers, L.C.; George B. Cheever to Henry Cheever, November 7, 1834, December 1834, Cheever Family Papers, A.A.S.

20 S. S. Jocelyn to Lewis Tappan, August 2, 1859, A.M.A. Papers, Dillard University; Cushing Strout, *The New Heavens and New Earth: Political Religion in America* (New York: Harper and Row, 1974), p. 155 (on Tappan); Lewis Tappan, "Who Are the Men?" July 21, 1870 (clipping), Lewis Tappan Papers, L.C.; George B. Cheever to Henry Cheever, December 1834, and to Charlotte B. Cheever, January 23, 1834, Cheever Family Papers, A.A.S.; George Whipple to Hamilton Hill, December 18, 1846, Oberlin College.

21 Jay is quoted on the antiabolition mobs in the *Emancipator* (New York), December 1, 1836. In the *Emancipator* (New York), July 15, 1834, Lewis Tappan used words like Jay's in the face of mob destruction of his house. Arthur Tappan's May 12, 1840, letter to Leavitt on the 1840 A.A.S.S. convention is quoted in the *Liberator* (Boston), May 22, 1840. For Lewis Tappan on Texas annexation, see Annie H. Abel and Frank J. Klingberg, eds., *A Side-Light on Anglo-American Relations, 1839–1858: Furnished by the Correspondence of Lewis Tappan and Others with the British and Foreign Anti-Slavery Society* (Washington, D.C.: Association for the Study of Negro Life and History, 1927), 195-6. George B. Cheever to Charlotte B. Cheever, April 23, 1843, Cheever Family Papers, A.A.S. S.S. Jocelyn to George Whipple, June 3, 1857, to Lewis Tappan, October 9, 1858, to George Whipple, February 10, 1859, March 20, 1861, A.M.A. Papers, Dillard University, shows Jocelyn's calm while administering A.M.A. activities. See Johnson, "The American Missionary Association," pp. 108-9, on Whipple's calm and confidence as an A.M.A. director. For examples of how Lewis Tappan remained confident in the face of crises, see his Journal, March 1, 1817, July 24, 1836, October 24, 1857, Lewis Tappan Papers, L.C. See William Jay's letters to Anna Jay, April 5, 1831, to Maria Jay Butterworth, November 21, 1831, June 19, 1832, January 7, 1833, John Jay Collection, Columbia University.

22 Abel and Klingberg, eds., *A Side-Light*, p. 67, quotes Lewis Tappan. George B. Cheever to Charles G. Finney, May 24, 1858, Charles Finney Papers, Oberlin College. Amos A. Phelps, *Lectures on Slavery and Its Remedy* (Boston: New England Anti-Slavery Society, 1834), p. 40, and Phelps's remark in the *Evangelist* (New York), October 11, 1834. S. S. Jocelyn to Sarah and Angelina Grimké, July 8, 1837, Weld-Grimké Collection, Clements Library, University of Michigan; S. S. Jocelyn to A. A. Phelps, April 5, 1842, B.P.L., Arthur Tappan is quoted in Lewis Tappan, *The Life of Arthur Tappan* (rpt., New York: Arno Press, 1970), p. 366. George Whipple to Levi Burnell, December 9, 1839, Oberlin College. Leavitt in J. C. Lovejoy, *Memoir of Rev. Charles T. Torrey* (Boston: John P. Jewett, 1847), p. 239. William Jay to Harry G. Ludlow, October 25, 1834, John Jay Collection, Columbia University.

23 Bertram Wyatt-Brown, "Three Generations of Yankee Parenthood: The Tappan Family: A Case Study of Antebellum Nurture," *Illinois Quarterly*, XXXVIII, no. 1 (fall 1975), 24-5, Lewis Tappan Diary, October 27, 1816, Lewis Tappan Papers, L.C. William Jay to John Jay, June 3, 1831, to Maria B. Butterworth, November 21, 1831, June 19, 1833, January 7, 1833, John Jay Collection, Columbia University.

24 Lewis Tappan Journal, December 18, 1819, Lewis Tappan Papers, L.C.

25 Sorin, *New York Abolitionists*, p. 72; Lois Wendland Banner, "The Protestant Crusade: Religious Missions, Benevolence, and Reform in the United States, 1790-1840" (Ph.D. dissertation, Columbia University, 1970), pp. 253-4; Wyatt-Brown, *Lewis Tappan*, pp. 43-4, 228-32; Lewis Tappan Journal, August 30, 1855, Lewis Tappan Papers, L.C.; Lewis Tappan to Benjamin Tappan, September 6, 1829, January 8, 1833, Benjamin Tappan Papers, L.C.; Lewis Tappan, *Is It Right to Be Rich?* (New York: Anson Randolph, 1869), p. 14.

26 Theodore D. Weld to Theodore Grimké Weld, October 4, 1855, Weld-Grimké Papers, Clements Library; Theodore D. Weld, *First Annual Report of the Society for Promoting Manual Labor in Literary Institutions, Including the Report of their General Agent, Theodore D. Weld, January 28, 1833* (New York, 1833), pp. 59-60; Barnes and Dumond, eds., *Weld-Grimké Letters*, 2, p. 994. George B. Cheever in the *Evangelist* (New York), June 24, 1837, October 11, 1845; William Jay to Salmon P. Chase, March 24, 1845, Salmon P. Chase Papers, Pennsylvania Historical Society; Lewis Tappan Journal, July 11, 1836, Lewis Tappan Papers, L.C. (on Jocelyn); S. S. Jocelyn to Lewis Tappan, September 8, 1854, A.M.A. Papers, Dillard University; George Whipple to Gerrit Smith, January 29, 1850, Gerrit Smith Papers, Syracuse University. For evidence that early nineteenth-century English evangelical reformers espoused this same ideal of vigorous business activity pursued with Christian morality, see Ian Bradley, *The Call to Seriousness: The Evangelical Impact on the Victorians* (New York: Macmillan, 1976), pp. 156-8.

27 Theodore Dwight Weld, *American Slavery As It Is: Testimony of a Thousand Witnesses* (New York: American Anti-Slavery Society, 1839), pp. 187, 205-6, 210; George B. Cheever, *God against Slavery: and the Freedom and Duty of the Pulpit to Rebuke It, as a Sin against God* (New York: Joseph H. Ladd, 1857), pp. 117, 134; Phelps, *Lectures on Slavery*, pp. 52-3; Lewis Tappan in the *Friend of Virtue* (Boston), September 1, 1857; William Jay, *Inquiry into the Character and Tendency of the American Colonization, and American Anti-Slavery Societies* (New York: R. G. Williams, 1838), p. 195.

28 Lewis Tappan Journal, March 25, 1836, Lewis Tappan Papers, L.C.; Wyatt-Brown, *Lewis Tappan*, p. 21; Thomas, *Weld*, p. 110, and Weld in Barnes and Dumond, eds., *Weld-Grimké Letters*, 1, pp. 286, 496; George B. Cheever, *The Salvation of the Country Secured by Immediate Emancipation* (New York, 1861), pp. 23-4; Jay in the *Evangelist* (New York), December 12, 1835; George Whipple to Hamilton Hill, December 18, 1846, Oberlin College.

29 For good general discussions of evangelical reformers exalting the northern countryside and fretting over urban immoralities, see Paul Boyer, *Urban Masses and Moral Order in America, 1820-1920* (Cambridge, Mass.: Harvard University Press, 1978), especially pp. 15-18, and Allan S. Horlick, "Countinghouses and Clerks: The Social Control of Young Men in New York, 1840-1860" (Ph.D. dissertation, University of Wisconsin, 1969), particularly pp. 96-8.

30 Robert Trendel, "William Jay and the International Peace Movement," *Peace and Change*, II, no. 3 (fall 1974), 17-23, provides the most thorough assessment of Jay's pacifist role. Mabee, *Black Freedom*, pp. 18-19, notes Lewis Tappan's longtime peace career. See York, "Cheever," particularly p. 118. See also Peter Brock, *Radical Pacifists in Antebellum America* (Princeton, N.J.: Princeton University Press, 1968).

31 Cheever is quoted in the *Evangelist* (New York), March 12, 1846. Weld, *Report of Society for Promoting Manual Labor*, especially p. 52. See Jocelyn in the *Liberator*, (Boston), December 17, 1836, and S. S. Jocelyn to George Whipple, November 1, 1859, A.M.A. Papers, Dillard University. For clear articulations of Lewis Tappan's pacifist views, see Lewis Tappan to Joseph Sturge, January 9, 1849, Tappan Letterbook, Lewis Tappan to L. S. Chamesovozow, May 20, 1855, both in the Lewis Tappan Papers, L.C.; Lewis Tappan to Lysander Spooner, October 7, 1858, B.P.L. Jay's peace outlook is best described in *An Address Delivered before the American Peace Society, at Its Annual Meeting, May 26, 1845* (Boston: American Peace Society, 1845).

32 See, e.g., Simeon S. Jocelyn to Amos A. Phelps, December 6, 1837, B.P.L.; Jocelyn in the *Liberator* (Boston), December 17, 1836; Barnes and Dumond, eds., *Weld-Grimké Letters*, 2, pp. 513–14; *Evangelist* (New York), September 5. 1835 (letter by A.A.S.S. executive committee); Lewis Tappan to Joseph Sturge, January 9, 1849 (Letterbook), February 17, 1856, and Tappan to John Fee, November 7, 1857 (Letterbook), all in Lewis Tappan Papers, L.C.; Jay, *Address Delivered before American Peace Society.*

33 Lewis Tappan to James G. Birney, September 8, October 21, 1846, James G. Birney Papers, Clements Library, University of Michigan, and Lewis Tappan's address in "The Slave's Friend," II, no. 5 [1836?], Juvenile Anti-Slavery Society of Chatham Street Chapel, in B.P.L. William Jay, *Miscellaneous Writings on Slavery* (Boston: John P. Jewett, 1853), p. 429, and Jay in *Proceedings of the New York Anti-Slavery Convention, Held at Utica, October 21, and New York Anti-Slavery State Society, Held at Peterboro, October 22, 1835* (Utica, 1835), p. 41. Leavitt in the *Evangelist* (New York), July 26, 1834. Cheever in W. D. Weatherford, *American Churches and the Negro* (Boston: Christopher Publishing, 1957), p. 209, and "Dred Scott in 'The Church of the Puritans': Rev. Dr. Cheever's Second Bull against the Supreme Court," n.d. [1857], Scrapbook, Cheever Family Papers, A.A.S. Phelps, *Lectures on Slavery*, p. 199. S. S. Jocelyn to George Whipple, September 23, 1851, A.M.A. Papers, Dillard University.

34 Leavitt in the *Emancipator* (Boston), November 27, 1844, November 12, 1845; Jay, *Miscellaneous Writings*, pp. 487, 629; Jay, *The American Tract Society, Withdrawal from* (London: Clarke, Beeton, 1853 [?]), pp. 8, 13–14; York, "Cheever," pp. 157–9.

35 William Jay, *Letters Respecting the American Board of Commissioners for Foreign Missions and the American Tract Society* (New York: Lewis J. Bates, 1853), pp. 11–12; Wyatt-Brown, *Lewis Tappan*, p. 293. George Whipple to Gerrit Smith, February 12, 1849, Gerrit Smith Papers, Syracuse University. Lewis Tappan to Thomas Boutelle, January 11, 1848 (Letterbook), to Charles Cleveland, October 26, 1849 (Letterbook), Lewis Tappan Journal, November 20, 1855, Lewis Tappan, "For the Congregational Herald," December 9, 1854, all in Lewis Tappan Papers, L.C. A. Knighton Stanley, *The Children Is Crying: Congregationalism among Black People* (New York: Pilgrim Press, 1979), pp. 20–3.

36 Lewis Tappan to Asa Mahan, February 13, 1848 (Letterbook), Lewis Tappan Papers, L.C. Robert H. Abzug, "Theodore Weld: A Biography" (Ph.D. dissertation, University of California, Berkeley, 1977), p. 294, quotes Weld.

37 George B. Cheever, *The Christian's Duty, in a Time of Revival* (New York: Dunn, 1858), p. 6; Arthur Tappan in the *Liberator* (Boston), June 19, 1840; Jay, *Miscellaneous Writings*, p. 634; A. A. Phelps to Lewis Tappan, December 18, 1837, Lewis Tappan Papers, L.C.; Lewis Tappan to A. A. Phelps, December 27, 1837, B.P.L.; Lewis Tappan Journal, July 15, 1836 (on Weld), Lewis Tappan Papers, L.C.

38 Barnes and Dumond, eds., *Weld-Grimké Letters*, 2, pp. 810–11.

39 Quoted in Merrill, *Against Wind and Tide*, p. 152.

40 Lewis Tappan to W. L. Garrison, September 6, 1839 as quoted in the *Liberator* (Boston), September 13, 1839; Lewis Tappan to Theodore Weld, May 26, 1840, Lewis Tappan Papers, L.C.; Lewis Tappan to Gerrit Smith, April 12, 1839, Gerrit Smith Papers, Syracuse University.

41 A. A. Phelps to W. L. Garrison, February 19, 1839 in the *Liberator* (Boston), February 22, 1839; Phelps to J. G. Whittier, August 17, 1837, B.P.L.; Phelps to Gerrit Smith, April 10, 1839, Gerrit Smith Papers, Syracuse University; Bayard Tuckerman, *William Jay and the Constitutional Movement for the Abolition of Slavery* (rpt., New York: Negro Universities Press, 1969), p. 113; Jay in the *Emancipator* (New York), July 2, 1840; Leavitt in the *Emancipator* (New York), October 21, 1838; Arthur Tappan to Amos A. Phelps, January 17, 1835, B.P.L.; Weld in Barnes and Dumond, eds., *Weld-Grimké Letters*, 1, pp. 426–27. For Jay's packhorse analogy, see Jay to Committee on Arrangements, American Anti-Slavery Society, April 17, 1840, John Jay Collection, Columbia University.

42 A. A. Phelps, *A Sketch of the Proceedings of the Convention for the Discussion of the Sabbath, the*

Ministry, and the Church (New York: American Society for the Promotion of Christian Morals, 1842), pp. 26–8. For Lewis Tappan's observations, see Bannan, "Arthur and Lewis Tappan," p. 139; Wyatt-Brown, *Lewis Tappan*, p. 186; Lewis Tappan to L. M. Blanchard, January 5, 1855, Lewis Tappan Papers, L.C. York, "Cheever," p. 116. S. S. Jocelyn to A. A. Phelps, December 6, 1837, B.P.L. William Jay to Ellis Gray Loring, September 13, 1843 (copy), B.P.L., and Jay to Lewis Tappan, June 11, 1849, Lewis Tappan Papers, L.C.

43 York, "Cheever," p. 52; George I. Rockwood, *Cheever, Lincoln, and the Causes of the Civil War* (Worcester, Mass., 1936), p. 46; George B. Cheever, *Fourth of July Address* (Salem, 1833), p. 56; George B. Cheever to Charlotte Cheever, June 29, 1835, Cheever Family Papers, A.A.S.; Wyatt-Brown, *Lewis Tappan*, pp. 185, 248, 262, 310, 322; Mabee, *Black Freedom*, p. 16; Lewis Tappan to John Greenleaf Whittier, April 1847, Whittier-Packard Manuscripts, Houghton Library, Harvard University; (Lewis Tappan), *Letter from a Gentleman in Boston to a Unitarian Clergyman of that City* (Boston, 1828), p. 6; Joshua Leavitt, *A Letter from a Trinitarian to a Unitarian* (Greenfield, Mass., 1820); Joshua Leavitt to George B. Cheever, January 14, 1836, Cheever Family Papers, A.A.S.; Lewis Tappan Journal, December 31, 1819, William Jay to Lewis Tappan, August 22, 1836, Lewis Tappan to Mrs. L. E. Sturge, July 10, 1855, all in Lewis Tappan Papers, L.C.; George Whipple in *American Missionary*, XII, no. 4 (April 1868), 83–4.

44 Lewis Tappan Journal, November 14, 1839, Lewis Tappan Papers, L.C.; *Emancipator* (New York), September 19, October 17, November 14, December 12, 16, 1839.

45 Lewis Tappan to Joshua Leavitt, n.d., as quoted in *Friend of Man* (Utica), December 4, 1839; *Emancipator* (New York), November 14, December 12, 1839; Mabee, *Black Freedom*, p. 411; Lewis Tappan to Gerrit Smith, March 24, 1840; February 7, 1842, Gerrit Smith Papers, Syracuse University; *Liberator* (Boston), December 27, 1839; Lewis Tappan to Benjamin Tappan, October 26, 1839 (Letterbook), Lewis Tappan to Gamaliel Bailey, March 6, 1843, both in Lewis Tappan Papers, L.C.

46 William Jay to Lewis Tappan, September 22, 1840, John Jay Collection, Columbia University; Richard H. Sewell, *Ballots for Freedom: Antislavery Politics in the United States, 1837–1860* (New York: Oxford University Press, 1976), p. 111; Gerald Sorin, *Abolitionism: A New Perspective* (New York: Praeger, 1972), p. 80; Walter M. Merrill and Louis Ruchames, eds., *The Letters of William Lloyd Garrison*, 6 vols. (Cambridge, Mass.: Harvard University Press, Belknap Press, 1971–81), 2, p. 566 (vol. 1, *I Will Be Heard! 1822–1835*; vol. 2, *A House Dividing against Itself, 1836–1840*; vol. 3, *No Union with Slaveholders, 1841–1849*; vol. 4, *From Disunionism to the Brink of War, 1850–1860*; vol. 5, *Let the Oppressed Go Free, 1861–1867*; vol. 6, *To Rouse the Slumbering Land, 1868–1879*; individual volumes are cited as *Letters of Garrison* with the volume number); Thomas, *Weld*, pp. 189–90; Lewis Perry, " 'We Have Had Conversation in the World': The Abolitionists and Spontaneity," *Canadian Review of American Studies*, VI, no. 1 (spring 1972), 24 *n.* 32.

47 Joshua Leavitt to Myron Holley, July 12, 1839, Myron Holley Papers, New York Historical Society; Joshua Leavitt to Gerrit Smith, August 3, 1840, Gerrit Smith Papers, Syracuse University; Dumond, ed., *Letters of Birney*, 2, pp. 660, 716; *Emancipator* (New York), September 10, November 12, 1840; Lewis Tappan to Amos A. Phelps, May 19, 1840, B.P.L.

48 Joshua Leavitt to Gerrit Smith, June 30, 1840, and Lewis Tappan to Gerrit Smith, August 28, 1840, both in Gerrit Smith Papers, Syracuse University; Sorin, *New York Abolitionists*, pp. 69–70; Lewis Tappan to Nathaniel Rogers, January 16, 1844 (Letterbook), Lewis Tappan Papers, L.C.

49 William Jay to Salmon P. Chase, June 5, 1843, Salmon P. Chase Papers, Pennsylvania Historical Society; John R. Hendricks, "The Liberty Party in New York State, 1838–1848" (Ph.D. dissertation, Fordham University, 1959), p. 107; Sorin, *New York Abolitionists*, pp. 80–1; *Emancipator* (Boston), September 28, 1843.

50 Phelps in *Emancipator* (Boston), September 1, 1842; Amos A. Phelps to Gerrit Smith, December 8, 1843, Gerrit Smith Papers, Syracuse University.

51 Wyatt-Brown, *Lewis Tappan*, p. 264; Lewis Tappan to Gerrit Smith, September 9, 1843, Lewis Tappan to Joshua Leavitt, October 10, 1843, both in the Letterbooks of the Lewis Tappan Papers, L.C.; Abel and Klingberg, eds., *Side-Light*, p. 186.

52 Abel and Klingberg, eds., *Side-Light*, p. 167; Theodore Clarke Smith, *The Liberty and Free Soil Parties of the Northwest* (New York: Longmans, Green, 1897), p. 111; McPherson, "Fight Against the Gag Rule," pp. 194–5; Alan Morton Kraut, "The Liberty Men of New York: Political Abolitionism in New York State, 1840–1848" (Ph.D. dissertation, Cornell University, 1975), p. 146; Lewis Tappan to F. J. Le Moyne, December 18, 1848, in "Letters of Dr. F. J. Le Moyne, an Abolitionist of Western Pennsylvania," *Journal of Negro History*, XVIII, no. 4 (October 1933), 453.

53 George Whipple to Gerrit Smith, February 12, 1849, Theodore D. Weld to Gerrit Smith, May 1, 1852, both in Gerrit Smith Papers, Syracuse University; Theodore D. Weld to James G. Birney, July 18, 1851, Lewis Tappan to James G. Birney, February 2, 1852, both in the James G. Birney Papers, Clements Library; Lewis Tappan to Gerrit Smith, November 18, 1848, Gerrit Smith Papers; Cheever in the *Radical Abolitionist* (New York), III, no. 11 (June 1858); William Jay to Salmon P. Chase, August 22, 1845, Salmon P. Chase Papers, Pennsylvania Historical Society.

54 Edmund Quincy to R. D. Webb, March 28, 1847, Quincy–Webb Correspondence, B.P.L.

CHAPTER 4. VOLUNTARISTS OF THE BURNED-OVER-DISTRICT

1 Gerrit Smith to Amos A. Phelps, December 28, 1838, Elizur Wright, Jr., Papers, Library of Congress [L.C.]; Gerrit Smith to William Lloyd Garrison, February 9, 1839, as published in the *Liberator* (Boston), February 22, 1839; Gerrit Smith to Amos A. Phelps, April 20, 1839, Boston Public Library [B.P.L.]; Gerrit Smith to Theodore Dwight Weld, July 11, 1840, in Gilbert H. Barnes and Dwight L. Dumond, eds., *Letters of Theodore Dwight Weld, Angelina Grimké Weld, and Sarah Grimké*, 2 vols. (New York and London: D. Appleton-Century, 1934), 2, pp. 849–50; Gerrit Smith to Lewis Tappan, June 19, 1840, to Oliver Johnson, July 6, 1840, both in 1827–43 Letterbook, Gerrit Smith Papers, Syracuse University; Gerrit Smith to Elizur Wright, Jr., April 20, 1840, Elizur Wright, Jr., Papers, L.C.

2 Henry C. Wright to W. L. Garrison, September 8, 1840, B.P.L.; Henry Wright to Gerrit Smith, June 28, 1846, Smith Papers, Syracuse University; Henry Wright in the *Non-Resistant* (Boston), April 20, 1839; Henry Wright to George W. Benson, February 20, 1840, B.P.L. In *Life and Times of Frederick Douglass* (New York: Macmillan, Collier, 1962), p. 229, Douglass also recalled the existence of this Smith "school" in central New York.

3 The Gerrit Smith Papers, Syracuse University, house vast quantities of biographical data on all group participants. Other pertinent sources for group social characteristics are the Slavery Manuscripts and the Alvan Stewart Papers in the New York Historical Society; the Stewart Papers in the New York State Historical Association; Muriel L. Block, "Beriah Green, the Reformer" (M.A. thesis, Syracuse University, 1935); M. Leon Perkal, "William Goodell: A Life of Reform" (Ph.D. dissertation, City University of New York, 1972); Ralph Volney Harlow, *Gerrit Smith, Philanthropist and Reformer* (New York: Henry Holt, 1939); Luther Rawson Marsh, ed., *Writings and Speeches of Alvan Stewart, on Slavery* (New York: A. B. Burdick, 1860); Elizur Wright, Jr., *Myron Holley; and What He Did for Liberty and True Religion* (Boston: Elizur Wright, 1882). *Liberator* (Boston), August 16, 1850, provides an excerpt from the *Washington Bee* containing crucial data on Chaplin's background. The *National Anti-Slavery Standard* (New York), January 16, 1851, also has a useful sketch of Chaplin.

4 Two Ph.D. dissertations are particularly informative regarding the Smith group's antislavery in the late 1830s and early 1840s: Alice Hatcher Henderson, "The History of the New York State Anti-Slavery Society" (University of Michigan, 1963), and

John R. Hendricks, "The Liberty Party in New York State, 1838–1848" (Fordham University, 1959). See also Harlow, *Smith*, p. 146; Marsh, ed., *Writings of Stewart*, p. 27; Richard H. Sewell, *Ballots for Freedom: Antislavery Politics in the United States, 1837–1860* (New York: Oxford University Press, 1976), pp. 45, 49–58; *Emancipator Extra* (New York), August 25, 1841.

5 For a most comprehensive analysis of the Smith constituency, see Alan M. Kraut, "The Liberty Men of New York: Political Abolitionism in New York State, 1840–1848" (Ph.D. dissertation, Cornell University, 1975), and Kraut, "The Forgotten Reformers: A Profile of Third Party Abolitionism in Antebellum New York," in *Antislavery Reconsidered: New Perspectives on the Abolitionists*, ed., Lewis Perry and Michael Fellman (Baton Rouge: Louisiana State University Press, 1979), pp. 119–45.

6 For data on friendships and antagonisms in the group, see Marsh, ed., *Writings of Stewart*, pp. 28–9; Block, "Green," pp. 88–9; Perkal, "Goodell," p. 213; Beriah Green to Gerrit Smith, April 19, 1839, January 1, 1841, October 26, 1842, December 26, 1849, Smith Papers, Syracuse University; Chaplin on Jackson in the *Albany Patriot*, May 12, 1847; Holley on Green in the *Rochester Freeman*, September 4, 1839; Dwight L. Dumond, ed., *Letters of James Gillespie Birney, 1831–1857*, 2 vols. (New York: D. Appleton-Century, 1938), 2, p. 1064.

7 Charles A. Hammond, *Gerrit Smith: The Story of a Noble Life* (Geneva, N.Y.: W. F. Humphrey, 1908), pp. 18–19; E. P. Tanner, "Gerrit Smith: An Interpretation," *Bulletin of the New York Historical Society*, V (1924), 26; Harlow, *Smith*, p. 22; Lawrence Ladner, *The Bold Brahmins: New England's War against Slavery, 1831–1863* (New York: E. P. Dutton, 1961), p. 127; Benjamin Quarles, "Sources of Abolitionist Income," *Mississippi Valley Historical Review*, XXXII, no. 1 (June 1945), 63–4.

8 William Goodell to Josiah Cady, April 1831 (?), William Goodell Papers, Berea College, on Goodell's 1830 trip to Peterboro. Henderson, "New York State Anti-Slavery Society," pp. 275–6, and Smith to Myron Holley, January 17, 1839, Miscellaneous Manuscripts, New York Historical Society on Smith's donations for antislavery newspapers. Block, "Green," p. 55, and Smith to Beriah Green, August 14, 1837, 1827–43 Letterbook, Smith Papers, Syracuse University, on Smith's support for Oneida Institute. For Smith's donations to free Chaplin, see Harlow, *Smith*, pp. 290–4; Philip S. Foner, ed., *The Life and Writings of Frederick Douglass*, 4 vols. (New York: International Publishers, 1950–5), 2, p. 560 *n.* 20 (vol. 1, *Early Years, 1817–1849*; vol. 2, *Pre–Civil War Decade, 1850–1860*; vol. 3, *The Civil War, 1861–1865*; vol. 4, *Reconstruction and After*; individual volumes are cited as *Life and Writings of Douglass* with the volume number); *National Era* (Washington, D.C.), October 10, 1850. Information on Smith's intervention in Jackson's behalf is provided in Henderson, "New York State Anti-Slavery Society," pp. 336–7, and *Friend of Man* (Utica), September 28, 1841.

9 See, e.g., Gerrit Smith to Beriah Green, October 5, 1837, to Alvan Stewart, July 20, 1840, to John Norton, December 7, 1840, to Beriah Green, April 14, 1842, to Allan Pinkerton, May 1, 1851, to William Steward, September 11, 1850, all in Letterbook, Smith Papers, Syracuse University; Marsh, ed., *Writings of Stewart*, p. 33; Gerrit Smith, "[Letter to] Edward C. Delavan, April 16, 1852" (n.p., 1852) and "Letter of Gerrit Smith to the Liberty Party of New Hampshire, March 18, 1848" (n.p., 1848), both broadsides in the Smith Papers, Syracuse University; Gerrit Smith in the *National Era* (Washington, D.C.), October 10, 1850.

10 Alvan Stewart to Gerrit Smith, October 2, 1835, Beriah Green to Smith, October 11, 1836, October 3, 1837, April 18, 1839, September 15, 1842, February 27, 1844, James C. Jackson to Smith, September 9, 1850, December 29, 1854, all in Smith Papers, Syracuse University; William Goodell to Josiah Cady, April 20, 1831, Goodell Papers, Berea College; Chaplin in *Albany Patriot*, June 16, 1847; Dumond, ed., *Letters of Birney*, 1, pp. 518–19; James Caleb Jackson to Maria Weston Chapman, March 10, 1840, B.P.L.

11 Perkal, "Goodell," pp. 95–6, 266, 296; William Goodell to Henry Catlin, December 14, 1855, 1855–57 Letterbook, Smith Papers, Syracuse University; William Goodell to A.

A. Phelps, April 13, 1837, B.P.L.; Smith to William Goodell, June 29, 1839, in *Rochester Freeman*, July 17, 1839.

12 See, e.g., Gerrit Smith, "[Letter to] President Green, Whitesboro, April 4, 1849," broadside (n.p., 1849), Smith to Beriah Green, January 5, 1850, Green to Smith, February 26, 1840, all in Smith Papers, Syracuse University; Green to A. A. Phelps, May 22, 1844, B.P.L.

13 Edward Pritchett to Elizur Wright, Jr., October 22, 1839, Elizur Wright, Jr., Papers, L.C.; Gerrit Smith to W. L. Chaplin, February 24, 1848, in the *Liberty Press* (Utica), March 9, 1848; James C. Jackson to Gerrit Smith, September 9, 1850, August 20, 1872, Smith Papers, Syracuse University; Chaplin in the *Albany Patriot*, May 26, June 23, 1847; Jackson in the *Liberty Press* (Utica), December 6, 1842.

14 William Goodell, *The Democracy of Christianity; or, An Analysis of the Bible and Its Doctrines in Relation to the Principle of Democracy*, 2 vols. (New York: Cady and Burgess, 1849–52), 2, pp. 32–9, 265, 299, 518; Goodell, *Slavery and Antislavery* (New York: William Harned, 1852), particularly pp. 447–8.

15 For Gerrit Smith's thoughts, see Octavius Brooks Frothingham, *Gerrit Smith: A Biography* (New York: G. P. Putnam, 1878), p. 216; *Emancipator* (New York), May 17, 1838; Gerrit Smith, *Three Discourses on the Religion of Reason* (New York, 1859), pp. 30, 69. Holley's ideas are in the *Rochester Freeman*, June 26, July 3, 1839; Myron Holley to James G. Birney, November 16, 1839, Miscellaneous Manuscripts, New York Historical Society. Alvan Stewart to Uriel Stewart, June 12, 1830, as quoted in Gerald Sorin, *The New York Abolitionists: A Case Study of Political Radicalism* (Westport, Conn.: Greenwood Publishing, 1971), p. 49. Green in *Friend of Man* (Utica), December 24, 1836; Jackson in the *Emancipator* (Boston), January 18, 1844.

16 Holley in the *Lyons Countryman*, May 3, 1831, and *Rochester Freeman*, June 12, 1839; Beriah Green to Gerrit Smith, February 26, 1840, in Harlow, *Smith*, pp. 31–2; Perkal, "Goodell," p. 64; Smith in *Fifth Annual Report of the American Anti-Slavery Society* (New York, 1838), p. 36; Goodell, *The American Slave Code in Theory and Practice* (New York: American and Foreign Anti-Slavery Society, 1853), pp. 104, 372; Goodell, *Slavery and Anti-Slavery*, p. 1; Goodell in the *Friend of Man* (Utica), July 7, 1836; *Albany Patriot*, December 18, 1844 (Green), February 26, 1845 (Jackson).

17 Gerrit Smith, *A Discourse on Creeds, and Ecclesiastical Machinery, Delivered at Peterboro, February 21, 1858* (Boston: John P. Jewett, 1858), pp. 15–16; Gerrit Smith to Martin Mitchell, November 9, 1841, 1827–43 Letterbook, Smith Papers, Syracuse University; *Albany Patriot*, October 23, 1844 (by Jackson), December 16, 1846 (by Goodell); Chaplin in the *Emancipator* (Boston), June 20, 1843, July 17, 1844; Alvan Stewart to Mr. and Mrs. Uriel Stewart, March 27, 1816, Alvan Stewart Papers, New York Historical Society.

18 *Emancipator* (Boston), August 25, December 22, 1842, February 8, 1844; *Albany Patriot*, February 16, 1843; Henderson, "New York State Anti-Slavery Society," pp. 114–15, 269–70; Harlow, *Smith*, pp. 55–6, 61. Gerrit Smith to Abigail Kelley Foster, June 24, 1843, 1827–43 Letterbook, Smith Papers, Syracuse University, contains Smith's remark on locality-centered antislavery. See also Smith to Edward C. Delavan, September 11, 1833, Smith to Duplessis Nash, December 2, 1846, Smith Papers, Syracuse University.

19 *Friend of Man* (Utica), October 2, 1839, quotes the general attack on the A.A.S.S. executive committee. Stewart is quoted in Gilbert Hobbs Barnes, *The Antislavery Impulse, 1830–1844* (New York: Harcourt, Brace and World, Harbinger, 1964), p. 151; William L. Chaplin to A. A. Phelps, March 13, 1838, B.P.L.; Chaplin in Barnes and Dumond, eds., *Letters of Weld-Grimké*, 1, p. 490; Gerrit Smith to James G. Birney, May 11, 1839, Smith Papers, Syracuse University, and Smith in the *Massachusetts Abolitionist* (Boston), May 30, 1839; Anne Warren Weston to Deborah Weston, April 8–11, 1839, B.P.L.; Lewis Perry, *Radical Abolitionism: Anarchy and the Government of God in Antislavery Thought* (Ithaca, N.Y.: Cornell University Press, 1973), p. 168, quotes Henry Wright.

20 For background on the origins of Smith's Church of Peterboro, see Carleton Mabee, *Black Freedom: The Nonviolent Abolitionists from 1830 through the Civil War* (New York: Macmillan, 1970), pp. 227–8; Harlow, *Smith*, pp. 204–5; Victor B. Howard, "The Anti-Slavery Movement in the Presbyterian Church, 1835–1861" (Ph.D. dissertation, Ohio State University, 1961), pp. 144–5; Abishai Scofield to A. Rand, July 3, 1848, Abishai Scofield Manuscripts, Burton Historical Collection, Detroit Public Library. Smith comments on the meaning of the Church of Peterboro in Smith to H. P. Crozier, May 17, 1849, to William Goodell, July 4, 1847, 1843–55 Letterbook, Smith Papers, Syracuse University; Smith to Joseph A. Dugdale, April 9, 1853, in *Proceedings of the Pennsylvania Yearly Meeting of Progressive Friends, Held at Old Kennett, Chester County, Fifth Month, 1853* (New York, 1853), p. 50; Smith, *A Discourse on Creeds*, p. 17; Ralph Volney Harlow, "Gerrit Smith and the Free Church Movement," *New York History*, XVIII, no. 3 (July 1937), 276.

21 Kraut, "Liberty Men of New York," p. 380, on the pervasiveness of nondenom-inational churches in the Burned-over-District. William Goodell, *Come-Outerism: The Duty of Secession from a Corrupt Church* (New York: American Anti-Slavery Society, 1845), especially p. 28. For further information on Goodell's position, see Perkal, "Goodell," p. 5; Mabee, *Black Freedom*, p. 228. Sorin, *New York Abolitionists*, p. 56, and Block, "Green," pp. 83–4, comments on Green. For Holley, see John White Chadwick, ed., *A Life for Liberty: Anti-Slavery and Other Letters of Sallie Holley* (New York and London: G. P. Putnam, 1899), p. 32, and Sewell, *Ballots for Freedom*, pp. 54–5. James C. Jackson to Gerrit Smith, June 26, 1838, Smith Papers, Syracuse University. Chaplin as quoted in the *Liberator* (Boston), January 19, 1844.

22 *Speeches of Gerrit Smith in Congress* (New York: Mason, 1855), pp. 11, 102, 242, 263–4, 284; Goodell in the *Liberator* (Boston), June 26, 1840; Chaplin in the *Albany Patriot*, June 16, 1847, Jackson in the *Emancipator* (Boston), January 18, 1844; *Radical Abolitionist* (New York), IV, no. 3 (October 1858); Walter M. Merrill and Louis Ruchames, eds., *The Letters of William Lloyd Garrison*, 6 vols. (Cambridge, Mass.: Harvard University Press, Belknap Press, 1971–81), 4, p. 561 n. 2 (vol. 1, *I Will Be Heard!, 1822–1835*; vol. 2, *A House Dividing against Itself, 1836–1840*; vol. 3, *No Union with Slaveholders, 1841–1849*; vol. 4, *From Disunionism to the Brink of War, 1850–1860*; vol. 5, *Let the Oppressed Go Free, 1861–1867*; vol. 6, *To Rouse the Slumbering Land, 1868–1879*; individual volumes are cited as *Letters of Garrison* with the volume number); Gerrit Smith, "Keep Government within Limits," n.d., Gerrit Smith Papers, New York Public Library; *The True Office of Civil Government, A Speech in the City of Troy, by Gerrit Smith* (New York: S. W. Benedict, 1851); Dumond, ed., *Letters of Birney*, 2, pp. 1079–80; Gerrit Smith, "Letter on Internal Improvements" (n.p., 1839), and Smith, "To the Voters of the Counties of Oswego and Madison, November 5, 1852" (n.p., 1852), both broadsides in the Smith Papers, Syracuse University.

23 For cogent analyses of this institutional–cultural transformation, see Michael B. Katz, *The Irony of Early School Reform: Educational Innovation in Mid-Nineteenth-Century Massachusetts* (Cambridge, Mass.: Harvard University Press, 1968); David J. Rothman, *The Discovery of the Asylum: Social Order and Disorder in the New Republic* (Boston: Little, Brown, 1971); George R. Taylor, *The Transportation Revolution, 1815–1860* (New York: Rinehart, 1951); William G. Rothstein, *American Physicians in the Nineteenth Century: From Sects to Science* (Baltimore: Johns Hopkins University Press, 1972), pp. 63–121; Matthew A. Crenson, *The Federal Machine: Beginnings of Bureaucracy in Jacksonian America* (Baltimore, Md.: Johns Hopkins University Press, 1975); William B. Skelton, "Professionalization in the United States Army Officer Corps during the Age of Jackson," *Armed Forces and Society*, I, no. 4 (summer 1975), 443–71; and especially John Higham, *From Boundlessness to Consoli-dation: The Transformation of American Culture, 1848–1860* (Ann Arbor, Mich.: William L. Clements Library, 1969).

24 *Address of the Macedon Convention, by William Goodell; and Letters of Gerrit Smith* (Albany: S. W. Green, 1847), especially p. 4. Goodell in the *Albany Patriot*, January 28, 1847.

25 Alvan Stewart to Samuel Webb, August 11, 1846, and Luther Marsh, "Alvan Stewart" (n.d.), both in Alvan Stewart Collection, New York State Historical Association; Stewart in the *Emancipator* (Boston), June 16, 1842.

26 For very early instances of group members looking beyond their locality to cure the ills of land monopoly, intemperance, and warfare, see, e.g., Alvan Stewart to Francis Jackson, July 23, 1838, B.P.L.; Stewart in *Herald of Freedom* (Concord), June 2, 1838; Gerrit Smith in the *Liberator* (Boston), May 26, 1837; Smith in the *Friend of Man* (Utica), May 31, 1837; *Letter of Gerrit Smith to Edward C. Delavan* (Whitesboro, N.Y.: Press of the Friend of Man, 1837), p. 17. Smith's plea for annexation of Canada and Cuba is printed in the *Congressional Globe*, 33d Cong., 1st sess., XXIII, appendix, pp. 1016–17.

27 The *Friend of Man* (Utica), October 18, 1837, reprints the Stewart speech before the N.Y.S.A.S.S. For useful commentaries on the speech, see William M. Wiecek, *The Sources of Antislavery Constitutionalism in America, 1760–1848* (Ithaca, N.Y.: Cornell University Press, 1977), pp. 254–5; Jacobus tenBroek, *The Antislavery Origins of the Fourteenth Amendment* (Berkeley and Los Angeles: University of California Press, 1951), pp. 43–7; Sorin, *New York Abolitionists*, pp. 50–1. Sewell, *Ballots for Freedom*, p. 50, and Hugh Houck Davis, "The Reform Career of Joshua Leavitt" (Ph.D. dissertation, Ohio State University, 1969), p. 177, covers Stewart's 1838 plea before the A.A.S.S. The *Emancipator* (Boston), November 9, 1843, printed Stewart's 1843 proclamation, while Marsh, ed., *Writings of Stewart*, pp. 272–367, prints several of Stewart's mid-1840s enunciations of radical constitutionalism and cultural voluntarism. See also Stewart to Samuel Webb, September 30, 1840, Stewart Papers, New York Historical Society.

28 Henderson, "History of N.Y.S.A.S.S.," p. 183, reports on Smith's defense of Stewart at the 1838 A.A.S.S. convention. For Smith's subsequent radical constitutionalism–cultural voluntarism, see Octavius Frothingham, *Gerrit Smith* (New York: G. P. Putnam, 1878), pp. 175–6, 188; *Letter of Gerrit Smith to S. P. Chase, on the Unconstitutionality of Every Part of American Slavery* (Albany: S. W. Green, 1847). For Stewart's pronouncements, see the *Rochester Freeman*, June 12, July 10, 1839. Perkal, "Goodell," p. 193; Goodell to George B. Cheever, July 4, 1857, Cheever Family Papers, American Antiquarian Society; William Goodell, *Our National Charters: For the Millions . . .* (New York: J. W. Alden, 1864). Chaplin in the *Albany Patriot*, May 26, 1847, and the *National Era* (Washington, D.C.), August 15, 1850.

29 Alvan Stewart to Myron Holley, December 16, 1839, Myron Holley Manuscripts, New York Historical Society; Henderson, "History of N.Y.S.A.S.S.," p. 150; Myron Holley to Gerrit Smith, January 12, 1839, Smith Papers, Syracuse University; Smith to William Goodell, October 9, 1838, in the *Friend of Man* (Utica), October 17, 1838; Smith to Goodell, February 8, 1840, in the *Friend of Man* (Utica), February 9, 1840; Holley in the *Rochester Freeman*, September 18, 25, 1839.

30 Holley in the *Rochester Freeman*, June 19, December 18, 25, 1839; *Emancipator* (New York), August 15, 1839; *Friend of Man* (Utica), August 14, 1839; Holley to Henry C. Wright, February 24, 1840, Miscellaneous Manuscripts, New York Historical Society. Alvan Stewart to Gerrit Smith, August 24, 1843, Smith Papers, Syracuse University; Stewart to Myron Holley, December 16, 1839, Stewart Papers, New York Historical Society; Stewart in the *Emancipator* (New York), November 18, 1841, and the *Liberator* (Boston), December 3, 1841; Stewart notation of May 6, 1844, in Western Anti-Slavery Society Album, n.d., Western Anti-Slavery Society Manuscripts, L.C. *Friend of Man* (Utica), October 17, 1838 (Green), March 23, April 1, 1840 (Goodell); *Albany Patriot*, December 18, 1844 (Green), March 5, 19, 1845 (Chaplin); *Liberty Press* (Utica), August 22, 1843 (Jackson); *Madison County Abolitionist* (Peterboro), December 7, 1841 (Smith and Green); *Emancipator* (New York), March 4, 1842 (Green); Frothingham, *Smith*, p. 157; Sorin, *New York Abolitionists*, p. 96. *Massachusetts Abolitionist* (Boston), September 5, 1839 (Goodell).

31 Hendricks, "Liberty Party in New York State," pp. 114–15; Chaplin to J. G. Birney, December 24, 1840, in Dumond, ed., *Letters to Birney*, 2, p. 619; Smith to Daniel Dickey

and George Ellingwood, March 21, 1845, Letterbook, Smith Papers, Syracuse University; Smith to James G. Birney, November 12, 1851, and Smith, "Report from the County of Madison," November 13, 1843, both in Birney Papers, Clements Library, University of Michigan; Stewart to Francis Jackson, July 23, 1838, B.P.L.; Stewart to Thomas Lafon, August 25, 1846, American Missionary Association Papers, Dillard University; *Emancipator* (Boston), May 25, 1843 (Jackson), December 7, 1843 (Smith); *Massachusetts Abolitionist* (Boston), October 31, 1839 (Smith).

32 *Model Worker* (Utica), November 24, 1848, quotes the resolution of the 1843 Buffalo convention. The best discussion of the Liberty party's nationally oriented organizational structure is provided in Alan M. Kraut, "The Politics of Reform: An Institutional Approach to Third Party Abolitionism" (paper presented at the annual meeting of the Southern Historical Association, Atlanta, November 1976), pp. 9–11. Lynn L. Marshall demonstrates well the national orientation of the major parties' structures in "The Strange Stillbirth of the Whig Party," *American Historical Review*, LXXII, no. 1 (January 1967), 445–68, and "The Genesis of Grass-Roots Democracy in Kentucky," *Mid-America*, XLVII, no. 4 (October 1965), 269–87.

33 [William Goodell], *Address Read at the New-York State Liberty Convention, Held at Port Byron, on Wednesday and Thursday, July 25, and 26, 1845* (Albany: Patriot [1845]); Sewell, *Ballots for Freedom*, p. 117.

34 Hendricks, "Liberty Party in New York State," p. 147; Kraut, "Liberty Men of New York," pp. 132–3; Chaplin in the *Emancipator* (Boston), May 13, 1846; Goodell to Mrs. Nicholson, July 30, 1846, in Clare Taylor, ed., *British and American Abolitionists: An Episode in Transatlantic Understanding* (Edinburgh: Edinburgh University Press, 1974), p. 274; Green to James G. Birney, September 23, 1846, in Dumond, ed., *Letters of Birney*, 2, p. 1027; Stewart to Samuel Webb, November 6, 1847, Stewart Papers, New York Historical Society.

35 *Address of the Macedon Convention by William Goodell; and Letters of Gerrit Smith* (Albany: S. W. Green, 1847), contains the Liberty League platform. See James Brewer Stewart, *Joshua R. Giddings and the Tactics of Radical Politics* (Cleveland: Press of Case Western Reserve University, 1970), pp. 156–7; Hugh H. Davis, "The Failure of Political Abolitionism," *Connecticut Review*, VI, no. 2 (April 1973), 83; Wiecek, *Sources of Antislavery Constitutionalism*, pp. 250–1; *Albany Patriot*, June 2, 1847 (Chaplin), July 7, 1847 (Jackson).

36 Sewell, *Ballots for Freedom*, pp. 131–69, 285–7; Wiecek, *Sources of Antislavery Constitutionalism*, p. 251; Theodore Clarke Smith, *The Liberty and Free Soil Parties of the Northwest* (New York: Longmans, Green, 1897), especially pp. 118–20; Kraut, "Liberty Men of New York," p. 151; Bertram Wyatt-Brown, *Lewis Tappan and the Evangelical War against Slavery* (Cleveland: Press of Case Western Reserve University, 1969), p. 332; Gerald Sorin, *Abolitionism: A New Perspective* (New York: Praeger, 1972), p. 88; Stewart, *Giddings*, pp. 260–1.

37 *Radical Abolitionist* (New York), I, no. 12 (July 1856), quotes Smith's 1856 remark on the presidency. For related data on the increasingly national orientation of Smith and his group from the late 1840s on, see Harlow, *Smith*, pp. 331, 427; Frothingham, *Smith*, pp. 189–92; Wendell Phillips Garrison and Francis Jackson Garrison, *William Lloyd Garrison, 1805–1879: The Story of His Life as Told by His Children*, 4 vols. (New York: Century, 1885–9), 2, pp. 405–6 (vol. 1, *1805–1835*; vol. 2, *1835–1840*; vol. 3, *1841–1860*; vol. 4, *1861–1879*; individual volumes are cited as *Garrison* with the volume number); Dumond, ed., *Letters of Birney*, 2, 1080; Goodell to John Fee, January 21, 1856, 1855–7 Letterbook, American Abolition Society Papers, Oberlin College; Smith to William Jay, February 23, 1849, Smith to F. Le Moyne, May 25, 1850, August 29, 1851, both in 1843–55 Letterbook, Smith Papers, Syracuse University; Smith, "Autobiographical Sketch," n.d., Smith Papers, Syracruse University; Smith, "[Letter to] Governor Chase, January 30, 1856," broadside (n.p., 1856), Smith Papers, Syracuse University; Smith to W. D. Phillips, March 23, 1855, Smith Papers, New York Historical Society; *Speeches of Smith in Congress*, especially p. 305.

38 For national, New York state, and central New York voting data for 1840-7, see Perkal, "Goodell," p. 144; Kraut, "Liberty Men of New York," pp. 162-3, 187, 308-19; Sorin, *New York Abolitionists*, pp. 128-9; Henderson, "History of N.Y.S.A.S.S.," p. 320; Lee Benson, *The Concept of Jacksonian Democracy: New York as a Test Case* (Princeton, N.J.: Princeton University Press, 1970), p. 133; Alan M. Kraut and Phyllis F. Field, "Politics versus Principles: The Partisan Response to 'Bible Politics' in New York State," *Civil War History*, XXV, no. 2 (June 1979), 116.

39 Drew Gilpin Faust, *A Sacred Circle: The Dilemma of the Intellectual in the Old South, 1840-1860* (Baltimore, Md.: Johns Hopkins University Press, 1977), p. 132. Theodore M. Mills, *The Sociology of Small Groups* (Englewood Cliffs, N.J.: Prentice-Hall, 1967), p. 18, cogently summarizes sociological literature on the structural-functional model and notes that when the group does not fulfill its survival requirements, disintegration sets in.

40 Beriah Green to James G. Birney, February 27, 1840, in Dumond, ed., *Letters of Birney*, 1, pp. 533-5; Green to Amos A. Phelps, May 22, 1844, B.P.L.; Mabee, *Black Freedom*, pp. 152, 363; Block, "Green," p. 95. Green's attacks on Stewart are printed in the *Emancipator* (Boston), February 19, 1845, and in Dumond, ed., *Letters of Birney*, 2, 1032-3. For the attacks on Goodell, see Green to Gerrit Smith, December 26, 1849, Smith Papers, Syracuse University, and Dumond, ed., *Letters of Birney*, 2, pp. 1066-7; see also Goodell to Beriah Green, September 12, 1856, in American Abolition Society Letterbook, 1855-57, Oberlin College. For good examples of how Smith tried to blunt Green's attacks, see Smith to Beriah Green, February 23, August 4, 1850, 1843-55 Letterbook, Smith Papers, Syracuse University. *Model Worker* (Utica), March 30, 1849, prints one of Green's attacks on Smith's conciliatory efforts.

41 Sewell, *Ballots for Freedom*, p. 98 n. 44, notes the discord between Stewart and the others over the Negro suffrage issue in 1846. Alvan Stewart to Elliot W. Stewart, September 15, 1846, Stewart Papers, New York Historical Society, attacks his Smith circle colleagues as "used up." For Stewart's subsequent attacks on the Smith circle, see Stewart to Samuel Webb, November 6, 1847, Stewart Papers, New York Historical Society; Marsh, ed., *Writings of Stewart*, pp. 22-3; *Albany Patriot*, March 22, May 10, 1848. Smith's remarks to Stewart are printed in "Letter of Gerrit Smith to the Liberty Party of New Hampshire, March 18, 1848," broadside (n.p., 1848), Smith Papers, Syracuse University, and *Albany Patriot*, May 10, 1848.

42 Sorin, *New York Abolitionists*, p. 95; *Dictionary of American Biography* (New York: Charles Scribner, 1932), 5, p. 547. James C. Jackson to Gerrit Smith, September 8, December 18, 1848, December 29, 1854, April 24, 1855, Smith Papers, Syracuse University.

43 *Albany Patriot*, March 17, 1847, covers the Chaplin-Goodell dispute.

44 For data on the Chaplin fugitive slave episode and the resulting erosion of the relationship between Smith and Chaplin, see Harlow, *Smith*, pp. 290-4; *Liberator* (Boston), August 16, 30, 1850; *National Era* (Washington, D.C.), August 15, September 5, 1850; Foner, ed., *Life and Writings of Frederick Douglass*, 2, p. 560 n. 20; *Commonwealth* (Boston), January 17, 1851; Gerrit Smith to D. H. Hall, February 7, 1851, March 27, June 26, 1852, Smith Papers, Syracuse University.

45 *Albany Patriot*, February 9, 1848, prints Goodell's public letter on freedom from group activity. See the *Chronotype* (Boston), September 25, 1848, on the Goodell difference with Smith over flirtations with Free Soilers. Gerrit Smith, "[Letter to] William Goodell, November 1, 1854," broadside (n.p., n.d.), Smith Papers, Syracuse University, notes Goodell's attack on Smith's proposed annexation of Cuba. Goodell to Gerrit Smith, June 25, 1856, American Abolition Society Letterbook 1855-57, Oberlin College, attacks Smith's call to arms in bleeding Kansas. Goodell attacks Smith on compensated emancipation in Goodell to T. B. McCormick, September 3, 1857, American Abolition Society Letterbook, 1857-59, Oberlin College, and in Goodell to Smith, February 13, 1856, Smith Papers, Syracuse University. For expressions of Goodell's envy over Smith's power of the purse, see Goodell to William Burr, March 20, 1857, and Goodell to Gerrit Smith, April 22, 1857, both in American Abolition Society

Letterbook 1855-57, Oberlin College. Perkal, "Goodell," pp. 293-6, provides cogent analysis of Goodell's final break with Smith. *Liberator* (Boston), September 28, 1860, prints Goodell's repudiation of Smith's presidential candidacy.

CHAPTER 5. "DISTINCTIONS OF SEX"

1 *Liberator* (Boston), June 19, 1840 (emphasis added).

2 For discussions of the benevolent movement's gender pattern, see Barbara J. Berg, *The Remembered Gate: Origins of Feminism: The Woman and the City, 1800-1860* (New York: Oxford University Press, 1978); Lois Wendland Banner, "The Protestant Crusade: Religious Missions, Benevolence, and Reform in the United States, 1790-1840" (Ph.D. dissertation, Columbia University, 1970), pp. 291, 304-5. For abolitionist defenses of this benevolent movement pattern of operation, see Garrison in Wendell Phillips Garrison and Francis Jackson Garrison, *William Lloyd Garrison, 1805-1879*, 4 vols. (New York: Century, 1885-9), 1, pp. 136-7 (vol. 1, *1805-1835*; vol. 2, *1835-1840*; vol. 3, *1841-1860*; vol. 4, *1861-1879*; individual volumes are cited as *Garrison* with the volume number), and in the *Journal of the Times* (Bennington, Vt.), December 12, 1828; Joshua Leavitt in *Evangelist* (New York), September 15, 1832.

3 For general discussions of gender roles at the 1833 A.A.S.S. organizational meeting, see Dwight L. Dumond, *Antislavery: The Crusade for Freedom in America* (New York: W. W. Norton, 1966), p. 275; Sandra Tyler Wood, "The Abolitionists and 'the Woman Question,' 1830-1840" (M.A. thesis, University of Georgia, 1972), pp. 40-1; Alma Lutz, *Crusade for Freedom: Women of the Antislavery Movement* (Boston: Beacon Press, 1968), p. 51. See also *First Annual Report of the American Anti-Slavery Society* (New York, 1834), p. 36.

4 Quoted in Phillip Green Wright and Elizabeth Q. Wright, *Elizur Wright: The Father of Life Insurance* (Chicago: University of Chicago Press, 1937), p. 72.

5 See, e.g., *Commemoration of the Fiftieth Anniversary of the Organization of the American Anti-Slavery Society, in Philadelphia, 1884.* (Philadelphia: Thomas S. Dando, 1884), pp. 34-7; Ann Davis Hallowell, ed., *James and Lucretia Mott: Life and Letters* (Boston: Houghton Mifflin, 1884), p. 113.

6 For general data on the continuing benevolent society pattern after 1833, see Ellen Carol DuBois, *Feminism and Suffrage: The Emergence of an Independent Women's Movement in America, 1848-1869* (Ithaca and London: Cornell University Press, 1978), p. 32; John B. Jentz, "Artisans, Evangelicals, and the City: A Social History of Abolition and Labor Reform in Jacksonian New York" (Ph.D. dissertation, City University of New York, 1977), p. 195; William Chaplin in the *Liberty Press* (Utica), August 13, 1844.

7 Grew in *Proceedings of the American Anti-Slavery Society, at its Third Decade, Held in Philadelphia, December 3d and 4th, 1863* (New York: American Anti-Slavery Society, 1864), pp. 125-8.

8 For delineations of this ideology, see Barbara Welter, "The Cult of True Womanhood, 1820-1860," *American Quarterly*, XVIII, no. 2, pt. 1 (summer 1966), 151-74; Ronald W. Hogeland, " 'The Female Appendage': Feminine Life-Styles in America, 1820-1860," *Civil War History*, XVII, no. 2 (June 1971), 101-14; Lawrence J. Friedman, *Inventors of the Promised Land* (New York: Alfred A. Knopf, 1975), chap. 4; Nancy F. Cott, *The Bonds of Womanhood: 'Woman's Sphere' in New England, 1780-1835* (New Haven: Yale University Press, 1977).

9 Walter M. Merrill and Louis Ruchames, eds., *The Letters of William Lloyd Garrison*, 6 vols. (Cambridge, Mass.: Harvard University Press, Belknap Press, 1971-81), 1, p. 71 (vol. 1, *I Will Be Heard! 1822-1835*; vol. 2, *A House Dividing against Itself, 1836-1840*; vol. 3, *No Union with Slaveholders, 1841-1849*; vol. 4, *From Disunionism to the Brink of War, 1850-1860*; vol. 5, *Let the Oppressed Go Free, 1861-1867*; vol. 6, *To Rouse the Slumbering Land, 1868-1879*; individual volumes are cited as *Letters of Garrison* with the volume number); John G. Whittier, "Justice and Expediency" in *Anti-Slavery Reporter*, I, no. 4 (September 1833), 61. See Friedman, *Inventors*, pp. 127-30, for a broad survey of abolitionist espousals of Woman's Sphere.

10 For cogent analyses of these "positive" aspects of Woman's Sphere, see Cott, *Bonds of Womanhood*, pp. 62, 67; Cott, "Passionlessness: An Interpretation of Victorian Sexual Ideology, 1790–1850," *Signs*, IV, no. 2 (winter 1978), 229; Vivian Fox, "The Rise of Women's Equality and the Mythical Decline of the Family," *Psychohistory: Bulletin of the International Psychohistorical Association*, II, no. 2 (fall 1978), 25; Daniel Scott Smith, "Family Limitation, Sexual Control, and Domestic Feminism in Victorian America," *Feminist Studies*, I, no. 3–4 (winter–spring 1973), 51–53.

11 Fuller is quoted in Keith M. Melder, *Beginnings of Sisterhood: The American Woman's Rights Movement, 1800–1850* (New York: Schocken Books, 1977), p. 30. For sophisticated studies of nineteenth-century sorority, see Carroll Smith-Rosenberg, "The Female World of Love and Ritual: Relations between Women in Nineteenth-Century America," *Signs*, I, no. 1 (autumn 1975), 1–29; Cott, *Bonds of Womanhood*, chap. 5; Lillian Faderman, "Female Same-Sex Relationships in Novels by Longfellow, Holmes, and James," *New England Quarterly*, LI, no. 3 (September 1978), 309–32; Christopher Lasch and William R. Taylor, "Two 'Kindred Spirits': Sorority and Family in New England, 1839–1846," *New England Quarterly*, XXXVI, no. 1 (March 1963), 23–41. For cogent if different analyses of nineteenth-century fraternity, see G. J. Barker-Benfield, *The Horrors of the Half-Known Life: Male Attitudes toward Women and Sexuality in Nineteenth-Century America* (New York: Harper and Row, 1976), and Drew Faust, *The Sacred Circle: The Dilemma of the Intellectual in the Old South, 1840–1860* (Baltimore, Md.: Johns Hopkins University Press, 1977). See also Lionel Tiger, *Men in Groups* (New York: Random House, 1969). Leslie Fiedler's *Love and Death in the American Novel* (New York: Criterion Books, 1960) remains the most penetrating analysis of gender relations within the nineteenth-century novel and is most attentive to the failings of heterosocial relationships.

12 Clare Taylor, ed., *British and American Abolitionists: An Episode in Transatlantic Understanding* (Edinburgh: Edinburgh University Press, 1974). The correspondence between James G. Birney and Gerrit Smith illustrates, most blatantly, the wives' practice of attaching supplementary letters to each other (James G. Birney Papers, Clements Library, University of Michigan; Gerrit Smith Collection, Syracuse University).

13 Gerrit Smith to Theodore D. Weld, July 30, 1836, Slavery Manuscripts, Box 2, New York Historical Society; Smith to James G. Birney, November 6, 1850, Birney Papers, Clements Library; Theodore D. Weld to James G. Birney, February 9, 1853, Birney Papers, Clements Library; Lewis Tappan to A. A. Phelps, Letterbook, September 10, 1844, Lewis Tappan Papers, Library of Congress [L.C.]; Ellis Gray Loring to James G. Whittier, March 4, 1837, Ellis Gray Loring Letterbook, Houghton Library; Henry C. Wright to George B. Cheever, February 26, 1835, Cheever Family Papers, American Antiquarian Society [A.A.S.].

14 Irving H. Bartlett, *Wendell Phillips: Brahmin Radical* (Boston: Beacon Press, 1961), p. 306, notes the cheek-kissing ritual. Merrill and Ruchames, eds., *Letters of Garrison*, 4, p. 248, and "Letters of Dr. F. J. Le Moyne, an Abolitionist of Western Pennsylvania," *Journal of Negro History*, XVIII, no. 4 (October 1933), 471, note the custom of holding hands. Katharine DuPre Lumpkin, *The Emancipation of Angelina Grimké* (Chapel Hill: University of North Carolina Press, 1974), p. 181, notes the importance of Mrs. Sprigg's boardinghouse. Elizur Wright, Jr., "London Clubs," April 8, 1844, Elizur Wright, Jr., Typescripts, Boston Public Library [B.P.L.].

15 For the Weld and Whittier pledges, see Blanche G. Hersh, *The Slavery of Sex: Feminist-Abolitionists in America* (Urbana: University of Illinois Press, 1978), p. 240. W. P. and F. J. Garrison, *Garrison*, 1, p. 43. Gary L. Williams, "The Psychosexual Fears of Joshua Speed and Abraham Lincoln, 1839–1842" (paper presented at the annual meeting of the Organization of American Historians, San Francisco, April 1980). For an excellent discussion of male anxiety about virility, see Charles E. Rosenberg, "Sexuality, Class, and Role in Nineteenth-Century America," *American Quarterly*, XXV, no. 2 (May 1973), 140–1.

16 The Ladies' Anti-Slavery Society of New York City is quoted in Gilbert H. Barnes

and Dwight L. Dumond, eds., *Letters of Theodore Dwight Weld, Angelina Grimké Weld, and Sarah Grimké, 1822–1844*, 2 vols. (New York and London: D. Appleton-Century, 1934), 1, pp. 374–5.

17 See Welter, "Cult of True Womanhood," p. 74, and Cott, *Bonds of Womanhood*, pp. 197–9, for cogent discussions of this point.

18 Philadelphia Female Anti-Slavery Society Minutes for 1833–1838 (December 8, 1836; December 14, 1837), Pennsylvania Historical Society; "Address of the Boston Female Anti-Slavery Society to the Women of New England," January 1838, B.P.L.

19 Stanton is quoted in the *Liberator* (Boston), May 18, 1860; Kelley is quoted in Merton L. Dillon, *The Abolitionists: The Growth of a Dissenting Minority* (DeKalb: Northern Illinois University Press, 1974), p. 58; Stone is quoted in the *Liberator* (Boston), May 17, 1850.

20 Melder, *Beginnings of Sisterhood*, especially chaps. 5–8. Support for Melder is found in Frances E. Kearns, "Margaret Fuller and the Abolition Movement," *Journal of the History of Ideas*, XXV, no. 1 (January–March 1964), 120, and Lumpkin, *Grimké*, p. 107.

21 Mary Grew to Isabel Howland, April 27, 1892, Howland Correspondence, Sophia Smith Collection, Smith College.

22 Katherine L. Herbig, "Friends for Freedom: The Lives and Careers of Sallie Holley and Caroline Putnam" (Ph.D. dissertation, Claremont Graduate School, 1977), p. 163. See also Herbig, "Friends," pp. 90–2, 104–8, 164; John White Chadwick, ed., *A Life for Liberty: Anti-Slavery and Other Letters of Sallie Holley* (New York and London: G. P. Putnam, 1899); Jane H. Pease and William H. Pease, "The Role of Women in the Antislavery Movement," *Historical Papers of the Canadian Historical Society* (June 7–10, 1967), 171. Sallie Holley to Ann Phillips, March 17, 1870, Crawford Blagden Collection, Houghton Library, Harvard University.

23 The basic facts of the Stuart–Weld relationship are noted in Benjamin P. Thomas, *Theodore Weld: Crusader for Freedom* (New Brunswick, N.J.: Rutgers University Press, 1950), pp. 16–17; Fred Landon, "Captain Charles Stuart: A Figure of Importance in the Struggle over Slavery," in *Amherstburg Echo*, September 3, 1953; Anthony J. Barker, "Captain Charles Stuart and the British and American Abolition Movements: 1830–34," *Slavery and Abolition*, I (fall 1980), 48–9.

24 Robert H. Abzug, "Theodore Weld: A Biography" (Ph.D. dissertation, University of California, Berkeley, 1977), pp. 26–30, on the improbability of extensive sexual conduct between Weld and Stuart. For their feelings toward one another, as quoted, see Charles Stuart to Theodore Weld, April 11, 1846, September 9, 1861, April 22, 1852, December 26, 1845, Weld-Grimké Papers, Clements Library; Theodore Weld to Elizabeth Smith Miller, June 30, 1888, Weld to Lewis Tappan, December 3, 1845, Weld-Grimké Papers, Clements Library. Lorman Ratner, *Pre–Civil War Reform: The Variety of Principles and Programs* (Englewood Cliffs, N.J.: Prentice-Hall, 1967), p. 13, quotes Weld wondering whether God intended him to marry. Unfortunately, although we have an abundance of letters from Stuart to Weld and know that Weld often wrote to Stuart, researchers have yet to uncover those letters.

25 For cogent analysis of the intellectual content of immediatist sorority, see Hersh, *Slavery of Sex*, chap. 6; Melder, *Beginnings of Sisterhood*, chaps. 5–7.

26 Quoted in Alice S. Rossi, ed., *Essays on Sex Equality by John Stuart Mill and Harriet Taylor Mill* (Chicago: University of Chicago Press, 1970), p. 96.

27 *Liberator* (Boston), September 6, 1834, quotes Garrison's admonition on the distinction of the sexes. Judith Nies, *Seven Women: Portraits from the American Radical Tradition* (New York: Penguin Books, 1977), pp. 25–6, notes Garrison's support of Sarah Grimké, and Garrison, *Garrison*, 3, pp. 310–11, prints Garrison's address to a women's rights gathering in 1850.

28 Samuel J. May, *The Right of Colored People to Education, Vindicated* (Brooklyn, Conn.: Advertiser Press, 1833), pp. 6, 10, on the Prudence Crandall episode; Thomas James Mumford, *Memoir of Samuel Joseph May* (Boston: Roberts, 1837), p. 190. See also Samuel J. May, *The Rights and Conditions of Women* (Syracuse: Stoddard and Babcock, 1846), pp. 9–10.

29 Samuel May, Jr., to Mary Carpenter, October 18, 1844, B.P.L. See also Samuel May, Jr., to J. B. Estlin, November 10, 1850, in Taylor, ed., *British and American Abolitionists*, p. 354.

30 The *Anti-Slavery Bugle* (Salem, Ohio), August 11, 1849, quotes Johnson; *National Anti-Slavery Standard* (New York), August 27, 1840, quotes Rogers; *Liberator* (Boston), May 3, 1850, for Henry Wright; Sallie Holley comments cogently on Pillsbury in Chadwick, ed., *A Life of Liberty*, p. 81.

31 Lewis Perry and Michael Fellman, eds., *Antislavery Reconsidered: New Perspectives on the Abolitionists* (Baton Rouge: Louisiana State University Press, 1979), pp. 275–6; Douglas C. Stange, *Patterns of Antislavery among American Unitarians, 1831–1860* (Rutherford, N.J.: Fairleigh Dickinson University Press, 1977), p. 127.

32 Octavius Brooks Frothingham, *Gerrit Smith: A Biography* (New York: G. P. Putnam, 1878), p. 124, quotes Smith's letter to Anthony; Gerrit Smith to Elizabeth Cady Stanton, December 19, 1853, Elizabeth Cady Stanton Papers, L.C.; Gerrit Smith, "[Letters to] Elizabeth C. Stanton, December 1, 1855," broadside (n.p., 1855), Gerrit Smith Papers, Syracuse University.

33 Gerrit Smith to Sallie Holley in Chadwick, ed., *A Life of Liberty*, p. 83.

34 Jackson in the *Albany Patriot*, January 15, 1845; J. C. Hathaway to J. C. Jackson, August 12, 1839, B.P.L.

35 Aileen S. Kraditor, *Means and Ends in American Abolitionism: Garrison and His Critics on Strategy and Tactics, 1834–1850* (New York: Random House, Vintage, 1970), pp. 61, 76 n. 75; Elizur Wright, Jr., to A. A. Phelps, August 17, 1838, Elizur Wright, Jr., Papers, L.C.; Jane H. Pease and William H. Pease, *Bound with Them in Chains: A Biographical History of the Antislavery Movement* (Westport, Conn.: Greenwood Press, 1972), p. 232; Wright and Wright, *Elizur Wright*, p. 197.

36 Lewis Tappan to Mrs. Bigelow, January 14, 1844, Letterbook, Lewis Tappan Papers, L.C.; Whipple in the *American Missionary*, II, no. 4 (February 1848).

37 A. A. Phelps to Elizur Wright, Jr., August 2, 1838, Elizur Wright, Jr., Papers. L.C.; Phelps in the *Liberator* (Boston), February 26, 1841; Phelps in the *American Missionary*, I, no. 11 (September 1847); William Jay to Anna Maria Jay Pierpont, April 11, 1839, John Jay Collection, Columbia University; *Liberator* (Boston), November 27, 1840 (Whittier).

38 See Hogeland, " 'The Female Appendage,' " pp. 101–14, and Lewis Perry, *Childhood, Marriage, and Reform: Henry Clarke Wright, 1797–1840* (Chicago and London: University of Chicago Press, 1980), p. 228, for cogent discussion of this point.

39 For penetrating analyses of this marital pattern as it emerged in the late eighteenth century, see Mary Beth Norton, *Liberty's Daughters: The Revolutionary Experience of American Women, 1750–1800* (Boston: Little, Brown, 1980), pp. 229–38, and Carl N. Degler, *At Odds: Women and Family from the Revolution to the Present* (New York: Oxford University Press, 1980), especially pp. 16–19.

40 Ira V. Brown, "Miller McKim and Pennsylvania Abolitionism," *Pennsylvania History*, XXX, no. 5 (January 1963), 63–6; Elizabeth Bancroft Schlesinger, "Two Early Harvard Wives: Eliza Farrar and Eliza Follen," *New England Quarterly*, XXXVIII, no. 2 (June 1965), 159–63; Martin Duberman, *James Russell Lowell* (Boston: Beacon Press, 1966), and Duberman on Lowell in "The Abolitionists and Psychology," *Journal of Negro History*, XLVII, no. 3 (July 1962), 188–9; M. Leon Perkal, "William Goodell: A Life of Reform" (Ph.D. dissertation, City University of New York, 1972), pp. 22–3; Oliver Johnson to Gerrit Smith, July 17, 1872, Smith Papers, Syracuse University; Mumford, *S. J. May*, pp. 276–9; Ralph V. Harlow, *Gerrit Smith, Philanthropist and Reformer* (New York: Henry Holt, 1939), p. 16; Elizabeth Cady Stanton, *Eighty Years and More (1815–1897)* (London: T. Fisher Urwin, 1898), p. 70, on the Smith marriage; Gerrit Smith to Ann Fitzhugh Smith, March 20, 1831, Smith Papers, Syracuse University; Hallowell, ed., *Mott*, pp. 262, 337, 379; Wright and Wright, *Elizur Wright*, pp. 136, 198.

41 For data on Henry Wright's marriage, see Perry, *Childhood, Marriage, and Reform*, especially pp. 70, 173, 181–2. Information on Pillsbury's marriage may be found in Parker

Pillsbury to Marius and Emily _____, September 15, 1865, Alma Lutz Collection, Schlesinger Library, Ratcliffe College, and Edmund Quincy to R. D. Webb, June 1863, Quincy-Webb Correspondence, B.P.L. For the Philleo-Crandall marriage, see Hersh, *Slavery of Sex*, p. 229; David O. White, "The Crandall School and the Degree of Influence by Garrison and the Abolitionists upon It," *Connecticut Historical Society Bulletin*, XLIII, no. 4 (October 1978), 105–6. Peter F. Walker, *Moral Choices: Memory, Desire, and Imagination in Nineteenth-Century American Abolition* (Baton Rouge: Louisiana State University Press, 1978), pp. 111–35, on Swisshelm.

42 Lumpkin, *Grimké*, pp. 115–95, provides the most thorough analysis of the early Weld–Grimké marriage. Robert W. Tolf, "Edmund Quincy: Aristocrat Abolitionist" (Ph.D. dissertation, University of Rochester, 1957), pp. 92, 135, 147. For data on the early Phillips marriage, see Bartlett, *Phillips*, pp. 39–40, 77–80; Perry and Fellman, eds., *Antislavery: Reconsidered*, pp. 178–9; and especially the 1837–41 letters between the couple in the Crawford Blagden Collection at Harvard's Houghton Library. For Lewis Tappan's early marriage, see Bertram Wyatt-Brown, *Lewis Tappan and the Evangelical War against Slavery* (Cleveland: Press of Case Western Reserve University, 1969), pp. 38, 300; Wyatt-Brown, "Three Generations of Yankee Parenthood: The Tappan Family, A Case Study of Antebellum Nurture," *Illinois Quarterly*, XXXVIII, no. 1 (fall 1975), 19. For data on Garrison's engagement and early years of marriage, see Walter McIntosh Merrill, "A Passionate Attachment: William Lloyd Garrison's Courtship of Helen Eliza Benson," *New England Quarterly*, XXIX, no. 2 (June 1956), 200–1; Friedman, *Inventors*, p. 278; Thomas, *Weld*, p. 297 n. 12; Helen Benson to W. L. Garrison, February 11, 1834, Benson–Garrison Correspondence, Houghton Library; Garrison to George W. Benson, September 4, 1835, B.P.L. For data on the early Kelley–Foster marriage, see Abby Kelley [Foster] to Stephen Foster, July 30, 1843, April 7, August 18, September 3, 9, 28, 1847, Stephen Foster to Abbey Kelley [Foster], April 11, 1850, July 27, 1851, all in the Kelley–Foster Papers, A.A.S.

43 Lumpkin, *Grimké*, pp. 195–214, brilliantly analyzes the improvement in the Grimké–Weld marriage. The Edmund Quincy Journals for 1832 to 1850 (Quincy Papers, Massachusetts Historical Society) reveal the change, in the mid-1840s, in the relationship between husband and wife. See also Edmund Quincy to Caroline H. Dall, November 13, 1844, Francis Jackson Collection, Massachusetts Historical Society, concerning the couple's practice of reading French together.

44 For information on the improvements in the Phillips marriage, see Bartlett, *Phillips*, p. 80; Merrill and Ruchames, eds., *Letters of Garrison*, 2, pp. 498–9 n. 1; Edmund Quincy to R. D. Webb, December 13, 1845, March 9, 1848, January 13, 1853, all in the Quincy-Webb Correspondence, B.P.L. Ann Phillips to Wendell Phillips, May 8, 1856 (reflecting on thirty years of marriage), and Wendell Phillips to Ann Phillips, n.d. [1874] reflecting on almost fifty years of marriage, both in the Blagden Collection, Houghton Library.

45 For data on Lewis Tappan's second marriage, see Wyatt-Brown, *Tappan*, pp. 301–4, and Lewis Tappan to Mary Dean, April 1, 1855, Lewis Tappan Papers, L.C.

46 For the late years of the Garrison marriage, see William Lloyd Garrison, *Helen Eliza Garrison: A Memorial* (Cambridge, Mass., 1876), pp. 27, 30, 31; Walter M. Merrill, *Against Wind and Tide: A Biography of William Lloyd Garrison* (Cambridge, Mass.: Harvard University Press, 1963), p. 306.

47 Abby Kelley Foster to Wendell Phillips, April 21, 1849, Blagden Collection, Houghton Library, and Stephen S. Foster to Abby Kelley Foster, September 26, 1850, Kelley–Foster Papers, A.A.S. See also Stephen S. Foster to Abby Kelley Foster, April 11, 1850, July 27, 1851, April 16, October 31, 1854, October 12, 1855, and Abby Kelley Foster to Alla Foster, April 17, 1852, all in Kelley–Foster Papers, A.A.S.

48 About the Myron Holley marriage, see Elizur Wright, Jr., *Myron Holley; and What He Did for Liberty and True Religion* (Boston: Elizur Wright, 1882), p. 37; Chadwick, ed., *A Life for Liberty*, pp. 19–21; Pease and Pease, "Role of Women," pp. 170–1. For the Scofield marriage, see Abishai Scofield to Elizabeth Scofield, June 15, 1857, and Elizabeth

Scofield to Abishai Scofield, October 15, 1872, Abishai Scofield Manuscripts, Burton Historical Collection, Detroit Public Library. For pertinent details on the Loring marriage, see Ellis Gray Loring to Louisa Loring, May 14, 1840; to Anna Loring, April 2, 1856; to Louisa and Anna Loring, May 13, 1858; all in Ellis Gray Loring Family Papers, Schlesinger Library, Ratcliffe College. Gertrude K. Burleigh to Samuel May, Jr., November 14, 1857, B.P.L., analyzes her relationship to her recently deceased husband Charles. For an excellent analysis of the marriage of David and Lydia Child, see Kirk Jeffrey, "Marriage, Career, and Feminine Ideology in Nineteenth-Century America: Reconstructing the Marital Experience of Lydia Maria Child, 1828-1874," *Feminist Studies*, II, no. 2/3 (1975), 113-30. Raimund E. Goerler, "Family, Self, and Anti-Slavery: Sydney Howard Gay and the Abolitionist Commitment" (Ph.D. dissertation, Case Western Reserve University, 1975), p. 163.

49 Henry Wright's many private journal books are deposited in Harvard University's Houghton Library and in the Boston Public Library. By far the most sensitive analysis of the sexual message of those journals is provided in Perry, *Childhood, Marriage, and Reform*, Wright's biography.

50 Duberman, *Lowell*, pp. 89-90.

51 William Lloyd Garrison to Abigail Kelley Foster, July 25, 1859, Kelley-Foster Papers, A.A.S.

52 Robert Samuel Fletcher, *A History of Oberlin College: From Its Foundation through the Civil War* (Oberlin: Oberlin College, 1943), 1, pp. 291, 382; 2, pp. 636, 639; Ronald W. Hogeland, " 'Co-Education of the Sexes' at Oberlin College: A Study of Social Ideas in Mid-Nineteenth Century America," *Journal of Social History*, VI, no. 2 (winter 1972-73), 160-76; Shirley S. Cook, "Traditional Sex Roles at Early Oberlin College: A Case Study of Female Education" (M.A. thesis, Bowling Green State University, 1975).

53 Fletcher, *Oberlin*, 1, p. 113, cites the 1850 removal of the ban on female study of the classics. Ibid., 1, p. 293, notes how Finney opened options for Antoinette Brown. Herbig, "Friends," pp. 48-9, on the courses Oberlin College women could take with male students by the time of the Civl War. James H. Fairchild, "Coeducation of the Sexes," *American Journal of Education*, XVII (1868), 395.

54 Child is quoted in the *Liberator* (Boston), September 6, 1839. For Mott's 1839 remark, see Lutz, *Crusade for Freedom*, p. 155.

55 *Liberator* (Boston), May 18, 1860, quotes Stanton. Merrill and Ruchames, eds., *Letters of Garrison*, 2, p. 326, prints Garrison's observation on the Grimkés, while [Theodore Weld, ed.], *In Memory of Angelina Grimké Weld* (Boston: George H. Ellis, 1880), pp. 28-30, quotes Phillips. Chadwick, ed., *Life of Liberty*, p. 17, quotes Samuel J. May. Edmund Quincy to R. D. Webb, January 29, 1843, Quincy-Webb Correspondence, B.P.L.

56 "Letters of Dr. F. J. LeMoyne," pp. 467-70, notes the relationship between LeMoyne and Caroline and quotes Caroline. Chadwick, ed., *Life of Liberty*, pp. 81-3, on the Gerrit Smith-Sallie Holley relationship.

57 Amy Swerdlow, "Abolition's Conservative Sisters: The Ladies' New York City Anti-Slavery Societies, 1834-1840" (paper presented at the Third Berkshire Conference on the History of Women, June 1976). Lydia Child in the *Liberator* (Boston), September 6, 1839. Lucy Stone as quoted in Fletcher, *Oberlin*, 1, p. 290. In a most sensitive essay dealing with abolitionist child-rearing practices, Bertram Wyatt-Brown suggests that because evangelical abolitionists active in the benevolent societies desired so intensely to achieve immortality and transcend conventional patterns of living, they often withdrew entirely from domestic responsibilities. (Bertram Wyatt-Brown, "The Missionary Impulse in the Old Republic: The Psychology of Commitment to a Noble Cause," manuscript [Cleveland: Case Western Reserve University, 1971], p. 24). This may help to explain why steward immediatists were most resistant to expanding female roles; they may have felt the need to confine women rigidly to the hearth in order to free themselves.

58 Wendell Phillips to Ann Phillips, n.d. [1874], Blagden Collection, Houghton Library;

Wendell Phillips, "The Boston Mob," *Speeches, Lectures, and Letters*, 1st ser. (Boston, 1894), p. 226; Wendell Phillips to R. D. Webb, June 29, 1842, B.P.L.

CHAPTER 6. "THE CHORD OF PREJUDICE"

1 Walter M. Merrill and Louis Ruchames, eds., *The Letters of William Lloyd Garrison*, 6 vols. (Cambridge, Mass.: Harvard University Press, Belknap Press, 1971–1981), 1, pp. 458–9 (vol. 1, *I Will Be Heard! 1822–1835*; vol. 2, *A House Dividing against Itself, 1836–1840*; vol. 3, *No Union with Slaveholders, 1841–1849*; vol. 4, *From Disunionism to the Brink of War, 1850–1860*; vol. 5, *Let the Oppressed Go Free, 1861–1867*; vol. 6, *To Rouse the Slumbering Land, 1868–1879*; individual volumes are cited as *Letters of Garrison* with the volume number).

2 David McBride, "Black Protest against Racial Politics: Gardner, Hinton and their Memorial of 1838," *Pennsylvania History*, XLVI, no. 2 (April 1979), 148, on Hinton's role in the A.A.S.S. Declaration of Sentiments; John Barkley Jentz, "Artisans, Evangelicals, and the City: A Social History of Abolition and Labor Reform in Jacksonian New York" (Ph.D. dissertation, City University of New York, 1977), p. 174; Elizur Wright, Jr., to Beriah Green, November 26, 1833, Elizur Wright Transcripts, Boston Public Library [B.P.L.] and Wright in the *Massachusetts Abolitionist* (Boston), August 20, 1839; Robert H. Abzug, "Theodore Weld: A Biography" (Ph.D. dissertation, University of California, Berkeley, 1977), pp. 108–9; Lawrence Ladner, *The Bold Brahmins: New England's War against Slavery, 1831–1863* (New York: E. P. Dutton, 1961), p. 271; Anna Davis Hallowell, ed., *James and Lucretia Mott: Life and Letters* (Boston: Houghton Mifflin, 1884), p. 266.

3 James Oliver Horton and Lois E. Horton, *Black Bostonians: Family Life and Community Struggle in the Antebellum North* (New York: Holmes and Meier, 1979), particularly pp. 58, 81–2; James O. Horton, "Black Activism in Boston, 1830–1860" (Ph.D. dissertation, Brandeis University, 1973), pp. 54–6, 61, 73; James O. Horton, "Generations of Protest: Black Families and Social Reform in Ante-Bellum Boston," *New England Quarterly*, XLIX, no. 2 (June 1976), 249, 251; "Abolition Letters Collected by Captain Arthur B. Spingard," *Journal of Negro History*, XVIII, no. 1 (January 1933), 79; Charles H. Wesley, "The Negroes of New York in the Emancipation Movement," *Journal of Negro History*, XXIV, no. 1 (January 1939), 76.

4 August Meier and Elliott Rudwick, "The Role of Blacks in the Abolitionist Movement," in *Blacks in the Abolitionist Movement*, ed. John H. Bracey, Jr., August Meier, and Elliott Rudwick (Belmont, Calif.: Wadsworth, 1971), pp. 112–14; Minute Book of the Junior Antislavery Society of Philadelphia, 1836–46, Pennsylvania Historical Society.

5 For the black leadership role, see Meier and Rudwick, "Role of Blacks in Abolitionist Movement," p. 112; Hugh Houck Davis, "The Reform Career of Joshua Leavitt" (Ph.D. dissertation, Ohio State University, 1969), pp. 165–66; William E. Ward, "Charles Lenox Remond: Black Abolitionist, 1838–1873" (Ph.D. dissertation, Clark University, 1977), pp. 167–68; Jane H. Pease and William H. Pease, *They Who Would Be Free: Blacks' Search for Freedom, 1830–1861* (New York: Antheneum, 1974), pp. 79–80. See Horton, "Generations of Protest," pp. 242–56, for discussion of the leadership role of blacks in the New England Anti-Slavery Society. The role of black lecturer and pamphleteer is discussed in Larry Gara, "The Professional Fugitive in the Abolition Movement," *Wisconsin Magazine of History*, XLVIII, no. 3 (spring 1965), 196–204; Philip S. Foner, ed., *The Life and Writings of Frederick Douglass*, 4 vols. (New York: International Publishers, 1950–5), 1, p. 46 (vol. 1, *Early Years, 1817–1849*; vol. 2, *Pre–Civil War Decade, 1850–1860*; vol. 3, *The Civil War, 1861–1865*; vol. 4, *Reconstruction and After*; individual volumes are cited as *Life and Writings of Douglass* with the volume number).

6 Richard O. Curry, "The Abolitionists and Reconstruction: A Critical Appraisal," *Journal of Southern History*, XXXIV, no. 4 (November 1968), 530–1; *Colored American* (New York), July 28, 1838; Jocelyn in *Friend of Man* (Utica), October 27, 1836; Records of the New

England Anti-Slavery Society, 1831–3, B.P.L.; Bertram Wyatt-Brown, *Lewis Tappan and the Evangelical War against Slavery* (Cleveland: Press of Case Western Reserve University, 1969), p. 180; Charles Sumner Brown, "The Genesis of the Negro Lawyer in New England," *Negro History Bulletin*, XXII (April 1959), 149.

7   See, e.g., *Colored American* (New York), June 27, July 11, July 18, August 8, 1840; *Northern Star and Freeman's Advocate* (Rochester), March 17, 1842; *Friend of Man* (Utica), September 27, 1837; *Massachusetts Abolitionist* (Boston), March 12, 1840; Jane H. Pease and William H. Pease, "Negro Conventions and the Problem of Black Leadership," *Journal of Black Studies*, II, no. 1 (September 1971), 30; Gerald Sorin, *Abolitionism: A New Perspective* (New York: Praeger, 1972), p. 110.

8   *National Anti-Slavery Standard* (New York), July 2, 1840 (Ward); *Colored American* (New York), November 4, 1837; *Friend of Man* (Utica), September 27, 1837 (Wright).

9   For examples of black abolitionist comments on demonic prejudice in whites, see, e.g., *Friend of Man* (Utica), September 27, 1837; Sorin, *Abolitionism*, p. 108. Horton, "Black Activism in Boston," p. 57, notes that Garrison was publicizing only activities that he favored in the Boston black community, while the *National Anti-Slavery Standard* (New York), July 2, 1840, quotes Samuel Ringgold Ward on white attitudes toward civil liberties when whites themselves were endangered. Carleton Mabee, *Black Freedom: The Non-Violent Abolitionists from 1830 through the Civil War* (New York: Macmillan, 1970), p. 106, quotes Whipper.

10 Lewis Tappan, "Report of Committee on Inducing Colored Persons to the Useful Arts," March 2, 1836, American Missionary Association Papers, Dillard University; Edmund Quincy, *Introductory Lecture Delivered before the Adelphis Union, November 19, 1839* (Boston, 1839), pp. 5, 17; Gilbert H. Barnes and Dwight L. Dumond, eds., *Letters of Theodore Dwight Weld, Angelina Grimké Weld, and Sarah Grimké, 1822–1844*, 2 vols. (New York and London: D. Appleton-Century, 1934), 1, p. 263; William Lloyd Garrison, *An Address, Delivered before the Free People of Color in Philadelphia, New York, and Other Cities during the Month of June, 1831* (Boston, 1831), pp. 6–7.

11 Executive Committee of the American Anti-Slavery Society to its Agents, n.d. [1834?], B.P.L.; Records of the New England Anti-Slavery Society, 1831–33, May 28, 1832, B.P.L.; Gerrit Smith to Samuel and Harriet Russell, October 1, 1841, Letter Copy Book, 1827–43, Gerrit Smith Papers, Syracuse University; Phyllis Mary Bannan, "Arthur and Lewis Tappan: A Study in New York Religious and Reform Movements" (Ph.D. dissertation, Columbia University, 1950), p. 71; Leavitt in the *Emancipator* (New York), January 28, 1841; [Simeon Smith Jocelyn], *College for Colored Youth: An Account of the New-Haven City Meeting and Resolutions, with Recommendations of the College, and Strictures upon the Doings of New-Haven* (New York, 1831), p. 2; Garrison in the *Liberator* (Boston), January 23, 1832.

12 Beriah Green, *Four Sermons, Preached in the Chapel of the Western Reserve College, on the Lord's Day, November 18th and 25th, and December 2nd and 9th, 1832* (Cleveland, 1833), pp. 38–39. Jane H. Pease and William H. Pease, "Black Power – The Debate in 1840," *Phylon*, XXIX, no. 1 (spring 1968), 20, on orders that the A.A.S.S. gave to agents in the early 1830s. Weld is quoted in the *Evangelist* (New York), April 5, 1834. For other clear examples of white missionary paternalism, see the *Emancipator* (New York), February 3, 1835; Gerrit Smith to J. Leavitt, S. Jocelyn, L. Tappan, September 8, 1839, Smith Letterbook, 1827–43, Smith Papers, Syracuse University; William Jay to Robert Smith, January 2, 1834, John Jay Collection, Columbia University; S. S. Jocelyn to A. A. Phelps, March 20, 1843, B.P.L.

13 Paul Boyer, *Urban Masses and Moral Order in America, 1820–1920* (Cambridge, Mass.: Harvard University Press, 1978), p. 56, affords an excellent discussion of the ethnocentric missionary mentality. In a provocative case study, Carol V. R. George demonstrates how white immediatist contacts tended to be confined to the better educated middle-class minority among black clergy. See George, "Widening the Circle: The Black Church and the Abolitionist Crusade, 1830–1860," in *Antislavery Reconsidered:*

New Perspectives on the Abolitionists, ed. Lewis Perry and Michael Fellman (Baton Rouge: Louisiana State University Press, 1979), pp. 75-95.

14 Lydia Maria Child, ed., *The Oasis* (Boston 1834), p. ix; Minute Book of the Junior Antislavery Society of Philadelphia, September 16, 1837, Pennsylvania Historical Society.

15 For extensive discussion of the acute distaste that white immediatists felt for amalgamation under Southern slavery, see Ronald G. Walters, "The Erotic South: Civilization and Sexuality in American Abolitionism," *American Quarterly*, XXV, no. 2 (May 1973), 177-201. For examples of vehement attacks by white immediatists of the 1830s on amalgamation in the South, see Sarah R. Miller to Lucretia Mott, May 9, 1835, Philadelphia Female Anti-Slavery Society Papers, Pennsylvania Historical Society; Merrill and Ruchames, eds., *Letters of Garrison*, 2, p. 30; Amos A. Phelps, *Lectures on Slavery and Its Remedy* (Boston: New England Anti-Slavery Society, 1834), p. 236; George Bourne, *Slavery, Illustrated in Its Effects upon Woman and Domestic Society* (Boston: Isaac Knapp, 1837), pp. 73, 96; Henry Clarke Wright, *Human Life: Illustrated in My Individual Experience as a Child, a Youth, and a Man* (Boston: Bela Marsh, 1849), p. 366; *Philanthropist* (Cincinnati), June 10, 1836.

16 Lydia Child to Wendell Phillips, May 3, 1842, Blagden Collection, Houghton Library.

17 Ronald Takaki, "The Black Child-Savage in Ante-Bellum America," in *The Great Fear: Race in the Mind of America*, ed. Gary B. Nash and Richard Weiss (New York: Holt, Rinehart and Winston, 1970), pp. 29-35.

18 For the stereotype of blacks as children, see, e.g., Maria Weston Chapman to W. L. Garrison, January 19, 1841, B.P.L.; Hiram Carpenter in *Friend of Man* (Utica), January 26, 1837; Dwight L. Dumond, ed., *Letters of James Gillespie Birney, 1831-1857*, 2 vols. (New York: D. Appleton-Century, 1938), 1, p. 499; Martin Duberman, *James Russell Lowell* (Boston: Houghton Mifflin, 1966), p. 79; Phelps, *Lectures on Slavery*, pp. 222-3; Lewis Tappan to Gerrit Smith, January 4, 1839, Gerrit Smith Papers, Syracuse University; Merrill and Ruchames, eds., *Letters of Garrison*, 1, p. 350. For overtly paternalistic remarks of whites acting as "our brother's keepers" toward childlike blacks, see, e.g., *Liberator* (Boston), February 18, 1832 (E. M. Chandler); Leon F. Litwack, "The Abolitionist Dilemma: The Antislavery Movement and the Northern Negro," *New England Quarterly*, XXXIV, no. 1 (March 1961), 61-2; Hiram Wilson in the *Massachusetts Abolitionist* (Boston), December 26, 1839; Helen Benson to W. L. Garrison, May 22, 1834, Benson-Garrison Correspondence, Houghton Library, Harvard University.

19 "I.G.B." in *Herald of Freedom* (Concord), November 10, 1838; Angelina E. Grimké, *Appeal to the Christian Women of the South* (rpt., New York: Arno Press, 1969), p. 2; Henry C. Wright Journal, XII, December 31, 1834, Houghton Library; Lydia Child in *National Anti-Slavery Standard* (New York), October 6, 1842; Garrison on David Walker in the *Liberator* (Boston), January 8, 1831; Merrill and Ruchames, eds., *Letters of Garrison*, 2, p. 319; Dumond, ed., *Letters of Birney*, 1, p. 97; Birney in *African Repository*, IX, no. 10 (December 1833), 312.

20 Phillips in the *Massachusetts Abolitionist* (Boston), September 5, 1839; *Emancipator* (Boston), October 22, 1845; *Correspondence between the Hon. F. H. Elmore and James G. Birney* (New York: American Anti-Slavery Society, 1838), p. 50; Garrison in the *Liberator* (Boston), May 7, 1831; Simeon S. Jocelyn to Gerrit Smith, April 2, 1836, Smith Papers, Syracuse University.

21 See, e.g., Gerrit Smith to John H. Cocke, December 11, 1840, Letter Copy Book, 1827-43, Smith Papers, Syracuse University; Simeon S. Jocelyn to W. L. Garrison, September 20, 1831, B.P.L.; *Fifth Annual Report of the American Anti-Slavery Society* (New York, 1838), p. 32.

22 *National Anti-Slavery Standard* (New York), June 18, 1840.

23 Lewis Tappan in [Ninth] *Annual Report of the American and Foreign Anti-Slavery Society, Presented at New York, May 8, 1849* (New York, 1849), p. 58; Samuel J. May in the *Liberator* (Boston), July 31, 1831; Lydia Maria Child, *An Appeal in Favor of That Class of*

Americans Called Africans (New York: John S. Taylor, 1836), p. 195; *Liberator* (Boston), June 14, 1834 (Garrison), December 10, 1841 (Quincy); William Jay, *Miscellaneous Writings on Slavery* (Boston: John P. Jewett, 1853), pp. 372–73.

24 Angelina Grimké as quoted in Gerda Lerner, "Black and White Women in the Nineteenth Century: Interaction and Confrontation" (paper presented at the Fifty-fourth annual meeting of the Association for the Study of Negro Life and History, Birmingham, Ala., October 8–12, 1969), p. 16, and in Sorin, *Abolitionism*, p. 70. Sarah Grimké in *Proceedings of the Anti-Slavery Convention of American Women Held in Philadelphia May 15th, 16th, 17th, and 18th, 1838* (Philadelphia: Merrihew and Gunn, 1838), p. 8. Elizur Wright, Jr., in *Massachusetts Abolitionist* (Boston), June 27, 1839; Beriah Green to Gerrit Smith, March 25, 1834, Smith Papers, Syracuse University; William Lloyd Garrison to Ebenezer Dole, June 29, 1832, B.P.L.; Dumond, ed., *Letters of Birney*, 2, pp. 945–7; Joshua Leavitt to Chloe Leavitt, May 10, 1842, Joshua Leavitt Papers, Library of Congress [L.C.].

25 Horton, "Black Activism in Boston," pp. 59–60; Charles Beecher, ed., *Autobiography, Correspondence, etc., of Lyman Beecher*, 2 vols. (New York: Harper, 1864–5), 2, pp. 323–6; Leonard L. Richards, *"Gentlemen of Property and Standing": Anti-Abolition Mobs in Jacksonian America* (New York: Oxford University Press, 1970), p. 41; Juanita D. Fletcher, "Against the Consensus: Oberlin College and the Education of American Negroes, 1835–1865" (Ph.D. dissertation, American University, 1974).

26 Lerner, "Black and White Women," cogently discusses such activity by white female immediatists.

27 Green in the *American Anti-Slavery Reporter*, I (June 1834), 88; Smith in *Fifth Annual Report of A.A.S.S.* (1838), p. 35; Henry Wright Journal, IV, January 28, 1834, Houghton Library; Catharine Birney, *The Grimké Sisters: Sarah and Angelina Grimké: The First Advocates of Abolition and Woman's Rights* (Boston: Lee and Sheppard, 1885), pp. 248–50, on the Grimké sisters and Sarah Douglass.

28 See, e.g., the *Liberator* (Boston), March 11, 1853, and March 16, 1860, for continued sympathy for white abolitionists by Nell and Rock. The *National Anti-Slavery Standard* (New York), February 3, 1855, prints James McCune Smith's attack on the A.A.S.S. and the A. & F.A.S.S. for "yellow" and not "black" speakers. *Frederick Douglass' Paper* (Rochester), April 15, 1853, and May 18, 1855, on the white immediatist failure to employ blacks. Also see Thomas Van Rensselaer in the *Colored American* (New York), October 10, 1840, on the failure of the Liberty party. For black complaints of the Boston Clique, see, e.g., Horton, "Black Activism in Boston," pp. 61–5, 132–3; David B. Davis, "Slavery and the American Mind," in *Perspectives and Irony in American Slavery* (Jackson: University Press of Mississippi, 1976), p. 68; James Brewer Stewart, *Holy Warriors: The Abolitionists and American Slavery* (New York: Hill and Wang, 1976), p. 129.

29 Garnet quoted in Stewart, *Holy Warriors*, p. 127; Ward, "Remond," p. 232; Martin R. Delaney, *The Condition, Elevation, Emigration, and Destiny of the Colored People of the United States* (Philadelphia, 1852), p. 10; Meier and Rudwick, "Role of Blacks in Abolitionist Movement," pp. 113–14, quotes Douglass.

30 *Frederick Douglass' Paper* (Rochester), May 18, 1855.

31 Pease and Pease, "Negro Conventions," 30; Howard H. Bell, "Expressions of Negro Militancy in the North, 1840–1860," *Journal of Negro History*, XLV, no. 1 (January 1960), 19; Richard P. McCormick, "William Whipper: Moral Reformers," *Pennsylvania History*, XLIII, no. 1 (January 1976), 45 *n*. 85; Benjamin Quarles, ed., "Letters from Negro Leaders to Gerrit Smith," *Journal of Negro History*, XXVII, no. 4 (October 1942), 450–1.

32 George Whipple in the *American Missionary*, III, no. 10 (August 1849).

33 Annie H. Abel and Frank J. Klingberg, eds., *A Side-Light on Anglo-American Relations, 1839–1858: Furnished by the Correspondence of Lewis Tappan and Others with the British and Foreign Anti-Slavery Society* (Washington, D.C.: Association for the Study of Negro Life and History, 1927), p. 190; Edmund Quincy to R. D. Webb, March 9, 1848, Quincy-Webb Correspondence, B.P.L.; Gerrit Smith to Charles Ray in the *Model Worker* (Uti-

ca), November 24, 1848; David M. Potter, *The Impending Crisis, 1848–1861* (New York: Harper and Row, 1976), p. 132; Wyatt-Brown, *Lewis Tappan*, p. 176; Elizur Wright, Jr., *Perforations in the 'Latter-Day Pamphlets,' by One of the 'Eighteen Millions of Bores'* (Boston: Phillips, Sampson, 1850), p. 41; Theodore Parker to Wendell Phillips, May 14, 1859, and n.d., both in Blagden Collection, Houghton Library; *Liberator* (Boston), September 15, 1865 (Sallie Holley); *Commonwealth* (Boston), February 5, 1864 (Elizur Wright to Samuel G. Howe).

34   Arthur Harry Rice, "Henry B. Stanton as a Political Abolitionist" (Ph.D. dissertation, Columbia University, 1968), p. 249, on Morris's vice-presidential candidacy. Stewart is quoted in the *Emancipator and Weekly Chronicle* (Boston), April 9, 1845. John Mayfield, *Rehearsal for Republicanism: Free Soil and the Politics of Antislavery* (Port Washington: Kennikat Press, 1980), pp. 116–17, on Liberty party coalitionists of 1848. Lewis Perry, "The Panorama and the Mills: A Review of the Letters of John Greenleaf Whittier," *Civil War History*, XXII, no. 3 (September 1976), 239. For some indication of the great extent to which white immediatists deemphasized Northern civil rights in favor of eradicating Southern slavery, see D. B. Davis, "Slavery and American Mind," pp. 67–8; Stewart, *Holy Warriors*, p. 129; Larry Gara, *The Liberty Line: The Legend of the Underground Railroad* (Lexington: University of Kentucky Press, 1961), p. 73. Douglass is quoted in *Frederick Douglass' Paper* (Rochester), April 5, 1856.

35   James G. Birney, *Examination of the Decision of the Supreme Court of the United States, in the Case of Strader, Gorman and Armstrong vs. Christopher Graham* (Cincinnati: Truman and Spofford, 1852). George Fredrickson, *The Black Image in the White Mind: The Debate on Afro-American Character and Destiny, 1817–1914* (New York: Harper and Row, 1971), p. 149, notes Smith endorsing the Blair Bill, while the broadside "Gerrit Smith to Montgomery Blair" (Peterboro, N.Y., 1862) contains his remark on blacks "naturally" moving toward the Equator. Bailey in the *National Era* (Washington, D.C.), March 22, 1849. Salmon P. Chase to Frederick Douglass, May 4, 1850 (copy), and Leicester King to J. W. Piatt, August 22, 1842, both in Salmon P. Chase Papers, Pennsylvania Historical Society.

36   Bertram Wyatt-Brown, "William Lloyd Garrison and Antislavery Unity: A Reappraisal," *Civil War History*, XIII, no. 1 (March 1967), 13, quotes a New York City steward threatening to disown a black editor. Oliver Johnson to Wendell Phillips, September 11, 1854, Blagden Collection, Houghton Library, on black lecturers who violated insurgent principles.

37   For cogent analyses of these qualities in Northern black activists, see Horton, *Black Bostonians*; Pease and Pease, *They Who Would Be Free*; Benjamin Quarles, *Black Abolitionists* (New York: Oxford University Press, 1969).

38   Charles H. Wesley, "The Participation of Negroes in Anti-Slavery Political Parties," *Journal of Negro History*, XXIX, no. 1 (January 1944), 44–45, and Sorin, *Abolitionism*, p. 113, on the 1843 Buffalo convention of the Liberty party. Frank W. Hale, "Frederick Douglass: Antislavery Crusader and Lecturer," *Journal of Human Relations*, XIV, no. 1 (first quarter 1966), 107, on the selection in 1860 of Douglass as elector-at-large for the Radical Abolitionist party. Donald M. Jacobs, "The Nineteenth Century Struggle over Segregated Education in the Boston Schools," *Journal of Negro Education*, XXXIX (winter 1970), 76–85, included data on the Boston Clique cooperation with blacks against a racist school admission policy. Meier and Rudwick, "Role of Blacks in Abolitionist Movement," pp. 120–1, on the change in the vigilance committees. Benjamin Quarles, *Allies for Freedom*, on abolitionist biracialism in Brown's raid on Harpers Ferry.

39   For examples of this strong commitment to environmentalism, see Lewis Tappan to Frederick Douglass, December 27, 1856, Letterbook, Lewis Tappan Papers, L.C.; Samuel J. May, *Some Recollections of Our Antislavery Conflict* (Boston: Fields, Osgood, 1869), p. 272; Richard Sewell, *Ballots for Freedom: Anti-Slavery Politics in the United States, 1837–1860* (New York: Oxford University Press, 1976), pp. 188–9; *The Anti-Slavery Papers of James Russell Lowell*, 2 vols. (Boston and New York: Houghton Mifflin, 1902), 2,

p. 85. For instances of repulsion with major-party leaders, see, e.g., Lewis Tappan to Frederick Douglass, November 27, 1856, Letterbook, Lewis Tappan Papers, L.C.; James Birney Diary, November 4, 1852, Birney Manuscripts, L.C.; Gerrit Smith to James G. Birney, February 7, 1852, Birney Papers, Clements Library, University of Michigan; Elizur Wright in the *Commonwealth* (Boston), March 4, 1851. The environmentalist posture taken by first-generation immediatists against the "romantic racialism" of newer antislavery recruits is cogently discussed in James M. McPherson, "A Brief for Equality: The Abolitionist Reply to the Racist Myth, 1860-65," in *The Antislavery Vanguard: New Essays on the Abolitionists*, ed. Martin Duberman (Princeton, N.J.: Princeton University Press, 1965), 156-77.

40 Henry C. Wright to Gerrit Smith, January 15, 1861, Gerrit Smith Papers, Syracuse University; Lewis Tappan to Samuel Rhoads, January 2, 1855, Lewis Tappan Papers, L.C.; Edmund Quincy to Caroline Weston, July 2, 1847, B.P.L. John Blassingame's thoughtful article, "Using the Testimony of Ex-Slaves: Approaches and Problems," *Journal of Southern History*, XLI, no. 4 (November 1975), 473-93, prompts an interesting question regarding this matter of empathy. After extensive analysis of both white abolitionist editors of slave narratives in the antebellum period and Works Progress Administration (W.P.A.) interviewers of ex-slaves in the 1930s, Blassingame concluded that the abolitionists less frequently interjected their own views in the slave's own story. It is crucial to determine whether this was because abolitionists felt more distant from and less involved with the slave than the W.P.A. interviewers felt.

41 Henry C. Wright to Wendell Phillips, September 27, 1844, Blagden Collection, Houghton Library.

42 See, e.g., Benjamin Quarles, "The Breach between Douglass and Garrison," *Journal of Negro History*, XXIII, no. 2 (April 1938), 144-54; William H. Pease and Jane H. Pease, "Boston Garrisonians and the Problem of Frederick Douglass," *Canadian Journal of History*, II, no. 2 (September 1967), 29-48; Tyrone Tillery, "The Inevitability of the Douglass-Garrison Conflict," *Phylon*, XXXVII, no. 2 (June 1976), 137-49; Philip S. Foner, *Frederick Douglass: A Biography* (New York: Citadel Press, 1964), particularly pp. 75-83, 136-54.

43 For some of the most pertinent facts in the Garrison-Douglass dispute, see Hale, "Frederick Douglass," pp. 104-7; Pease and Pease, "Boston Garrisonians," pp. 29-44; Merrill and Ruchames, eds., *Letters of Garrison*, 3, p. 533 n. 3; Horton, "Black Activism in Boston," pp. 78-9; Ward, "Remond," pp. 170-2, 183; Foner, ed., *Life and Writings of Douglass*, 2, pp. 52-4; Nathan I. Higgins, *Slave and Citizen: The Life of Frederick Douglass* (Boston: Little, Brown, 1980), p. 65.

44 See, e.g., Pease and Pease, *They Who Would be Free*, p. 195 n. 73, and Ward, "Remond," p. 45.

45 For evidence that Garrison and other Clique members discouraged black editors, see Meier and Rudwick, "Role of Blacks in Abolitionist Movement," pp. 116-17; Garrison in the *Liberator* (Boston), December 20, 1839, July 23, 1847; Edmund Quincy to R. D. Webb, March 9, 1848, Quincy-Webb Correspondence, B.P.L., Horton, *Black Bostonians*, pp. 63-4, 82-3, Higgins, *Douglass*, p. 39.

46 Peter F. Walker, *Moral Choices: Memory, Desire, and Imagination in Nineteenth Century American Abolition* (Baton Rouge: Louisiana State University Press, 1978), pp. 245-57, sensitively demonstrates the restraint in Douglass' correspondence with Boston Clique members. Frederick Douglass to Wendell Phillips, April 28, 1846, Blagden Collection, Houghton Library, on his inability to approach Phillips "familiarly." *Frederick Douglass' Paper* (Rochester), December 9, 1853, quotes his explanation of "incurring the displeasure of the Garrisonians." Frederick Douglass, *Life and Times of Frederick Douglass* (New York: Macmillan, Collier, 1962), pp. 259-60, quotes Douglass realizing in 1847 that insurgents treated him like a child. Foner, ed., *Life and Writings of Douglass*, 2, p. 210, quotes Douglass commenting on Clique insurgents' view of his position vis-à-vis Garrison.

47 *North Star* (Rochester), December 3, 1847 quotes Douglass on the purpose of an independent black newspaper. For other useful data on Douglass' quest for a sense of blackness and rapport with Northern blacks, see Hale, "Frederick Douglass," 106–7, Pease and Pease, *They Who Would Be Free,* p. 245.

48 Edmund Quincy to R. D. Webb, March 29, 1845, Webb–Quincy Correspondence, B.P.L. Walker, *Moral Choices,* pt. 3, particularly p. 258.

49 Edmund Quincy to R. D. Webb, December 13, 1845, May 23, 1846, Quincy–Webb Correspondence, B.P.L.; Merrill and Ruchames, eds., *Letters of Garrison,* 3, pp. 532–3; Samuel J. May to J. B. Estlin, October 31, 1847, B.P.L.; Garrison on Douglass in the *Liberator* (Boston), November 18, 1853; Parker Pillsbury to Wendell Phillips, October 22, 1860, Blagden Collection, Houghton Library.

50 For the Clique's general characterizations of Douglass in primitive, savagelike terms, see, e.g., Samuel May, Jr., to R. D. Webb, January 12, 1858, September 13, 1859, B.P.L.; Merrill and Ruchames, eds., *Letters of Garrison,* 3, pp. 532–3; 4, pp. 693–4. Abby Kelley Foster to Maria Weston Chapman, October 5, 1847, B.P.L. Richard Webb to Maria W. Chapman, February 26, 1846, B.P.L. Wendell Phillips to Elizabeth Pease, December 4, 1852, B.P.L.

51 Benjamin Quarles, *Frederick Douglass* (Washington, D.C.: Associate Publishers, 1948), pp. 73–4, and Higgins, *Douglass,* p. 46, outline Smith's financial and editorial arrangements with Douglass. Frederick Douglass to Gerrit Smith, May 1, 1851 (on being won over to Smith's voluntarist positions); Douglass to Smith, July 14, 1852 (praising Smith for sustaining his paper and his spirits), both in Gerrit Smith Papers, Syracuse University. See also Douglass to Smith, March 30, 1849, Smith Papers, Syracuse University.

52 Gerrit Smith, "[Letter to] Elder Charles B. Ray, Nov. 16, 1848," broadside (n.p., 1848), Smith Papers, Syracuse University. Gerrit Smith to Theodore Wright, Charles B. Ray, S. McCune Smith, November 14, 1846, Smith to Nathan Lord, November 2, 1845, both in Letter Copy Book, 1843–55, Smith Papers, Syracuse University. Lewis Tappan to Frederick Douglass. December 8, 19, 27, 1856, Frederick Douglass Papers, L.C.; Wyatt-Brown, *Lewis Tappan,* pp. 332–3.

53 Gerrit Smith, "Letter to John Thomas, Esq., Syracuse, Chairman of the Jerry Rescue Committee, August 27, 1859," broadside (n.p., 1859), Smith Papers, Syracuse University, on blacks in despair about "loud-mouthed abolitionists." *Model Worker* (Utica), October 6, 1846, quotes Smith on the *Ram's Horn* editorial. According to Benjamin Quarles, ed., "Letters from Negro Leaders to Gerrit Smith," *Journal of Negro History,* XXVII, no. 4 (October 1942), 432–6, more than two-thirds of the 277 letters blacks wrote to Smith contained requests for financial help. But one is struck, in many of these same letters, by the blacks' pleased surprise at Smith's empathy.

54 Foner, ed., *Life and Writings of Douglass,* 2, pp. 205, 170, 158, 174, 269; Frederick Douglass to Gerrit Smith, February 13, 1852, and August 22, 1854, Smith Papers, Syracuse University; Douglass, *Life and Times,* p. 453. In his well-known study, *Frederick Douglass: A Biography,* p. 151, Philip S. Foner, unlike most scholars, grasped the importance of Smith's empathy for Douglass. But Foner did not explain how this empathy was linked with Douglass' dispute with Boston Clique insurgents.

CHAPTER 7. RIGHTEOUS VIOLENCE

1 For characterizations of violent means as a logical response to external events, see, e.g., Carleton Mabee, *Black Freedom: The Nonviolent Abolitionists from 1830 through the Civil War* (New York: Macmillan, 1970), p. 377; Merton L. Dillon, *Elijah P. Lovejoy, Abolitionist Editor* (Urbana: University of Illinois Press, 1961), p. 179; John Demos, "The Antislavery Movement and the Problem of Violent 'Means,' " *New England Quarterly,* XXXVII, no. 4 (December 1964), 501–26; Jane H. Pease and William H. Pease, "Confrontation and Abolition in the 1850s," *Journal of American History,* LVIII, no. 4 (March

1972), 923-37. That support for violence resulted from the immediatists' image of themselves as agents for the Lord is argued in Lewis Perry, *Radical Abolitionism: Anarchy and the Government of God in Antislavery Thought* (Ithaca: Cornell University Press, 1973), pp. 231-67 and Ronald G. Walters, *The Antislavery Appeal: American Abolitionism after 1830* (Baltimore, Md.: Johns Hopkins University Press, 1976), pp. 32-3. George Fredrickson, *The Inner Civil War: Northern Intellectuals and the Crisis of the Union* (New York: Harper & Row, 1965), best exemplifies the emphasis on the Civil War experience as a cause.

2   Records of the New England Anti-Slavery Society, 1831-33, Boston Public Library [B.P.L.] (preamble to 1832 Constitution); Gerald Sorin, *Abolitionism: A New Perspective* (New York: Praeger, 1972), p. 89, quotes the American Anti-Slavery Society in 1833; John Greenleaf Whittier, *The Conflict with Slavery: Politics and Reform: The Inner Life Criticism* (Boston and New York: Houghton Mifflin, 1889), p. 76; Sorin, *Abolitionism*, p. 91, quotes Ladd.

3   Garrison on *Walker's Appeal* in the *Liberator* (Boston), January 8, 1831; Theodore D. Weld, *First Annual Report of the Society for Promoting Manual Labor in Literary Institutions, Including the Report of their General Agent, Theodore D. Weld, January 28, 1833* (New York, 1833), p. 52; Jocelyn in the *Liberator* (Boston), December 17, 1836.

4   Robert H. Abzug, "The Influence of Garrisonian Abolitionists' Fear of Slave Violence on the Antislavery Argument, 1829-1840," *Journal of Negro History*, LV, no. 1 (January 1970), 15-28. For evidence on noninsurgent immediatist admonitions against slave violence, see the *Evangelist* (New York), September 5, 1835, and Ronald G. Walters, *American Reformers, 1815-1860* (New York: Hill and Wang, 1978), p. 98. Gilbert H. Barnes and Dwight L. Dumond, eds., *Letters of Theodore Dwight Weld, Angelina Grimké Weld, and Sarah Grimké, 1822-1844* (New York and London: D. Appleton-Century, 1934), 1, p. 378, quotes Sarah Grimké's warning to Smith.

5   Kenneth Keniston, *Young Radicals: Notes on Committed Youth* (New York: Harcourt, Brace and World, 1968), p. 255.

6   Garrison in Walter M. Merrill and Louis Ruchames, eds., *The Letters of William Lloyd Garrison*, 6 vols. (Cambridge, Mass.: Harvard University Press, Belknap Press, 1971-81), 2, p. 237 (vol. 1, *I Will Be Heard! 1822-1835*; vol. 2, *A House Dividing against Itself, 1836-1840*; vol. 3, *No Union with Slaveholders, 1841-1849*; vol. 4, *From Disunionism to the Brink of War, 1850-1860*; vol. 5, *Let the Oppressed Go Free, 1861-1867*; vol. 6, *To Rouse the Slumbering Land, 1868-1879*; individual volumes are cited as *Letters of Garrison* with the volume number). Jabez D. Hammond to Gerrit Smith, March 15, 1836, Gerrit Smith Papers, Syracuse University; Mabee, *Black Freedom*, pp. 38-9, on Arthur Tappan's orders during the 1834 New York riots; Elizur Wright, Jr., to Clarissa Wright, September 16, 1834, Elizur Wright Transcripts, B.P.L.; Gerrit Smith to Leonard Bacon, October 24, 1835, Gerrit Smith Papers, Syracuse University, on resort to arms against the Utica mob; Benjamin P. Thomas, *Theodore Weld: Crusader for Freedom* (New Brunswick, N.J.: Rutgers University Press, 1950), p. 107, on the Ohio Anti-Slavery Society's resort to weapons; Mabee, *Black Freedom*, p. 40, on Birney's arming of his home; Sarah Grimké in Barnes and Dumond, eds., *Weld-Grimké Letters*, 1, p. 377.

7   Jacques Lacan, "The Mirror Stage as Formative of the Function of the 'I' as Revealed in Psychoanalytic Experience," in *Écrits* (New York: W. W. Norton, 1977), p. 6.

8   Minute Book of the Junior Antislavery Society of Philadelphia (January 5, 1838), Pennsylvania Historical Society; Henry Wright in the *Liberator* (Boston), December 1, 1837; Angelina Grimké in the *Liberator* (Boston), December 22, 1837; Sarah Grimké in Barnes and Dumond, eds., *Weld-Grimké Letters* 1, pp. 480-1.

9   Lydia Maria Child to Abby Kelly [sic], October 1, 1838, Kelley-Foster Papers, American Antiquarian Society [A.A.S.]; William H. Burleigh, "Rev. E. P. Lovejoy, Murdered by a Mob at Alton, Illinois, November 7th 1837," November 24, 1837, Album, Western Anti-Slavery Society Manuscripts, Library of Congress [L.C.]; Phillips in the *Liberator* (Boston), January 5, 1838; Beriah Green, *The Martyr: A Discourse, in*

Commemoration of the Martyrdom of the Rev. Elijah P. Lovejoy (New York: American Anti-Slavery Society, 1838), pp. 15–16; Amos A. Phelps in the *Liberator* (Boston), January 5, 1838; Hugh Houck Davis, "The Reform Career of Joshua Leavitt" (Ph.D. dissertation, Ohio State University, 1969), p. 179; Elizur Wright, Jr., in *Fifth Annual Report of the American Anti-Slavery Society* (New York, 1838), p. 107. The action at the 1838 annual meeting of the A.A.S.S. on the Whittier resolution condemning Lovejoy is reported in the *National Anti-Slavery Standard* (New York), February 4, 1842. See also Minutes of the Executive Committee of the American Anti-Slavery Society, November 20, 1837, American Antislavery Society Papers, B.P.L.

10 Lewis Tappan in the *Liberator* (Boston), January 5, 1838; S. S. Jocelyn to A. A. Phelps, December 6, 1837, B.P.L.; Goodell in the *Liberator* (Boston), September 6, 1839, and *Friend of Man* (Utica), November 22, 29, 1837; Garrison in the *Liberator* (Boston), January 5, February 16, 1838, and in Merrill and Ruchames, eds., *Letters of Garrison*, 2, pp. 328, 332; Rogers in the *Herald of Freedom* (Concord), October 27, 1838; Maria Weston Chapman, "The Anniversary of Lovejoy's Martyrdom," n.d., Ellis Gray Loring Family Papers, Schlesinger Library, Ratcliffe College; *Sixth Annual Report of the Board of Managers of the Massachusetts Anti-Slavery Society* (Boston, 1838), p. 38; *Liberator* (Boston), November 24, 1837, on reaction to Lovejoy by the board of managers of the Massachusetts Anti-Slavery Society.

11 Foster's effort to persuade the Massachusetts Governor is noted in Anne Warren Weston to "Misses Weston," January 23, 1845, B.P.L. George B. Cheever, *Punishment by Death: Its Authority and Expediency* (New York, 1842). Luther Rawson Marsh, ed., *Writings and Speeches of Alvan Stewart, on Slavery* (New York: A. B. Burdick, 1860), p. 268. Sarah B. Shaw to Maria W. Chapman, November 2, 1842, B.P.L.

12 Sorin, *Abolitionism*, p. 92, on the slave revolt aboard the *Creole* in 1841. Walters, *Antislavery Appeal*, p. 26, quotes the 1844 Liberty party platform on slave uprisings. Jay in the *American and Foreign Anti-Slavery Reporter* (Extra Edition), December 1840. Alvan Stewart to Samuel Webb, June 25, September 30, 1840, December 2, 1841, Alvan Stewart Papers, New York Historical Society; Smith in the *National Anti-Slavery Standard* (New York), February 24, 1842, and in Bertram Wyatt-Brown, "William Lloyd Garrison and Antislavery Unity: A Reappraisal," *Civil War History*, XIII, no. 1 (March 1967), 11; Nathaniel Peabody Rogers, *A Collection from the Miscellaneous Writings of Nathaniel Peabody Rogers* (Boston: Benjamin B. Mussey, 1849), p. 15, and Rogers in the *Liberator* (Boston), October 23, 1840. Garnet is quoted in Jane H. Pease and William H. Pease, *Bound with Them in Chains: A Biographical History of the Antislavery Movement* (Westport: Greenwood Press, 1972), p. 180.

13 Robert Trendel, "William Jay and the International Peace Movement," *Peace and Change*, II, no. 3 (fall 1974), 17–23; Mabee, *Black Freedom*, pp. 18–19; Betty Fladeland, *James Gillespie Birney: Slaveholder to Abolitionist* (Ithaca, N.Y.: Cornell University Press, 1955), 258–9.

14 Samuel May, Jr., to J. B. Estlin, May 30, September 26, 1846. Garrison in Clare Taylor, ed., *British and American Abolitionists: An Episode in Transatlantic Understanding* (Edinburgh: Edinburgh University Press, 1974), p. 312; see also Garrison in the *Liberator* (Boston), May 7, 1847. Robert W. Tolf, "Edmund Quincy: Aristocrat Abolitionist" (Ph.D. dissertation, University of Rochester, 1957), pp. 224–5, and Edmund Quincy to R. D. Webb, May 23, 1846, Quincy–Webb Correspondence, B.P.L. Abigail Kelley Foster in the *Chronotype* (Boston), May 27, 1846.

15 Arthur H. Rice, "Henry B. Stanton as a Political Abolitionist" (Ed.D. dissertation, Columbia University, 1968), p. 3, and Elizur Wright, Jr., in the *Chronotype* (Boston), May 23, 1846.

16 Henry Wright in *National Anti-Slavery Standard* (New York), June 6, 1850, and in Mabee, *Black Freedom*, p. 296. Angelina Grimké Weld to Gerrit Smith, June 10, 1855, Smith Papers, Syracuse University. Gerald Sorin, *The New York Abolitionists: A Case Study of Political Radicalism* (Westport: Greenwood Publishing, 1971), p. 77, on Lewis Tappan.

Merrill and Ruchames, eds., *Letters of Garrison*, 4, p. 212 *n.* 1, on May's and Smith's roles in the rescue of Jerry McHenry. Chaplin in *National Anti-Slavery Standard* (New York), January 16, 1851.

17   Stephen Foster in the *Liberator* (Boston), October 11, 1850. Lydia Maria Child, *Letters of Lydia Maria Child* (Boston: Houghton, Mifflin, 1833), p. 73. William H. Pease and Jane H. Pease, "Freedom and Peace: A Nineteenth Century Dilemma," *Midwest Quarterly*, IX, no. 1 (October 1967), 36, for May on the rescue of Burns. Thomas James Mumford, *Memoir of Samuel Joseph May* (Boston: Roberts, 1873), p. 220, quotes May on the rescue of Jerry McHenry.

18   M. Leon Perkal, "William Goodell: A Life of Reform" (Ph.D. dissertation, City University of New York, 1972), pp. 257–8, quotes Smith; see also Smith, "To the Abolitionists and Prohibitionists of the County of Madison, August 16, 1858," broadside (n.p., 1858), Smith Papers, Syracuse University. Fredrickson, *The Inner Civil War*, p. 41, on Phillips. Foster in the *Liberator* (Boston), December 12, 1856. Sarah Grimké in Robert H. Abzug, "Theodore Weld: A Biography" (Ph.D. dissertation, University of California, Berkeley, 1977), pp. 328–9. Sorin, *Abolitionism*, p. 95, quotes Angelina Grimké Weld.

19   Lewis Tappan to Joseph Sturge, February 17, 1856, Lewis Tappan Papers, L.C.; Tappan to Gerrit Smith, May 22, 1856, Smith Papers, Syracuse University. W. L. Garrison to Samuel J. May, March 21, 1856, B.P.L.; Fredrickson, *The Inner Civil War*, p. 41, and Sorin, *Abolitionism*, p. 95, on Garrison. William Goodell to Gerrit Smith, April 23, September 23, 1856, American Abolition Society Letterbook for 1855–57, Oberlin College.

20   Anne Warren Weston to Mary A. Estlin, February 5, 1855, B.P.L. Francis Jackson to Lysander Spooner, December 3, 1858, B.P.L.

21   Brown is quoted in Benjamin Quarles, *Allies for Freedom: Blacks and John Brown* (New York: Oxford University Press, 1974), p. 124. Irving H. Bartlett, *Wendell Phillips: Brahmin Radical* (Boston: Beacon Press, 1961), pp. 210–11. Ralph Volney Harlow, *Gerrit Smith: Philanthropist and Reformer* (New York: Henry Holt, 1939), pp. 37, 405, and Sorin, *New York Abolitionists*, p. 37, on Smith.

.22   *Liberator* (Boston), November 4, 1859, January 13, 1860; Barbara Louise Faulkner, "Adin Ballou and the Hopedale Community" (Ph.D. dissertation, Boston University, 1965), p. 228; Perry, *Radical Abolitionism*, p. 265. Garrison's retort to Ballou appeared in the *Liberator* (Boston), January 13, 1860.

23   Samuel May, Jr., to R. D. Webb, October 31, December 7, 1859, B.P.L. William S. Heywood, ed., *Autobiography of Adin Ballou* (Lowell, Mass.: Vox Populi Press, 1896), p. 419, quotes the resolution of the Worcester County South Division Anti-Slavery Society. Nathaniel Colver to Henry Wise, November 16, 1859, John Brown Papers, L.C. Spooner's plan is noted in Bartlett, *Wendell Phillips*, pp. 211–12, and in William O. Reichert, *Partisans of Freedom: A Study in American Anarchism* (Bowling Green, Ohio: Bowling Green University Popular Press, 1976), p. 122. Phillips in the *Liberator* (Boston), November 11, December 2, 1859.

24   Garrison in James Redpath, ed., *Echoes of Harper's Ferry* (Boston: Thayer and Eldridge, 1860), p. 309; Bertram Wyatt-Brown, "The Abolitionist Controversy: Men of Blood, Men of God," in *Men, Women and Issues in American History*, ed. Howard Quint and Milton Cantor (Homewood, Ill.: Dorsey Press, 1975), 1, p. 215; *Liberator* (Boston), December 3, 9, 16, 1859; June 1, 1860; Merrill and Ruchames, eds., *Letters of Garrison*, 4, pp. 703–4.

25   Henry Wright to Wendell Phillips, November 19, 1859, Blagden Collection, Houghton Library; Samuel J. May in Pease and Pease, "Freedom and Peace," 33; Quincy in *National Anti-Slavery Standard* (New York), November 12, 1859; Henry C. Wright to W. L. Garrison, February 3, 1860, B.P.L.; Lydia Child and C. C. Burleigh in the *Liberator* (Boston), December 23, 1859; Lewis Tappan in *American Missionary*, III, ser. 2 (December 1859), 280; David L. Smiley, "Cassius M. Clay and John Fee: A Study in Southern Anti-Slavery Thought," *Journal of Negro History*, XLII, no. 3 (July 1957),

210–11; John G. Whittier to Charles Sumner, December 8, 1859, Charles Sumner Papers, Houghton Library.

26 For the pertinent stanza in "Brown of Ossawatomie," see *The Complete Poetical Works of John Greenleaf Whittier* (Boston, 1883), p. 258.

27 Walter M. Merrill, *Against Wind and Tide: A Biography of William Lloyd Garrison* (Cambridge, Mass.: Harvard University Press, 1963), pp. 276–91, thoroughly covers Garrison's thoughts and actions during the war years. Merrill and Ruchames, eds., *Letters of Garrison*, 5, pp. 106–7, 168, and Mabee, *Black Freedom*, pp. 348, 349, 422, covers Garrison's attitude toward his sons. Garrison's remark supporting the federal war effort is quoted in John S. Rosenberg, "Toward a New Civil War Revisionism," *American Scholar*, XXXVIII, no. 2 (spring 1969), 262. For evidence that Garrison's was the majority position of first-generation immediatists during the Civil War, see, e.g., Mabee, *Black Freedom*, pp. 341–2, 345–9, 359–63, 366–7, 422 *n.* 23 and *n.* 31; Maria Weston Chapman to "Mrs. Mitchell," January 1861, B.P.L. During the war years, Garrison was naturally disposed to "prove" his majoritarian position and, accordingly, printed many abolitionist statements that echoed it in the *Liberator* (Boston). It is, therefore, striking that the *Liberator* also contained several antiwar statements similar to those of Adin Ballou and Beriah Green.

28 Quoted in Taylor, ed., *British and American Abolitionists*, p. 407. See also Douglas C. Riach, "Richard Davis Webb and Antislavery in Ireland," in *Anti-Slavery Reconsidered: New Perspectives on the Abolitionists*, ed. Lewis Perry and Michael Fellman (Baton Rouge: Louisiana State University Press, 1979), p. 161 .

29 Herbert C. Kelman, "Violence without Moral Restraint: Reflections on the Dehumanization of Victims and Victimizers," in *Varieties of Psychohistory*, ed. George M. Kren and Leon H. Rappoport (New York: Springer, 1976), p. 310, cogently accounts for this sort of perspective: "Violence can offer a person the illusion that he is in control, that he is able to act on his environment, that he has found a means of self-expression."

30 James Redpath to Thomas W. Higginson, November 13, 1859, B.P.L. William Henry Furness, *A Word of Consolation for the Kindred of Those Who Have Fallen in Battle, a Discourse of September 28, 1862* (n.p., 1862), p. 7.

31 Spooner in Wendell Phillips Garrison and Francis Jackson Garrison, *William Lloyd Garrison, 1805–1879*, 4 vols. (New York: Century, 1885–9), 3, p. 406 (vol. 1, *1805–1835*; vol. 2, *1835–1840*; vol. 3, *1841–1860*; vol. 4, *1861–1879*; individual volumes are cited as *Garrison* with the volume number). L. Maria Child to Anne Warren Weston, December 22, 1859, B.P.L.; Sorin, *New York Abolitionists*, p. 36, quotes Smith; Tolf, "Quincy," pp. 261–2.

32 Maria W. Chapman to Anne Greene Chapman, July [?] 21, 1862, B.P.L.

33 Henry Wright in the *Non-Resistant* (Boston), April 30, 1839. Samuel May, Jr., to Edmund Quincy, July 9, 1842, Edmund Quincy Papers, Massachusetts Historical Society; Merrill and Ruchames, eds., *Letters of Garrison*, 2, 215.

34 Various students of social psychology characterize this general process of moving outward with different labels. Jacques Lacan, "Mirror Stage," pp. 5–6, calls it transformation from the "spectacular I," where all of life must "mirror" one's own qualities, to the "social I," where there is significant identification with people having qualities unlike one's own. Heinz Kohut characterizes it as a movement from the "grandiose self," which cannot differentiate its own personage from other people and things, to the "cohesive self," which can enjoy give and take with other people and values. See Paul H. Ornstein, ed., *The Search for Self: Selected Writings of Heinz Kohut: 1950–1978* (New York: International Universities Press, 1978), especially 1, pp. 22, 56–7. In *The Imperial Self: An Essay in American Literary and Cultural History* (New York: Alfred A. Knopf, 1971), pp. 19, 40, Quentin Anderson describes it as a process where the "Imperial Self" discovers that it must establish relationships with clearly distinguishable "Others" if it is to function effectively within the world.

35 James Brewer Stewart, *Holy Warriors: The Abolitionists and American Slavery* (New York: Hill and Wang, 1976), pp. 153–4.
36 Garrison and Garrison, *William Lloyd Garrison*, 4, 21–2, 30; Gay in the *National Anti-Slavery Standard* (New York), April 10, 1851. Octavius Brooks Frothingham, *Gerrit Smith: A Biography* (New York: G. P. Putnam, 1878), pp. 233–4; *Speeches and Letters of Gerrit Smith (from January, 1863 to January, 1864) on the Rebellion* (New York: John A. Gray and Green, 1864), p. 13; and Fredrickson, *The Inner Civil War*, p. 123, on Smith. Tilden G. Edelstein, *Strange Enthusiasm: A Life of Thomas Wentworth Higginson* (New Haven and London: Yale University Press, 1968), p. 194. Sorin, *Abolitionism*, p. 151, on the demand for abolitionist speakers throughout the North during the Civil War. Goodell in the *Principia* (New York), December 21, 1861. Bartlett, *Phillips*, p. 247, on the winter 1861–62 lecture tour and Ann Phillips to Wendell Phillips, April 3, 1862, Blagden Collection, Houghton Library, Harvard University (written at the end of the tour).
37 Thomas Wentworth Higginson, *Wendell Phillips* (Boston: Lee and Shepard, 1884), vii–ix. James C. Jackson in the *Albany Patriot*, January 29, 1845. Anne Warren Weston to Wendell Phillips, April 22, 1851, and Oliver Johnson to Wendell Phillips, August 10, 1860, both in the Blagden Collection, Houghton Library. Michael Fellman, "Theodore Parker and the Abolitionist Role in the 1850s," *Journal of American History*, LXI, no. 3 (December 1974), 666–84. T. W. Higginson to Wendell Phillips, November 12, 1861, Blagden Collection, Houghton Library. Louis Filler, "Liberalism, Antislavery, and the Founders of the *Independent*," *New England Quarterly*, XXVII, no. 3 (September 1954), 296 *n.* 12, on the Tappan–Bowen relationship. Anne Warren Weston to Mary A. Estlin, January 21, 1855, B.P.L., on the relationship with the Beecher children, particularly Harriet Beecher Stowe.

CHAPTER 8. IMMEDIATISTS AND RADICALS

1 Edward Magdol, *Owen Lovejoy: Abolitionist in Congress* (New Brunswick, N.J.: Rutgers University Press, 1967), pp. 24, 89, 123–4, 141. As early as 1848, it should be noted, Barnburner Democrats supporting the Van Buren presidential candidacy were characterized as the "Radical Democracy."
2 *Bureau County* (Illinois) *Republican*, n.d. [July 1858], "Extra," publishing the "Remarks of Mr. Lovejoy on Receiving the Nomination at the Convention at Joliet, June 30th."
3 In " 'Historical Topics Sometimes Run Dry': The State of Abolitionist Studies," *Historian*, XLIII, no. 2 (February 1981), 177–94, I elaborate upon these historical approaches to immediatists and radicals.
4 Comparison of Gerald Sorin, *The New York Abolitionists: A Case Study of Political Radicalism* (Westport, Conn.: Greenwood Publishing, 1971), in its comprehensive delineation of first-generation immediatist social traits with Robert Montgomery's delineation of the social traits of radicals (*Beyond Equality: Labor and the Radical Republicans, 1862–1872* [New York: Alfred A. Knopf, 1967], pp. 72–89) reveals the basic similarity of radicals and immediatists as social types. See also Eric Foner, *Free Soil, Free Labor, Free Men: The Ideology of the Republican Party before the Civil War* (New York: Oxford University Press, 1970), pp. 105–9, Margaret Shortreed, "The Antislavery Radicals: From Crusade to Revolution, 1840–1868," *Past and Present*, XVI (November 1959), 72, and Hans L. Trefousse, *The Radical Republicans: Lincoln's Vanguard for Racial Justice* (New York: Alfred A. Knopf, 1969), pp. 5–10, 26, for evidence confirming this similarity.
5 Joshua Giddings to George W. Julian, December 5, 1858, and George Julian to Francis Bird, Robert Carton, F. H. Underwood, April 29, 1853, both in Giddings–Julian Papers, Library of Congress [L.C.]; George Julian to E. A. Stansbury, September 14, 1855, Miscellaneous Manuscripts, L.C.; Israel Washburn to J. L. Stevens, April 27, 1856, Israel Washburn Papers, L.C. Amory Battles as quoted in Gaillard Hunt, *Israel, Elihu, and Cadwallader Washburn: A Chapter in American Biography* (New York: Macmillan, 1925), p. 64. H. L. Trefousse, *Benjamin Franklin Wade: Radical Republican from Ohio* (New

York: Twayne Publishers, 1963), p. 108. Gamaliel Bailey to Thaddeus Stevens, March 8, 1854, Thaddeus Stevens Papers, L.C.; Robert F. Horowitz, *The Great Impeacher: A Political Biography of James M. Ashley* (New York: Brooklyn College Press, 1979), pp. 47–8. Carl Schurz to Gerrit Smith, September 14, 1858, Gerrit Smith Papers, Syracuse University. "Diary and Correspondence of Salmon P. Chase," *Annual Report of the American Historical Association for the Year 1902*, 2 vols. (Washington, D.C.: U.S. Government Printing Office, 1903), 2, pp. 109, 274; S. P. Chase to E. S. Hamlin, November 4, 1854, and to William Seward, March 11, 1858, both in S. P. Chase Papers, L.C.

6   Lewis Tappan to Charles Sumner, June 19, 1860, Charles Sumner Papers, Houghton Library; Edward L. Pierce, *Memoir and Letters of Charles Sumner*, 4 vols. (Boston: Roberts, 1877–93), 3, p. 508 (vol. 1, *1811–1838*; vol. 2, *1838–1845*; vol. 3, *1845–1860*; vol. 4, *1860–1874*; individual volumes are cited as *Memoir and Letters of Sumner* with the volume number); Samuel May, Jr., to R. D. Webb, February 8, 1857, Boston Public Library [B.P.L.]; George W. Julian, *Political Recollections 1840 to 1872* (Chicago: Jansen, McClurs, 1884), p. 23.

7   For a sample of the abundant evidence of radical–immediatist friendships, see Trefousse, *Radical Republicans*, pp. 15–16; Patrick W. Riddleberger, *George Washington Julian Radical Republican: A Study in Nineteenth-Century Politics and Reform* (Indianapolis: Indiana Historical Bureau, 1966), p. 36; Douglas A. Gamble, "Joshua Giddings and the Ohio Abolitionists: A Study in Radical Politics," *Ohio History*, LXXXVIII, no. 1 (winter 1979), 40; James M. Smith, "The 'Separate but Equal' Doctrine: An Abolitionist Discusses Racial Segregation and Educational Policy during the Civil War," *Journal of Negro History*, XLI, no. 2 (April 1956), 146–7; Charles Sumner to Wendell Phillips, September 15, 1852, and William H. Herndon to Wendell Phillips, March 19, 1857, both in Blagden Collection, Houghton Library, Harvard University; S. P. Chase to Gerrit Smith, November 8, 1852 and Smith to Chase, June 8, 1859, S. P. Chase Papers, L.C.; Franklin B. Sanborn to R. W. Emerson, August 3, 1857, Franklin B. Sanborn Papers, L.C.

8   See, e.g., Thomas Wentworth Higginson, *Cheerful Yesterdays* (Boston and New York: Houghton, Mifflin, 1899), p. 237; Richard H. Abbott, *Cobbler in Congress: The Life of Henry Wilson, 1812–1857* (Lexington: University Press of Kentucky, 1972), p. 25; Frank Otto Gatell, *John Gorham Palfrey and the New England Conscience* (Cambridge, Mass.: Harvard University Press, 1963), p. 198; William L. Garrison to George W. Julian, November 10, 1853, Giddings–Julian Papers, L.C.; Henry Wilson to E. A. Stansbury, January 31, 1851, Henry Wilson Papers, L.C.

9   Henry Wright in the *Liberator* (Boston), September 7, 1855; George Julian to Salmon P. Chase, July 22, 1856, S. P. Chase Papers, L.C.

10   Stephen Foster in the *Liberator* (Boston), June 6, 1856; Ann Phillips to Wendell Phillips, December 5 [1855], Blagden Collection, Houghton Library; Samuel J. May to Charles Sumner, July 17, 1860, Charles Sumner Papers, Houghton Library; Minute Book of the Western Anti-Slavery Society (resolution 4 of 1857 annual meeting), unpublished manuscript, L.C.; "Speech of Hon. Henry Wilson" (clipping of speech given before the Massachusetts A.S.S., January 1851), Henry Wilson Papers, L.C.; Charles Sumner to Cornelius C. Fenton, April 9, 1850, Sumner Papers, Houghton Library; William S. Robinson to Wendell Phillips, August 30, 1861, Blagden Collection, Houghton Library; Laura E. Richards, ed., *Letters and Journals of Samuel Gridley Howe*, 2 vols. (Boston: Dana Estes, 1906–9), 2, pp. 405–6. (vol. 1, *The Greek Revolution*; vol. 2, *The Servant of Humanity*).

11   For cogent discussions of this difference between radical and immediatist concepts of "slavery" and "freedom," see Eric Foner, "Abolitionism and the Labor Movement in Antebellum America," in *Anti-Slavery, Religion, and Reform: Essays in Memory of Roger Anstey*, ed. Christine Bolt and Seymour Drescher (Folkestone, England: Dawson, 1980), p. 267; Foner, "The Causes of the American Civil War: Recent Interpretations and New Directions," *Civil War History*, XX, no. 3 (September 1974), 205–9; Abbott,

Cobbler in Congress, pp. 4–5, 263; Shortreed, "Antislavery Radicals," 73. Wilson is quoted in the *Whig* (Boston), May 11, 1847.

12 Wade in the *Congressional Globe*, 33 Cong., 1st sess., appendix, pp. 763–5; *Speech of Hon. Charles Sumner in the Senate of the United States, 19th and 20th May, 1856* (Boston: John P. Jewett, 1856), pp. 40–1; Ashley in Trefousse, *Radical Republicans*, p. 28; Chase and Seward in Russel B. Nye, *Fettered Freedom: Civil Liberties and the Slavery Controversy, 1830–1860* (East Lansing: Michigan State College Press, 1949), pp. 181, 184. Leavitt's contrast of the free labor North with the stagnant South is discussed particularly well in Hugh Houck Davis, "The Reform Career of Joshua Leavitt" (Ph.D. dissertation, Ohio State University, 1969). Edmund Quincy in the *National Anti-Slavery Standard* (New York), October 13, 1855, May 10, July 26, 1856. Garrison as author of the *Annual Report of the American Anti-Slavery Society, 1855* (New York, 1855), p. 70.

13 Quoted in the *Bulletin* (Natick, Mass.), November 5, 1870.

14 Abby K. Foster to Wendell Phillips, March 29, _____, Blagden Collection, Houghton Library, and Foster in Merrill and Ruchames, eds., *Letters of Garrison*, 4, p. 630 *n.* 2. W. H. Furness to Edmund Quincy, December 29, 1851, Quincy Family Papers, Massachusetts Historical Society. Ann Phillips to Wendell Phillips, December 5 [1855], Blagden Collection, Houghton Library.

15 Salmon P. Chase to Wendell Phillips, December 26, 1852, Blagden Collection, Houghton Library; Joshua Giddings to Gamaliel Bailey, November 11, 1855, Giddings–Julian Papers, L.C.; Bailey in Dwight L. Dumond, ed., *Letters of James Gillespie Birney, 1831–1857*, 2 vols. (New York: D. Appleton-Century, 1938), 2, p. 726; William H. Herndon to Wendell Phillips, December 28, 1860, Bladgen Collection, Houghton Library.

16 Frederick J. Blue, *The Free Soilers: Third Party Politics, 1848–54* (Urbana: University of Illinois Press, 1973), pp. 185–6, on Giddings's and Lewis's view of Chase leaving the Ohio Free Soilers. Foster and Phillips in the *Liberator* (Boston), June 6, 1856.

17 James M. Ashley to Salmon P. Chase, October 21, 22, 1855, January 18, 1856, February 17, 1858, S. P. Chase Papers, L.C. Henry Wilson to Charles Sumner, January 19, 1857, Charles Sumner Papers, Houghton Library, revealing radical efforts to make immediatists "keep silent." *Liberator* (Boston), February 20, 1857, reports that Garrison was advised to go public and to respond to the radicals. According to Godfrey T. Anderson, "The Slavery Issue as a Factor in Massachusetts Politics from the Compromise of 1850 to the Outbreak of the Civil War" (Ph.D. dissertation, University of Chicago, 1944), pp. 100–1, 122–8, this tactic helped the radicals stave off even worse defeat in the 1854 Massachusetts election than they incurred. Lydia Child's letter to Trumbull is quoted in Kenneth M. Stampp, *The Imperiled Union: Essays on the Background of the Civil War* (New York: Oxford University Press, 1980), p. 120.

18 William Jay to Joel Doolittle, February 11, 1836, John Jay Collection, Columbia University; Gerrit Smith in the *Model Worker* (Utica), September 22, 1848. Historian Ronald Formisano comments cogently on this antiparty temperament of stewards and voluntarists who supported the Liberty party in "Political Character, Antipartyism and the Second Party System," *American Quarterly*, XXI, no. 5 (winter 1969), 705.

19 Larry Wertheim, "Garrisonian Abolitionists and the Republican Party, 1854–1861," seminar paper (Madison: University of Wisconsin, 1972), pp. 8–9, cogently analyzes this insurgent view of Republicans as erring "children." For specific illustrations, see, e.g., the *National Anti-Slavery Standard* (New York), June 9, 1855 (Stephen Foster), November 15, 1856; Oliver Johnson to Salmon P. Chase, July 9, 1855, S. P. Chase Papers, L.C.

20 Foner, *Free Soil, Free Labor, Free Men*, p. 147, on the radical willingness to bolt the Republican party. Seward and Sumner are quoted in Richard Hofstadter, *The Idea of a Party System: The Rise of a Legitimate Opposition in the United States, 1780–1840* (Berkeley and Los Angeles: University of California Press, 1969), pp. 268–9.

21 Aileen S. Kraditor, *Means and Ends in American Abolitionism: Garrison and His Critics on*

Strategy and Tactics, 1834–1850 (New York: Pantheon Books, 1969). James Brewer Stewart, *Joshua R. Giddings and the Tactics of Radical Politics* (Cleveland: Press of Case Western Reserve University, 1970), p. 228, on Giddings's greater comfort within an established national party. Riddleberger, *George Washington Julian*, p. 25, on Julian's 1844 posture. George W. Julian to T. W. Higginson, October 24, 1857, Giddings–Julian Papers, L.C. Benjamin Wade to Samuel Hendry, December 16, 1838, Joel Blakeselee Papers, Western Reserve Historical Society. Preston King to Jabez D. Hammond, August 11, 1852, Preston King Papers, New York Historical Society. W. G. Weld to Samuel May, Jr., October 24, 1860, B.P.L.

22   Salmon P. Chase to Thaddeus Stevens, April 8, 1842, Thaddeus Stevens Papers, L.C. Chase to _____, July 4, 1852; Chase, "Autobiographical Sketch," June 10, 1853; Chase to [Gerrit Smith], February 15, 1856; all in S. P. Chase Papers, L.C. Chase to Joshua Giddings, January 7, 1857, Joshua Giddings Papers, Ohio Historical Society. Trefousse, *Radical Republicans*, p. 17; Gamble, "Joshua Giddings," p. 48.

23   Blue, *The Free Soilers*, p. 90; Fawn M. Brodie, *Thaddeus Stevens: Scourge of the South* (New York: W. W. Norton, 1966), p. 106; Gamble, "Joshua Giddings," pp. 48–9; Gamaliel Bailey to George Julian, September 7, 1852, George Julian to T. W. Higginson, October 24, 1857, both in Giddings–Julian Papers, L.C.; Benjamin Wade in *New York Tribune*, February 7, 8, 1854; Ernest Paul Muller, "Preston King: A Political Biography" (Ph.D. dissertation, Columbia University, 1957), p. 376; C. S. Seldon in Richard H. Sewell, *Ballots for Freedom: Antislavery Politics in the United States, 1837–1860* (New York: Oxford University Press, 1976), p. 309.

24   Garrison in Sewell, *Ballots*, p. 340. Smith in the *Chronotype* (Boston), September 25, 1858. *Address to the Friends of Liberty, by the Executive Committee of the American and Foreign Antislavery Society* (n.p., n.d. [1848]), p. 4.

25   Chapter 2 on the Boston Clique and Chapter 4 on the Gerrit Smith circle discuss the differing insurgent and voluntarist attitudes on the Constitution and slavery. For a comprehensive study of immediatist and radical constitutional thought, see William M. Wiecek, *The Sources of Antislavery Constitutionalism in America, 1760–1848* (Ithaca, N.Y.: Cornell University Press, 1977).

26   For a few good examples of the considerable number of voluntarist expressions along these lines on nonextension, see William Goodell, *The Kansas Struggle of 1856, in Congress and in the Presidential Campaign, with Suggestions for the Future* (New York: American Abolition Society, 1857); Gerrit Smith to Salmon P. Chase, April 15, 1855, March 1, August 13, 1856, January 26, 1857, S. P. Chase Papers, Historical Society of Pennsylvania; "Address Reported by Gerrit Smith to Jerry Rescue Convention, held in Syracuse, October 1, 1857," broadside (n.p., 1857), Franklin B. Sanborn Papers, L.C. For choice examples of insurgent expressions of this sort against nonextension, see the 1854 to 1856 portions of the Minute Book of the Western Antislavery Society (unpublished), L.C.; W. L. Garrison to Wendell Phillips, August 21, 1848; and T. W. Higginson to Wendell Phillips, March 2, 1853, both in the Blagden Collection, Houghton Library.

27   Pillsbury in the *Sentinel* (Ashtabula, Ohio) September 12, 19, 26, October 3, 1857. William Goodell to William H. Seward, March 17, 1858, William H. Seward Papers, Rush Rhees Library, University of Rochester, and Goodell in M. Leon Perkal, "American Abolition Society: A Viable Alternative to the Republican Party?" *Journal of Negro History*, LXV, no. 1 (winter 1980), 64. John Pierpont to Charles Sumner, June 16, 1860, Charles Sumner Papers, Houghton Library; *Pennsylvania Freeman* (Philadelphia), December 7, 1848.

28   Foner, *Free Soil, Free Labor, Free Men*, p. 282; Foner, "Politics and Prejudice: The Free Soil Party and the Negro, 1849–1852," *Journal of Negro History*, L, no. 4 (October 1965), 249; *Congressional Globe*, 36th Cong., 1st sess., p. 1684; Foner, "Racial Attitudes of the New York Free Soilers," *New York History*, XLVI, no. 4 (October 1965), 316; Riddleberger, *George Washington Julian*, p. 89; Horwitz, *Great Impeacher*, p. 37.

29 For Giddings, see Stampp, *Imperiled Union*, p. 111, Foner, "Politics and Prejudice," p. 242, and the *Congressional Globe*, 35th Congress, 2d sess., p. 346. For Chase, see Foner, *Free Soil, Free Labor, Free Men*, pp. 295-6, and S. P. Chase to John Mercer Langston, November 11, 1850, S. P. Chase Papers, L.C.

30 Muller, "Preston King," pp. 265, 616. Seward in the *Congressional Globe*, 35th Cong., 2nd sess., 1, p. 944. Eugene H. Berwanger, *The Frontier against Slavery: Western Anti-Negro Prejudice and the Slavery Extension Controversy* (Urbana: University of Illinois Press, 1967), p. 133, and *Liberator* (Boston), November 9, 1860, on Owen Lovejoy. Benjamin F. Wade to Mrs. Wade, December 29, 1851, Benjamin Wade Papers, L.C. Stampp, *Imperiled Union*, p. 110 (Trumbull), pp. 111-12 (Wade). Michael F. Holt, *The Political Crisis of the 1850s* (New York: John Wiley, 1978), p. 310 (Williams). *Great Speech of Hon. Lyman Trumbull on the Issues of the Day* (Chicago, 1858), p. 13. Charles Buxton Going, *David Wilmot, Free Soiler* (rpt., Gloucester, Mass.: Peter Smith, 1966), p. 174, and Foner, "Racial Attitudes," p. 317 (Wilmot).

31 David Charles French, "The Conversion of an American Radical: Elizur Wright, Jr., and the Abolitionist Movement" (Ph.D. dissertation, Case Western Reserve University, 1970), p. 139; Wright in the *Observer and Telegraph* (Hudson, Ohio), July 12, August 18, September 6, 13, November 8, 1832; Beriah Green, *Four Sermons, Preached in the Chapel of the Western Reserve College, on Lord's Days, November 18th and 25th, and December 2nd and 9th, 1832* (Cleveland, 1833); Elizur Wright, *The Sin of Slavery and Its Remedy* (New York, 1833); Elizur Wright to Carroll Cutler, June 12, 1876, Elizur Wright, Jr., Papers, L.C.

32 French, "Conversion of American Radical," pp. 192-4, 206; Jane H. Pease and William H. Pease, *Bound with Them in Chains: A Biographical History of the Antislavery Movement* (Westport, Conn.: Greenwood Press, 1972), pp. 224-35; Gilbert Barnes and Dwight L. Dumond, eds., *Letters of Theodore Dwight Weld, Angelina Grimké Weld, and Sarah Grimké, 1822-1844*, 2 vols. (New York and London: D. Appleton-Century, 1934), 1, pp. 95 *n*. 1, 203-4; Elizur Wright to Beriah Green, December 15, 1838, and to Mr. and Mrs. Elizur Wright, Sr., December 5, 1839, both in Elizur Wright, Jr., Papers, L.C.

33 Elizur Wright, Jr., to Beriah Green, October 10, 1839, Elizur Wright, Jr., Typescripts, B.P.L.; Wright to Gerrit Smith, March 20, 1840, Gerrit Smith Papers, Syracuse University; Edmund Quincy to R. D. Webb, June 27, 1843, Edmund Quincy Papers, Massachusetts Historical Society.

34 *Chronotype* (Boston), May 28, 1846; February 1, April 26, June 1, 26, September 20, 23, 1848; Pease and Pease, *Bound with Them in Chains*, pp. 237, 241; Philip Green Wright and Elizabeth Q. Wright, *Elizur Wright: The Father of Life Insurance* (Chicago: University of Chicago Press, 1937), pp. 184-5; Reinhard O. Johnson, "The Liberty Party in New England, 1840-48: The Forgotten Abolitionists" (Ph.D. dissertation, Syracuse University, 1976), chap. 2.

35 Frank Preston Stearns, *Cambridge Sketches* (rept., Freeport, N.Y.: Books for Libraries Press, 1968), pp. 166, 295-6, 301; P. and E. Wright, *Elizur Wright*, pp. 200, 278.

36 *Francis William Bird, A Biographical Sketch, by His Children* (Boston: Norwood Press, 1897), pp. 32-4, 37; Stearns, *Cambridge Sketches*, pp. 172-3, 219; Francis W. Bird to Charles Sumner, April 17, 1859, Charles Sumner Papers, Houghton Library; Richard H. Abbott, "Massachusetts: Maintaining Hegemony," in *Radical Republicans in the North: State Politics during Reconstruction*, ed. James C. Mohr (Baltimore, Md.: Johns Hopkins University Press, 1976), p. 4, Montgomery, *Beyond Equality*, pp. 120-1.

37 See Abbott, "Massachusetts," pp. 2-17; Foner, *Free Soil, Free Labor, Free Men*, p. 243, and information dispersed throughout Kinley Brauer, *Cotton versus Conscience: Massachusetts Whig Politics and Southwestern Expansion, 1843-1848* (Lexington: University of Kentucky Press, 1967).

38 *Commonwealth* (Boston), May 9, 1851, November 2, 1867; Merrill and Ruchames, eds., *Letters of Garrison*, 5, pp. 469-70 *n*. 1; James W. Stone to John Andrew, February 25, 1861, and George L. Stearns to John Andrew, n.d. [1863], John Andrew Papers,

Massachusetts Historical Society; Samuel G. Howe to Theodore Parker, May 17, 1859, Howe–Sumner Correspondence, Houghton Library; Francis Bird to Lydia M. Child, May 29, 1863, B.P.L.; Abbott, "Massachusetts," p. 4.

39 Bird in *Proceedings of the State Disunion Convention* (Boston, 1857), pp. 6–11; Francis Bird to Charles Sumner, February 14, September 14, 1858, June 8, 1859, January 20, 1860, February 17, 1861, all in the Charles Sumner Papers, Houghton Library; Samuel G. Howe to Moncure Conway, September 13, 1859, Samuel Gridley Howe Papers, Massachusetts Historical Society; Samuel G. Howe to Charles Sumner, November 6, 1858, to Theodore Parker, February 27, 1860, to Francis Bird, January 30 [1861], all in Howe–Sumner Correspondence, Houghton Library.

40 Samuel G. Howe to Charles Sumner, June 19, 1859, Howe–Sumner Correspondence, Houghton Library; *Francis William Bird*, p. 36; Francis Bird to John Andrew, January 31, 1861, and Charles Sumner to John Andrew, January 8, 1861, both in the John Andrew Papers, Massachusetts Historical Society. Charles Slack in the *Commonwealth* (Boston), August 11, 1866.

41 *Francis William Bird*, p. 34; *"Warrington" Pen Portraits: A Collection of Personal and Political Reminiscences from 1848 to 1876, from the Writings of William S. Robinson* (Boston: Mrs. W. S. Robinson, 1877), p. 497; James W. Stone to Charles Sumner, March 23, 1859, Charles Sumner Papers, Houghton Library; P. and E. Wright, *Elizur Wright*, pp. 278–9; Elizur Wright to Charles Sumner, January 19, August 11, 1860, Sumner Papers, Houghton Library; Elizur Wright to Nathaniel P. Banks, n.d. [January 3, 1861], Elizur Wright, Jr., Papers, L.C.

42 Elizur Wright to Dr. Gregory, February 10, 1851, B.P.L. Richards, ed., *S. G. Howe*, 2, p. 331, reports on Wright's contemplated subeditorial role on the *Commonwealth* (Boston). Wright in the *Chronotype* (Boston), January 1, 1851, characterizing his contemplated role on the *Commonwealth*. Richards, ed., *S. G. Howe*, 2, pp. 340–1, quotes Howe in February 1851 on Wright's damage to Sumner. Harold Schwartz, *Samuel Gridley Howe, Social Reformer, 1801–1876* (Cambridge, Mass.: Harvard University Press, 1956), pp. 177–9; Elizur Wright to "Brother and Sister," July 23, 1851, Elizur Wright Transcripts, B.P.L.; Samuel E. Sewall to Elizur Wright, May 13, 1852, E. Wright Papers, L.C.

43 See Brauer, *Cotton versus Conscience*, p. 145, and Martin B. Duberman, *Charles Francis Adams, 1807–1886* (Boston: Houghton Mifflin, 1961), p. 108, for Wright's role in the Texas annexation crisis and perceptions of his role. Pease and Pease, *Bound with Them in Chains*, p. 241, on Wright running for state representative in 1849 and 1850. See P. and E. Wright, *Elizur Wright*, p. 211, and Charles Francis Adams, *Richard Henry Dana: A Biography* (Boston and New York: Houghton Mifflin, 1891), 1, p. 222, on the "Shadrach" case. Henry Wilson, *History of the Rise and Fall of the Slave Power in America* (Boston and New York: Houghton Mifflin, 1872), 1, p. 259 provides a good example of how Bird Club members had come to characterize Wright.

44 Elizur Wright to Beriah Green, October 8, November 3, 1860, Wright to _____, October 12, 1860, both in E. Wright Papers, L.C.; Pease and Pease, *Bound with Them in Chains*, p. 241. See also Wright in the *Chronotype* (Boston), October 16, 1848, justifying support for Van Buren over Gerrit Smith and in the *Chronotype*, January 3, 1850, criticizing Wendell Phillips for ineffective antislavery activity.

45 Wright in the *Commonwealth* (Boston), May 28, 1851; Elizur Wright to _____, June 14, 1860, Friends Historical Library, Swarthmore College.

46 Elizur Wright to Charles Scribner, May 19, 1854, Elizur Wright Typescripts, B.P.L.

CHAPTER 9. A TROUBLED JUBILEE

1 May, Jr., in *National Anti-Slavery Standard* (New York), April 22, 1865; William Lloyd Garrison to Helen Garrison, April 7, 1865, Boston Public Library [B.P.L.]. See also Edwin M. Stanton to William Lloyd Garrison, September 18, 1865, B.P.L.

2   Carlos Martyn, *Wendell Phillips: The Agitator*, rev. ed. (London and New York: Funk and Wagnalls, 1890), p. 340.

3   James M. McPherson, *The Abolitionist Legacy: From Reconstruction to the NAACP* (Princeton, N.J.: Princeton University Press, 1975), pp. 396–405, conveniently lists birth and death dates. Perceptions of aging by romantic writers are cogently analyzed in W. Andrew Achenbaum, *Old Age in the New Land: The American Experience since 1790* (Baltimore, Md.: Johns Hopkins University Press, 1978), pp. 33–7.

4   See, e.g., Alma Lutz, *Crusade for Freedom: Women of the Antislavery Movement* (Boston: Beacon Press, 1968), p. 268; Parker Pillsbury to George B. Cheever, April 26, 1864, Cheever Family Papers, American Antiquarian Society [A.A.S.]; Samuel May, Jr., to R. D. Webb, November 7, 1858, B.P.L.; *Albany Patriot*, February 9, 1848 (Goodell); Lewis Tappan to William Jay, July 26, 1857, Letterbook, Lewis Tappan Papers, Library of Congress [L.C.]; *Sentinel* (Ashtabula, Ohio), November 13, 1854 (Smith).

5   John Greenleaf Whittier, *The Conflict with Slavery: Politics and Reform: The Inner Life Criticism* (Boston and New York: Houghton Mifflin, 1889), p. 146; Parker Pillsbury to Samuel May, Jr., October 25, 1859, B.P.L.; Samuel May, Jr., to R. D. Webb, November 6, 1860, to Charles C. Burleigh, September 20, 1857, B.P.L.

6   Oliver Johnson to Wendell Philips, August 10, 1860, Blagden Collection, Houghton Library, Harvard University; Oliver Johnson to Samuel May, Jr., August 18, 1860, B.P.L.; Leavitt in Dwight L. Dumond, ed., *Letters of James Gillespie Birney, 1831–1857*, 2 vols. (New York: D. Appleton-Century, 1938), 2, p. 1172.

7   Maria Weston Chapman to Samuel E. Sewall, August 9, 1857, Robie–Sewall Papers, Massachusetts Historical Society. James Miller McKim to R. D. Webb, February 1, 1862, B.P.L., offers an observation much like Chapman's.

8   Oliver Johnson to Wendell Phillips, February 8, August 10, 1860, Blagden Collection, Houghton Library, on Lewis Tappan and Cheever. James M. McPherson, *The Struggle for Equality: Abolitionists and the Negro in the Civil War and Reconstruction* (Princeton, N.J.: Princeton University Press, 1964), p. 106 (on Cheever and Weld); W. L. Garrison to Oliver Johnson, May 5, 1863, B.P.L.; Robert M. York, "George B. Cheever, Religious and Social Reformer 1807–1890," *University of Maine Bulletin*, LVII, no. 12 (April 1, 1955), 157, on Cheever. Walter M. Merrill and Louis Ruchames, eds., *The Letters of William Lloyd Garrison*, 6 vols. (Cambridge, Mass.: Harvard University Press, Belknap Press, 1971–81), 4, p. 233 n. 5, on Stanton (vol. 1, *I Will Be Heard! 1822–1835*; vol. 2, *A House Dividing against Itself, 1836–1840*; vol. 3, *No Union with Slaveholders, 1841–1849*; vol. 4, *From Disunionism to the Brink of War, 1850–1860*; vol. 5, *Let the Oppressed Go Free, 1861–1867*; vol. 6, *To Rouse the Slumbering Land, 1868–1879*; individual volumes are cited as *Letters of Garrison* with the volume number). Henry C. Wright to Gerrit Smith, January 13, 1862, Gerrit Smith Papers, Syracuse University, and William L. Garrison to J. M. Forbes, March 22, 1864, Garrison Papers, Massachusetts Historical Society (on Smith). Wendell Phillips Garrison and Francis Jackson Garrison, *William Lloyd Garrison, 1805–1879*, 4 vols. (New York: Century, 1885–9), 3, pp. 329–30, and 4, p. 37 (on Goodell); 4, p. 88, on the mending of the Garrison–Tappan relationship (vol. 1, *1805–1835*; vol. 2, *1835–1840*; vol. 3, *1841–1860*; vol. 4, *1861–1879*; individual volumes are cited as *Garrison* with the volume number).

9   Martyn, *Phillips*, p. 472, on Phillips's donations. Garrison and Garrison, *Garrison*, 4, pp. 251–2, on the Samuel J. May donation. Luther Rawson Marsh to Anna H. Weld, June 17, 1892, August 1892, Weld–Grimké Papers, Clements Library, University of Michigan; William Jay to Wendell Phillips, February 28, 1853, Blagden Collection, Houghton Library; Garrison and Garrison, *Garrison*, 4, p. 257, on immediatists urging Garrison to pen his autobiography; see also Oliver Johnson to W. L. Garrison, November 21, 1859, B.P.L.

10 Joshua Leavitt to Salmon P. Chase, November 7, 1860, Salmon P. Chase Papers, L.C.; Garrison in Merrill and Ruchames, eds., *Letters of Garrison*, 4, p. 698; James M. McPherson, "The Ballot and Land for the Freedmen, 1861–1865," in *Reconstruction: An Anthol-*

ogy of Revisionist Writings, ed. Kenneth Stampp and Leon Litwack (Baton Rouge: Louisiana State University Press, 1969), p. 142, on Goodell's call for land redistribution; John G. Whittier to Charles Sumner, November 1, 1862, Charles Sumner Papers, Houghton Library; William L. Garrison to Gerrit Smith, September 5, 1861, Gerrit Smith Papers, Syracuse University.

11 Wendell Phillips, *Speeches, Lectures, and Letters* (Boston, 1863), p. 376; Jocelyn in Lewis Tappan, *The Life of Arthur Tappan* (New York: Hurd and Houghton, 1870), p. 224; Mary Grew in *Twenty-Eighth Annual Report of the Philadelphia Female Anti-Slavery Society* (Philadelphia, 1862), pp. 18–19; Lydia Child to Gerrit Smith, January 7, 1862, Smith Papers, Syracuse University.

12 Maria W. Chapman to W. L. Garrison, n.d. [fall 1861], to J. Miller McKim, November 2 [1861], to E. B. Chapman, February 16, 1862, to Mary [Estlin], February 20, [1862], all in B.P.L. McKim as quoted in *National Anti-Slavery Standard* (New York), May 3, 1862. J. Miller McKim to Edmund Quincy, January 1, 1862, Edmund Quincy Papers, Massachusetts Historical Society. Garrison in the *Liberator* (Boston), May 10, 1862. S. S. Foster to Wendell Phillips, November 3, 1861, Blagden Collection, Houghton Library. Edmund Quincy to R. D. Webb, November 22, 1863, Quincy–Webb Correspondence, B.P.L. Irving H. Bartlett, *Wendell Phillips: Brahmin Radical* (Boston: Beacon Press, 1961), p. 287.

13 *Proceedings of the American Anti-Slavery Society, at its Third Decade, Held in the City of Philadelphia, December 3d and 4th, 1863* (New York: American Anti-Slavery Society, 1864), p. 3, prints Garrison's circular letter of invitation.

14 *Proceedings of A.A.S.S., at Third Decade, 1863*, p. 34 (McKim), pp. 90–2 (Foss), p. 146 (Thurston); p. 130 (Grew), pp. 40–1 (Samuel J. May).

15 *Proceedings of A.A.S.S., at Third Decade, 1863*, pp. 5, 7, 27.

16 McPherson, *Struggle for Equality*, pp. 287–8; *Liberator* (Boston), February 6, 1863; January 8, 1864; *National Anti-Slavery Standard* (New York), December 26, 1863; *Proceedings of A.A.S.S., at Third Decade, 1863*, pp. 73, 111–12.

17 *Proceedings of A.A.S.S., at Third Decade, 1863*, pp. 80–2.

18 Merrill and Ruchames, eds., *Letters of Garrison*, 5, p. 147.

19 *Liberator* (Boston), February 3, 1865; McPherson, *Struggle for Equality*, p. 305; Russel B. Nye, *William Lloyd Garrison and the Humanitarian Reformers* (Boston: Little, Brown, 1955), p. 187; Walter M. Merrill, *Against Wind and Tide: A Biography of William Lloyd Garrison* (Cambridge, Mass.: Harvard University Press, 1963), p. 437.

20 *Liberator* (Boston), February 17, March 24, May 19, 26, December 22, 29, 1865; Oliver Johnson, *William Lloyd Garrison and His Times* (Boston: B. B. Russell, 1880), p. 388; Garrison and Garrison, *Garrison*, 4, p. 126; Merrill and Ruchames, eds., *Letters of Garrison*, 5, p. 282; Bartlett, *Phillips*, p. 286.

21 *Liberator* (Boston), December 29, 1865 (Samuel J. May and Marius Robinson); Benjamin P. Thomas, *Theodore Weld: Crusader for Freedom* (New Brunswick, N.J.: Rutgers University Press, 1950), p. 255; Lewis Tappan, *Arthur Tappan*, p. 378; Lewis Tappan to Gerrit Smith, October 3, 1864, Gerrit Smith Papers, Syracuse University; *Liberator* (Boston), February 3, December 29, 1865 (Henry Wright), and Lewis Perry, *Childhood, Marriage, and Reform: Henry Clarke Wright, 1797–1870* (Chicago: University of Chicago Press, 1980), p. 59.

22 Johnson, *Garrison*, pp. 388–9; *Liberator* (Boston), November 24, December 1, 22, 29, 1865; *National Anti-Slavery Standard* (New York), April 22, May 6, 1865, February 3, 1866; *New York Times*, May 15, 1865 (Quincy); Oliver Johnson to Maria W. Chapman, May 4, 1865, B.P.L.

23 For Wendell Phillips's evolving position on restructuring Southern power relations, see the *National Anti-Slavery Standard* (New York), February 13, May 14, 21, June 18, 1864, June 3, 1865. See also Robert D. Marcus, "Wendell Phillips and American Institutions," *Journal of American History*, LVI, no. 1 (June 1969), 52–3.

24 *Liberator* (Boston), February 10, 1865.

25 For Phillips's full delineation of his antidissolution position, see the *National Anti-Slavery Standard* (New York), May 13, August 11, October 21, November 4, 1865 and the *Liberator* (Boston), April 28, 1865. See also Edmund Quincy to R. D. Webb, October 16, 1865, Quincy–Webb Correspondence, B.P.L., for a perceptive analysis of Phillips's motivations.

26 *Liberator* (Boston), June 9, 1865 (Cheever); January 27, February 3, 1865 (Foster). For Pillsbury see the *Liberator* (Boston), June 2, 1865; *National Anti-Slavery Standard* (New York), November 4, 1865; McPherson, *Struggle for Equality*, p. 306; and Parker Pillsbury to Wendell Phillips, February 15, 1865, Blagden Collection, Houghton Library. Smith in the *Liberator* (Boston), September 22, 1865, the *National Anti-Slavery Standard* (New York), January 13, 1866; "Gerrit Smith to General Ashley, Februry 6, 1865" (n.p., 1865), and "Gerrit Smith to Senator Sumner, February 5, 1866" (n.p., 1866), both broadsides in Gerrit Smith Papers, Syracuse University.

27 For an example of Garrison's strong pro–Negro suffrage position, see his editorial in the *Liberator* (Boston), July 14, 1865. Quincy in the *National Anti-Slavery Standard* (New York), April 1, 1865, and Sewall in the *Liberator* (Boston), December 29, 1865.

28 *National Anti-Slavery Standard* (New York), February 3, 1866, reports Garrison's remark at the Massachusetts Anti-Slavery Society meeting. Anne Weston to Mary Estlin, October 17, 1866, B.P.L. *National Anti-Slavery Standard* (New York), February 2, 1867 (Stephen Foster), June 15, 1867 (Abigail Kelley Foster), June 2, 1866 (Pillsbury).

29 Merrill and Ruchames, eds., *Letters of Garrison*, 5, p. 440; Garrison to Samuel May, Jr., January 24, May 7, 1867, B.P.L.; Merrill, *Against Wind and Tide*, pp. 315–16; Martyn, *Phillips*, pp. 357–8; *National Anti-Slavery Standard* (New York), August 10, 24, September 7, 1867; Bartlett, *Phillips*, p. 292; McPherson, *Struggle for Equality*, p. 401; *Commonwealth* (Boston), September 7, 1867; Mary Grew to Wendell Phillips, July 23, 1867, Blagden Collection, Houghton Library.

30 McPherson, *Struggle for Equality*, p. 430; *National Anti-Slavery Standard* (New York), May 15, 1869; March 5, April 16, 1870. To be sure, the National Reform League claimed to be a successor to the A.A.S.S., but it did little and dissolved in 1872.

31 *National Anti-Slavery Standard* (New York), February 3, 1866, December 5, 1868, May 11, 22, June 5, 1869, April 16, 1870; Parker Pillsbury, *Acts of the Anti-Slavery Apostles* (Concord, N.H., 1883), pp. 501–2; Stephen Foster to George Thompson, January 15, 1870, Kelley–Foster Papers, American Antiquarian Society; Abigail Kelley Foster to Gerrit Smith, April 19, 1869, Smith Papers, Syracuse University; Jane H. Pease, "The Freshness of Fanaticism: Abby Kelley Foster: An Essay in Reform" (Ph.D. dissertation, University of Rochester, 1969), p. 238; James M. McPherson, "Abolitionists, Woman Suffrage, and the Negro, 1865–1869," *Mid-America*, XLVII, no. 1 (January 1965), 40–1; Jane H. Pease and William H. Pease, *Bound with Them in Chains: A Biographical History of the Antislavery Movement* (Westport, Conn.: Greenwoood Press, 1972), p. 216. Stephen Foster and especially Pillsbury also opposed A.A.S.S. dissolution because they believed that the organization could be used to fight for woman suffrage.

32 *Commonwealth* (Boston), February 5, April 30, 1870; *National Anti-Slavery Standard* (New York), February 20, May 22, June 5, 1869; January 29, April 16, 1870; McPherson, *Struggle for Equality*, pp. 378, 427–8; Martyn, *Phillips*, pp. 370–2; Bartlett, *Phillips*, p. 315.

33 Richard O. Curry, "The Abolitionists and Reconstruction: A Critical Appraisal," *Journal of Southern History*, XXXIV, no. 4 (November 1968), 543.

34 See, e.g., *National Anti-Slavery Standard* (New York), May 29, December 4, 25, 1869; April 2, 16, July 30, 1870; *Thirty-Sixth and Final Annual Report of the Philadelphia Female Anti-Slavery Society* (Philadelphia, 1870), pp. 3, 28, 33; McPherson, *Struggle for Equality*, p. 427.

35 Stephen and Abigail Kelley Foster's accusations are noted in Merrill, *Against Wind and Tide*, p. 433, and in Bartlett, *Phillips*, p. 285. Lydia and David Child as quoted in *National Anti-Slavery Standard* (New York), April 16, 1870.

36 McPherson, *Struggle for Equality*, p. 401 *n.* 28, on the general easing of bitterness among

immediatists during the 1870s. Wendell Phillips to W. L. Garrison, October (?), November (?), 1870, B.P.L. Johnson, *Garrison*, pp. x–xi, quotes Whittier. Pillsbury, *Acts*, p. 495.

37   Quoted in *Chicago Tribune*, June 10, 1874.

38   Larry Gara, "A Glorious Time: The 1874 Abolitionist Reunion in Chicago," *Journal of the Illinois State Historical Society*, LXV, no. 3 (autumn 1972), 282–4, 287; *Chicago Tribune*, June 10, 1874. A printed invitation to this Chicago reunion is found in the Zebina Eastman Papers, Chicago Historical Society.

39   *Chicago Tribune*, June 11, 1874 (Douglass and Whittier letters); June 13, 1874 (Stebbins's remark); June 11, 1874 (letters by Whittier and Amos Dresser stressing physical intimacy of immediatists).

40   *Chicago Tribune*, June 10, 1874; Gara, "Glorious Time," 287.

41   *Chicago Tribune*, June 12, 13, 1874; Gara, "Glorious Time," 290–1.

42   *Chicago Tribune*, June 10, 1874 (Garrison), June 13, 1874 (Fee and Walker); Merton L. Dillon, "The Abolitionists as a Dissenting Minority," in *Dissent: Explorations in the History of American Radicalism*, ed. Alfred F. Young (DeKalb: Northern Illinois University Press, 1968), pp. 103–4 (Dresser); Sallie Holley to Zebina Eastman, June 8, 1874, Zebina Eastman Papers, Chicago Historical Society.

43   James C. Klotter, "The Black South and White Appalachia," *Journal of American History*, LXVI, no. 4 (March 1980), 832–49, sensitively demonstrates a shift in the focus of the missionary reform impulse beginning in the 1870s from Southern blacks toward Appalachian whites. Klotter finds several old immediatists encouraging this shift.

BIBLIOGRAPHICAL NOTE

There is no shortage of comprehensive and detailed bibliographies covering abolitionist historiography and primary documents. Consequently, no more than a short commentary on the materials that were most essential to the construction of *Gregarious Saints* is required.

Most certainly a number of somewhat dated studies of the abolitionists continue to be valuable. Gilbert Hobbs Barnes's volume, *The Anti-Slavery Impulse, 1830–1844* (1933), remains, for example, the best study of the evangelical missionary underpinnings of immediatist social psychology. Similarly, sensitive biographies like Irving Bartlett's *Wendell Phillips: Brahmin Radical* (1961) and John Thomas's *The Liberator: William Lloyd Garrison* (1963) continue to serve as effective reminders that immediatist character was both convivial and devout. This is not to belittle the importance of more recent works. David Davis's *The Problem of Slavery* volumes (1966, 1975) brilliantly cast antislavery thought within the context of broader social and intellectual developments in Western culture. Lewis Perry's *Radical Abolitionism: Anarchy and the Government of God in Antislavery Thought* (1973) is a remarkably probing exploration of immediatist ideas. Ronald Walters's *The Antislavery Appeal: American Abolitionism after 1830* (1976) skillfully and creatively delineates the cultural features of the immediatist crusade. Finally, Peter Walker's *Moral Choices: Memory, Desire, and Imagination in Nineteenth-Century American Abolition* (1978) uses autobiography in unusually imaginative ways to illustrate the interplay between individual personality, ideas, and culture.

Many old abolitionist manuscript collections in the major archives of the Northeast and the Midwest have served generations of historians. But two relatively recent archival developments are noteworthy. In 1974 the Microfilming Corporation of America completed transforming the massive Gerrit Smith Collection of 1,000 volumes and 61,500 pieces into seventy-seven reels of microfilm. M.C.A. added a precise eighty-one-page index revealing the contents of each reel. Consequently the enormous number of letters to Smith from immediatists of every sort have become available to scholars at a relatively low cost. Long and expensive trips to Syracuse University to study the original letters are no longer necessary. The availability of the Crawford Blagden Collection at Harvard's Houghton Library represents an even more significant archival development. Early in 1977 Wendell Phillips's great-great-nephew, Crawford Blagden, opened a forgotten crate of papers in the basement of his home in Tuxedo Park. His discovery was the most important in abolitionist studies since Gilbert Barnes uncovered a trunk full of Theodore Weld's correspondence in a farmhouse near Allston, Massachusetts, almost half a century ago. Blagden found about 7,000 items. In the main, these were letters to Wendell Phillips from about 1,500 correspondents. Concentrating on the 1855–75 period, the letters came from the obscure as well as the prominent within the abolitionist ranks. Predictably, a preponderance of the letters were written by Wendell Phillips's New England insurgent colleagues.

My first chapter, "Young Missionaries," benefited enormously from Gilbert Barnes's work. It also profited from thoughtful general scholarship on the social and cultural dimensions of missionary endeavor. David Heise's "Prefatory Findings in the Sociology of Missions," *Journal of the Scientific Study of Religion,* VI (1967), 49–58, and Elmer Miller's "The Christian Missionary: Agent of Secularization," *Missiology,* I (1973), 99–107, were particularly useful. Moreover, there is value in reviewing the rich scholarship concerning New England Puritan missions to the Indians. Francis Jennings's "Goals and Functions of Puritan Missions to the Indians," *Ethnohistory,* XVIII (1971), 197–212, and Neal Salisbury's "Red Puritans: The 'Praying Indians' of Massachusetts Bay and John Eliot," *William and Mary Quarterly,* XXXI (1974), 27–54 are especially insightful. But three brilliant studies of nineteenth-century American missionary activity make it abundantly clear that abolitionists must be understood within the context of a larger evangelical missionary social-cultural nexus: *Salvation and the Savage: An Analysis of Protestant Missions and American Indian Response, 1787–1862* (1965), by Robert Berkhofer, Jr.; Paul Boyer's *Urban Masses and Moral Order in America, 1820–1920* (1978); and Bertram Wyatt-Brown's "The Missionary Impulse in the Old Republic: The Psychology of Commitment to a Noble Cause," in his soon to be published *Yankee Saints and Southern Sinners.* Finally, Donald Scott's *From Office to Profession: The New England Ministry, 1750–1850* (1978) is most useful in understanding the relationship between young men's clerical training and their embrace of immediatism.

Chapter 2 on the Boston Clique was, of course, largely constructed from the *Liberator,* the *National Anti-Slavery Standard,* and especially letters in the old Garrison collection at the Boston Public Library. Two bound volumes in that collection containing the Edmund Quincy–Richard Davis Webb correspondence are particularly valuable. Week after week, Quincy related to Webb all sorts of confidential information concerning Clique successes, reverses, and internal bickering. The Boston Public Library papers are nicely supplemented by the new Blagden Collection at the Houghton Library. Drawing on the Blagden Papers, Irving Bartlett published a most instructive essay, "New Light on Wendell Phillips: The Community of Reform, 1840–1880," *Perspectives in American History,* XII (1979), 1–57. Lewis Perry's subtle and fascinating biography, *Childhood, Marriage, and Reform: Henry Clarke Wright, 1797–1870* (1980) offers important insights into the more eccentric, unpredictable side of Boston Clique existence. The more structured, genteel side is sensitively characterized in Robert Sparks's dissertation, "Abolition in Silver Slippers: A Biography of Edmund Quincy" (Boston College, 1978). James Stewart's short essay, "Garrison Again, and Again, and Again, and Again . . . ," *Reviews in American History,* IV (1976), 539–45, is probably the most sophisticated assessment of Garrison's complex and dynamic leadership qualities. Still, it was owing to Aileen Kraditor's ground-breaking study, *Means and Ends in American Abolitionism: Garrison and His Critics on Strategy and Tactics, 1834–1850* (1969) that historians became aware of the political skills of Garrison and other Clique insurgents. Finally, in "Explosive Intimacy: Psychodynamics of the Victorian Family," *History of Childhood Quarterly,* I (1974), 437–61, Stephen Kern outlines ways in which the very closeness of the members of a small group can become basic sources of collective discontent. The relevance of Kern's insight to the evolution of the Boston Clique is apparent.

Chapter 4 concerned steward immediatism and centered on Lewis Tappan's intimacy circle. Betram Wyatt-Brown's *Lewis Tappan and the Evangelical War against Slavery* (1969) remains the principal point of departure for investigation of the topic. It is the single most provocative analysis of steward personality and culture. Ian Bradley helps to locate this personality within an Anglo-American context in his important volume, *The Call to Seriousness: The Evangelical Impact on the Victorians* (1976). Although Theodore Weld was hardly a typical Tappan circle steward, one can also learn a great deal from Robert Abzug's sensitive volume, *Passionate Liberator: Theodore Dwight Weld and the Dilemma of Reform* (1980). While the Lewis Tappan Papers in the Library of Congress and the Weld-Grimké Papers at the Clements Library remain the most useful collections on the Tappan circle, the rich American Missionary Association Archives of the Amistad Research Center at Dillard University must not be neglected. The A.M.A. Papers are now available on microfilm.

Voluntarist immediatism revolving around the Gerrit Smith circle in central New York was the topic of Chapter 4. The vast Smith Collection at Syracuse University was, of course, my principal source. But the value of upstate voluntarist newspapers such as the *Liberty Press* (Utica), the *Albany Patriot*, the *Rochester Freeman*, and the *Friend of Man* (Utica) cannot be underestimated. Alan Kraut's dissertation, "The Liberty Men of New York: Political Abolitionism in New York State, 1840–1848" (Cornell University, 1975) represents an exceedingly thorough study of upstate New Yorkers who voted for the Liberty party. Moreover, it contains much useful detail on abolitionism in Madison County, where Gerrit Smith lived. But Mary Ryan's *Cradle of the Middle Class: The Family in Oneida County, New York, 1790–1865* (1981) is the richest and most sophisticated analysis of any upstate county where the Smith men were active. Unfortunately, we lack adequate biographies of the men in the Smith circle. Ralph Harlow's *Gerrit Smith, Philanthropist and Reformer* (1939) is tarnished by the simplistic if not irrelevant characterization of immediatists as impractical moralists. With additional research and historiographical updating, M. Leon Perkal's dissertation, "William Goodell: A Life of Reform" (City University of New York, 1972) could become a fine publication. Not even a promising beginning can be reported on full-scale biographies of the other men of the Smith circle. But Gerald Sorin's important volume, *The New York Abolitionists: A Case Study of Political Radicalism* (1971) affords reliable biographical data about them as well as about several of their upstate associates.

Because of a paucity of appropriate scholarship, Chapter 5 on gender relationships within immediatism was most difficult to organize. To be sure, a number of helpful studies of female abolitionists have been published in recent years. Three are particularly useful: Blanche Hersh, *The Slavery of Sex: Feminist-Abolitionists in America* (1978); Ellen DuBois, *Feminism and Suffrage: The Emergence of an Independent Women's Movement in America, 1848–1869* (1978); and Keith Melder, *Beginnings of Sisterhood: The American Woman's Rights Movement, 1800–1850* (1977). Yet there is no systematic general analysis of relationships between male and female immediatists. Case studies of abolitionist marriages can provide the building blocks for such a general analysis, as excellent studies of three marriages make abundantly clear: Kirk Jeffrey, "Marriage, Career, and Feminine Ideology in Nineteenth-Century America: Reconstructing the Marital Experience of Lydia Maria Child, 1828–1874," *Feminist Studies*, II (1975), 113–30; Katherine Lumpkin, *The Emancipation of Angelina Grimké* (1974) on the Weld–Grimké relationship; and Jane Pease, "The Freshness of Fanaticism: Abby Kelley Foster: An Essay in Reform" (Ph.D. dissertation, University of Rochester, 1969) concerning the Stephen Foster–Abby Kelley marriage.

Unlike gender relationships among immediatists, there is no paucity of literature on race relations within the crusade. Benjamin Quarles's numerous books and articles on the topic merit close examination. So do several publications by Jane and William Pease, particularly "Anti-slavery Ambivalence: Immediatism, Expediency, Race," *American Quarterly*, XVII (1965), 682–95, and "Ends, Means, and Attitudes: Black–White Conflict in the Antislavery Movement," *Civil War History*, XVIII (1972), 117–28. James and Lois Horton's *Black Bostonians: Family Life and Community Struggle in the Antebellum North* (1979) is a remarkably thorough study of the changing social context within which black immediatists labored. Finally, it is important to consult two broad but contrasting studies of the deepening racism in national culture that white immediatists reflected. George Fredrickson's *The Black Image in the White Mind: The Debate on Afro-American Character and Destiny, 1817–1914* (1971) is a comprehensive intellectual history that underscores the varieties of white racism. Ronald Takaki's *Iron Cages: Race and Culture in Nineteenth-Century America* (1979) represents an effective fusion of Marxian and Freudian assumptions; it emphasizes the fundamental similarities in white racial prespectives.

There is also an abundance of literature concerning the immediatist shift from pacifism to righteous violence (Chapter 7). Carleton Mabee's *Black Freedom: The Nonviolent Abolitionists from 1830 through the Civil War* (1970) is filled with useful data. It is also profitable to consult Merton Dillon's excellent *Elijah P. Lovejoy, Abolitionist Editor* (1961), and Stephen Oates's fascinating volume, *To Purge This Land with Blood: A Biography of John Brown* (1970).

Probing analyses of the general turn to violence are to be found in John Demos, "The Antislavery Movement and the Problem of Violent 'Means,'" *New England Quarterly*, XXXVII (1964), 501–26; Jane and William Pease, "Confrontation and Abolition in the 1850s," *Journal of American History*, LVIII (1972), 923–37; and Bertram Wyatt-Brown, "The Abolitionist Controversy: Men of Blood, Men of God," in *Men, Women, and Issues in American History*, ed. Howard Quint and Milton Cantor, 2 vols. (1975), 1, pp. 215–33. In "Violence and John Brown," *Journal of Social Philosophy*, V (1974), 9–12, Richard King provides a skillful critique of the philosophic justifications for Brown's use of righteous violence. Much can also be learned about the general social psychology of the immediatists' acceptance of violence from Herbert Kelman, "Violence without Moral Restraint: Reflections on the Dehumanization of Victims and Victimizers," in *Varieties of Psychohistory*, ed. George Kren and Leon Rappoport (1976), pp. 282–314. Most important of all, Heinz Kohut's *The Analysis of the Self* (1971) and *The Restoration of the Self* (1977) allow one to understand connections between a depreciated sense of self-worth and aggressive words and deeds.

Despite the frequency and importance of immediatist contacts with radical Republicans, there was surprisingly little background literature on this specific topic to help me with Chapter 8. In *The Radical Republicans: Lincoln's Vanguard for Racial Justice* (1969), Hans Trefousse offers some useful contrasts between radicals and insurgent immediatists but does not extend his comparison to stewards and voluntarists. Similarly, Eric Foner's brilliant *Free Soil, Free Labor, Free Men: The Ideology of the Republican Party before the Civil War* (1970) offers bits of useful data and some provocative insights concerning the general immediatist–radical relationship but provides no comprehensive analysis of the topic. Biographies of both immediatists and radicals supply some useful data. Moreover, collections such as the Charles Sumner papers at the Houghton Library and such as two more at the Library of Congress – the Salmon P. Chase Papers and the Giddings–Julian Papers – do contain very useful information. If it is difficult to research immediatist–radical relationships in general, it is even more difficult to find information about Elizur Wright's relationship with his Bird Club associates. Two interesting doctoral dissertations help us learn something of Wright's complex personality and ideology: David French, "The Conversion of an American Radical: Elizur Wright, Jr., and the Abolitionist Movement" (Case Western Reserve University, 1970), and Lawrence Goodheart, "Elizur Wright, Jr., and the Abolitionist Movement, 1820–1865" (University of Connecticut, 1978). But to understand the details of Wright's experience with Bird Club radicals, there is no substitute for long and tedious digging in the Wright Papers at the Library of Congress, the Sumner Papers and the Howe–Sumner Correspondence at the Houghton Library, and the Howe and Andrew collections at the Massachusetts Historical Society.

The final chapter on the decision to dissolve immediatist organizations was the easiest to research. Both the *National Anti-Slavery Standard* and the *Liberator* covered the details of the American Anti-Slavery Society dissolution debates. Two fine books by James McPherson were also exceedingly helpful: *The Struggle for Equality: Abolitionists and the Negro in the Civil War and Reconstruction* (1964) and *The Abolitionist Legacy: From Reconstruction to the NAACP* (1975). But neither the two newspapers nor the two volumes by McPherson indicate quite why the antidissolutionists of 1865 led by Wendell Phillips became the dissolutionists of 1870. Nor, regrettably, do any of the letters in the new Crawford Blagden Collection. Finally, Larry Gara's "A Glorious Time: The 1874 Abolitionist Reunion in Chicago," *Journal of the Illinois State Historical Society*, LXV (1974), 280–92 analyzes one of the most important of the last hurrahs for antebellum immediatists. Thanks to detailed reporting by the *Chicago Tribune*, it is possible to follow the proceedings of the 1874 gathering quite closely.

INDEX